OXFORD CLASSICAL MONOGRAPHS

Published under the supervision of a Committee of the
Faculty of Literae Humaniores in the University of Oxford

Divinity and History

The Religion of Herodotus

THOMAS HARRISON

CLARENDON PRESS · OXFORD

OXFORD

UNIVERSITY PRESS

Great Clarendon Street, Oxford OX2 6DP

Oxford University Press is a department of the University of Oxford
and furthers the University's aim of excellence in research, scholarship,
and education by publishing worldwide in

Oxford New York

Auckland Bangkok Buenos Aires Cape Town Chennai
Dar es Salaam Delhi Hong Kong Istanbul Karachi Kolkata
Kuala Lumpur Madrid Melbourne Mexico City Mumbai Nairobi
São Paulo Singapore Taipei Tokyo Toronto

and an associated company in Berlin

Oxford is a registered trade mark of Oxford University Press

Published in the United States
by Oxford University Press Inc., New York

For my father, †Martin Harrison, and my mother, Reziya

The moral rights of the author have been asserted
Database right Oxford University Press (maker)

First published 2000
First published in paperback 2002

British Library Cataloguing in Publication Data

Data available

Library of Congress Cataloging in Publication Data
Harrison, Thomas E. H., 1969–
Divinity and history: the religion of Herodotus / Thomas Harrison.
p. cm.—(Oxford classical monographs)
Includes bibliographical references and indexes
1. Herodotus. History. 2. Herodotus—Religion. I. Title. II. Series.
D58.H36 2000   938′.007202—dc21   99–039300

ISBN 0–19–815291–4
ISBN 0–19–925355–2 (pbk.)

1 3 5 7 9 10 8 6 4 2

Typeset in Imprint
by Joshua Associates Ltd., Oxford
Printed in Great Britain
on acid-free paper by
Biddles Ltd., Guildford & King's Lynn

Preface

Herodotus, Felix Jacoby wrote, 'is not a subject for *dissertationes inaugurales,* the young authors of which appreciate one side only of this complicated figure (which is at the same time so simple as a whole), and see that side incompletely or from a wrong angle' (*Atthis* (Oxford, 1949), 321 n. 5). This book—a discussion of one aspect of Herodotus' work, his religious beliefs—began life as an Oxford D. Phil thesis. Despite some attempts to disguise those origins, I am sure that they will be evident.

If it avoids even to a small degree the pitfalls described by Jacoby, the credit is due to a number of teachers, colleagues and friends. Foremost among these is Robert Parker, who has overseen the slow progress of the thesis and of its transformation into a book with unfailing kindness, and whose advice (even when I have been unable to realize it) has always been wise. Peter Derow first introduced me to Greek history and to Herodotus and inspired me to pursue both further; he has remained a constant source of encouragement and guidance. The late George Forrest—despite claiming that he found my ideas profoundly dangerous—engaged with them regularly for the first years of my research with an extravagant kindness. Other teachers also—Theo Zinn, Eric Pratt, Charles Low, Peter Southern, Dave Cook, Peter Heather, and Henrietta Leyser—have all left me greatly in their debt. A number of others have read and commented on the whole thesis or book: my examiners, John Davies and Chris Pelling, Michael Crawford, Hugh Johnstone, and Robin Osborne. Many more have been kind enough to comment on substantial sections or to discuss my work with me: amongst them, David Asheri, Robert Fowler, David Gribble, Alan Griffiths, Stephen Halliwell, Robin Lane Fox, Rosalind Thomas, Henk Versnel, and Stephanie West. In my time as a graduate student, I was lucky to have as contemporaries three other Greek historians, Andronike Makris, Henri de Marcellus, and Graham Oliver: to them, to Claude Eilers, and to other friends, particularly John Kingman, Paola De Carolis, Amra Mustovic, David Colclough, Lucinda Platt, and Frances Harrison, I owe whatever good humour I may still have. To all of these, and for the institutions that have sheltered me, especially Wadham College Oxford, the School of Greek, Latin, and Ancient History of the University of St Andrews, the History Department of University College London, the Classics Department of Royal Holloway, the libraries of the Ashmolean and the London Institute of Classical Studies, and not least the British Academy, I am enormously grateful.

One other debt of gratitude towers above all others, and is reflected in the dedication.

T.H.

Preface to the paperback edition

The occasion of a paperback edition has allowed me to make a number of typographical and other minor corrections. It also gives me the opportunity to record new thanks: to Hilary O'Shea, Enid Barker, Georga Godwin, Lucy Qureshi, and Lavinia Porter of Oxford University Press, for all their work on the book; to Esther Godfrey, Jon Hesk, and Jonathan Williams, for a variety of practical help and advice; and, not least, to Richard Gordon for presenting me with an embarrassing catalogue of errors and infelicities of style.

The period since I first submitted my typescript to Oxford University Press (late 1998) has seen an unprecedented spate of publications on Herodotus, many of which are directly relevant to the themes of this book. (The year 2002 will also see the publication of the first of two 'Companions' to Herodotus, both to contain alternative accounts of Herodotean religion.) The original edition has already provoked a number of, often very fruitful, reactions. I have resisted the temptation, however, to try to take into account, or respond to, new work. Those who would like to set my book against the background of other approaches to Herodotus might consult the (far from exhaustive) additional bibliography (p. viii). Included there are also two forthcoming pieces of my own: a more explicit statement of the importance of religious beliefs to the 'origins of history', and an account of the religious dimension (amongst others) of Herodotus' narrative of the Persian wars. My attempt in these pages to sketch a picture of Greek religious belief (for a general discussion, see pp. 18–23) will be developed further in a forthcoming book, *Greek Religion. Belief and Experience*.

In one area, finally, I should like to clarify or reiterate my position. My insistence on the importance of religious beliefs in the *Histories* should not be taken to suggest that I mean to champion a 'fundamentally conservative' or archaic Herodotus; nor should my conviction that recent work on Herodotus' literary artistry raises important questions be interpreted as seeking to return to the dark-age view of the *Histories* as a 'naïve compilation of colourful anecdotes and ethnographic excursuses' (in the phrase of Edith Hall), or as a denial of his sophistication or familiarity with contemporary intellectual trends. My position—clearly enough expressed, I hope, in Chapter 10—is that such sophistication is, on the contrary, *compatible* with the possession of religious convictions. I could think of nothing more unfortunate for the study of Herodotus than its polarization into 'archaizing' and 'modernizing' camps.

THOMAS HARRISON
St Andrews
February 2002

ADDITIONAL BIBLIOGRAPHY TO THE PAPERBACK EDITION

BOEDEKER, D. (2000), 'Herodotus's Genres', in M. Depew and D. Obbink (eds.) *Matrices of Genres. Authors, Canons, and Society* (Cambridge Mass.), 97–114.

CHAMBERLAIN, D. (2001), '"We the Others": Interpretative Community and Plural Voice in Herodotus', *ClAnt* 20, 5–34.

DORATI, M. (2000), *Le Storie di Erodoto: etnografia e racconto* (Pisa).

HARTOG, F. (1999), '"Myth into logos": the case of Croesus or the historian at work', in R. Buxton (ed.), *From Myth to Reason? Studies in the Development of Greek Thought* (Oxford), 183–95.

HARRISON, T. (forthcoming 2003), '"Prophecy in reverse?" Herodotus and the origins of history', in P. S. Derow and R. Parker (eds.) *The World of Herodotus. Essays in Memory of W. G. Forrest* (Oxford).

—— (forthcoming 2002), 'The Persian invasions', in E. Bakker, I. De Jong and H. van Wees (eds.) *Brill's Companion to Herodotus* (Leiden).

HORNBLOWER, S. (2001), 'Epic and epiphanies: Herodotus and the "New Simonides"', in D. Boedeker and D. Sider (eds.) *The New Simonides. Contexts of Praise and Desire* (New York).

LURAGHI, N. (ed.) (2001), *The Historian's Craft in the Age of Herodotus* (Oxford).

MUNSON, R. V. (2001), '*Ananke* in Herodotus', *JHS* 121, 30–50.

NESSELRATH, H.-G. (1999), 'Dodona, Siwa und Herodot—ein Testfall für den Vater der Geschichte', *MH* 56, 1–14.

PIETSCH, C. (2001), 'Ein Spielwerk in den Händen der Götter? Zur geschichtlichen Kausalität des Menschen bei Herodot am Beispiel der Kriegsentscheidung des Xerxes', *Gymnasium* 108, 205–21.

SHAPIRO, S. O. (2000), 'Proverbial wisdom in Herodotus', *TAPhA* 130, 89–118.

THOMAS, R. (2000), *Herodotus in Context. Ethnography, Science and the Art of Persuasion* (Cambridge).

ZINGROSS, M. (1998), *Herodotus' Views of Nature* (Athens).

Contents

Abbreviations

Herodotus is cited from the Oxford Classical Texts edition of C. Hude (Oxford, 1908), though any divergences from Hude's text in Rosén's new Teubner edition which have a significant impact on the argument are always noted. References in the format 9. 65. 2 are—unless specified—to Herodotus. Translations of Herodotus are my own, though sometimes based on those of Henry Cary (London, 1847). Transliterations of Greek proper names follow no consistent pattern.

References to secondary literature are by the surname of the author and date of publication. In addition to abbreviations of journal titles (which follow the conventions of *L'Année Philologique*) the following abbreviations are used.

Asheri i	*Erodoto. Libro I*, D. Asheri (Fondazione Lorenzo Valla, Verona, 1988)
Asheri iii	*Erodoto. Libro III*, D. Asheri (Fondazione Lorenzo Valla, Verona, 1990)
CAH	*Cambridge Ancient History*
CEG	*Carmina Epigraphica Graeca*, ed. P. A. Hansen (Berlin, 1983–9)
CIG	*Corpus Inscriptionum Graecarum* (1828–77)
Corcella	*Erodoto. Libro IV*, A. Corcella (Fondazione Lorenzo Valla, Verona, 1993)
DK	*Die Fragmente der Vorsokratiker*, H. Diels, rev. W. Kranz (6th edn., Berlin, 1951–2)
FGH	*Die Fragmente der griechischen Historiker*, F. Jacoby *et al.* (Berlin and Leiden, 1923–)
Fraenkel	*Aeschylus: Agamemnon*, E. Fraenkel, 3 vols. (Oxford, 1950)
GDI	*Sammlung der griechischen Dialekt-Inschriften*, ed. H. Collitz *et al.* (Göttingen, 1884–1915)

Giannantoni	*Socratis et Socraticorum Reliquiae* vol. i, G. Giannantoni (Naples, 1990)
HHD	*The Homeric Hymn to Demeter*, ed. N. J. Richardson (Oxford, 1974)
Hornblower	*A Commentary on Thucydides*, S. Hornblower, 2 vols. (Oxford, 1991–6)
How and Wells	*A Commentary on Herodotus*, W. W. How and J. Wells, 2 vols. (Oxford, 1912)
KA	*Poetae Comici Graeci*, R. Kassel and C. F. L. Austin (Berlin, 1983–)
Legrand	*Hérodote. Histoires*, Ph.-E. Legrand (Budé edn., Paris, 1939–64)
Lloyd i	*Herodotus Book II, Introduction*, A. B. Lloyd (Leiden, 1975)
Lloyd ii	*Herodotus Book II, Commentary 1–98*, A. B. Lloyd (Leiden, 1976)
Lloyd iii	*Herodotus Book II, Commentary 99–182*, A. B. Lloyd (Leiden, 1988)
Macan iv	*Herodotus. The Fourth, Fifth and Sixth Books*, R. W. Macan (London, 1895)
Macan vii	*Herodotus. The Seventh, Eighth and Ninth Books*, R. W. Macan (London, 1908)
Marg	*Herodot. Eine Auswahl aus der neueren Forschung*, ed. W. Marg (Darmstadt, 1962)
Masaracchia viii	*Erodoto. La Battaglia di Salamina. Libro VIII delle Storie*, A. Masaracchia (Fondazione Lorenzo Valla, Verona, 1977)
Masaracchia ix	*Erodoto. La Sconfitta dei Persiani. Libro IX delle Storie*, A. Masaracchia (Fondazione Lorenzo Valla, Verona, 1978)
ML	R. Meiggs and D. Lewis, *A Selection of Greek Historical Inscriptions to the End of the Fifth Century BC* (revised edn., Oxford, 1988)
Nauck	*Tragicorum Graecorum Fragmenta*, A. Nauck (2nd edn., Leipzig, 1926)
Nenci	*Erodoto. Libro V*, G. Nenci (Fondazione Lorenzo Valla, Verona, 1994)
OCD[3]	*The Oxford Classical Dictionary*, 3rd. edn.,

	ed. S. Hornblower and A. J. Spawforth (Oxford, 1996)
PMG	*Poetae Melici Graeci,* ed. D. L. Page (Oxford, 1962)
Powell	*A Lexicon to Herodotus,* J. E. Powell (Cambridge, 1938)
Pritchett	*The Greek State at War,* W. K. Pritchett (Berkeley, 1974– , vol. i first published as *Ancient Greek Military Practices* (Berkeley, 1971))
Rawlinson	*A History of Herodotus,* ed. G. Rawlinson (4th edn., London, 1880)
RE	*Real-Encyclopädie der classischen Altertumswissenschaft,* ed. A. Pauly and G. Wissowa, 83 vols. (Stuttgart, 1894–1980)
Rosén	*Herodoti Historiae,* ed. H. B. Rosén, 2 vols. (Leipzig, 1987–97)
Sayce	*The Ancient Empires of the East. Herodotos I–III,* A. H. Sayce (London, 1883)
SEG	*Supplementum Epigraphicum Graecum*
SLG	*Supplementum Lyricis Graecis,* ed. D. L. Page (Oxford, 1974)
Stein	*Herodotos,* ed. H. Stein (Berlin, 1881–96)
West	*Iambi et Elegi Graeci,* ed. M. L. West, 2 vols. (Oxford, 1971–2)
Wiedemann	*Herodots Zweites Buch,* A. Wiedemann (Leipzig, 1890)

I

Introduction: Divinity and History

> As for his ideas, let us not, for goodness' sake, place them
> at the head of the series, the starting point for our own
> ideas. A savage who makes fire by energetically whirling a
> stick in the hollow of a piece of dry wood is extremely
> ingenious. And if he thought up the technique himself, he
> is a savage of genius. For all that, we are not going to list
> him as one of the inventors of the electric stove.
>
> (Lucien Febvre, *The Problem of Unbelief in the Sixteenth
> Century. The Religion of Rabelais.*[1])

Herodotus has been growing increasingly ingenious in recent
years. Once the credulous recorder of everything he heard or
saw, useful precisely because he was uncritical,[2] he has
emerged as a figure almost sinisterly clever, creating patterns
of reciprocity, setting up expectations which he then subverts,
manipulating his characters and their preoccupations like
puppets. Herodotus' portrayal of character has been compared
to the technique of a 'master-musician',[3] the architecture of his
Histories to the 'pedimental structure' of a Greek temple.[4]

In most respects, there is no cause for mourning the loss of
Herodotus' innocence. Recent criticism of Herodotus has
made a number of significant advances: it has shown, for
example, how he threads a delicate commentary on the events
of his day through his narrative of the Persian wars;[5] it has
highlighted the structuring patterns of his *Histories*, rarely
made explicit: the manner, for example, in which his last
chapters echo the opening of his work.[6] A new subtlety has

---

[1] Febvre (1982: 461), originally published in 1942 as *Le Problème de
l'incroyance au XVIe siècle: la religion de Rabelais*.

[2] Explicitly stated by e.g. Salmon (1956: 329).

[3] Gammie (1986: 176).

[4] Myres (1953: 86–7).   [5] See esp. Fornara (1971*a*).

[6] See esp. Boedeker (1988), Moles (1996: 271–7), Dewald (1997),

also developed in the analysis of Herodotus' use of sources, no longer merely written but also oral,[7] or in treating the affinities in method or argumentation between Herodotus and his contemporaries, historians or medical writers.[8] But there have also been some dangerous side-effects. Herodotus has, in some hands, become excessively ingenious. When Richmond Lattimore wrote his classic article on the 'Wise Adviser' in the *Histories*, the repeated motif of the royal lieutenant whose recommendations of caution and humility are routinely ignored by his—or, in the case of Artemisia, at least, her— master, he described the Adviser as a 'mode of understanding . . . in the mind of Herodotus'; 'a certain situation calls for, it may even create a sage'.[9] If we compare a more recent treatment of a similar motif, Donald Lateiner's discussion of the 'Laughing Tyrant', a significant difference is apparent: 'so from their blind chortling, Herodotus imaginatively and soberly develops a pattern and creates expectations in us that Xerxes' laughter too augurs him no good.'[10] The difference between these two approaches might appear at first sight to be one only of language. But there is a deeper change in approach: where Lattimore sees room for what we might crudely term a Herodotean unconscious—we might talk alternatively of underlying cultural patterns or of a narrative drive—for Lateiner there is apparently no aspect, however small, of the *Histories* that has not been fashioned with care by its author.

This growth in Herodotus' imagined ingenuity has occurred in tandem with another change: he has also become more of a historian. (Even those such as Detlev Fehling who believe that

---

A. Griffiths (1999); for an excellent introduction to the structure of the *Histories*, see also Dewald (1998).

[7] See esp. Murray (1987). It is necessary, however, to draw a distinction between (residual) elements of an oral style and oral performance. I am sceptical e.g. of the suggestion, made by Stadter (1992: 783; 1998), that sections of the *Histories* could not have been performed in certain cities: see the useful corrective of W. A. Johnson (1995).

[8] See Fowler (1996) for a comparison with contemporary historians, Lateiner (1986) and esp. now R. Thomas (1997) for medical writers.

[9] Lattimore (1939a: 34). Likewise Myres describes Herodotus' much-derided 'pedimental structure' as 'rather a habit of mind than an artifice or a memoria technica' (1953: 86–7).   [10] Lateiner (1977: 182).

Herodotus was writing a type of pseudo-history require a well-developed *conception* of history on Herodotus' part in order for him to have mimicked it.[11]) This idea of Herodotus as a historian may ultimately be a sustainable position, but only after one has established the differences between his idea of history and our own. More often it is a prejudice rather than a reasoned conclusion. In the phrase of Wilamowitz, we 'tend to attach more importance to the label of the bottle than its contents':[12] we presume that Herodotus was a historian and we then explain away whatever features of his *Histories* conflict with our own idea of history.[13] That idea may, of course, vary. Different writers on Herodotus have differing conceptions of the proper scope of history: some, for example, see Herodotus as the earliest exemplar of an *Annales*-style 'total history',[14] others as a scrupulous sifter of his sources.[15] Whatever their preference, however, they are all equally likely to project their own model of the proper limits of history onto Herodotus. 'It is not for history to give the ultimate sense of things or to measure in full the relevance of gods to men': that 'the intervention of gods in human affairs is neither constant nor too patent' was, according to Arnaldo Momigliano, taken for granted by Herodotus, 'an implicit acceptance, an exploitation, of the general trend of Greek thought in the fifth century rather than a programmatic aim'.[16] Modern critics assume wrongly, Immerwahr tells us, 'that Herodotus has not fully grasped that history is first of all the history of human action, and that its purpose should not be to prove a point outside of history itself'.[17] Perhaps most strikingly, Kenneth Waters opens his

[11] Fehling (1989) with the comments of Murray (1987: 101 n. 12), Dover (1998: 220). For Fehling and the so-called 'Liar School', see further below, this chapter.   [12] Cited by Picard (1952).

[13] Such a syndrome is particularly marked in the case of Waters (1971), Carbonell (1985), Shimron (1989); it is observed by Heidel (1935: 57), Raubitschek (1960: 178), de Ste Croix (1977: 142).

[14] See e.g. the comments of Immerwahr (1966: 2).

[15] See e.g. Waters (1971: 65): Herodotus 'if the obvious may be restated without offence, was writing history and had to select and arrange the material offered by his sources'.

[16] Momigliano (1978: 7–8); contrast Momigliano (1985: 4). For a critique of the allegedly secular nature of classical historiography focusing on the end of that tradition, see Harrison (1999a).

[17] Immerwahr (1954: 18).

study *Herodotos on Tyrants and Despots. A Study in Objectivity* by offering the reader a simplistic choice between Herodotus the historian and Herodotus the moralizer, on the assumption that the two are mutually exclusive:

The purpose of this study is to examine the reports given by Herodotos of . . . the Greek tyrants and the kings of Persia, and to determine whether he has treated these, often the subject of tendentious and prejudiced discussion in his own and in later days, in the manner befitting a historian, or whether he has used them for the purposes of moralising and to preach a particular world view; that is, in a non-scientific, anti-historical way.[18]

A number of strategies have been deployed in order to buttress such definitions of Herodotus' sense of history. One such modernizing strategy is to pass the responsibility for what are deemed less admirable features of the *Histories* onto Herodotus' contemporary audience or readership. According to this theory, the work as we have it reflects a compromise between Herodotus' historical aspirations and the meagre intelligence and education of his public. Among the features explained away in this fashion, the evidence of religious belief is particularly prominent. The 'concepts of Nemesis and the like', Waters writes again, 'are often useful to the writer, to assist in presenting to his audience, mainly persons of little historical perceptiveness and obviously having no historical training at all, certain facts and features of the history he was recording'.[19] According to Pearson, Herodotus was obliged to say that the Greek victory in the Persian wars was due to the gods in order to avoid giving offence.[20] Russell Meiggs speaks

---

[18] Waters (1971: 1); cf. Waters (1970: 505): 'the historian of war is not bound to provide his readers with a complete philosophy and theology.'

[19] Waters (1971: 47).

[20] Pearson (1954: 140); see also Pearson (1941: 337); Waters (1970: 507), 'a genuine historian, who in the nature of the case paid a certain respect to the tastes of his audience'; Lateiner (1980; 1989: 141), 'for his audience, *tisis* was a more convenient and familiar way of linking events than the original historiographical analysis of cause that Herodotus invented'; and Vandiver (1991: 139). Lateiner also passes responsibility for the supernatural onto Herodotus' sources, absolving his audience (1990: 235): 'some supernatural appearances and disappearances are reported almost as if they are ordinary, because the people who related these events to Herodotus accepted their possibility. Those who first heard or read his retelling these stories of the

of Herodotus 'paying lip-service to the mythologists'.[21] Much
more can be explained in this fashion, however. Herodotus' use
of dramatization reflects the skill with which he used literary
means for a 'genuine, historical purpose'.[22] Speeches provide
pellets of editorial in the midst of news reports. And Herodotus' stress on individual motivation is also, according to
Waters, not really his own:[23]

the correct conclusion about Herodotus' presentation of grievances or
other personal motives as pretexts for action is that it represents a way
of writing about history rather than a way of thinking about it.
Herodotus shows that he is capable of thinking about history in a
logical and impersonal way; but he must temper the wind of scientific
history to the shorn lambs of his unsophisticated public—unsophisticated certainly in the matter of historical studies, with which
Herodotus was the first man to make them acquainted. To communicate the results of his researches to the man in the agora, he needed a
technique which would satisfy tastes accustomed to epic (and also
drama); and that technique is found in the dramatised presentation of
cause and motivation.

In so far as it constitutes an assumption rather than an argued
position, this tendency to attempt to vindicate Herodotus, to
affirm his status as the Father of History, is plainly unhistorical. Speeches or dialogues may in certain instances contain
within them Herodotus' own historical judgements. So, for
example, before Marathon, Miltiades seeks to impress Callimachus of the advantages of joining battle with the Persians by
arguing that if they were to win, not only would Athens be free
but 'the first of the cities of Greece' (6. 109. 6): implicit here is
a historical judgement that the cities of Greece were not only
fighting for freedom from the Persians but jostling for position
amongst themselves. The fact, however, that this judgement is
expressed through a speech—where the modern historian
would choose to express it more directly—is not a casual or a
slight difference. Moreover, that dramatization can be a vehicle

fantastic may have enjoyed the human experience of condescending to other
people's gullibility.'
    [21] Meiggs: (1957: 738).
    [22] Waters (1966: 157); for speeches as vehicles for Herodotus' interpreta-
tion see also Solmsen (1943; 1944).
    [23] Waters (1966: 170-1).

for the delivery of historical lessons need not mean that it is always or exclusively so: dramatization may also constitute an end in itself.

Our suspicions should surely be aroused by the very convenience of this 'entertainment-theory'. At one stroke it can rid us of every troublesome feature of the *Histories*, allowing us complete licence to refashion a Herodotus in our own image. Of course, Herodotus must have been detached to a certain extent from the presuppositions of his contemporaries. He was doubtless capable, again to a certain extent, of accommodating his audience's tastes, or of subverting their expectations. We can also accept that his work was designed to entertain, even to be humorous,[24] that Herodotus was capable of speaking in different idioms at different times. But, equally clearly, we should be wary of classifying certain passages of his work as somehow less characteristic of his real purpose than others; there must also have been limits to this detachment, limits to his creative role as author, a sense in which he was—in the clichéd phrase—'rooted in his own age'.[25] It may be difficult, if not actually impossible, to establish those areas where Herodotus' and his audience's presuppositions coincide or overlap; it is still, however, an important truth that there must have been such areas. In the fine phrase of Fornara, Herodotus 'wrote his work under the impression that it was capable of being read between two covers without causing aesthetical indigestion'.[26] Some modern readings of Herodotus, by contrast, convey the impression that Herodotus has casually condescended to touch down in his own world. Herodotus 'does not dissemble his Hellenic bias towards women'.[27] How could he, we might ask, dissemble such a deep-rooted set of attitudes? He 'knew well enough', according to Immerwahr,

[24] See Shimron's appropriately humourless discussion (1989: 58 ff.).

[25] A more subtle view of Herodotus' readership is taken by e.g. Starr (1966; 1989), Asheri (1990: 331–4), Fornara (1990: 164 n. 4), Pritchett (1993: 328–53), and especially by Fornara (1971a).

[26] Fornara (1971a: 7). Fornara's reconstruction tends often to be overdrawn, as when Herodotus is said to have 'observed the cancerous nature of imperialism' (p. 88), 'to have 'been 'devoted to the ideal of freedom' or to have deplored his contemporaries' 'ignorant hatred of Athens' (p. 80). See now the sensible comments of Derow (1995: esp. 36).

[27] Lateiner (1985a: 94).

'that it is a mistake for a historian to treat his subject with an excessive amount of theory, and he goes to some lengths to avoid even the type of theorizing familiar from Thucydides':[28] Herodotus was possessed of so much ingenuity that he knew how not to show it.

Another result of the entertainment hypothesis is that the book fragments into serious and non-serious segments.[29] Gibbon said of Herodotus that he wrote 'sometimes for philosophers, sometimes for children'. This may be the impression that Herodotus gives to us, but it clearly does not follow that this was either the impression intended by the author or registered by his audience. Arguably we should be looking for a certain degree of coherence or unity of purpose.[30] The tendency to break the *Histories* down into classified sections, the 'Arabian logos' or the 'Egyptian digression'—digression from what?—is a deep-seated one.[31] But at any rate, we cannot simply conclude that the non-serious exists simply or primarily to serve as a sweetener for the serious; we cannot suppose that one is more characteristic of the essence of the *Histories* than the other.[32] This appears to be the assumption beneath the frequent observation that the later books of the *Histories* contain fewer marvels and miracles than the earlier

[28] Immerwahr (1966: 324); cf. p. 12.

[29] This fragmentation of serious and anecdotal sections of the *Histories* is observed and rejected by Flory (1987: 16); cf. Balcer (1987: 78), Benardete (1969: 3).

[30] See here Fornara (1971a: 6).

[31] As Lattimore remarks (1958: 14) on 3. 4. 3–9. 4, 'this passage has been called the Arabian Logos; and if there is any such thing as an Arabian Logos, this must be it. But it is no organised free-standing anthropology of Arabia or the Arabians, rather a sequence of notices which grows organically out of its place of occurrence in the Persian progress.' Contrast e.g. Wardman (1960: 406): 'The whole point of digressions, with their mythical apparatus, was to give the reader a rest.'

[32] See Fornara's comments (1971a: 14 n. 18) on the tendency of modern writers to see Herodotus as a 'pure geographer': 'the word "pure" comes up again and again'. Waters (1971: 2) places Herodotus' priorities in strict order: 'Herodotus was a historian in the first place. In the second place, no doubt, a teller of tales and purveyor of curious information. Occasionally, and as an afterthought, he is a moralist, but a dramatist, never (except in the skill with which he composes dialogue).' See van der Veen (1996) for the significance of the 'insignificant' in the *Histories*.

books. The 'view of Herodotus as a teller of fairy-tales' can be
rejected, Simon Hornblower remarks, on the grounds that 'it
draws its strength from the more remote and anecdotal, i.e. the
earlier, books; in the period from the Ionian revolt onwards . . .,
there is *much less to object to*'.[33] It might be right to suppose that
there are fewer stories with a folktale element in the later than
in the earlier books—although miracles, oracles and portents
are arguably just as common—but even if this were indispu-
tably true, what are we therefore to conclude about the
Histories as a whole? Can we privilege the less marvellous,
less anecdotal passages over all others? Can we conclude simply
that Herodotus could, had he chosen to, have written exclusively in the manner of the later books, and turn a blind eye to
the evidence that for half of his *Histories* he chose not to?[34]

Another technique for syphoning off elements of the *Histories* objectionable to modern sensibilities might be termed the
'idea of the traditional'.[35] Herodotus stands at the gateway of
two worlds, two eras of history. Though Myres described him
as a pioneer,[36] Herodotus is more often given the task of

[33] Hornblower (1987: 21) (the italics are mine). Contrast, however, Murray
(1987: 107), Flory (1987: 47), Gould (1989: 123).

[34] See also Murray's argument (1987: 105–7), expressed less delphically at
(1980: 28–32), for a distinction between material gathered by Herodotus from
Delphic or east Greek traditions, on the one hand, and mainland aristocratic
family tradition, on the other: in the former, events are preserved 'in a
framework in which the hero moves from prosperity to over-confidence and
a divinely sanctioned reversal of fortune'; in the latter (for example, in the
traditions of Cleomenes or Themistocles), there is a 'comparative absence of
moralizing folk-tale motifs'. Murray is not, it should be insisted, seeking to
devalue the moralizing framework of the *Histories* either by passing responsibility onto Herodotus' sources or by painting it as a purely literary imposi-
tion. It may be the case that Murray's 'moral and aesthetic patterning' is more
marked in, for example, the stories of Croesus or of Polycrates; however, the
assumptions underpinning these moralizing stories can be seen to inform a far
wider range of material in the *Histories* (see Ch. 2), material concerning both
the mainland and east Greece.

[35] A less subtle approach might be to fall back on the catch-all idea of
'genius'—as Flory says of the idea of Herodotean charm (1969: 100), 'always a
discouragement to further analysis rather than an invitation to it'.

[36] Myres (1953: 47); contrast Myres (1908: 125) on Herodotus as the father
of anthropology: 'If Herodotus was not in advance of his age, then his age was
abreast of Herodotus.' Cf. Segal (1971: 40), 'Bacchylides' narrative [of Solon
on the pyre] points back to the Archaic world; Herodotus' points ahead to the

salvaging, interpreting the values of a bygone age: in the words of de Sainte Croix, Herodotus 'belonged to an older, less rational world'.[37] Proverbs, maxims, or commonplaces, ideas of fate and nemesis and so on are the leftovers of a traditional—and therefore outmoded—folk wisdom.[38] Just as an earlier generation of critics found signs in the *Histories* of the order of its composition,[39] we may hunt for hints of a primitive mentality from which Herodotus has—by his genius—broken free. So, for example, Sealey posits a progression through the works of Herodotus and Thucydides from a system of causation based on grievances to a historiography based on conscious, rational explanation.[40] John Gould sees Herodotus' 'sense of what was going to happen' not as 'the language of one who holds a theory of historical necessity' or of one 'who sees the whole of human experience as constrained by inevitability and without room for human choice or human responsibility' but as 'the *traditional language* of a teller of tales'.[41]

It would be a slur against any of these writers to suggest that they do not take these 'traditional' features of Herodotus' narrative seriously. However, it often seems only a short step from marking something as traditional to thinking of it as redundant. As when we talk of a rhetorical *topos*, or of formulae, the word 'traditional' seems inevitably to carry with it the lazy sense of *only* traditional.[42] This implication

Classical'; or the curious suggestion of Flory (1980) that the length of the *Histories* made them unlikely to be popular in the 5th cent.

[37] De Ste Croix (1977: 147). See also Evans (1992: 60) on Herodotus as 'a transitional figure', and Immerwahr (1966: 31), asserting that the form of Herodotus' work 'and its underlying philosophy must have seemed strange to contemporaries'. On Herodotus' 'archaic mentality' see more cogently Pippidi (1960: 76); contrast Pearson (1939: 21), and Dewald (1987: 152) criticizing the 'early 20th. c. idea' of Herodotus as a 'pious anachronism'.

[38] Cf. Lang (1984a: 52): 'in Herodotus' use of proverbs, maxims, or commonplaces we see the continued operation and influence of traditional folk wisdom.'   [39] See e.g. J. E. Powell (1939).

[40] Sealey (1957; 1975: 95–6).   [41] Gould (1989: 77–8), my italics.

[42] See here Rhodes's marvellous attack on what he describes as the 'topos-fallacy' (1994: 157–8); see also Fornara (1990: 26–7), and the remark of Pritchett (1993: 328) on the observation that Herodotus has lapsed into a 'literary tradition . . .whatever that may mean'. As Denis Feeney has put it in another context, 'the challenge is to put the right adverb in front of the word "literary": not "merely" but "distinctively"' (1998: 41).

has frequently been made explicit. Herodotus' 'conviction that
"human happiness never continues long in one stay" ' has been
described as 'flavouring for the narrative rather than . . . a
philosophy of history'.[43] Herodotus' proverbial remarks may
'prepare the reader for what is to come, introducing a note of
foreboding', but 'they do not *explain* anything'.[44] They may
have 'rhetorical value' but 'no merit as an expression of
historical causation'.[45] To say after the event that that event
had been bound to happen may indeed not '*explain* anything' in
our terms, but if one man is prone to such gnomic pronouncements and another not, that is surely one meaningful way of
distinguishing them. The possibility cannot be discounted,
moreover, that such pronouncements may be more than
purely literary, that they may reflect deep-seated assumptions
about the way the world works. We should not then disallow
apparently traditional features of Herodotus' narrative, but
isolate them.

This is in a sense what John Gould and other recent critics
have done—by their concentration on the structuring ideas of
the *Histories*, the theme of reciprocity or 'give-and-take', or the
'ever-increasing list of narrative patterns'[46] such as the 'laughing tyrant'. Once we have collected the evidence of such motifs,
however, we must interpret them.[47] Every child who has ever
been to a pantomime knows that villains chuckle. Is this
pattern then the result of a consciously developed narrative
technique or (in large part, at least) merely the function of
Herodotus' unconscious assumption, his own belief—a term to

[43] Bowden (1992: p. xxv). Fornara (1990: 37) sees these expressions that *x*
or *y* was bound to come to a bad end as an 'integral part of . . . Herodotus'
metaphysical system'. Waters (1985: 104) recants his earlier view that these
expressions were 'meaningless formulae'.

[44] Bowden (1992: p. xxv); cf. Derow (1994: 76).

[45] Lang (1984a: 52); the similarity of Homeric to Herodotean maxims
suggests also, however, that they are 'basically human'. Cf. Lang (1968: 27):
Herodotus 'himself sees disasters as invariably the result of human error
(except when for the sake of brevity he uses the δεῖ γενέσθαι κακῶς formula)'.

[46] Dillery (1996: 217).

[47] Contrast the remarks of Flory (1978a: 145): 'Writers often describe
similar events in a similar way. In Herodotus' writing we find examples of
such repetitions which form motifs in his narrative. These aspects occur in
meaningful patterns and constitute one aspect of the unit of the historian's
work.' But how are they meaningful?

which it will be necessary to return—in the pattern of the rise and fall of tyrants? Obviously in any particular instance, the answer to this question is unlikely to be black and white. The 'laughing tyrant' is very likely the function both of unconscious assumptions and of literary technique. Frequently, however, such patterns have been put down exclusively to Herodotus' conscious intent[48]—and so a gap opens up between Herodotus and his audience, and it becomes impossible to use the *Histories* as evidence of any beliefs, assumptions, attitudes except his own.[49]

This study is an attempt to describe one area of Herodotus' 'world view', his religious beliefs. This is a particularly difficult area for this modernizing approach to the *Histories*. As Gould has written, there is a 'constant and recurring unhappiness' over the role of religion in the *Histories*:[50]

This unhappiness is of two, rather different, kinds. One kind is a sort of generalized unhappiness which finds it difficult, even impossible, to accept that Herodotus really gave such weight as superficially he appears to do to the presence of divinity in human affairs—a sort of incredulity that things present themselves to him as they seem to do, a feeling that he 'must have been' more sceptical than he seems; and a determination to make him so. The other is somewhat more specific, a sort of disappointment with an author otherwise admired, a sense that Herodotus fails to display his usual sharpness of observation, the analytical clarity and sensitivity of response that we expect of him . . .

History is imagined to be necessarily secular: either then Herodotus' residual obscurantism is seen as a regrettable qualification to his achievement as the Father of History, or—more usually—the Father of History is forced to conform to this ideal.

The rejection of religious traces in the *Histories* can take a number of forms. The crudest is simply to ascribe a modern

---

[48] As Mabel Lang has written (1984a: 4), you cannot automatically divine Herodotus' purpose from the result: 'just because it is possible to identify a skeleton of causation, it is not necessary or even desirable to believe . . . that the narrative was constructed in this way, that it was conceived first as a causally articulated skeleton and then fleshed out with narrative.'

[49] Cf. Pritchett (1993: 352) on the Liar School.

[50] Gould (1994: 91 ff.).

rationalism to Herodotus: miracles do not happen; therefore Herodotus could not have believed them to have happened.[51] A more subtle technique is to deny not that Herodotus held religious beliefs—he was doubtless a 'sincerely pious man'— but that they were significant. Herodotus, in one view, recognized that it would be inappropriate to express his piety in the course of his *Histories*: 'whatever theory or belief a historian may hold, he cannot allow it to vitiate his objectivity, or he will not be able to write good history.'[52] Just as modern-day religious parties in Israel 'in daily practical politics . . . act according to purely human, rational considerations', so Herodotus knew that history was fundamentally a secular reserve.[53] This is a view that superficially derives some support from two passages in Book 2 (2. 3. 2 and 2. 65. 2) in which Herodotus appears to express the opinion that he means to exclude 'the divine' from his *Histories*. On closer examination Herodotus' discretion can be seen to refer only to certain details of the myth and cult of Egypt.[54] However, even if Herodotus were indeed to have made a programmatic statement of his exclusion of the divine, we would then have to judge that he himself broke this 'ban'.[55] There are further problems, however, with such a distinction. Whether or not a separation of religion and politics is possible in contemporary Israel is itself disputable, but the difficulty of supposing that Herodotus could consciously have kept his beliefs from influencing his *Histories* is surely of an even greater order, presupposing an enormous degree of

[51] 'Miracles', according to Shimron (1989: 37), 'are records of phenomena that are deviations from the natural laws and therefore unacceptable as facts'; Shimron ignores the possibility that an ancient writer may have thought differently.

[52] Shimron (1989: 78).

[53] Shimron (1989: 56). The behaviour of the religious parties in the Israeli Knesset scarcely supports Shimron: when (*The Independent*, Mon. 19 Dec. 1994) in the debate on the Nobel Peace Prize awarded to Peres, Rabin, and Arafat, religious members declared King David a hero, and accused Peres of giving up Israeli territory, Peres replied, in reference to David's 'assignation with Bathsheba', that 'not everything that King David did on the ground, or on the roofs, is acceptable to a Jew'. The religious parties then precipitated a confidence vote on the subject.

[54] See further, Ch. 8.

[55] Language characteristic of Linforth, e.g. (1928: 205).

detachment on Herodotus' part—as if 'religion' were seen as a distinct category apart from other 'secular' concerns.[56]

It is possible to see Herodotus' beliefs as unimportant without also supposing that he thought them so. 'God' for Herodotus 'provided a metaphysical framework, an umbrella under which men operated in the way that men do.'[57] Herodotus' 'piety and belief in fate are seen', in Fornara's paraphrase, 'as a sort of embroidery that dresses up his history but does not compromise the pragmatic sequence of events of which it consists'.[58] It is perhaps hard to see how a belief in fate can *not* have a significant impact on the writing of history. Nevertheless, this is a position which it is impossible to refute simply: one purpose of this book is to demonstrate the many ways in which Herodotus' religious beliefs do indeed affect his *Histories*.

Another, more insidious approach to the 'problem' of Herodotus' religious beliefs is to latch on to disconnected instances of religious scepticism on Herodotus' part and to present them as evidence of a *general* scepticism.[59] Herodotus distances himself (on occasions) from miraculous stories. He is apparently sceptical of the idea of the divine parentage of men. He is aware of the possibility that oracles may be bribed or that prophets may be corrupt. It should come as no surprise, however, that Herodotus is not exclusively credulous. Scepticism over one form of divine intervention need not entail

[56] For the idea of the secular, see esp. Dover (1974: 252), Connor (1988). For an argument, however, which I mean to address elsewhere that Thucydides 'had the vocabulary for distinguishing the religious from the non-religious sphere', see Hornblower (1992a). The idea of Herodotus' 'interest' in religion, e.g. Grant (1983: 284), also presumes an arguably impossible detachment.

[57] Forrest (1979: 312). Cf. also Lateiner (1989: 200): Herodotus 'detects a pattern of divine action, but he suggests that it is distinct from historical causation, his particular concern'.

[58] Fornara (1990: 26). Fornara does not share this view, although he does then (p. 25) place Herodotus 'in the line of historians who believed the human condition subject to purely human explanation'.

[59] So e.g. Linforth asserts (in the context of Herodotus' 'religious discretion' at 2. 3. 2 and 2. 65. 2) that 'there can be little doubt that Herodotus must plead guilty to a charge of skepticism in religion': (1924: 286). Linforth is then forced again and again to establish classes of exception to what he claims that Herodotus intends to exclude, e.g. (1924: 272; 1928: 205, 217).

scepticism in other areas. Scepticism or credulity, moreover, cannot be measured on a single scale: we cannot, for example, adduce Herodotus' knowledge of the corruption of Delphi as suggestive of a moderate religiosity, a traditional belief tempered by rationalism, still less introduce his appreciation of the importance of seapower as if it constituted evidence of his fundamental secularism.[60] At the same time, scepticism or credulity cannot be understood except in their relation to one another.[61] Scepticism in one area may indeed actually reinforce belief in another:[62] to condemn one diviner as a fraud, for example, presupposes that there are others whose insights are genuine.[63] If we cease to imagine that every instance of Herodotean scepticism, however limited its focus, is representative of a scepticism over the intervention of the gods in general, then Herodotus' speculations become evidence, in fact, of an *interest* in divine intervention.[64] Likewise, if we suspend our assumption that Herodotus 'despised myth', his criticisms of individual myths become evidence of a basic trust in the structures of myth. 'Demythologization', as Paul Veyne has wisely argued, 'is not the same thing as irreligion.'[65]

   In describing Herodotus' religious beliefs then, we should not simply map out the areas of Herodotus' scepticism and credulity case by case.[66] Any single passage can only properly be understood in the context of all analogous sections of his work. A good illustration of the way in which the object of

[60] Shimron (1989: 89–92): Shimron in general imagines only two starkly opposed positions for Herodotus. It is arguably one fault of the excellent article of Asheri (1993) that belief and scepticism are envisaged on a simple sliding scale. Carbonell (1985: 139) has measured the proportion of the *Histories* taken up with non-historical *logoi* (14. 6 per cent) and 'mytho-histoire' (2 per cent, 'une très faible part des *Histoires*'): Carbonell's criteria are a mystery.

[61] 'There is no belief without disbelief': Feeney (1998: 22); cf. G. E. R. Lloyd (1979: 10).

[62] Cf. D. H. Johnson (1994: 333).   [63] See further, Ch. 5.

[64] Cf. Sourvinou-Inwood (1997: 185), distinguishing the 'explanation' of religion from 'criticism'.

[65] Veyne (1988: 98). For such religious speculation as common, see G. E. R. Lloyd (1979: 14).

[66] Cf. Feeney (1998: 14): 'Addressing the problem of belief is not simply a matter of tallying up all the evidence of scepticism in one column and all the evidence for credulity or allegiance to cult in another.'

Herodotean scepticism can be sharpened by an analysis of comparable passages is his famous observation on the Peneius gorge (7. 139. 4). The Thessalians say, Herodotus tells us, that the gorge was made by Poseidon—reasonably (οἰκότα λέγοντες): for whoever considers that Poseidon shakes the earth would conclude that the gorge was the work of Poseidon, as it was certainly the result of an earthquake. This has been taken as evidence that Herodotus is sceptical of the possibility of divine intervention through earthquakes, or of natural miracles alto-gether;[67] Herodotus' natural explanation of the gorge, that it was the result of an earthquake, excludes, it is imagined, a parallel divine explanation. On another occasion, however, Herodotus explicitly states that an earthquake was caused by 'the god'. His doubt in the story of the Peneius gorge may then be only as to whether it is possible to ascribe such miracles to Poseidon in particular. Yet another passage, moreover, his description of the Potidaea floodtide, makes clear that it is possible to ascribe some natural miracles to Poseidon. Her-odotus' scepticism may then refer only to the possibility of ascribing a particular form of natural miracle to a particular god. Herodotus has not apparently envisaged (in this instance) a natural explanation as excluding a parallel divine cause.

The intention behind this book is, by the same method, to expose Herodotus' religious beliefs in all their complexity. It is necessary also to describe Herodotus' more conscious beliefs, those which he was capable of expressing directly, and what we might term his theological speculations, side by side with his less conscious beliefs. In cases such as those discussed above, the Peneius gorge and the Potidaea floodtide, Herodotus makes evident the logic of his deduction; but in these as in other cases, Herodotus' conscious religious judgements are based on pre-mises of which he was not aware. Herodotus seems to take for granted, for example, that certain crimes will inevitably be punished by divine retribution.[68] A description of any single

---

[67] For a full discussion of this passage, see Ch. 3.

[68] As Gomme asserts (1954: 151), we cannot look solely for simple statements of belief; for unconscious presuppositions, see also Cartledge (1990: 30), and the comments of Lloyd-Jones on the tendency to see the moral-religious thought of Aeschylus as a distinct, 'theological' position: (1956: 57).

strand of Herodotus' religious beliefs—his beliefs concerning
divine retribution, for example, or in divination—must clearly
embrace both his presuppositions *and* his conscious theological
explanations, both those aspects of his belief which serve from
our perspective to 'explain things' and which may appear only
'colouring', both those beliefs which seem to us sophisticated
and 'forward-looking' and those which appear traditional or
naïve.

At the same time, however, Herodotus' religious beliefs
cannot simply be broken down step by step, distinction by
distinction, into a single consistent plan. In describing the
pattern of his beliefs, there is a constant danger of improving
upon it, of constructing a coherent theology where none exists.
It is not always easy to tell, in using one passage to elucidate
another, whether we are indeed comparing like with like. In the
case of the Peneius gorge and the Potidaea floodtide, for
example, might some other element—the fact that the victims
of the floodtide were the same men who had earlier committed
an act of sacrilege against Poseidon—make the passage incom-
parable to his discussion of the Peneius gorge? Might Herodotus not simply be inconsistent? Some contradictions in
Herodotus' belief—most notably, as we will see, the contradictions surrounding his belief in predestination—are blatant
and irreducible. Our inability to reconcile these contradictions
should not, however, be construed as a failure. In the first
place, no 'system' of religious beliefs is entirely consistent: a
belief in predestination, while the conclusion that an event was
fated may itself constitute a deduction from the nature of such
events, must entail contradiction in order for that belief to be
sustainable. Indeed a more positive emphasis is necessary.
Inconsistencies in belief are not just an inevitable flaw of all
religions, but actually a *means* whereby belief is maintained.[69]

No author can be seen in isolation. Nevertheless, this study
will in the first instance attempt to do so. 'Why Herodotus?',
it might be asked. Though other authors—Hesiod in his
Works and Days, for example, the Attic tragedians or orators,
Xenophon in his *Anabasis*—provide evidence similarly of a

---

[69] For inconsistency as a method of maintaining belief, see esp. Versnel
(1990a: 1–38). See below, this chapter, for the compatibility of beliefs and
experience.

wide range of (sometimes conflicting) beliefs, the evidence provided by Herodotus has several advantages. The first is simply the sheer quantity of material included in his *Histories* which sheds light on Greek religious belief. Moreover, though it can hardly be claimed that we can see straight through to the religious views of Herodotus—I will return to discuss some of the difficulties in using his evidence below—the problems entailed in examining a historical writer such as Herodotus are arguably of a different order from those encountered in discussing genres such as didactic poetry or Greek tragedy.[70] Finally, though it is right to be wary of clichés of 'ages of anxiety' or individuals at 'intellectual crossroads', and though, as we have recently been reminded by Robert Parker, 'doubt, criticism and revision' were in fact traditional to Greek religion,[71] few would doubt that the late fifth century has left us at least with greater evidence of diversity in religious opinion. This may make the decision to treat Herodotus in isolation all the more surprising, but it provides in fact the strongest reason. Put negatively, the explanation might be said to be the danger of judging Herodotus' thought—which beliefs are traditional and which are forward-looking—on the basis of other authors. More positively, it is important first to judge the variety of religious beliefs of one man, the variety of beliefs, most importantly, that can be held *in combination* with one another, before then turning to that man's intellectual context. This way, it is easier to conclude whether the differences between two authors reflect differences of personal outlook, a chronological shift in opinion, or simply the complexity of Greek religious belief. As will be seen, Herodotus' 'system of beliefs' succeeds in accommodating—even where he does not accept—many of the sceptical opinions of the late fifth century. By looking at Herodotus initially apart from his intellectual context, we may be able to tell more about that context: we may no longer

[70] See esp. Parker (1997), Sourvinou-Inwood (1997); for ritual, Easterling (1988).

[71] Parker (1996: 210); 5th-cent. innovations (p. 153) 'allow us to observe, with unusual clarity and precision, a quite normal operation of polytheism'. Cf. Feeney (1998: 5) for Roman religion. For these questions of religious change, see Ch. 10.

need, for example, to imagine Herodotus and Thucydides as living in two separate, hermetically (or chronologically) sealed worlds.

The picture that will ultimately be derived of Greek religion will be significantly different from that presented in many recent treatments of the subject. In particular, a number of ideas will be addressed that together have begun to form something of an orthodoxy in the treatment of Greek religion. The main tenets of this orthodoxy are often phrased in terms of a sharp contrast between Greek religion and modern preconceptions of the nature of religion.[72] Some facts are undeniable: the lack of any body of sacred scriptures, or of an organized priesthood, let alone a church. Greek religion, it is further said, was centred on the community and not the individual. What was important was not the state of mind of the participant in ritual acts but simply the performance.[73] In the words of Louise Bruit Zaidman and Pauline Schmitt Pantel,[74]

> Greek religion may then fairly be said to be ritualistic in the sense that it was the opposite of dogmatic: it was not constructed around a unified corpus of doctrines, and it was above all the observance of rituals rather than fidelity to a dogma or belief that ensured the permanence of tradition and communal cohesiveness.

It is perhaps important to offer some qualifications to what may be seen as a caricature of a modern consensus. Detailed discussion often presents a different impression from these generalizing formulations. Bruit Zaidman and Schmitt Pantel continue to say that this 'ritualism did not exclude either religious "thought" or religious "belief"'. Bremmer acknowledges that Greek religion 'gave meaning and explanation to life', that dreams or shipwrecks 'all could be traced back to

---

[72] See e.g. Price (1984: ch. 1), Burkert (1985a: 8, 275), Osborne (1994: 144–5), Bremmer (1994: 1–10). Cf. the strictures of Staal (1989: 390–1, 393) concerning the Western misunderstanding of 'eastern' religions.

[73] The primacy of ritual over belief has been a feature of the vast majority of studies of ancient religion this century, as observed by Versnel (1990a: 26); already in 1889 Robertson Smith declared that 'ritual and practical usage were the sum total of ancient religions' (p. 20). For the idea of the primacy of action over belief in anthropological treatments of religion, see also the discussion of Skorupski (1976: 46–8).

[74] Bruit Zaidman and Schmitt Pantel (1992: 27).

particular gods and . . . given a recognizable and clear place in the Greek world-view'.[75] Much of the drive behind such generalizing formulations for ancient religion derives from the study of Roman religion, where historically there has been a greater need to establish the authenticity of religion.[76] Historians of Greek religion, by contrast, have sporadically continued to use terms such as 'belief' without apparent qualms.[77]

Nevertheless, there are a number of significant overstatements in this modern creed that need to be challenged. The most evident differences between Christian and Greek religion—the lack in Greek religion of a body of scripture or of a priesthood—are the basis at best for relative distinctions:[78] texts and a church demonstrably fail to ensure more than a degree of uniformity in Christian doctrine or practice. Conversely, though the restraints on religious innovation may be relatively loose, the Greek world is not a world without any form of, or focus for, religious authority.[79] To describe Greek religion as primarily or exclusively concerned with the performance of ritual acts is also an extreme overstatement. Religious belief, as will be seen, provides for the Greeks (as for Christians) a means for the explanation of events that is compatible with experience.[80] The beliefs that make up this

[75] Bremmer (1994: 6).

[76] As Feeney has said (1998: 10), 'ritual has become a kind of trump card: if you can prove that something has reference to cult, you are proving that it means something'; see also the comments of Nock cited by Phillips (1986: 2697). See, however, Burkert (1985a: 275) on the danger in Greek religion also of dismissing 'a piety without faith, love, and hope as extrinsic and superficial, not attaining the essence of religion'.

[77] See e.g. Sourvinou-Inwood (1997: 161) for tragedy as a source for 'theology and belief', or Parker's definition of the 'religious act' (1996: 1) as a group of worshippers approaching a god 'via a set of traditional procedures, acting on the basis (or at least 'as if' on the basis) of certain beliefs'. For 'religious mentality', see Versnel (1981; 1990a), Pleket (1981). The term 'belief' is used by I. Morris (1993) (whilst approving of Price's strictures, p. 24), and quite unselfconsciously by Yunis (1988).

[78] See Tambiah (1968: 181).

[79] The complex relation between religion and the state, and the process by which the state became 'increasingly the main framework of religious activity' are well sketched by Davies (1988); for religious comformity and 'tolerance', see Garnsey (1984: 3–6).

[80] For this approach to Greek religion, see esp. Easterling (1973: 5–6),

'system', though many might be described as dependent on or
secondary to the performance of ritual acts—most obviously,
taboos over ritual purity—can by no means in general be
characterized as a subset of ritual. Though this study will
concentrate on describing Herodotus' beliefs rather than the
religious practices he describes, Herodotus' treatment of 'foreign religions', for example, reveals a far more complex
relationship between ritual and belief than is suggested by
any such general formulation. To seek to describe Greek
religion by means of a stark opposition of ritual and dogma is
little more than to offer a choice of two caricatures.

Such questions of the nature of Greek religion will re-
emerge throughout the course of this book. One point requires
particular emphasis in advance. The term 'belief' has been
used already to describe both Herodotus' conscious statements
concerning religion and his unconscious presuppositions. It is
not a term that is prominent in studies of Greek religion. The
reason for this nervousness is the term's associations with
Christianity, its reflection, in the phrase of Simon Price, of
'Christianizing assumptions' of the nature of religion:[81]

'Belief' as a religious term is profoundly Christian in its implications;
it was forged out of the experience which the Apostles and Saint Paul
had of the Risen Lord. The emphasis which 'belief' gives to spiritual
commitment has no necessary place in the analysis of other cultures.

'Belief', Price comments, is not a 'distinct and natural capacity
which is shared by all human beings'. Ritual, on the other
hand, 'is what there was'.[82] Ironically, it might be claimed that
this position falls into exactly the trap that it seeks to avoid.
For to avoid the term 'belief' on the grounds of its association
with Christianity is surely to privilege Christianity, and the
Christian definition of belief as a personal 'spiritual commitment', unduly.[83] The idea of measuring the believer by the

Gould (1985). For the compatibility of beliefs and experience, cf. Evans-
Pritchard (1976; 1956) on the Azande and Nuer; Lienhardt on Dinka religion
'rather phenomenological than theological' (1961: 32); see also Hallpike (1979:
466–74), Skorupski (1976: 4–5) on the idea of 'blocks to falsifiability' as
originating with Tylor.

[81] Price (1984: 11); cf. Beard and Crawford (1985: 26–7).
[82] Price (1984: 10–11).
[83] Cf. Beard, North, and Price (1998: p. x), distinguishing 'issues of belief'

extent to which they accord belief to, or withold it from, a core of doctrines[84] may be alien to ancient (and many modern) religions. As Denis Feeney has commented in paraphrasing Price, 'not all religions place as high a value on belief in key dogmas as does modern Christianity'.[85] A stress on the emotional state of the participant in cult may also arguably be a more common feature of Christianity than of other religions.[86] However, the state of mind of an individual can hardly be used as a necessary criterion even of Christian religious experience. As Evans-Pritchard commented, it would be absurd to say that 'when a priest is saying Mass, he is not performing a religious act unless he is in a certain emotional state'; 'anyhow', he added, 'who knows what his emotional state might be?'[87] In practice, the means—the 'let-out clauses' or 'blocks to falsifiability'—by which belief in the presence of a Christian god is sustained are little different to those whereby the ancient belief in divination or epiphanies was maintained—or indeed whereby any unverifiable proposition is supported.[88] Christianity also is riven with contradictions and inconsistencies.[89] Christian belief too is *in practice* inherited, not only a matter of personal choice; it too

from 'personal belief' (see also pp. 48–50). For the question of whether the Greeks had a conception of belief, see Fahr (1969), and below, Ch. 8.

[84] A phrase adapted from Feeney (1998: 22).

[85] Feeney (1998: 13). He qualifies his remark with the expression 'to put it most modestly'; elsewhere (pp. 2–3) he characterizes the Christian and Greek models of belief as, respectively, 'salvation, morality, belief', and 'ritual and mythology of corporate significance'.

[86] Though, for the idea of a relationship of *philia* between man and god, see Parker (1998b: 122–3).

[87] Evans-Pritchard (1965: 44); cf. Skorupski (1976: 144).

[88] See esp. the racist jazz fan of Versnel (1990a: 11), or Versnel (1990b: 43–4) on the proposition that all redheads are alchoholics.

[89] See Evans-Pritchard (1965: 108): 'It may, indeed, be true, that primitive beliefs are vague and uncertain, but it does not seem to have occurred to these writers that so are those of ordinary people in our own society; for how could it be otherwise when religion concerns beings which cannot be directly apprehended by the senses or fully comprehended by reason?' Cf. Geertz (1973: 109–10), or Lienhardt's comments on Tylor (1956: 387): 'A little reflection upon the religion of his own day would have persuaded him that though reason and argument by analogy may support a faith, they do not found one.'

is socially reinforced through ritual.[90] Even in the case of a
religion with sacred texts, these shed light only on a small part
of a much larger picture: Evans-Pritchard went so far as to
describe such texts as, for the anthropologist, 'the least
significant part of religion'.[91]

Rather than dismissing 'belief' then, we need to reclaim it.
The relationship between belief and ritual may not, we can
allow, be a simple or a direct one. A ritual action may not be
directly motivated by a corresponding belief. Nonetheless,
ritual cannot be seen in isolation from the attitudes that
frame and structure it: it would be absurd to see, for example,
the practice of divination in the *Histories* apart from Herodotus' observations concerning divination. At the same time, as
we will see, religious beliefs have other functions than simply
to validate ritual: the explanation of personal misfortune, of
earthquakes or other natural disasters, or indeed as a means of
explaining any reversal in human fortune. Belief, in this sense,
is a term that can be applied to the analysis of all societies; the
word need have no association with the Christian emphasis on
'belief in key dogmas'. The most important distinction is that
suggested by Feeney's reference to 'modern Christianity'. The
real difference arguably is not between Christianity and
ancient religion, but between an age today (in Britain)
where unbelief is envisaged as a normal, if not indeed as the
normal position—and so consequently 'religion' is envisaged
as something apart—and earlier ages, Christian as well, in
which complete unbelief was scarcely imaginable.[92] The
words of Lucien Febvre might again, with a few changes,
provide an accurate description of Herodotus and his contemporaries:[93]

---

[90] For the social context and reinforcement of belief, see e.g. Evans-
Pritchard (1956: 46, 54), Macintyre (1970: 73–4).

[91] Evans-Pritchard (1965: 119); cf. Lienhardt (1956: 383), Price (1984: 5–
6). Contrast Mikalson (1983: 3–4), regretting the lack of a religious confes-
sional literature.

[92] Cf. Bossy (1985: 170–1), Phillips (1986: 2700), Beard, North, and Price
(1998: 42–3). See also Evans-Pritchard's observations on the absence of the
idea of belief or unbelief among the Nuer (1956: 9).

[93] Febvre (1982: 336); referred to also by Bremmer (1982: 51–2).

Today we make a choice to be a Christian or not. There was no choice in the sixteenth century. One was a Christian in fact. One's thoughts could wander far from Christ, but these were plays of fancy, without the living support of reality. One could not even abstain from observance. Whether one wanted or not, one found oneself immersed from birth in a bath of Christianity from which one did not emerge even at death.

Finally, it is necessary to address some of the difficulties faced in the attempt to elucidate Herodotus' religious beliefs. Recent years have seen a revival in scholarly scepticism concerning Herodotus' reliability: the assertion, for example (associated particularly with Detlev Fehling) that Herodotus' source ascriptions are essentially fictional, or that he never in fact travelled to many of the lands of which he claims first-hand knowledge.[94] These are questions far too great and involved to admit of any easy solution—questions which, it might fairly be said, if you are not completely confused you have not begun to understand. A study of religious mentality avoids many of these hazards. It matters little for us whether Herodotus' account of Egyptian beliefs and practices, say, bears any resemblance to reality. No one doubts, I imagine, that his account of Egypt is heavily shaped or distorted by Greek 'perceptual filters'—regardless of whether he visited Egypt, regardless in other words of the stage at which these filters did their work. Where Fehling's Herodotus must be confronted is in his modernity and detachment. As Kenneth Dover has sharply observed, Fehling's analysis assumes a stark antithesis: '*either* systematic invention *or* puerile gullibility'.[95] If two sources are cited in support of a miracle (something inherently impossible) one or both of those citations must be invented.[96]

---

[94] See e.g. Fehling (1989), Armayor (1978*a*; 1978*b*; 1978*c*; 1980; 1985), West (1985; 1992). Against this 'Liar School' (in fact a fairly disparate group), see above all Pritchett (1993), more temperately Rhodes (1994: 160–1), A. B. Lloyd (1995) on Egyptian buildings; for a middle course, see Moles (1993), Derow (1994: 79), Fowler (1996: esp. 80–6), Dover (1998). West also seems occasionally to pursue a middle course, as when she asserts (1985: 294) that 'no doubt he sincerely believed that these Sehenswürdigkeiten were there to be seen', or that Herodotus' use of the first person was a 'literary convention'.

[95] Dover (1998: 224).

[96] See Fehling (1989: 12–14) on 8. 38–39. 1, his first example of 'demonstrably false source-citations'; contrast Pritchett (1993: 10–12).

The alternative that Herodotus might himself have believed in
the *possibility* of the impossible, that his tidy source-citations
are themselves the product of that belief, is not considered.[97]
Herodotus will be taken here at face value. We may, surely,
take it as highly probable that there were no constraints upon
Herodotus—even the pressure of audience expectations, discussed above—that might have led him to claim, for example, a
belief in prophecy (8. 77) when his personal view was at
variance with this. An even greater degree of disingenuousness
would be necessary to explain Herodotus' forgery of some of
what have been termed his religious presuppositions, the
assumption, for example, that certain actions will inevitably
receive retribution.

How then can we distinguish Herodotus' own opinions from
those reported in the *Histories*? Can we ever hope to establish
that in any instance Herodotus shares the opinion expressed,
except in those cases where he makes his agreement explicit?
Herodotus does not vouch for the truth of every report in his
Histories. As he famously remarks in the context of the
differing reports of the Argive role in the Persian wars, 'I am
bound to say what has been said ($\lambda\acute{\epsilon}\gamma\epsilon\iota\nu$ $\tau\grave{\alpha}$ $\lambda\epsilon\gamma\acute{o}\mu\epsilon\nu\alpha$), but I am
not at all bound to believe everything—and let this remark hold
for my whole history' (7. 152. 3).[98] This statement, clearly a
programmatic declaration of his procedure throughout the
Histories, has been seen as a failure on Herodotus' part to
'accept his responsibilities' as a historian.[99] More often, however, it is given a favourable interpretation, produced as a kind
of trump card in the arguments against claims of naïvety or in
favour of his status as a historian. Charges of credulity laid
against Herodotus, we are told by W. K. Pritchett, ignore this
statement.[100] Herodotus, in the words of another scholar, is
responsible for the inclusion of a logos but 'not at all for its
contents'![101] Such arguments tend to present the reader with an

---

[97] See esp. Dover's 'stretching' of oral tradition (1998).

[98] $\dot{\epsilon}\gamma\grave{\omega}$ $\delta\grave{\epsilon}$ $\dot{o}\phi\epsilon\acute{\iota}\lambda\omega$ $\lambda\acute{\epsilon}\gamma\epsilon\iota\nu$ $\tau\grave{\alpha}$ $\lambda\epsilon\gamma\acute{o}\mu\epsilon\nu\alpha$, $\pi\epsilon\acute{\iota}\theta\epsilon\sigma\theta\alpha\acute{\iota}$ $\gamma\epsilon$ $\mu\grave{\epsilon}\nu$ $o\dot{\upsilon}$ $\pi\alpha\nu\tau\acute{\alpha}\pi\alpha\sigma\iota\nu$ $\dot{o}\phi\epsilon\acute{\iota}\lambda\omega$, $\kappa\alpha\acute{\iota}$
$\mu o\iota$ $\tau o\hat{\upsilon}\tau o$ $\tau\grave{o}$ $\dot{\epsilon}\pi o\varsigma$ $\dot{\epsilon}\chi\acute{\epsilon}\tau\omega$ $\dot{\epsilon}\varsigma$ $\pi\acute{\alpha}\nu\tau\alpha$ $\lambda\acute{o}\gamma o\nu$.   [99] Veyne (1981: 5).

[100] Pritchett (1993: 286); see similarly Hooker (1989: 146); or (from a
different perspective and in a different context) Fehling (1989: 96): 'we have
become familiar with Herodotus' practice of providing miraculous stories
with a Confirmation that still safeguards his own credit'.

[101] Waters (1971: 14).

unattractive choice of two extremes. But the very desperation
with which some scholars cling to the passage might reasonably
lead one to doubt that it says quite what they suppose it to say.
Herodotus 'insulates himself', in Lateiner's words, 'from
seeming to believe'.[102] There is a grave danger that it is we
who insulate him.

Herodotus' distancing strategy has been broken down into a
number of discrete but related 'techniques'. Of these, one—the
so-called 'intrusive oblique infinitive'—has been relegated to
Appendix 1. Two others need to be addressed more directly,
however: the practice of offering 'alternative versions' of the
same event; and that of prefacing an account by 'it is said'
(λέγεται) or a similar expression. The strategy of 'alternative
versions' has been described by John Gould as a 'cautionary
mode of narrative . . . conspicuously adopted when there are
supernatural explanations among those offered by his informants'.[103] More crudely, the term λέγεται, it has been claimed,
is 'used by Herodotus in his own name as an expression of
doubt'. In the case of 'passages where the word introduces two
or more versions of a story', where the two techniques are
combined, 'the doubt is implicit in this fact'.[104]

The important point that needs to be made is that neither of
these phenomena *necessarily* suggests doubt or distance on
Herodotus' part. We cannot, of course, automatically assume
that any account ascribed to an individual or people and
reported by Herodotus without explicit comment comes, as it
were, with the author's guarantee of its truth. But equally we
cannot presume that Herodotus intends by reporting it in this
way to signal his doubt. One counter-example is enough to
disprove any such general rule. Herodotus presents a number
of alternative explanations for the death of Cleomenes (6. 75. 3,

[102] Lateiner (1989: 23). Lateiner's 'inventories' are of enormous use in
refuting his views.

[103] Gould (1994: 96).

[104] Gould (1989: 75). On λέγεται see also Lateiner (1989: 22): Herodotus
'employs this convenience for 1) what he has not seen and deems most
unlikely, 2) what is divine or miraculous . . ., 3) what seems best or worst
or otherwise superlative, and 4) when more than one account of a given event
is current and no secure resolution is discernible. These four categories
represent what he does not know, what he cannot know, and what cannot
be known by anyone.'

84):[105] that he died because he had bribed the Pythia, 'as most of the Greeks say' (ὡς μὲν οἱ πολλοὶ λέγουσι Ἑλλήνων, 6. 75. 3), 'as the Athenians say' because he had ravaged the shrine of the god at Eleusis (6. 75. 3), 'as the Argives say' because of his burning of a sacred grove, and 'as the Spartans themselves say' for no supernatural reason (ἐκ δαιμονίου μὲν οὐδενός, 6. 84. 1), but because he had learnt from some Scythian ambassadors to drink his wine neat. Herodotus then digresses to give the background for this explanation as for the others—and then concludes by expressing his own opinion that 'it seems to me that Cleomenes paid the price for his treatment of Demaratus' (ἐμοὶ δὲ δοκέει τίσιν ταύτην ὁ Κλεομένης Δημαρήτῳ ἐκτεῖσαι, 6. 84. 3). Nothing in Herodotus' reporting of the alternative versions of Cleomenes' death suggests his own view except this final statement. It follows then that, in the absence of any similar expression of preference (or of any analogous passages in which he does express a preference), we may not presume to know either which version Herodotus would have preferred *or* indeed that he would have preferred any.

Far from it being the case that *ta legomena* are for Herodotus inherently unreliable, reports of others' views are in fact the inevitable basis of the answers to many (if not all) historical questions. Frequently, of course, he professes that he cannot judge even when there are such reports,[106] sometimes explicitly on the grounds of the differences between accounts.[107] Even in these circumstances, Herodotus still often feels it necessary to record 'what has been said'—'I am not able to say except what has been said' (2. 130. 2)[108]—on one occasion even to add that his sources swear by their incredible account (4. 105. 2).[109]

---

[105] This is curiously the example chosen by Gould to illustrate 'alternative versions'. He concludes by saying that it 'should not surprise us that Herodotus gives his authorial approval to such an explanation, involving the anger of divinity'. It is hard to see then in what sense alternative versions constitute a 'cautionary mode of narrative'.

[106] e.g. 8. 8. 2: οὐκ ἔχω εἰπεῖν ἀτρεκέως, θωμάζω δὲ εἰ τὰ λεγόμενά ἐστι ἀληθέα; cf. also 1. 172. 1; 3. 116. 1; 4. 195. 2; 6. 82. 1, 124. 1.

[107] 4. 81. 1, 6. 14. 1, 9. 84. 1–2.

[108] οὐκ ἔχω εἰπεῖν πλὴν ἢ τὰ λεγόμενα; 6. 137. 1, 7. 152. 1.

[109] ἐμὲ μέν νυν ταῦτα λέγοντες οὐ πείθουσι, λέγουσι δὲ οὐδὲν ἧσσον, καὶ ὀμνῦσι δὲ λέγοντες (Saying these things they do not convince me, but they say so nonetheless, and they swear to the truth of their words).

Moreover, on those occasions in which Herodotus asserts that he cannot judge the truth of a question, the explanation that he gives is often also that 'it is not said' (οὐ λέγεται).[110] Another formula frequently employed is that 'no one can say', that 'no one can accurately say' or 'no one can clearly say':[111] the implication of these passages appears to be that because of the lack of second-hand information Herodotus too cannot accurately say.[112] Expressions such as 'in so far as we know' (ὅσον ἡμεῖς ἴδμεν)[113] suggest also that on the subject in question he has at his disposal no reliable or plausible report.

Herodotus' references to the clarity or to the accuracy of his would-be informants show, of course, that he is not likely to believe *any* report given to him: he applies criteria of clarity and of accuracy—whatever these might constitute for him—to the reports he receives. This is not in itself very surprising. Given, however, the common opinion that Herodotus *by definition* means to distance himself from his reports of others' stories, it is worth noting that, while he may indeed distance himself from his reports, he equally considers it possible that *ta legomena* might be clear, accurate, and reliable. This position is perfectly compatible with the passage with which this section began, 7. 152. 3, so long as that passage is not read with the presumption that any hint of an oral source spells doubt: what Herodotus is saying there is that he is not *obliged* to believe *all reports alike*. In other words Herodotus is asserting that he is critical, and that on some occasions he may report stories that he does not himself believe. 7. 152. 3 is a statement of principle—and a general one at that—not a legalistic record of procedure.[114]

---

[110] 1. 47. 2, 49; 7. 60. 1; 8. 128. 1, 133; cf. also 2. 19. 1, 28. 1; 3. 115. 2; 4. 16. 1 in which Herodotus pleads that he was unable to learn anything from (respectively) the priests (or anyone else), from the Egyptians, Libyans, and Greeks, or in the final two instances from any eyewitnesses.

[111] e.g. 2. 31 (οὐδεὶς ἔχει σαφέως φράσαι), 2. 34. 1 (οὐδεὶς ἔχει λέγειν), 2. 126. 1 (οὐ γὰρ δὴ τοῦτό γε ἔλεγον); 4. 25. 1 (οὐδεὶς ἀτρεκέως οἶδε φράσαι), 40. 2, 53. 4 (ἔχει οὐδεὶς φράσαι); 5. 9. 1 (οὐδεὶς ἔχει φράσαι τὸ ἀτρεκές).

[112] He may nevertheless speculate on the basis of probability: 1. 57. 1; 4. 180. 4; 8. 112. 2, 133; 9. 32. 2, 81. 2.

[113] 3. 98. 2, 417. 2; 4. 18. 3, 20. 2, 197. 2; 7. 111. 1.

[114] See, however, Shimron (1989: 77) envisaging 7. 152. 3 as his 'strongest dissociation from his λεγόμενα'. Moles (1993: 95) takes the more subtle line that 'this non-committal stance takes many forms—genuinely non-committal,

How then are we to ascertain Herodotus' own opinions or beliefs in those instances in which he makes no explicit judgement? Frequently we cannot. When, for example, in the course of his account of how the Psylli came to be buried in a sand-storm, an account containing apparently no other clues of his judgement, Herodotus asserts 'I say what the Libyans say' (λέγω δὲ ταῦτα τὰ λέγουσι Λίβυες, 4. 173), there is no reasonable cause to speak of Herodotus' 'doubts on [the] Libyan story of how [the] Psylli perished':[115] his remark may just as well be intended either as a quite neutral source ascription or even as an assurance of the likely truth of the story. There are no simple rules. Even stories told in direct speech 'in Herodotus' own words' cannot be held to come with a guarantee of their truth.[116] The chief way to judge Herodotus' opinion in the absence of any explicit comment is clearly by way of analogy to others in which he does express an opinion. In cases where no such analogy is available, for instance in the case of a character employing proverbial religious language which cannot be paralleled in any of Herodotus' own direct statements, it is useful to ask what function such language might serve other than as an expression of Herodotus' own beliefs: does it, for example, help to characterize the individual in question? If it apparently serves no such function, if on the other hand the same language is apparently employed by a large number of characters in different circumstances through the *Histories,* then the possibility increases that the language in question reflects Herodotus' own attitudes or beliefs. A test case of this problem, discussed in the following chapter, is the pattern of ideas on the unpredictability of human fortune expressed first by Solon in Book 1 and then repeated and developed through-out the *Histories,* often at crucial points in Herodotus' narrat-

or implying the untruth of the material, or implying, if not its untruth, at least its relative insignificance'.

[115] Lateiner (1989: 72).

[116] Cf. Cooper (1974: 28 n. 8): 'It must also be emphasized that Herodotus is capable of reporting something which he plainly quite disbelieves in Oratio Recta. Straightforward belief and straightforward disbelief are psychologically and therefore stylistically far more closely related to each other than irony is to either.' Lateiner (1989: 25) suggests that 'the greater the aura of verisimilitude, the more mimetic a story . . ., the less credence the author seems to give it'.

ive: it would be hard to see what function these passages might be intended to serve if they were not somehow—even if only as straw men to be thrown down[117]—an expression of an Herodotean philosophy.

Two questions remain. The first is that of the implications of Herodotus' procedure with regard to *ta legomena* for his status as a historian. The idea, rarely argued at any length, that such procedures *necessarily* constitute distancing techniques can clearly be seen to be rooted in the tendency to seek to defend Herodotus (as such critics see it) from charges of naïvety, to affirm his status as the Father of History. Having dismissed half of the *Histories* as unhistorical in Herodotus' own eyes, however, his self-styled defenders are left, surely, in an uncomfortable position. Herodotus' imagined integrity is preserved—but at what price for his work? The strategy of alternative versions may in certain instances be motivated by the consideration on Herodotus' part that others could employ the same data to form their own conclusions, that what men think about past events is as important as the truth of those events.[118] There is surely, however, a danger of special pleading in this portrayal of Herodotus the model anthropologist. It would be simpler to acknowledge that the criteria of truth or reliability, or even of verifiability, are not necessarily essential for the inclusion of material in the *Histories*. But another extreme position is equally unattractive. 7. 152. 3 has been described as revealing an awareness on Herodotus' part that 'there are only versions and no ultimate truth . . . He has no notion of getting at the *bare* facts, whatever that may mean. To him facts are always dressed.'[119] Much as this reading of Herodotus provides a fashionable twist to the question of his historical status, it does not adequately describe his work. Herodotus' concepts of accuracy and of reliability clearly show that he was, on occasion at least, concerned to undress his facts. It is in this, the extent to which the past was for him a 'field of critical study',[120] that his achievement as a historian lies.

---

[117] See e.g. the discussion of Glaucus, Ch. 4.
[118] Lateiner (1989: 77).
[119] Ligota (1982: 10).
[120] The phrase is Peter Derow's (1994: 73), used of Hecataeus.

Secondly, it is necessary to say something of the idea, alluded to above, that strategies such as that of 'alternative versions' are characteristically or more conspicuously adopted in the context of the supernatural or divine.[121] Even presuming that alternative versions do reflect a degree of distance or reserve, to prove that there is any correlation between such strategies and the presence of supernatural explanations is, at very least, a difficult proposition. A cursory run-through of Donald Lateiner's inventory of approximately 150 instances of alternative versions reveals no more than a handful of supernatural explanations.[122] Many of the questions to which Herodotus gives a number of alternative answers, moreover, turn out to be quite everyday. They follow no clear pattern: did Xerxes cross the Hellespont after or in the middle of his army (7. 55. 3)? did he return by sea or land (8. 117. 2–119)? was Ladice the daughter of Battus or of Critoboulus (2. 181. 2)? did the Alcmeonids show a shield at Marathon (6. 121–4)? was the exiled Demaratus loyal to Sparta (7. 239. 2)? Herodotus is sceptical of certain stories of divine intervention just as he is sceptical of rumours of political intrigue, or of false genealogy. It is probably more fruitful then to attempt to mark out the areas of Herodotus' scepticism or belief on the basis of the evidence that we have than to insinuate, let alone to seek to measure, the answers to such questions on the basis of statistics.

[121] Gould (1994: 96). See also Lateiner (1989: 22, 31–2; 1990: 231); Shimron (1989: 10); Bowden (1992: pp. xxvi–vii), introducing the reverse argument that 'most of his stories about divine activity are introduced as *logoi* told by others, which . . . suggests that he wanted to distance himself from them. They are included because they represent the traditions of his time . . .'. See also Shimron's attempt to prove (1989: 75–80) that λέγεται is used only for 'obviously non-political and very often unhistorical details'. Contrast the sensible conclusion of Groten (1963: 87) that Herodotus follows no 'common pattern of treatment'.

[122] 1. 95. 1, 182. 1; 2. 56. 1; 3. 33; 5. 1, 95. 1–96. 2; 7. 167. 2, 189. 3, 191. 2; 9. 91. For the complete inventory see Lateiner (1989: 84–90).

2

Solon and Human Fortune

> This is the display of the enquiries of Herodotus of Halicarnnassus, [written] so that the affairs of men (τὰ γενόμενα ἐξ ἀνθρώπων) should not become forgotten over time, and that great and marvellous deeds, both those displayed by Greeks and by barbarians, should not become lacking in due glory, especially the reason why they waged war with one another.

In these opening words of the *Histories*, Herodotus makes no mention of the gods, but only of men. Whereas Homer in the opening lines of the Iliad first claims divine inspiration for his work and then portrays the deaths of the Achaeans as being in fulfilment of the plans of Zeus, Herodotus speaks only of 'the affairs of men' (or 'events emerging from men'?) or of 'great and marvellous deeds', by implication again the deeds of men.[1] The miraculous is also conspicuously absent in Herodotus' subsequent telling of the stories of the thefts of Io, Europe, Medea, and Helen (1. 1–5. 2):[2] his Io, for example, is not forced to wander the earth in the form of a heifer, but is kidnapped by Phoenician merchants (in the version ascribed to the Persians) or (according, Herodotus says, to the Phoenicians themselves) is seen running away from home through a maidenly modesty, having become pregnant, voluntarily, at the hands of the Phoenician ship's captain. Herodotus' conclusion to these stories of reciprocal wife-stealing again emphasizes only the human (1. 5. 3–4):

[1] ἔργα, translated here as 'deeds', embraces both actions and monuments: so, for example, Moeris was the only one of a group of kings of Egypt to have displayed ἔργα of any distinction as he left as a memorial the gateway of Hephaestus, 2. 101. 1–2. Conversely, brave actions and even defiant, wise or epigrammatic remarks can be described as 'memorials': 6. 109. 3, 7. 226. 2, 9. 16. 2. See further Immerwahr (1960); contrast Raubitschek (1939), Grant (1983: 294–6).

[2] See e.g. Flory (1987: 23–8).

I will not say about these matters that it happened in this way or in
that. Rather, indicating the man whom I know to have been the first
to initiate unjust deeds against the Greeks, I will proceed with my
account, touching as I do so on both small and great cities of men
alike (ὁμοίως σμικρὰ καὶ μεγάλα ἄστεα ἀνθρώπων ἐπεξιών).[3] For of those
which were formerly great most have now become small, while those
which in my time were great were formerly small. Understanding
then that human fortune never remains for long in the same place (τὴν
ἀνθρωπηίην ὢν ἐπιστάμενος εὐδαιμονίην οὐδαμὰ ἐν τὠυτῷ μένουσαν), I will
recall both alike.

Herodotus' treatment of myths, the significance of his technique of 'demythologization', will be discussed more fully
below in Chapter 7. How, though, are we to interpret the
omission of any mention of the gods or of 'the divine' from
these opening chapters?

A common reading of the Proem is that Herodotus means to
announce his historical enterprise as an exclusively secular
one.[4] Herodotus certainly makes no claims of inspiration.
Unlike Homer, it is only rarely that he gives any glimpse into
the deliberations of the gods themselves, and such insights as
he does provide into the smoke-filled rooms in which the fates
of men are decided derive not from his own historical understanding but from oracles or prophets: the closest that we come
is the Pythia's justification of Apollo against Croesus' complaint of having been deceived (1. 91). However, a focus on the
'affairs of men' need not entail any exclusion of the divine. The
Histories indeed are saturated with instances of divine intervention. Such divine intervention is sometimes, as we will see,
ascribed to individual gods. Herodotus may even ascribe
motives for such intervention. But his characterization of the
divine is made up only of the broadest brush strokes. For,
unlike the characterizations of the gods in myth—sustained by
a certain suspension of disbelief and projected onto a distant
past—the conclusion that a god is angry or that he is jealous

---

[3] This is an echo of the Odyssey, Od. 1. 3. For other Homeric echoes in the
Proem, see Krischer (1965), Woodman (1988: 1–4); more broadly, Bowie
(1993), Moles (1993).

[4] So e.g. Wikarjak (1963: 42, 54), Drews (1973: 41), Fornara (1990: 29),
Darbo-Peschanski (1987: 23), acknowledging that the Histories are saturated
with the divine.

constitutes for Herodotus a deduction from the course of events. Quite simply, he felt no need in the Proem to mention the presence of the gods. As he himself says in conclusion to the coincidences between the battles of Mycale and Plataea (that they were both fought close by shrines of Demeter, that they were simultaneous, and that, despite this, a rumour reached Mycale of the victory at Plataea) 'the divine nature of affairs is clear by many proofs' (δῆλα δὴ πολλοῖσι τεκμηρίοισί ἐστι τὰ θεῖα τῶν πρηγμάτων, 9. 100. 2).

Other forms of divine intervention, through miracles, through divine retribution, and through divination, will be discussed in subsequent chapters. This chapter will treat possibly the most indirect, the most intangible form of divine intervention, intervention through reversals in human fortune. The instability of human fortune is, as we have seen, central to Herodotus' own definition of his task: his account will take in both small and great cities, as he understands that human fortune never resides long in the same place (1. 5. 4). It is also fundamental to the broader pattern of his religious beliefs. How can we be sure, however, that such reversals in human fortune are, in Herodotus' mind, the result of the divine?[5] The fullest exposition in the *Histories* of the idea of the instability of human fortune and of the divine cause of this instability comes in the words put into the mouth of the Athenian Solon during his encounter with Croesus early in Book 1. The question of whether or not Herodotus ascribes a divine cause to reversals in human fortune hinges primarily on what we consider to be the status of this passage. A fairly lengthy synopsis of the encounter between Solon and Croesus is necessary here.

Croesus orders his servants to take Solon on a tour of his treasury to show him his great fortune (πάντα ἐόντα μεγάλα τε καὶ ὄλβια, 1. 30. 1). Then Croesus asks Solon the very leading question of the identity of the 'most fortunate man' (ὀλβιώτατον, 1. 30. 2) that Solon has met on his travels. He fully expects Solon to give his own name. Solon's first candidate, however, is the

---

[5] The link between human instability and the divine is acknowledged by e.g. De Sanctis (1936: 7), Moles (1993: 96), denied by Waters (1971: 10), Lateiner (1989: 215–16), Shimron (1989: 28, 40) (though he appears also to express an opposite view at p. 49), Fornara (1990: 30).

Athenian Tellus (1. 30. 3).[6] His good fortune consisted in the
healthy state of his city during his lifetime, the possession of
noble children and of grandchildren, a life of relative comfort
and prosperity for an Athenian, a glorious death in battle for his
country, and a public burial (1. 30. 4–5). So, Herodotus says,
Solon admonished Croesus by telling him of the good pieces of
fortune of Tellus. The words Herodotus uses of Tellus' blessings, πολλά τε καὶ ὄλβια (1. 31. 1), by their echo of the similar
words that describe Croesus' treasure, imply a distinction
between two types of fortune, perhaps incompatible.[7]

Croesus then asks the identity of the next most fortunate
man (1. 31. 1). Solon again defies Croesus' expectation by
replying with the story of the Argive brothers Cleobis and
Biton. They were blessed with a wealth that was sufficient to
live on, a 'sufficient living' (βίος . . . ἀρκέων, 1. 31. 2), and
strength of body. They had both won prizes at Games. When
their mother needed to get to the festival of Hera, but their
oxen did not arrive from the fields in time, the brothers
dragged the cart in their stead for all of forty-five stades
(1. 31. 2). When they arrived, the men of the crowd praised
the strength of the young men, and the women praised their
mother (1. 31. 3).[8] Their mother prayed to the goddess to grant
them 'the best piece of fortune that was possible for man' (τὸ
ἀνθρώπῳ τυχεῖν ἄριστόν ἐστι, 1. 31. 4): having feasted and
sacrificed, the brothers promptly lay down in the temple and
died (1. 31. 5). So, according to Solon, 'the god showed
through these things how death is better for men than life'
(διέδεξέ τε ἐν τούτοισι ὁ θεὸς ὡς ἄμεινον εἴη ἀνθρώπῳ τεθνάναι

---

[6] For the *double-entendre* of Tellus' name, see Immerwahr (1966: 156 and
n. 21).

[7] For the meaning of *olbos* both in Herodotus and in earlier authors, see esp.
Immerwahr (1966: 155–7), with further refs. Immerwahr asserts (p. 155) both
that *olbos* in early Greek thought meant 'true (that is, lasting) prosperity' and
that this prosperity is 'reflected in external fortune and possessions; the word
has a very strong concrete connotation'. That is surely not the prevailing view
in Herodotus, where it is precisely concrete wealth that cannot be relied
upon—although it may describe Croesus' attitude.

[8] For the way in which the interests of women mirror those of men, see also
the story of Lycidas, 9. 5—stoned by the Athenians for suggesting that a
Persian 'peace-plan' should be put before the people, his wife and children
then subsequently stoned by the Athenians' wives—with Loraux (1985: 26–7).

μᾶλλον ἢ ζώειν, 1. 31. 3).[9] The Argives subsequently set up
statues of Cleobis and Biton at Delphi, Herodotus tells us
(1. 31. 5), 'as having displayed great excellence' (ὡς ἀνδρῶν
ἀρίστων γενομένων)[10]—statues which survive to this day.[11]
    Croesus is then openly enraged. Why does Solon not value
his good fortune (εὐδαιμονίη, 1. 32. 1)? Solon's reply makes
more explicit the divine cause of changes in human fortune,
already implied by the fulfilment of the prayer of Cleobis and
Biton's mother (1. 32. 1):

Croesus, you ask me, though I understand that the divine is completely jealous and prone to disturb us, you ask me about the affairs of
men! (Ὦ Κροῖσε, ἐπιστάμενόν με τὸ θεῖον πᾶν ἐὸν φθονερόν τε καὶ ταραχῶδες
ἐπειρωτᾷς ἀνθρωπηίων πρηγμάτων πέρι.)

A lifetime of seventy years contains twenty-six thousand, two
hundred and fifty days, no one of them like any other 'so
altogether subject to chance is man' (πᾶν ἐστι ἄνθρωπος συμφορή,
1. 32. 4). Croesus may be greatly wealthy (πλουτέειν μέγα) and
the king of many men. But a wealthy man is not more fortunate
(ὀλβιώτερος, 1. 32. 5) than a man with enough to live for a day
'unless he has the luck, with all his beautiful possessions, to end
his life well' (εἰ μή οἱ τύχη ἐπίσποιτο πάντα καλὰ ἔχοντα εὖ
τελευτῆσαι τὸν βίον). Many rich men are unfortunate (ἄνολβοι),

---

[9] Legrand asks, ad loc. (i. 48 n. 1), why it is that Cleobis and Biton only
won the second prize ('si c'est un bonheur pour l'homme que d'être mort, ils
ont eu cette chance plus tôt que l'Athénien'); his suggestion is that Herodotus
has merely put the more striking story second. Conrast S. O. Shapiro's
reading (1996: 351), that 'they did not live full lives and did not leave
descendants behind'. Unlike Shapiro (or Konstan 1983: 16), but with
M. Lloyd (1987), I cannot see how Herodotus can mean anything other
than death being better than life, e.g. that 'They died at their highest
moment.'

[10] Arguably the story reflects a democratic or at least populist ideology
(death levels all men?), as suggested by Schmid and Stählin (1934: i. 2. 621);
contrast, however, Fornara (1971a: 50 n. 24). For Cleobis and Biton as
sacrificial victims, see Sansone (1991: 121–3).

[11] For the identification, see Sansone (1991: 125–32). A possibility is that
the story of Cleobis and Biton grew out of the statues, and that the statues
were then seen as the proof of the story. For comparable cases, see Parke and
Wormell (1956: i. 116, 379), Parke (1984: 219), Flower (1991: 68–9); for this
process, Gabba (1981: 61), and Herodotus' interpretation of the story of
Mycerinus' daughter, 2. 131. 2–3.

many moderately well-off men lucky (εὐτυχέες). A rich man may be able to fulfil his desires and may be better equipped to withstand any disaster that falls upon him (1. 32. 6). But the poor man's good luck (εὐτυχίη) guards him from such disasters in the first place: he is sound of body, free from disease and suffering, blessed with fine children and beauty.[12] If such a man then also finishes his life well, he can be called fortunate (ὄλβιος), but until then only lucky (εὐτυχέα, 1. 32. 7). It is not possible for a man to possess every blessing any more than for a country. So it is necessary to look to the end of a man's life, as of any other matter, to see how it turns out. For often god gives man a glimpse of happiness only then to ruin him (πολλοῖσι γὰρ δὴ ὑποδέξας ὄλβον ὁ θεὸς προρρίζους ἀνέτρεψε, 1. 32. 9).[13]

Croesus was not at all pleased with Solon, nor did he take any account of what he had said, but sent him away: for he supposed that he was a fool who dismissed 'present blessings' and who recommended that it was necessary to look to the end of every affair (1. 33). Herodotus then concludes by apparently offering his own validation of Solon's wisdom (1. 34. 1):

After Solon left a great nemesis came upon Croesus, as far as one can reckon because he considered himself to be the most fortunate of all men. (Μετὰ δὲ Σόλωνα οἰχόμενον ἔλαβε ἐκ θεοῦ νέμεσις μεγάλη Κροῖσον, ὡς εἰκάσαι, ὅτι ἐνόμισε ἑωυτὸν εἶναι ἀνθρώπων ἁπάντων ὀλβιώτατον.)

The expression ὡς εἰκάσαι suggests a considered judgement. By referring Croesus' eventual nemesis to his opinion of his own good fortune, Herodotus appears completely to adopt Solon's terms.

What then is the status of the ideas presented by Solon? They are certainly not unique to Herodotus' *Histories*. There are, to begin with, enough parallels between the thoughts expressed by the Solon of the *Histories* and by the historical Solon in the extant fragments of his poetry to suggest that Herodotus intended in

---

[12] Contrast, however, the ugliness of the (later beautiful) wife of Ariston, a worse tragedy apparently for the wealth of her parents: 6. 61. 3.

[13] How and Wells, ad loc., judge the thought of 1. 32 'forced' and inconsistent; contrast, however, the sensible remarks of Audiat (1940). M. Lloyd (1987) attempts too strenuously to render Solon's philosophy consistent. De Romilly (1977: 42–6) by contrast demands too great a degree of consistency.

some sense to be faithful to the historical figure, to create, as it were, a collage of Solonian thought.[14] Perhaps the most significant affinity between the historical and Herodotean Solon is revealed by Solon's poem on the ages of man: a man who reaches 70 years of age will have met a timely death, Solon asserts (fr. 24. 17–18 West). Herodotus must surely have had this poem in mind when he made his own Solon calculate the precise number of days in 70 years.[15] Solon's remark that no one can know how any matter will end when it is just beginning (fr. 13. 65–6 West) perhaps finds an echo in a similar remark in Herodotus (1. 32. 9). Solon's list of the blessings of the fortunate man (ὄλβιος, fr. 23 West), dear children, horses, hounds, and 'a friend in foreign parts', is at least consistent with Herodotus' description of the blessings of Tellus, though in a different frame of mind he finds that 'no man is blessed' (μάκαρ) but 'all mortals are wretched whom the sun sees' (fr. 14 West). There are hints of the same promotion of self-sufficiency ahead of an excessive wealth: the man with great quantities of silver and gold, land and horses, is really no wealthier, he asserts in one poem (fr. 24 West), than the man with nothing but a sound body, for money cannot buy health in old age or an escape from death, nor can the rich man take his wealth to Hades. Wealth, for Solon, is no sure index of virtue—'many bad men are rich, and good poor' (fr. 15. 1 West)—nor is virtue a sure guide to happiness: the well-intentioned man without foreknowledge may fall into ruin whilst god rewards the evildoer (fr. 13. 67–70 West). There is, then, an element of randomness in the distribution of fortune. However, compared to Herodotus' Solon, there is perhaps in Solon's verse a greater degree of moralism, a greater emphasis on the inevitability of retribution, and in general a tidier, more secure vision

[14] For the 'adaption' of the historical Solon, see esp. Chiasson (1986), noting (pp. 254–5) a more optimistic attitude to old age.

[15] The figure of 70 and the habit of breaking down a lifetme into units of seven years is, however, very common (see e.g. Arist. *Pol.* 1335^{b}32–5, 1336^{b}37 ff.), just as 'three score years and ten' is a cliché in much English literature (cf. Psalm 90. 10): see further Musti (1990). Both Solon, fr. 20. 4 West, and Herodotus, 3. 22. 4, also allude to the figure of 80 years, albeit Herodotus gives it as the *upper limit* for a Persian lifetime. The Ichthyophagoi live generally to 120, 3. 23. 1. Aristotle, *Pol.* 1335^{a}7–11, also gives 70 as the age-limit for the male generation of children, though he later suggests a more practical figure of 50 (*Pol.* 1335^{b}32–8).

of the world and of man's place in it. Solon distinguishes, for example, between two types of wealth, a god-given or legitimate wealth which therefore is reliable, and ill-gotten wealth, the possession of which leads inevitably to retribution (frs. 13. 7 ff., 15 West). Safe possession of great wealth (πολὺς ὄλβος) depends on a 'straight mind' (νόος ἄρτιος, fr. 6. 3–4 West), without which qualification, *koros* will lead to *hybris*—and *hybris* to great pains (fr. 4. 7–8 West).

While then the Solon of the *Histories* is certainly—at least, in so far as we can tell from fragments—consonant with the historical Solon, a duty of historical accuracy does not seem greatly to have constrained Herodotus: it is unlikely that he would have felt many qualms in indulging in a certain number of 'variations on a theme'. Given indeed the existence of variant versions of the death of Croesus,[16] there must surely have been a number of alternative traditions of the encounter of Solon and Croesus for Herodotus to draw upon. The tradition of Solon's travels seems to have been well developed by Herodotus' time, unsurprisingly given his status in Athens as the founder of the democracy: Herodotus has him travel to the court of Amasis in Egypt (1. 30. 1), from where he took the law that every man in Athens should declare annually his means of making his living (2. 177. 2), and to Cyprus where he praised Philocyprus above all other tyrants (5. 113. 2). The anecdote, retold by Herodotus, of the visit of the Athenian Alcmeon to Sardis, leaving the King's treasury with his mouth and pockets bulging with gold (5. 125) or Herodotus' remark, introducing the encounter of Solon and Croesus, that Solon was merely one of a sequence of Greek sophists—Herodotus' own term—to visit Croesus' court (1. 29. 1) suggest also that the device of confronting a poor Greek with the wealth of Croesus, as a test of his moral fibre, was a common one.

But the ideas expressed by the Herodotean Solon have, of course, a far wider currency. Observations such as that 'no man is happy until he is dead',[17] that divine jealousy disturbs

---

[16] See below, n. 28.

[17] See e.g. Pind. *Ol.* 1. 33–4, Aesch. *Ag.* 928–30, Soph. *Trach.* 1–3, E. *Tro.* 509–10, Soph. *Ant.* 583, Soph. *Aj.* 131–3, E. *Alc.* 782 ff. The transitory nature of life is also a commonplace: e.g. Pind. *Pyth.* 8. 95–6, E. *Suppl.* 953, Soph. *OT* 1186–8.

human affairs,[18] human fortune is inevitably mixed,[19] or that
'death is better than life'[20] are myriad, especially in archaic
poetry or tragedy, though they find their reflections also in
pre-Socratic philosophy. The dangers of wealth are also well
explored in a number of sources.[21] These affinities between
Herodotus and other authors have a clear implication for the
status of the 'Solonian' philosophy of Book 1: such observations are unlikely to reflect long theological reflection on
Herodotus' part, but they form part rather of a body of
proverbial wisdom to a large extent taken for granted by
both Herodotus and his contemporaries.[22] Consequently, it
would be absurd to expect too high a level of consistency in
Herodotus' reiteration of this 'Solonian philosophy',[23] to sort

[18] For divine $\phi\theta\acuteo\nu o\varsigma$ in earlier authors, see Lloyd Jones (1971: 55 ff.), Parker
(1997: 151 n. 30); cf. e.g. Pind. *Pyth.* 10. 29 ff. (fortune mixed due to $\phi\theta\acuteo\nu o\varsigma$),
Xenophanes DK 21 B 25 ($\pi\acute\alpha\nu\tau\alpha\ \kappa\rho\alpha\delta\alpha\acute\iota\nu\epsilon\iota$), E. *Rhes.* 332 ($\acuteo\rho\alpha\ \tau\grave o\ \mu\acute\epsilon\lambda\lambda o\nu\cdot\ \pi\acuteo\lambda\lambda'$
$\acute\alpha\nu\alpha\sigma\tau\rho\acute\epsilon\phi\epsilon\iota\ \theta\epsilon\acuteo\varsigma$).
[19] See e.g. H. *Il.* 24. 525 ff., *Od.* 4. 236–7, Theogn. 135 ff., 165–6, 167–8,
171–2, 441, 585 ff., 659 ff., Hes. *Erga* 179, Bacchyl. *Ode* 5. 53–5, frs. 24, 54,
Soph. fr. 681, E. *IA* 21 ff., *Bacch.* 1388 ff., Alc. 1159–63, Med. 1415–9, Hel.
1688–92, And. 1284–8, Heraclidae 608 ff., Hipp. 980–1, Hec. 957. The mixed
nature of human fortune is seen as a good by Heraclitus, DK 22 B 110–11:
disease, for example, makes health sweet.
[20] See e.g. H. *Il.* 3. 172 ff., 22. 431 ff., Hes. *Erga* 174–5, Theogn. 819–20,
1178[a-b], Soph. *El.* 820–2, *OT* 1367–8, *Ant.* 461–4, 1328–32, *OC* 1725–8, 1751–
3, E. *Tro.* 636–7, *Suppl.* 821, Alc. 895 ff., Hel. 298, Bacchyl. *Ode* 3. 47, 5. 160.
[21] See e.g. Soph. *Ant.* 221–2 , Aesch. *Pers.* 823–6. A fatalistic position that
wealth brings evil (e.g. Theogn. 1155–6) coexists with another whereby
reversals in fortune are justified: so, for example, Theogn. 145–6 (choice of
piety and moderate wealth vs. wealth and injustice), Aesch. *Ag.* 378–84 (riches
encourage lack of justice). A more philosophical approach to fortune is
displayed by Menelaus, H. *Od.* 4. 90.
[22] Contrast, however, Waters (1971: 15): 'if one seeks Herodotus' thought,
it is not to be found in Novellismen' unless two conditions can be fulfilled: 'a)
that these logoi consistently reflect a certain cast of thought and b) (what is
more difficult) that this way of thinking is not merely that of Greek popular
tales or conventional morality.' Cf. also Waters (1974: 6): 'Solon is included
mainly as evidence for the cultural importance of Kroisos' kingdom' . . . 'the
"popular wisdom" is expanded for its own sake and for the two moralistic
anecdotes, which Herodotos perhaps thought he could tell better than the
current market-place retailers'; Croesus or Cyrus are both 'absolutely necessary to the historical action' whereas Solon is 'merely part of the décor'. For a
sensible critique of Waters, see Fisher (1992: 366).
[23] Equally Herodotus' concluding judgement to the encounter of Solon and

this philosophy into a number of discrete propositions—that the divine is jealous, that human fortune is inherently unstable, that no man can be called happy until he is dead[24]—and then to expect each of these constituent strands to find unequivocal corroboration in the text as a whole, or to be restated in an identical pattern. Equally, to claim a particular significance for any one strand—the concept of nemesis, for example (a term that appears only once in the *Histories*),[25] or divine jealousy—and to isolate that as the sole criterion of the relevance of Solon's ideas to the *Histories* as a whole,[26] gives again a misleading impression: that Herodotus too could look through to the bones and sinews of Solon's message, that he distinguished between these strands as clearly in writing as we do in (re-)reading. The philosophy of Herodotus' Solon is rather re-cast in a number of different patterns, both in consciously fashioned episodes such as the Persian debate on the expedition to Greece at the beginning of Book 7 and in passing, in contexts that suggest no theological reflection.

Herodotus' concluding judgement to the story of Solon's encounter with Croesus—that nemesis overtook the Lydian king (1. 34. 1)—points forward as well as back. Croesus'

Croesus—that nemesis overtook Croesus because of his estimation of his own good fortune (1. 34. 1)—may arguably, for example, imply a suggestion of Croesus' end as deserved that is at variance with the philosophy outlined by Solon. For Zeus as punishing boastful thoughts or words, see Aesch. *Pers.* 827–8, Soph. *Ant.* 127 ff., 1350–3, E. *Heraclidae* 387–8; see also de Romilly (1977: 42–3), 'it is a thought which the gods punish, not a situation'.

[24] See esp. S. O. Shapiro (1996), setting out to ask whether Herodotus 'agreed with' the views presented by Solon: her conclusions follow, nonetheless, very similar lines to those presented here.

[25] De Romilly (1971: 315).

[26] The 'most studied' system of explanation in the *Histories,* according to Lateiner (1989: 196), is the 'immoral and divine jealousy' endorsed by Solon, Amasis, Artabanus, and Themistocles: 'yet there are no other references to it in the *Histories*'. See similarly Lang (1968: 27; 1984a: 61), Gould (1989: 79–80), de Romilly (1977: 45) contending that Artabanus' ' "theory of *hybris*" . . . is not once supported by Herodotus's history', and that 'no theory . . . is supported by Herodotus . . . which explains the wrath of god by a religious fault'. More satisfactorily Fornara remarks (1971a: 79) that 'although to us Herodotus' philosophy is little more than a literary chestnut, so familiar are we with it, to him it was an immutable truth of central importance for mankind'.

subsequent history implies repeatedly the truth of Solon's words. Croesus had two sons, we are told: one dumb, the other excelling in every way other men of his age (1. 34. 2). Croesus loses his able son, Atys, when the suppliant Adrastus, whom Croesus had received into his house and had then charged to protect his son during a boar hunt, missed the boar with his spear and 'chanced' to hit Atys (τυγχάνει, 1. 43. 2). This first misfortune is in fulfilment of a dream (1. 34. 2), but it is also in fulfilment of Solon's words: the poor fortunate man is blessed with fine children (εὔπαις, 1. 32. 6); Croesus loses the son he cherishes, and is left only with a son who is dumb.[27] Adrastus, considering himself the 'most unfortunate of men' (βαρυσυμφορώτατος, 1. 45. 3), kills himself.

Croesus' second misfortune is his defeat in his war against Cyrus and the Persians, a war he had fully expected to win (1. 71).[28] After the capture of Sardis, one of the Persians came towards Croesus to kill him, but Croesus was saved by the intervention of his dumb son (1. 85. 3–4). Death is better than life, Solon had maintained (1. 31. 3). As the Persian ran towards him, Croesus did not care if he lived or died, but his son spoke for the first time to tell the Persian not to kill Croesus, and so saved his father's life. The Pythia had told Croesus that the boy would speak for the first time 'on an unfortunate day' (ἐν ἤματι . . . ἀνόλβῳ, 1. 85. 2).[29] In all respects other than his dumbness, he had been perfectly presentable (1. 85. 1); from now on, he spoke for the rest of his life (1. 85. 4).[30]

[27] Cf. the contrast between the two sons of Periander, 3. 53. 1; inevitably it is the able son, Lycophron, who is killed.

[28] For the alternative versions of Croesus' fall, see esp. the fascinating discussion of Burkert (1985c); cf. Segal (1971), Georges (1994: 170–1). For arguments on the plausibility of the different versions, see Evans (1978), Mallowan (1972: 12), speculating rather literal-mindedly that Bacchylides' version of Croesus' suicide is preferable on the grounds that the Persians would never have allowed 'the pollution of fire by human sacrifice'.

[29] Contrast Sebeok and Brady (1979), envisaging Croesus' son's intervention as positive (in the context of their attempt to see Herodotus' narrative as 'an account of man's attempt to communicate with ordering forces beyond themselves').

[30] The dumbness of Croesus' son is also picked up by the prophecy given him by the Pythia in the context of Croesus' test of various oracles, 1. 47. 3: 'I understand the dumb and hear him who does not speak.'

Cyrus then places Croesus and fourteen Lydian boys on a pyre: his motive was either to sacrifice them as first fruits to one of the gods or to test Croesus' reputation for piety, to see if a daimon would rescue him from being burnt (1. 86. 2). As he waits on his pyre for his own death, Croesus remembers the words of Solon which he had dismissed before as the words of a fool, and recognizes now that they were spoken, like prophecies, 'by divine inspiration' (σὺν θεῷ, 1. 86. 3).[31] Three times he groans out Solon's name. When Cyrus enquires as to what he is saying, Croesus takes this as the cue for a potted Solonian sermon: everything Solon had said had been fulfilled (1. 86. 5). Cyrus, on this occasion, appears to take in this lesson: realizing that he was about to set fire to a man no less fortunate once than himself, fearing vengeance, and 'understanding that nothing in human life is safely established' (ἐπιλεξάμενον ὡς οὐδὲν εἴη τῶν ἐν ἀνθρώποισι ἀσφαλέως ἔχον, 1. 86. 6), he orders the fire to be put out. An acknowledgement of, and submission to, the Solonian law of the mutability of fortune somehow, it seems, protects you from it. Putting out the fire takes a miracle, however: divine intervention in the form of a well-timed thunderstorm in answer to Croesus' prayer (1. 87. 1–2). Cyrus then asks Croesus why he had decided to make war in the first place (1. 87. 3). Croesus' reply again links human fortune and the divine:

O king, I did these things for your good fortune and my own ill fortune (τῇ σῇ μὲν εὐδαιμονίῃ, τῇ ἐμεωυτοῦ δὲ κακοδαιμονίῃ): the god of the Greeks was responsible (αἴτιος) for these things by encouraging me to go to war.

As he then discovers from the god at Delphi, however, he had been mistaken in his interpretation of the oracles given to him (1. 91. 6).

Many of the complications of Croesus' career—in particular, the contradiction between the fated nature of his fall and his responsibility—must be deferred.[32] At one level, Croesus' story is that of a good man whose goodness does not pay (1. 90. 2, 86. 2). The fact that Apollo saves Croesus from death on the pyre appears to confirm the reputation for piety tested by

---

[31] For this expression, see Ch. 5.
[32] See Chs. 8–9.

Cyrus. At the same time, however, he is a fool who defied Solon's wisdom and blithely accepted the meaning of oracles. His advice to Cyrus to stop his men from plundering Sardis, now that Sardis was Cyrus' own property, shows a certain practical wisdom, as does his recommendation that Cyrus should cynically use a tithe to Zeus as a means of controlling the plundering (1. 88–9), or his plan of turning the Lydians from warriors into women as a way of saving them from a worse fate (1. 155–6). However, his dedication at Delphi of the chains in which he had been bound by Cyrus (1. 90. 4), or his sarcastic questioning of whether it was customary for Apollo 'to deceive those men who act well' or for 'Greek gods to be ungrateful' (1. 90. 2, 4) in their assumption of a crude relationship of *quid pro quo* between gods and men, are not apparently the actions of a man who has learnt the Solonian lesson of humility and acquiescence to the divine. After the Pythia's response to his formal complaint, Croesus acknowledged that the error had been his and not the god's (1. 91. 6). He survives to provide a useful narrative foil to Cyrus and to Cambyses,[33] in whose careers in turn the same ideas are reproduced with variations.[34] But, as Cambyses later remarks sarcastically, Croesus had hardly made a good fist of looking after his own affairs, nor had his advice to Cyrus to cross the Araxes been obviously successful (3. 36. 3). Cambyses is clearly not an unquestionable witness, but the fact that such doubts are aired at all is perhaps significant. Whether Croesus' failure as an adviser reflects his own inability to learn the lessons of Solon or simply the inability of any man to avert fate remains an open question.

A similar pattern to that of Croesus' rise and fall can be seen in the life of Cyrus, itself interwoven with Croesus' second career as royal adviser. Cyrus' survival from death by exposure was, as Harpagus tells him, not mere chance, but the result of divine favour (1. 124. 1–2):[35] the gods look over him (σὲ γὰρ θεοὶ

---

[33] Cf. Stahl (1975: 12).

[34] Vidal-Naquet (1960: 68): 'Crésus est à bien des égards une première version de Xerxes'; Herodotus' characters are 'outside time'. See similarly Lombardo (1990: 173), Schadewaldt (1962: 193–4). The career of Cambyses in many ways reverses the usual model: immediately before his death, he goes through a striking period of lucidity.

[35] For the 'divine chance' of Cyrus' survival, see further Chs. 3, 6.

ἐπορῶσι), for otherwise he would never have had such luck; his survival was, Harpagus adds, due to the gods and him. Such good fortune was bound to turn sour, however.[36] Many were the things that urged him on in his campaign against the Massagetai, says Herodotus: first, that his birth seemed more than human; second, his 'good fortune' against his enemies (ἡ εὐτυχίη, 1. 204. 2). Croesus then reinforces the point (1. 207. 2). Cyrus has apparently forgotten the lesson taught to him earlier by Croesus. He has forgotten that he is a man.

If you think that you are immortal, and that the army that you command is immortal too, then there is no point in my expressing my judgements to you; but if, on the other hand, you know that you are a man, and that you command others who are also men, then learn this first: that there is a wheel of human affairs which, as it turns, does not allow the same men always to have good fortune (ὡς κύκλος τῶν ἀνθρωπηίων ἐστὶ πρηγμάτων, περιφερόμενος δὲ οὐκ ἐᾷ αἰεὶ τοὺς αὐτοὺς εὐτυχέειν).

As Hans-Peter Stahl has written, Cyrus' conversion scene 'must now appear as an empty lie, a beautiful idealization which does not stand up to the reality of human behaviour'.[37]

Croesus' advice to cross the Araxes is intended as a form of damage limitation (something in which he seems to have been a specialist; cf. 1. 155–6): should he be defeated, he would not lose his whole kingdom (1. 207. 3–4). This was advice that was arguably vindicated. The plan, however, again devised by Croesus (1. 207. 4–7), by which Cyrus aims to get the better of Tomyris and the Massagetai strongly implies a falling-off in

---

[36] This progression is traced at greater length by Avery (1972*b*). For the theme of instability in the early life of Cyrus, see esp. van der Veen (1996: ch. 3).

[37] Stahl (1975: 22). A similar picture of 'two distinct Cyruses' is drawn by Avery (1972*b*: 536 ff.). Even in the immediate aftermath of Cyrus' conversion there are arguably some dissonant notes struck: Cyrus' laughter (1. 90. 3) apparently in surprise at Croesus' not asking for a more worldly favour, or his question (1. 87. 3) as to 'which of men' had encouraged Croesus in his campaign. Admittedly, his tutorial is still in progress. Cyrus' treatment of the river Gyndes (1. 189–190. 1) also arguably fits into a pattern of the tyrannical abuse of nature: see below, ch. 9. Contrast S. O. Shapiro (1994), arguing against Stahl that Croesus and Artabanus keep their wisdom once acquired and (p. 352) that Cyrus 'does not forget his wisdom because he never really learnt it in the first place'.

the qualities of rustic simplicity by which Cyrus and the Persians acquired their empire:[38] the Persians leave a great feast of food and wine undefended; the Massagetai gorge themselves upon these unknown luxuries, fall asleep, and are killed or taken prisoner (1. 211). One other episode reveals even more clearly a blindness to the instability and unpredictability of human fortune. Cyrus dreams of Darius, then a relatively insignificant man of 20, with wings grown from his shoulders, wings that covered Asia and Europe (1. 209. 1).[39] He then summons Darius' father Hystaspes and informs him that his son is conspiring for the throne. In fact, of course, he had misinterpreted the dream: the daimon was merely indicating to Cyrus his own impending death and that the throne would devolve eventually on to Darius (1. 210. 1). Cyrus, however, had presented his interpretation as certain fact, the consequence of his special relationship with the gods: 'for the gods look after me, and show me in advance everything that will come to be' (ἐμεῦ θεοὶ κήδονται καί μοι πάντα προδεικνύουσι τὰ ἐπιφερόμενα, 1. 209. 4).

The history of Polycrates follows a similar pattern.[40] His power increased apparently never-endingly: wherever he campaigned, everything went 'fortunately' for him (εὐτυχέως, 3. 39. 3). His friend, however, the Egyptian king Amasis, was concerned at this good fortune (3. 40. 1). As he explains to Polycrates in a letter, such 'good fortune' (μεγάλαι εὐτυχίαι, 3. 40. 2) does not please a man like him who 'understands that the divine is jealous' (ἐπισταμένῳ τὸ θεῖον ὡς ἔστι φθονερόν). His words echo almost precisely Solon's reply to Croesus quoted above (1. 32. 1). Better, he continues, to alternate from good fortune to misfortune (εὐτυχέειν / προσπταίειν, 3. 40. 2) than 'to be fortunate in everything' (εὐτυχέειν τὰ πάντα): for the man who is fortunate in everything invariably 'comes to an utterly bad

[38] See 9. 122 with n. 82 below.

[39] The image of Darius' wings may reflect a distant familiarity with Persian iconography: Mallowan (1985: 394), Miller (1997: 106). Cf. 1. 107. 1, 108. 1; 7. 8. γ2–3, 19. 1, 54. 2; 8. 53. 2.

[40] Waters asserts extraordinarily (1971: 25 n. 67), that 'anything less metaphysical would be hard to imagine than the Polykrates story . . . the purpose is simply to tell the story of Polykrates with special relation to his situation between Greece and Persia.'

end' (ἐς τέλος οὐ κακῶς ἐτελεύτησε πρόρριζος, 3. 42. 3). The term πρόρριζος, 'root and branch' or 'utterly', echoes the phrase of Solon's, that 'the god, having shown a glimpse of happiness to many men, then overthrows them utterly' (1. 32. 9). On Amasis' advice, Polycrates then contrives to break his own run of luck— by throwing away the one possession that would most upset him were he to lose it (3. 40. 4).[41] The ring which he throws into the sea, however, comes back to him in the belly of a large fish presented to him by a fisherman (3. 42. 3). Polycrates 'recognized then that this event was divine' (τὸν δὲ ὡς ἐσῆλθε θεῖον εἶναι τὸ πρῆγμα, 3. 42. 4) and wrote to tell Amasis of it (3. 43. 1).[42]

When Amasis read the letter which came from Polycrates, he understood that it is not possible for a man to save another from what is about to happen (ἔμαθε ὅτι ἐκκομίσαι τε ἀδύνατον εἴη ἀνθρώπῳ ἄνθρωπον ἐκ τοῦ μέλλοντος γίνεσθαι πρήγματος), and that Polycrates was bound to end badly (οὐκ εὖ τελευτήσειν μέλλοι Πολυκράτης), being so fortunate in all things that he found what he threw away.

Polycrates duly did meet with a bad end, at the hands of Oroites, the Persian governor of Sardis. Oroites' motive was either a quarrel with Mitrobates or a grudge against Polycrates originating in a (perhaps imagined) snub (3. 120–1). But the means by which he plots Polycrates' death are to harness his ambition. He had heard of Polycrates' plan to rule the sea, to rule Ionia and the islands (3. 122. 2), and so he sends a messenger offering Polycrates the capital with which to realize his ambitions (3. 122. 3)—an offer bound to succeed, as Polycrates 'loved money greatly' (3. 123. 1). The wealth, however, was largely illusory: a messenger sent to Sardis is shown eight chests full of stones but with a layer of gold on the surface (3. 123. 2).[43] But, on the basis of his report, Polycrates

---

[41] Cf. Heraclitus DK 22 B 110: ἀνθρώποις γίνεσθαι ὁκόσα θέλουσιν οὐκ ἄμεινον.

[42] Van der Veen suggests (1993: 448 (cf. Marinatos 1982: 260–1)), that 'the ring is returned to Polycrates because the loss of it has not made him suffer'; he ought to have discarded his power. Certainly, one implicit theme is the question of what is man's most valuable possession: cf. 1. 86. 4, 5. 24. 3, 6. 62, 7. 237. 3. For interpretations in the light of scapegoat rituals, see Versnel (1977: 37), Ogden (1997: 119–27). See also, e.g. for marriage with the sea, Aly (1921: 90 ff.), Versnel (1977: 18 ff.), and van Ooteghem (1940); for a more worldly view of the relationship of Amasis and Polycrates, Wallinga (1991).

[43] For the comparable Thucydidean anecdote of Athenian ambassadors to

decided to travel to meet Oroites himself, despite the entreaties of his friends and the dream in which his daughter foresaw his death, and was duly killed, his body—in fulfilment of his daughter's dream—washed by Zeus and anointed by the sun as it hung from a cross (3. 124–5). His death, according to Herodotus, was 'worthy neither of him nor of his ambitions' (οὔτε ἑωυτοῦ ἀξίως οὔτε τῶν ἑωυτοῦ φρονημάτων, 3. 125. 2). His was not a deserved death[44]—though it is easy to see how it might have been presented as one. 'The great good fortune of Polycrates ended thus' (Πολυκράτεος μὲν δὴ αἱ πολλαὶ εὐτυχίαι ἐς τοῦτο ἐτελεύτησαν, 3. 125. 4). Polycrates' successful run ends precisely as predicted by Amasis, precisely on the Solonian model. The detail may not be entirely coincidental that Solon had indeed visited Amasis (1. 30. 1).

The story of Xerxes shows the same ideas developed further: it depends and builds on the Solonian model.[45] It is no longer merely a question of personal fortune, good or bad. The whole Persian empire is on a Polycratean roll of good fortune, which it is Xerxes' duty to maintain:[46] a god, he says, leads the Persians on; so long as they follow, their fortunes are invariably good (7. 8. α1). Xerxes reminds the Persians of the achievements of his predecessors, Cyrus, Cambyses, and Darius, omitting to mention the ends of their expeditions:[47] in his planned campaign against Greece, he has found a way to add further to the Persians' power (7. 8. α2). Mardonius then gives a number of

Segesta, see Thuc. 6. 46 with Hornblower's comments (1987: 22–3) on what he dubs the 'roving anecdote'.

[44] Fisher rightly observes (1992: 362) that the story of Polycrates is told in an 'unmoralised fashion'. For a historical reconstruction of Polycrates' fall, see Abramenko (1995).

[45] Contrast Immerwahr (1956: 273) judging 7. 1–18 as 'the climax of Herodotus' thought on the subject of causation' or as (p. 274) 'a summary of the whole work'; de Romilly (1977: 45) asserting that with Xerxes Herodotus 'ruins the pattern of *hybris* and *nemesis*' established in the case of Solon.

[46] Raaflaub (1987: 227–9) points up similarities with the image of the Athenians in Thucydides and tragedy; see further Harrison (1999b). For Persian expansionism, see Verdin (1982).

[47] For the continuity of imperial expansion between Persian kings (by contrast to Aeschylus' *Persians*), see esp. Said 1981; for modifications, Harrison (1998b; 2000: 85). For imperial expansion as a constant given in the *Histories*, see Verdin (1982).

reasons as to why the planned expedition cannot fail. He has
already revealed himself to be as deluded in his estimate of the
wealth of Greece as Polycrates had been in the wealth of
Oroites (7. 5. 3–6. 1). Nevertheless every effort must be made
to ensure success (7. 9. γ): 'let nothing then be untried: for
nothing happens of its own accord, but all things come to men
from their efforts.' Artabanus, however, reminds Xerxes of
how vulnerable Darius had been during his campaign against
the Scythians: he had depended entirely on one man, Histiaeus
of Miletus, who had prevented the other tyrants from breaking
up the Danube bridge (7. 10. α2–3; γ).[48] If he, Xerxes, were by
chance to be defeated, not even on both land *and* sea but merely
on sea, and if the Greeks should sail to the Hellespont and
break up the bridge, the consequences would be disproportio-
nately terrible (7. 10. β). Artabanus tells Xerxes to dissolve the
meeting and to think the matter through again (7. 10. δι–ζ):

> For to deliberate well is, I find, the greatest profit: for if one's wish
> meets with opposition, one's deliberations are no less good, but it is
> by chance that the plan is defeated. But if a man deliberates badly,
> and if chance is on his side (εἴ οἱ ἡ τύχη ἐπίσποιτο), he may meet with
> success, but his deliberations were no less bad. You see with living
> things how the god strikes with his thunderbolts those that stand out
> and does not allow them to make a show of themselves, whereas small
> things in no way provoke him. You see how it is always against the
> greatest buildings and the greatest trees that he hurls his bolts. For all
> things that stand out the god is prone to cut down (φιλέει γὰρ ὁ θεὸς τὰ
> ὑπερέχοντα πάντα κολούειν). And so even a great army may be destroyed
> by a small one if the god is envious and strikes them with fear or
> lightning so that they perish in a way unworthy of themselves. For the
> god does not allow any one other than himself to have high thoughts
> (οὐ γὰρ ἐᾷ φρονέειν μέγα ὁ θεὸς ἄλλον ἢ ἑωυτόν). Now to hurry in any
> matter gives rise to mistakes, from which it is likely for great harm to
> come to them. In delay, however, there are advantages, which, even if
> they are not immediately apparent, one will nevertheless discover in
> time.

There are again a number of echoes of Solon here: the mention
of god as jealous (cf. 1. 32. 1, 3. 40. 2), the discussion of luck or
good fortune (εἴ οἱ ἡ τύχη ἐπίσποιτο; cf. εἰ μὴ οἱ τύχη ἐπίσποιτο,
1. 32. 5). Artabanus' words, like Solon's earlier, are also

---

[48] Cf. Darius' earlier advice, 4. 83.

prophetic: god does indeed inflict fear, thunder and lightning on the invading Persians.[49]

Artabanus is subsequently persuaded of the wisdom of the campaign, and Xerxes' resolve is stiffened, by the succession of dreams that appear to them. But the solid Solonian grounds for resisting the campaign continue to reverberate through Herodotus' narrative. Just as Xerxes had been made great in a small time, so equally quickly, the dream threatens, he could be reduced to scale (7. 14): Xerxes' fear of reversal contributes to his fall. Even while Artabanus is actually recanting his 'warning' against Xerxes, the same message shines through (7. 18. 2–3):

I, O king, being a man, and one who has seen already many great powers falling at the hands of lesser ones (οἷα ἄνθρωπος ἰδὼν ἤδη πολλά τε καὶ μεγάλα πεσόντα πρήγματα ὑπὸ ἡσσόνων), do not allow you entirely to yield to youth, understanding (ἐπιστάμενος) that it is bad to desire many things, mindful (μεμνημένος) of the expedition of Cyrus against the Massagetai and how it turned out, mindful also (μεμνημένος) of that of Cambyses against the Ethiopians, and myself having taken part with Darius in the campaign against the Scythians. Understanding (ἐπιστάμενος) these things, I was of the opinion that if you remained quiet you would be called blessed by all men. But since this impulse has sprung up from some daimon (δαιμονίη τις γίνεται ὁρμή), and some heaven-sent destruction, as it seems, is overtaking the Greeks (καὶ Ἕλληνας, ὡς οἶκε, φθορή τις καταλαμβάνει θεήλατος[50]), I am myself converted and change my mind.

All of what Artabanus now says is true: Xerxes would have been happier otherwise; however, the god is at work in the matter, and so there is no choice. The language Artabanus uses (the phrases ἐπιστάμενος ὡς and μεμνημένος, for example) is reminiscent of Solon's words in Book 1. Herodotus all but makes explicit the analogy of Xerxes' campaign with the disastrously overreaching campaigns of earlier Persian kings.

Even Xerxes reveals some doubt. At Abydos, he decides for one of many times to review his troops. He does so from the vantage point of a hill, from where he could see 'the shore and

---

[49] See Ch. 3. Artabanus is not completely right in all of his predictions: Pelling (1991: 136).

[50] For the tragic connotations of θεήλατος, see Chiasson (1982: 159).

the plains of Abydos full of men' (7. 45). At that point he
suffers from a kind of ironic fit of Solonianism: then 'Xerxes
thought himself blessed, and after that he began to cry'.[51]
Artabanus, ever-present, asks him the reason. He had been
contemplating the brevity of human life, how none of the men
beneath him would be alive in a hundred years. He does not
comment on the brevity of his own life. Solon, of course, had
had a precise knowledge of the length of one man's life.
Artabanus finds something sadder still than this (7. 46. 3–4):

In so short a life there is no man alive, either of these men or of others,
who was born so happy (εὐδαίμων) that it will not occur to him, not
only once but often, to wish that he was dead rather than alive
(τεθνάναι βούλεσθαι μᾶλλον ἢ ζώειν). For disasters befall him, diseases
confound him, so that they make life, which is short, appear long. In
the same way, life is so wretched that death becomes the most
welcome refuge for men, and the god, giving us a taste of the
sweetness of human life, is discovered in his very gift to be envious
(ὁ δὲ θεὸς γλυκὺν γεύσας τὸν αἰῶνα φθονερὸς ἐν αὐτῷ εὑρίσκεται ἐών).

Once again there are a number of echoes of Solon. The
sentiment of death being preferable to life is first expressed
by Solon through the story of Cleobis and Biton (1. 31. 3).
Artabanus' final remark in this passage echoes Solon's final
words of wisdom to Croesus (1. 32. 9): πολλοῖσι γὰρ δὴ ὑποδέξας
ὄλβον ὁ θεὸς προρρίζους ἀνέτρεψε. The idea of the divine as jealous
occurs also in the mouths of Solon, Amasis, and Themistocles
(1. 32. 1, 3. 40. 2, 8. 109. 3). Other Solonian sentiments are
echoed later in the course of this discussion at Abydus:
'accidents rule men', Artabanus observes, 'and not men accidents' (αἱ συμφοραὶ τῶν ἀνθρώπων ἄρχουσι καὶ οὐχὶ ὥνθρωποι τῶν

---

[51] The fact that Xerxes calls *himself* blessed, unlike Cleobis and Biton,
acclaimed as blessed by their peers (ἐμακάριζον, 1. 32. 3), possibly reflects the
instability of his fortune relative to theirs. See here Flory (1978a), followed by
Konstan (1987: 63 ff.), for a discussion of other instances in which laughter
gives way to tears, esp. 8. 99 and 9. 16. In this second case, the Theban
banquet, Herodotus does not mention laughter, however; Flory takes for
granted (p. 146) 'the gaiety of the after-dinner drinking'. Another difference
between the Theban banquet and 7. 45, observed by Flory (p. 148), is that
Xerxes unlike the anonymous Persian is ignorant of the outcome of the war;
he has forebodings rather than knowledge. For laughter as presaging disaster,
see Lateiner (1977), though the laughter of the Ethiopian king, 3. 22. 2, is an
exception: Asheri iii. 246.

συμφορέων, 7. 49. 3; cf. 1. 32. 4). The sentiment that the end cannot be seen at the beginning is explicitly referred to by Artabanus as proverbial, an 'ancient saying, well said', that Xerxes should keep in mind (7. 51. 3).

A coda to this Solonian theme of the *Histories* is provided by the story of the banquet given to the Persians by the Theban Attaginus (9. 15. 4–16). Herodotus claims to have been told of the banquet by an eyewitness, Thersander of Orchomenus. A Persian, seated on the same couch as Thersander, addressed him in Greek and told him that, of all those feasting and of the Persian army in general, but a few would survive. Thersander was amazed and asked the Persian why he did not tell this to Mardonius. But the Persian replied (9. 16. 4):

Friend, what must come from the god, it is impossible for man to turn away (ὅ τι δεῖ γενέσθαι ἐκ τοῦ θεοῦ, ἀμήχανον ἀποτρέψαι ἀνθρώπῳ). For no one will listen to those who speak the truth. Many of us Persians understand these things, but we are bound by necessity to obey. This pain is the most hateful for men: to have much knowledge but no power.[52]

The Persian's prophetic remarks on the imminent death of Xerxes' army echo Xerxes' conversation with Artabanus on the brevity of human life, at the time of his review of his troops (7. 46. 2). Similar sentiments on the impossibility of avoiding fate are expressed by the Pythia and the dying Cambyses (1. 91. 1, 3. 65. 3); this is also the lesson said by Herodotus to have been learnt by Amasis from the story of Polycrates' ring (3. 43. 1).

This main skeleton of Solonian thought includes a number of recurring patterns. The story of Solon and Croesus, the conversations of Xerxes and Artabanus, and the Theban banquet are clearly also positioned at crucial moments in the *Histories*. Given this, given also the recurrence of ideas from one passage to another, and given hints such as Artabanus' reference to an 'ancient saying', it is hard to imagine that this skeleton has not been developed—in part consciously—either as an explanatory framework for the events of the *Histories* or

---

[52] Pippidi (1960: 82) sees the whole of the *Histories* as 'only the illustration of this sentence'; cf. Kroymann (1970: 175), ascribing the Persians' pessimism to the Persian master–servant relationship.

simply for the truth of Solon's sayings. Croesus from his pyre described Solon as a man who spoke 'to the whole of mankind' (ἐς ἅπαν τὸ ἀνθρώπινον, 1. 86. 5).

At the same time, however, fragments of what we might dub 'Solonian' ideas appear at times to be embedded in Herodotus' narrative: Herodotus may then be both evangelical in his presentation of Solonian thought and at other moments slip into it almost by reflex. Herodotus is frequently concerned, even in passing, to show how a certain man's fortunes were mixed. Ameinocles the Magnesian made a fortune overnight by picking gold and silver from the wrecks of the Persian ships off Cape Sepias where he farmed his land; 'the shipwreck was very good for Ameinocles at least' (7. 190).[53] The irony is Herodotus', I think. He was not, however, Herodotus adds, 'fortunate (εὐτυχέων) in other respects', but like Croesus he lost his son at his own hands (παιδοφόνος).[54] All men, Herodotus' remark suggests, suffer some such grief. Leutychidas 'did not grow old in Sparta' (6. 72. 1) but paid the price for his crime against Demaratus, his complicity in Cleomenes' bribery of the Delphic oracle to induce it to declare Demaratus illegitimate. Leutychidas was caught himself in the act of receiving a bribe; he was subsequently banished, his house razed to the ground; he then died in exile in Tegea (6. 72. 2). Although Leutychidas' end is obviously envisaged as the result of retribution, Herodotus clearly conceives of it also on the Solonian model: Leutychidas did not die happy at home with his children, or gloriously in battle for his city. Herodotus also emphasizes the extent of Demaratus' fall by concluding the story of his flight to Asia with a catalogue of his achievements (6. 70. 3):

So Demaratus did arrive in Asia and such was his fortune, having excelled in many respects among the Lacedaimonians both in his deeds and in his counsels, and in particular having won an Olympic

[53] Cf. Immerwahr (1966: 76), S. O. Shapiro (1996: 356). It was because the Macedonian Alexander was (like Solon's fortunate man, 1. 32. 6) κακῶν ἀπαθής, 5. 19. 1, that he invited disaster by exacting retribution for a Persian insult against Macedonian women. He manages, however, to avoid subsequent disaster, except that he is forced ironically to give his sister in marriage to a Persian, 5. 21. 2.

[54] Periander likewise represents his murder of his wife as a misfortune (συμφορή), made greater only by his own responsibility: 3. 52. 4.

victory in the four-horse chariot, being alone in doing this of all the kings of Sparta who have been.

Reversal can be for the better as well as the worse. Hermotimus, made into a eunuch as a boy, was not 'unlucky in all respects' (τὰ πάντα ἐδυστύχεε, 8. 105. 2), but came to be the most honoured of the eunuchs in Xerxes' service. Skythes, the monarch of the Zancleans, was forced to flee to the court of Darius, where the King, however, judged him the most just of all those many Greeks who had come to him, and he died exceedingly rich in old age (6. 24. 2). Though a death so far from home in one sense hardly fits the Solonian ideal, the detail of Skythes' comfortable old age, mitigating his fall from power, at the same time takes for granted that model.

Good fortune signals impending misfortune.[55] Good fortune indeed may only be a front for misfortune. Harpagus, for example, was delighted at the 'good piece of chance' of being invited to dinner by Astyages (1. 119. 1), unaware that his own son was on the menu. The enormously rich Lydian Pythius, after feasting Xerxes' entire army, offers the King all his gold and silver as a contribution to his campaign, for with his land and his slaves remaining to him he would still have a 'sufficient living' (ἀρκέων . . . βίος, 7. 28. 3), words echoing Solon's Cleobis and Biton (1. 31. 2). Xerxes is so pleased by Pythius' attitude that, far from taking his wealth, he adds to it, making up Pythius' gold to the round figure of four million Daric staters (7. 29. 2). 'Keep what you have acquired', the King tells Pythius in parting, 'and be intelligent enough to remain as you are; for if you behave in this way, neither now nor in the future will this be a cause of regret' (7. 29. 3). It is not wealth, however, that Pythius is destined to lose. Terrified by an eclipse, and encouraged by Xerxes' earlier generosity, he tells Xerxes that all of his five sons are on campaign, and asks the King, out of compassion for his old age, to release his eldest son from the campaign (7. 38). In punishment, Pythius' son is cut in two and Xerxes' army marched between his remains (7. 39. 3).[56] Apries also

---

[55] See esp. Lateiner (1982); see also Chiasson (1983) on the word περιχαρής, the one word that 'unfailingly indicates imminent danger'.

[56] For Near-Eastern parallels to the punishment of Pythius, see Masson (1950), West (1987); see also Evans (1988b).

mistook his ruin for his salvation. Apries was the most fortunate
of any of the kings of Egypt apart from Psammetichus (2. 161. 2).
He had led an army against Sidon, and fought a sea battle
against Tyre. He considered that his power was 'so safely
established' (οὕτω ἀσφαλέως ἑωυτῷ ἱδρῦσθαι, 2. 169. 2) that no
god would be able to end his rule. But he was 'bound to end
badly' (οἳ ἔδεε κακῶς γενέσθαι. . ., 2. 161. 3). Having sent a great
expedition against the people of Cyrene, he met with an equally
great disaster (στράτευμα μέγα . . . μεγάλως προσέπταισε, 2. 161. 4).
For the Egyptians revolted from him, supposing that he had
sent them away on campaign with the intention that they should
be destroyed, so that he then could rule the remaining Egyptians 'more securely' (ἀσφαλέστερον). Apries sent Amasis to put
down the rebellion, but Amasis instead became its leader. His
folly in appointing Amasis parallels that of Astyages in appointing Harpagus against Cyrus in spite of the treatment Harpagus
had received from Astyages. Astyages was θεοβλαβής, blinded by
the gods (1. 127. 2).[57] Harpagus had been the most trusted of
Astyages' lieutenants (1. 108. 3), just as Gyges had been the
right hand man of Candaules (1. 8. 1)—the man least likely,
ostensibly, to be the agent of his downfall.

Misfortune, contrary to Solon's wisdom, may strike even
after death. Cambyses, on invading Egypt, did not find Amasis
alive (3. 10. 2): Amasis had died, 'having ruled for four and
forty years, in the course of which no great misfortune had
happened to him'. He was then embalmed, and buried in the
tomb he himself had built in the temple, and his son became
king in his place. Herodotus then reverts to his account of
Cambyses' campaign. When Cambyses was victorious, he
disinterred Amasis' body, and ordered it to be scourged,
plucked of its hairs, pricked with goads, and finally burnt
(3. 16. 1–2).

The good fortune of a city or a people follows precisely the
same pattern as that of individuals: good fortune is either mixed
or it will be short-lived. Under Amasis, before Cambyses'
invasion, Egypt had never been more prosperous (2. 177. 1).
The Aeginetans were encouraged by their great prosperity to

---

[57] The same word is also used of the king who offered Perdiccas the sun in
place of wages, the sun that constituted his sovereignty, 8. 137. 4.

initiate a costly war against Athens (εὐδαιμονίη, 5. 81. 2).[58] Lydia was at its height at the arrival of Solon in Croesus' court (1. 29. 1). The affairs of Siphnos too were at their peak (ἤκμαζε) when Samian pirates came and deprived them of one hundred talents (3. 57. 2). The Spartans under Leon and Hegesicles were fortunate in all their campaigns—except one against the Tegeans (εὐτυχέοντες, 1. 65. 1). (After their transfer of the bones of Orestes, their success was uninterrupted, however, 1. 68. 6.) The Thebans, who changed sides to support the Persians at Thermopylae when they saw that the Persians were winning, and who then pleaded with the Persians for their lives by arguing that they had fought for the Greeks under compulsion, survived as a result (7. 233. 1–2), 'but they were not fortunate in every respect' (οὐ μέντοι τά γε πάντα εὐτυχήσαν, 7. 233. 2): for some of them were killed as they first approached the Persians, others, the majority, branded with the King's mark at Xerxes' order. At the outset of the Ionian revolt Naxos excelled all other islands in its prosperity (εὐδαιμονίη, 5. 28), and Miletus was at its peak (τότε ἀκμάσασα), the model, πρόσχημα, of Ionia:[59] Miletus and Naxos were two of the chief victims of the revolt (6. 18–20; 5. 33–4, 6. 96). Sybaris and Eretria too were at their peaks when Smindyrides the son of Hippocrates and Lysanies went to woo Agariste of Sicyon (6. 127. 1, 4): both their cities were subsequently taken, by the Crotoniates and Persians respectively (5. 44. 1; 6. 21. 1, 100–1).

In some such cases, there may be some suggestion of folly, that a people acted rashly on the basis of their present prosperity.[60] In other cases, misfortune is quite evidently undeserved. When a city is about to experience great misfortunes, signs tend to be given in advance (6. 27. 1). The Chians experienced two such signs: the death through plague of all but two of a hundred young men sent to Delphi as a chorus, and the death of all but one of a hundred and twenty children when their

[58] A group of Samian pirates settled happily at Cydonia on Crete for five years (εὐδαιμόνησαν), but in the sixth year the Aeginetans and some Cretans defeated them in a sea battle and sold them into slavery, 3. 59. 2.

[59] Miletus' fortune was even more mixed, as it had only recently recovered from a two-generation bout of stasis, 5. 28–30. 1. Cf. the change in the Spartan constitution and in Spartan fortune, 1. 65. 2 ff.

[60] Cf. Thucydides' judgement on the Chian revolt from Athens, 8. 24. 4–5.

school roof collapsed (6. 27. 2). These signs were sent by the god: for afterwards the city was brought to its knees by the sea battle at Lade (6. 27. 3). It was precisely because of their dogged refusal to give up the fight that they suffered so badly (6. 15). Many of their survivors met with an even more unfortunate death at the hands of fellow-Greeks: as they made their way home by land, the Ephesians mistook them for bandits come to steal away their women from the Thesmophoria, and killed them (6. 16).

Reversals, personal or communal, can also be given an extra sharpness by the subtlety of their presentation. The arrival in Susa of the news of the occupation of Athens was followed swiftly by that of the defeat of Salamis, plunging the people of Susa from celebration to mourning (8. 99). The Persians' reversal, by being presented obliquely, projected onto a small screen, is given an extra pathos. Characters also highlight the reversal in fortune of others: Leutychidas, himself shortly to be caught out, cruelly taunts Demaratus, the man whom he has replaced as king of Sparta, by asking 'what it is like to be a magistrate after being a king'. The question, Demaratus replied, would be the beginning of 'either countless evil or countless good fortune for the Spartans' (6. 67. 2–3). Harpagus likewise asks Astyages how slavery compares with freedom (1. 129. 1): Astyages replies by calling him the 'weakest and most unjust of men'—the weakest for not assuming the kingship himself, and the most unjust because he had enslaved the Medes to the Persians on account of his personal grudge (1. 129. 3).

Bad ends are also often implied rather than spelled out. Croesus answers Cambyses' question of whether he was as fortunate as his father Cyrus, by saying that he was less so in that he had no son such as Cyrus had (3. 34. 4–5). Whilst being simultaneously effective flattery (with which Cambyses is blindly delighted) it also highlights (according to Solonian thinking) a genuine misfortune: he indeed died childless (3. 66. 2). Pausanias in the aftermath of Plataea illustrates the foolishness of Xerxes' invasion by a comparison of a Persian and a Spartan banquet.[61] Pointing to the difference between the

---

[61] A good example of what Edward Hussey (in Oxford lectures) has termed a 'synchronous reversal'.

two, and laughing, Pausanias observed: ' "Men of Greece, I have called you together for this reason, because I wish to show you the folly of the Mede who, possessing such fare as this, came to us, who possess such humble fare, to take it from us." ' An additional irony, however, derives here from the reader's knowledge of Pausanias' later degeneration into Persian decadence and tyrannical excess.[62] Thucydides describes, for example, how Pausanias began to wear Persian dress and, most significantly, keep a Persian table (Thuc. 1. 130. 1).

Tyranny, as we have already seen in the case of Apries, is inherently unreliable. Periander's question to Thrasybulus— 'in what fashion he might establish affairs most securely and best rule the city' (ὄντινα ἂν τρόπον ἀσφαλέστατον καταστησάμενος τῶν πρηγμάτων κάλλιστα τὴν πόλιν ἐπιτροπεύοι, 5. 92. ζ2)?—hints already at the impossibility of maintaining his power without risk.[63] As the reader may already know, Periander would lose his son Lycophron largely through his own fault (3. 50. 7), whilst keeping his tyranny. Thrasybulus' advice to Periander that he should kill the most eminent (τοὺς ὑπερόχους) of his fellow-citizens (5. 92. η1)—displayed graphically by his cutting down (κολούων, 5. 92. ζ2) whichever ear of corn stood out (ὑπερέχοντα) among others in a cornfield—also gives intimations of this punishment: it is not accidentally reminiscent of Artabanus' description of the behaviour of the gods, that 'all things that stand out the god is prone to cut down' (φιλέει γὰρ ὁ θεὸς τὰ ὑπερέχοντα πάντα κολούειν, 7. 10. ε). Periander, by usurping the divine prerogative of the whimsical punishment of those who excel, is laying himself open to exactly such a fall.[64]

Herodotus develops the idea of personal reversal furthest in tragic, narrative terms, in the story of the downfall of Psammenitus, the son of Amasis.[65] When he sees his daughter and the daughters of the Egyptian nobles paraded in front of him

---

[62] Fornara (1971a: 62 ff.).

[63] The emphasis on the 'rooting' of Peisistratus' tyranny, e.g. 1. 60. 1, 64. 1, perhaps implies its eventual rooting out. Two royal treasuries, of Rhampsanitus and Sardanapallus, are also inevitably flawed: 2. 121. a, 150. 3.

[64] Cf. van der Veen (1996: 82–3); for a more positive reading, J. Salmon (1997).

[65] See Lloyd's excellent interpretation of this passage: (1988b: 51).

dressed as slaves and carrying water pitchers, Psammenitus
does not react, even though the fathers of the other girls are
weeping and shouting around him (3. 14. 2–3). He merely looks
down at the ground (3. 14. 3). Then when his son is marched
past, with two thousand other Egyptians, with ropes round
their necks and bridles in their mouths on their way to
execution, again he shows no sign of emotion (3. 14. 4–6).[66]
But when he then saw an old drinking partner who had fallen to
begging from the Persian soldiers, he cried out aloud, struck
his own head, and called to the man by name (3. 14. 7).[67] As he
explained to Cambyses, his own sufferings were too great to cry
at, but the grief of his friend, a man who had fallen 'from great
good fortune' (ἐκ πολλῶν τε καὶ εὐδαιμόνων) into beggary on the
threshold of old age, was worthy of tears.[68] Croesus, who was
on the scene, according to the Egyptians began to cry, as did
those Persians present. Even Cambyses was moved to pity
(3. 14. 11) and gave the order for Psammenitus' son to be
saved; but his messengers arrived too late (3. 15. 1). The pathos
of the scene is clearly heightened by the way in which
Psammenitus' grief at his own misfortune is displaced onto a
friend, and the way in which his hope of relief exists only to be
dashed. The death of one's children is on the Solonian model
an archetypal misfortune: Tellus' good fortune consisted to a
large extent in his possession of noble sons at the time of his
death in battle (1. 32. 4; cf. 1. 32. 6). One of Croesus'
misfortunes is the death of his one sound son Atys (1. 43. 2).
For Psammenitus to be made to witness his own child's death
parallels the awful vengeance enacted on the slave trader
Panionius by Hermotimus—whereby Panionius was forced to
castrate all of his four sons before they performed the same
operation on him (8. 106. 4),[69] according to Herodotus the most
awful vengeance of any of which he knows (8. 105. 1).

[66] Such stiff-upper-lip stoicism is apparently considered a virtue: cf.
Theogn. 445–6, 591–4, E. *Phoen.* 1763 (men must endure whatever the
gods send).

[67] See van der Veen's distinction (1996: 31): 'whereas δακρύειν is an
impulsive reaction, κλαίειν is preponderantly the stylised and intentional
demonstration of grief.'

[68] Flory (1978a: 149) adduces this as an example parallel to his 'laughter,
tears and wisdom' motif.

[69] For childlessness, see esp. 1. 109. 3 (Astyages and Harpagus), 2. 79. 3

Herodotus' discussion of the origins and the geographical definition of Egypt also arguably depends on a belief in the Solonian idea of reversals in human fortune (2. 13–14).[70] The priests told him that at the time of King Moeris, the Nile needed to rise by eight cubits to flood the land (2. 13. 1). In his own day, the river would fail to overflow unless it rose by at least fifteen or sixteen cubits. Herodotus then opines that, if the land were to continue to rise and grow because of the Nile's alluvial deposits, and the Nile were no longer to flood, the Egyptians would suffer permanently precisely the same fate that they said that the Greeks would some day suffer (2. 13. 2): for the Egyptians, on learning that Greece had rain and that the rivers did not flood, had said that the Greeks 'would one day suffer terrible hunger having been disappointed of their great hope' (ψευσθέντας κοτὲ ἐλπίδος μεγάλης κακῶς πεινήσειν, 2. 13. 3). What they meant, Herodotus adds, was that if in the future the god no longer wished to give them rain but decided to inflict a drought, they would suffer a famine; for they had no other source of water except that from Zeus. Herodotus then describes the effortless fashion in which the Egyptians below Memphis obtain their food (2. 14. 2):

For indeed at the moment these men bring in their harvest from the land with less labour than all other men and than the rest of the Egyptians: they do not have to labour to break up the furrows with the plough, nor to hoe, nor to do any of the other tasks at which other men labour for a crop, but when the river has come up of its own accord and flooded the fields, and then having done so retreats back again, then each man sows his own field, turns his pigs into it, and

(Linus song), 5. 48 (Cleomenes), 3. 66. 2 (Cleomenes), 6. 38. 2 (Stesagoras), 7. 39. 3 (Pythius), 7. 221 (Megistias). Cf. also E. *Suppl.* 1120–2: to see one's children dying is the greatest pain for mortals. Lateiner (1989: 142) points out the significant coincidence that 'seven violators of supra-national *nomoi* are said to be *childless*'. For the murder of one's enemy's children, 'not unusual or unGreek' according to Mossman (1995: 188), though excessive (pp. 175–6), cf. 9. 120. 4 (Artayctes), 3. 35. 1–4 (Prexaspes).

[70] Generally, however, as Fornara observes (1971a: 18), 'eloquent as was the history of Egypt of the transience of human fortune, it is no more than merely implicit in his account'. Wood develops the curious thesis (1972: 59–60 n. 3) that reversals in Egypt (with the exception of their one great reversal, the Persian conquest) are from low to high. Cf. the crocodile, 2. 68. 2, the animal that grows to the greatest size from being the smallest.

when the seed is trodden in by the pigs, he waits for harvest-time, and then having trodden in the corn with his pigs, he gathers it in.

Such an easy life is surely tempting fate, Herodotus seems to be saying. The sentiments apparently implied here are of a piece with the remarks of Demaratus in Book 7 (7. 102. 1): ' "Poverty has always been familiar in Greece, but virtue has been acquired, fashioned through wisdom and the strength of law: it is with these that Greece wards off poverty and tyranny." '[71] In one respect, however, the life of stability in Egypt has advantages: the Egyptians are, next to the Libyans, the most healthy people in the world, because their seasons are not liable to change: for men, Herodotus observes, 'are most subject to diseases at periods of change, and above all others at the change of the seasons' (2. 77. 3).

Solonian ideas seem also to be prominent amongst the foreign peoples whom Herodotus describes. The Massagetai sacrifice their sick and believe this to be a piece of fortune for the victim (1. 216. 2–3). The Trausi do everything in the same way as other Thracians except that they lament a man's birth and celebrate his death, for they think that 'human life is nothing but suffering' (5. 4).[72] At dinner parties of rich Egyptians, a servant carries around to all the guests a coffin with the image of a dead man painted on it, and as he shows it to each guest tells him to look on it, drink, and be merry, for when he dies he too will be like that (2. 78).[73] Other peoples are defined in opposition to Solonian values. The Indians kill and eat each other at the first opportunity, with the consequence

[71] For the correlation between freedom and poverty, see esp. 9. 122 with n. 82 below.

[72] Cf. Soph. *OC* 1751–3 (one should not mourn when death welcome). For the question of whether death really was welcome for the Trausi, see Kazarow (1940: 410–11); as Asheri points out (1990: 149), the Trausi's belief reflects a common Greek aphorism.

[73] This *carpe diem* philosophy was typically Egyptian: Lloyd ii. 337. Cf. the attitude to death of Mycerinus, 2. 133. 4–5. More frivolously, cats in Egypt are overcome by the divine (θεῖα πρήγματα καταλαμβάνει . . ., 2. 66. 3) and leap into the flames of fires: could the θεῖα πρήγματα with which the cats are inspired be the knowledge that death is better than life? According to Benardete (1969), the cats are inspired with the divine in the sense that they are compelled to jump; for further speculations, see Linforth (1928: 234).

that few reach old age (3. 99). The Persians are noticeably lacking in Solonian fatalism. In the words of Macan, they 'took a cheerful view of birthdays' (1. 139. 1).[74] Cyrus thought his luck would last (1. 204. 2). Xerxes imagined that his empire's expansion would continue (7. 8. *a*). Achaemenes petulantly accuses Demaratus and the Greeks of envying all good fortune (7. 236. 1), missing the point presumably that it is not the Greeks who envy fortune but the gods.[75]

Just as good fortune is never certain, always prone to sudden reversal, so too (by extension) human certainty over the future is also impossible.[76] 'Can anyone who is a man know with certainty what should be done?', Xerxes asks Artabanus (7. 50. 1). To what extent mistaken certainty is avoidable or blameworthy will be discussed in Chapter 9. The frequent misinterpretation of oracles or of other forms of divination is itself, however, an illustration of the truth of the Solonian principle of the instability of fortune. Herodotus not only frequently structures his narrative around the misinterpretation of oracles—much of Book 1, for example, is structured around the misinterpretations of Croesus—but he uses a number of techniques for highlighting in his narrative the false certainty of his characters: his lengthy description of Croesus' dedications, each act of dedication compounding Croesus' certainty in his success, is inevitably a prelude to his 'betrayal' by Delphi (1. 50–4). Equally, the thoroughness of Xerxes' preparations, again lavishly described, is a signal that the campaign is bound to end in failure: as Artabanus recognizes, their numbers will work against them (7. 49).[77]

While a certain sort of Solonian 'knowledge' or 'understanding' seems almost invariably to be vindicated (1. 96. 2, 2. 152. 3, 6. 17; cf. 1. 3. 1[78]), hopes and expectations are—equally invariably—confounded (7. 168. 2; 8. 10. 1, 24. 2, 77. 1, 140. 3; cf. 8. 12. 2).[79] Croesus' hopes are charted carefully by

---

[74] Macan iv. 1. 155.
[75] Artabanus is, of course, an exception to this rule.
[76] See Chs. 5–6. See also Masaracchia on 9. 16. 5 (p. 159) for further refs.
[77] See further Harrison (1998*b*; 2000: ch. 7).
[78] Cf. also the cunning of Rhampsanitus' thief, described in apparently Solonian terms, 2. 121. ζ2.
[79] For mad hope, see Avery (1972*a*: 19–20).

Herodotus through Book 1 (50. 1, 54. 1, 56. 1, 71. 1, 75. 2, 77. 4)
until eventually it is announced that 'his hope was destroyed'
(1. 80. 5). Histiaeus likewise 'hopes' or expects that he would
not be killed by Darius for his revolt from Persian power
(ἐλπίζων, 6. 29. 1). Chased by a Persian, and aware that if he
were caught he would be stabbed, he called out in the Persian
language that he was Histiaeus the Milesian (6. 29. 2). If he had
indeed been sent to Darius, he would most likely have been
spared, Herodotus opines, but Artaphernes had other ideas: he
was impaled then and there; the only part of him that was sent
on to the King was his pickled head (6. 30. 1). Histiaeus' death
presents almost a mirror image of the escape from death of
Croesus.[80]

The idea that cities' fortunes are subject to sudden reversals
is, as we have seen, enshrined even at the opening of Book 1
(1. 5. 3–4):

I will proceed with my account, touching as I do so on both small and
great cities of men alike (ὁμοίως σμικρὰ καὶ μεγάλα ἄστεα ἀνθρώπων
ἐπεξιών). For of those which were formerly great most have now
become small, while those which in my time were great were formerly
small. Understanding then that human fortune never remains for long
in the same place (τὴν ἀνθρωπηίην ὢν ἐπιστάμενος εὐδαιμονίην οὐδαμὰ ἐν
τὠυτῷ μένουσαν), I will recall both alike.

The Histories, it seems, are founded on the principle of the
instability of human fortune.[81] Herodotus' words here echo
closely those of Solon to Croesus and of Amasis to Polycrates;

[80] At the same time, though the assumption that the King would overthrow
the Greeks is shown to be a false one, this does not prevent characters in other
contexts from reasoning on the basis of probability rather than on the
probability of reversals of expectation. The Samians at the battle of Lade
realized that, in the event of a victory, the King would only send an even
larger fleet against them (6. 13. 1), an opinion from which Herodotus does not
dissent. Cf. 5. 124. 1: Aristagoras realizes that he cannot overthrow the King.

[81] See e.g. Stahl (1975: 1–2), Fornara (1971a: 77), S. O. Shapiro (1996:
356). Cf. also Raaflaub (1987: 234), envisaging 1. 5. 3 as 'the programmatic
heading for Herodotus' topical interpretation of history, both in a moral and
political sense', Immerwahr (1966: 153), seeing a fanciful connection with
Heracleitus 'on the coincidence of opposites, by which fortune and misfortune
may be identical actions affecting the two parties to a dispute in a different
way'. Immerwahr (1957) also sees this theme as providing the rationale for the
account of Samos, a city that had become small.

the same themes are picked up also in the very last chapter of the *Histories* (9. 122).[82] It has been suggested even that Herodotus saw his own role as enquirer and narrator as analogous to that of the travelling sage Solon.[83] At any rate, the *Histories* are deeply marked by Solonian ideas. Every reversal in the *Histories*, every demonstration of the rule of the mutability of fortune—of which the greatest of course is the reversal of the Persians' fortunes through their campaign to Greece—is also, moreover, an illustration of the force of the divine to disturb human affairs.[84]

This sense of the possibility of reversal in human affairs may also underlie Herodotus' inclusion in his *Histories* of reports which seem overtly to be marvellous or extraordinary. A Thracian people, he relates, the Sigynnai, claim to be Median colonists. Herodotus declares himself unable to judge the truth of the report—except to say that 'anything can happen, given time' (5. 9. 3; cf. 4. 195. 2).[85] This and the Solonian recommendation that 'it is necessary to look to the end of all things' are arguably not bad mottos for a historian.

---

[82] See esp. Redfield (1985); also Cartledge (1990: 40), and less convincingly Alonso-Nuñez (1988: 130); see also Ch. 7, n. 68.

[83] Redfield (1985: 102), Moles (1996: 264–5); cf. Raaflaub (1987: 248) for Herodotus as resembling his warners.

[84] There is nothing doctrinaire about Herodotus' belief in the mutability of human fortune; as Gomme sensibly observes (1954: 81) of the idea of *hybris*, it is the 'result of observation'. See also here Immerwahr (1966: 307): the pattern of rise and fall is 'neither theological nor moral, but existential'.

[85] Cf. van der Veen (1996: 4 and n. 12).

3

Miracles and the Miraculous

The reversals of fortune discussed in the previous chapter may in some instances run against common sense expectations. They may be improbable. Other reversals of expectation, however, are more drastic. The people of Cnidus, confronted by Cyrus' general Harpagus, planned to dig a canal across the Isthmus that divided their territory from the mainland of Caria (1. 174. 4):[1]

> But as they were carrying on the work with many hands, the workers appeared to incur more injuries and in a fashion more divine than was reasonable (μᾶλλον γάρ τι καὶ θειότερον ἐφαίνοντο τιτρώσκεσθαι οἱ ἐργαζόμενοι τοῦ οἰκότος), both around the body and in particular in the eyes due to the splintering of the rock, and so they sent ambassadors to Delphi to ask what was obstructing them.

It is the unreasonable, or at any rate the unusual, nature of the injuries that convinces the Cnidians to draw the logical deduction that they were of divine origin, and to reach the practical decision to enquire as to the most expedient course of action. The Cnidians should not, it transpires, have begun to dig the canal: 'for Zeus would have made [Cnidus] an island, if he had wished to' (1. 174. 5) The Cnidians' infringement of nature is met by another. There are 'natural laws' then. Indeed these natural laws, the god's reply suggests, are divinely ordained or sanctioned, an idea that recurs elsewhere in the *Histories*.[2] To believe in the divine cause of such inherently unlikely events is not to suspend all 'common sense' ideas of probability. In certain limited circumstances, however, these

---

[1] Cf. 2. 175 (Amasis takes sigh as omen and stops building), 2. 158. 5 (Necos stops building on advice of oracle) and, less directly, 8. 137. 3 (Perdiccas' loaf *always* doubles in size, and so the King realizes it to be a *teras* or omen). For comparable 'engineering superstitions', e.g. Plut. *Per.* 13. 7–8, see McCartney (1940).

[2] See esp. 3. 108. 2, discussed Ch. 9.

laws may be suspended.[3] The Cnidians, it should be said, ceased digging their canal and, as soon as Harpagus approached with his army, gave themselves up without a fight (1. 174. 6).

The story of the Cnidian ditch provides the clearest illustration of what in this chapter will be termed a miracle: an event deduced to be divine on the grounds that it would otherwise be impossible (or at least extremely improbable).[4] It is important to state at the outset, however, that the miraculous is by no means an exclusive category of divine intervention, nor is it one that Herodotus or his contemporaries would have been able to recognize or distinguish. The case of Cnidus might also be seen as an omen, a miracle with a message, the message to stop digging. The impossible may shade into the merely unusual or unlikely. The intention in this chapter is not to obscure these grey areas of overlap between different 'categories' of divine intervention but to highlight them.

In the example of the Cnidian ditch, although Herodotus' passing use of θειότερον suggests that the Cnidians' reasoning is one he naturally understands, he does not make his belief in miracles explicit.[5] In a number of other instances he does so. The same process of rational deduction can be seen, for example, in what we might term the 'moral miracle' of the shrine of Demeter at Plataea (9. 65. 2).

It is a wonder to me (θῶμα δέ μοι) how not a single one of those Persians fighting by the grove of Demeter appeared either to have entered or died in the precinct, yet most of them fell in unconsecrated ground

[3] See G. E. R. Lloyd (1979: 51): 'the category of the "supernatural" develops, in fact, *pari passu* with that of the "natural"'; Lloyd also discusses 1. 174 as an inference on Herodotus' part (p. 50 and n. 214). See also on this passage Legrand (1932: 133). For the idea of the supernatural, cf. Evans-Pritchard (1965: 109–10); see also Hallpike's argument (1979: 451–6) that 'primitive thought' lacks the conceptions of randomness or probability.

[4] Miracles, writes Shimron, 'are records of phenomena that are deviations from the natural laws and therefore unacceptable as facts' (1989: 37). Cf. Pind. *Pyth.* 10. 48–50, Soph. *Aj.* 86.

[5] For scepticism over Herodotus' belief in miracles, see e.g. Shimron (1989: 23), referring in the surprising context of 2. 54–7, to his 'consistent rejection of miracles that were connected with humans or done by them', or Vandiver (1991: 100 n. 2, 101): 'however, when natural phenomena are claimed as divinely inspired or are associated with miracles, he leaves the question of divine or heroic causation open'.

around the shrine. I reckon—if we may speculate about divine matters (δοκέω δέ, εἴ τι περὶ τῶν θείων πρηγμάτων δοκέειν δεῖ)[6]—that the goddess refused to receive the men who had burnt her temple in Eleusis.

Herodotus need not have drawn attention to the miraculous distribution of the Persians' bodies. The fact that he does so implies that in his mind it is important and that it requires an explanation: that explanation is then found in a past crime of the Persians in question.[7] Sceptical rationalizations—such as that the bodies were subsequently moved—do not appear to have crossed his mind. The expression 'it is a wonder to me' (θῶμα μοι) can in different circumstances be an expression of doubt: that the Alcmeonids should have raised a shield at Marathon as a signal to the Persians is, Herodotus tells us twice, a 'wonder' to him (6. 121. 1, 123. 1):[8] 'and I do not accept the story', he adds; 'I will not admit the slander'. The same expression can either then reflect the impossibility of an event or it may suggest divine intervention.

There are ample further illustrations of the same pattern. In the case of the 'wrath of Talthybius', the Spartan herald and hero, a wrath which arose from the Spartan killing of Persian ambassadors, the coincidence that vengeance was visited on the sons of the same men who had once volunteered to die in expiation of the crime is proof once again for Herodotus of the involvement of the divine (7. 137. 1–2).[9] A similar deduction is made in the case of the battle of Mycale, and the coincidences between Mycale and Plataea (9. 100. 1–101. 2):

When therefore the Greeks were prepared, they advanced towards the barbarians; and as they were advancing, a rumour flew through the whole army, and a herald's staff was seen lying on the shoreline: the

---

[6] Herodotus' qualification has been construed as evidence that Herodotus thought such a divine explanation inadequate: see further Ch. 7.

[7] Cf. 8. 129. 3 (the Potidaea floodtide), for which see below, this chapter. For the miraculous distribution of Persian bodies, cf. 8. 39. 2 where the rocks that fall on the Persians all stop within the precinct of Athena Pronaia.

[8] Cf. 8. 8. 2, Skyllias' dive (θωμάζω δὲ εἰ τὰ λεγόμενά ἐστι ἀληθέα). Mardonius' institution of democracy in Ionia would be a μέγιστον θῶμα according to Herodotus, 6. 43. 3, to those Greeks who did not accept that Otanes had earlier spoken in favour of democracy; but those who wondered in this way would be wrong. Cf. also 2. 21: one of the theories of the Nile is θωμασιωτέρη. Contrast the eccentric survey of the Greek historians' terms of disbelief of Packman (1991).   [9] Cf. Vandiver (1991: 216).

rumour that spread among them was this, that the Greeks had conquered the army of Mardonius in battle in Boeotia. Divine involvement in human affairs is clear by many proofs (δῆλα δὴ πολλοῖσι τεκμηρίοισί ἐστι τὰ θεῖα τῶν πρηγμάτων): for, on the same day on which the defeat at Plataea took place and on which that at Mycale was about to happen, a rumour reached the Greeks there with the result that the army was enormously encouraged and wished more eagerly to risk danger. There was also this other coincidence (καὶ τόδε ἕτερον συνέπεσε γενόμενον), that there were shrines of Eleusinian Demeter close by both engagements: for the battle at Plataea, as I mentioned before, took place by the Demetrion and that at Mycale was about to do likewise. The rumour that the Greeks under Pausanias had prevailed turned out to be correct (ὀρθῶς σφι ἡ φήμη συνέβαινε ἐλθοῦσα): for the battle at Plataea was fought while it was still early in the day, that at Mycale towards evening. That both happened on the same day and in the same month became very soon evident when men looked into it.

There are a number of elements that point towards divine intervention here: that the battles occurred on the same day; that they both took place by shrines of Eleusinian Demeter; the physical evidence of the herald's staff found lying on the shore; and, most importantly perhaps, the fact that the rumour of Plataea reached Mycale before it could have done so by normal means.[10] Divine intervention and human motivation, interestingly, are not mutually exclusive here: the intervention of the divine occurs at a crucial moment psychologically for the Greeks.[11] Curiously, the plausibility of the rumour—the fact that Plataea was in actual fact fought earlier in the day than Mycale—appears to be adduced as evidence of the divine origins of the rumour: it may bend nature through its inordinate speed, but it is not in any way prophetic.[12]

[10] For comparable divine rumours (without quite the background of evidence of their divine origin), cf. H. *Il.* 2. 93 ff., *Od.* 1. 282–3, 3. 215, Soph. *Aj.* 998–9. It is possible that the story of the divine rumour is connected to the watchword given at Mycale, 9. 98. 3, possibly Hera rather than Hebe as conjectured now by Rosén. Diodorus, 11. 35, and Polyaenus, 1. 33, rationalize the rumour as a stratagem of Leutychidas.

[11] Cf. the answer to Pausanias' prayer at Plataea, 9. 62; also H. *Il.* 8. 251–2.

[12] If Plataea had been fought after Mycale, would it not also have been miraculous, but prophetic too? If the rumour had been false, had the Greeks been defeated at Plataea, might the rumour not still have been construed as divine?

The unlikely or impossible events of Mycale prove not only divine intervention in this instance but more broadly the possibility of divine intervention at any moment in human history:[13] divine involvement in human affairs is clear by many proofs. This is a moral which is probably latent in many of the miracles recorded by Herodotus. It is often hard to establish certainly, however. In the case of the intervention of the hero Protesilaus, for example, it is a character in the *Histories,* the sacrilegious Persian Artayctes, rather than Herodotus who spells out the broader moral (9. 120. 1–2). According to the Chersonitans, one of the men who had been put to guard Artayctes as he awaited his execution was cooking some fish when suddenly the fish began to jump into life. The guards were all amazed (ἐθώμαζον). Artayctes, however, summoned the man and spoke to him:

My Athenian friend, do not be afraid of this marvel (τὸ τέρας). For it is not to you but to me that Protesilaus of Elaeus sends this sign (σημαίνει) that even though he is dead and dried [i.e. like the fish] he still has power from the gods to punish the man who acts unjustly (δύναμιν πρὸς θεῶν ἔχει τὸν ἀδικέοντα τίνεσθαι).

By virtue of its position in the *Histories*—the story of the punishment of Artayctes continues until the penultimate chapter of Book 9—the moral of the story is amplified: that wrongdoers are punished is a message of the *Histories* as a whole.[14] It is again here the impossibility of the event—of fish returning to life—that prompts Artayctes to infer a divine origin. But in this case the moral of the miracle is more specific than simply the proposition that the gods and heroes are latent in human history (though that more general moral may also be implicit). Having deduced that the event is divine, Artayctes interprets it as an omen. The knowledge of his own act of sacrilege against Protesilaus, the clue of the fish being dead and dried like the hero, together prompt the conclusion that Protesilaus is exacting his vengeance on him for his act of sacrilege. Having interpreted the omen correctly, Artayctes then attempts to evade its fulfilment. He offers to dedicate

[13] Possibly also the actual presence of a divinity: see Versnel (1987: 52).
[14] For Artayctes and Protesilaus, see esp. Boedeker (1988); for an interpretation of Herodotus' religion as polemical, Fornara (1990).

one hundred talents to the hero in place of the wealth he had plundered and a further two hundred talents to the Athenians for his life and that of his son (9. 120. 4). These terms are refused: Artayctes is nailed to a plank overlooking the Hellespont, his son stoned to death in front of him. Ironically then the omen of the fish, as interpreted by Artayctes, is fulfilled through his own death.

There are many other such 'miracles-with-messages'. In the course of Xerxes' occupation and destruction of Athens, for example, the olive tree planted on the Acropolis by Athena in the course of her contest with Poseidon[15] was, according to the Athenians, burnt to the ground by the barbarians (8. 55). But on the second day from the burning, the Athenians sent by Xerxes to sacrifice on the Acropolis saw a new shoot already a cubit in length. The implication, of course, is that such growth would normally have been impossible; the regrowth of the olive tree is a sign of the resurgence of Athens herself. A slight variation is presented by the story of the miraculous apparition of the Eleusinian procession seen by the Spartan king Demaratus and by the Athenian exile Dicaeus. Herodotus, as if to assert the authenticity of the story, ascribes the story to Dicaeus himself[16] who, he claims, appealed to the testimony of Demaratus 'and other witnesses' (8. 65. 6). Dicaeus deduced that the sound of the procession was divine from the fact that there was no other possible source (8. 65. 2):

This is evident (τάδε γὰρ ἀρίδηλα): that, since Attica is deserted, the words uttered are divine (θεῖον τὸ φθεγγόμενον), and that they are coming from Eleusis to the assistance of the Athenians and their allies.

Dicaeus—and here is the variation—then puts the apparition to use in a form of impromptu divination:[17] from the direction the procession then takes, towards Salamis rather than the

---

[15] See further Parker (1987: 198–200).

[16] For the theory of Dicaeus as a written source for Herodotus (c.470), rightly criticized by Macan vii. 1. 2. 454 as a 'suggestive fancy', see Trautwein (1890), Mathieu (1931). The memoirs of Dicaeus, Hauvette commented (1894: 493), exist only in the imagination of M. Trautwein. Macan vii. 1. 1. 7 himself fancied that Dicaeus was one of the shadowy Peisistratids of 7. 6. 2–5.

[17] For the shadow of the Peloponnesian war behind the pairing of an Athenian and a Spartan, see Boedeker (1987: 200).

Peloponnese, he calculates that it is Xerxes' fleet rather than his land force that would soon suffer (7. 65. 3, 6).

While miracles may imply messages, there are other areas of overlap (discussed further in Chapter 5) between the miraculous and the prophetic. Though oracles and other forms of divination are rightly seen as guides to human action rather than merely a form of fortune-telling, they do nevertheless give access to knowledge impossible by other means. Croesus was reassured that Delphi was a true source of prophecy when the god discovered something that it was 'impossible to discover' (τὰ ἦν ἀμήχανον ἐξευρεῖν, 1. 48. 2). He had charged his ambassadors to ask the oracle what he himself was doing on the hundredth day from their departure (1. 47. 2); on the appointed day he had cut up a tortoise and a lamb and stewed them together in a bronze cauldron with a bronze lid (1. 48. 2).[18] The question posed of the oracle—the nature of Croesus' activity on a fixed day—is not, it should be stressed, in essence undiscoverable except by special insight: it is only the distance in space between Croesus and Delphi that makes such knowledge impossible except through the divine. In some cases, the miraculous authority of a prophecy is reinforced also by the manner of its delivery. If the priestess replies in advance of a question, for example (1. 47. 2),[19] this may not show greater prescience on the part of the god, but it is at least an impressive sign of that prescience. When a Greek prophet of the oracle of Apollo Ptous gives an answer in Carian (8. 135), this too must help to reinforce the impression of the truth of the prophecy.[20]

---

[18] For similar proofs of prophetic insight, cf. the token given by Melissa to Periander, 5. 92. η2, or the story of the Telmessian seers, 1. 78. 3 (for which see Ch. 5); the precise coincidence of the two prophecies given to Croesus, 1. 53. 1, also constitutes a miraculous proof of their authority. For the similarities between Croesus' 'test oracle' and the Homeric Hymn to Hermes, see Dobson (1979).

[19] Cf. the prophecy to Lycurgus, 1. 65. 2: the Pythia's reply seems not to refer to any question, however. See here also Parke (1962), but contrast Fontenrose (1978: 116): 'the spontaneous response is characteristic of Legendary material.'

[20] For the question of whether this detail is authentic, see Flacelière (1946: 200 ff.), Robert (1950), Picard (1952), Daux (1957). Cf. Tambiah (1968: 177–8), describing Sinhalese *mantra* spoken in a 'hierarchy of languages'.

There may also be a miraculous element to the fulfilment of oracles and divination. This is not to say that the events through which such fulfilment takes place are necessarily miraculous in themselves—it may be rather the impossibly detailed mirroring of the original prophecy that is miraculous—but that can also be the case. A good example of this, and more broadly of the interrelatedness, the permeability, of these categories of divine intervention, is the story of the series of miracles that occur around Delphi at the time of the Persians' arrival there. These could be seen as fulfilling the remark of the god, in response to the question of whether the Delphians should evacuate his treasures, that he was able to look after his own possessions (8. 37–38):[21]

When the barbarians came near in their approach and saw the temple, the prophet, whose name was Aceratus, saw that the sacred arms that lay within, those which it is impious for any man to touch, had been carried out from the shrine. He therefore went to point out the marvel (σημανέων τὸ τέρας) to those of the Delphians who were present. But when the barbarians hurrying came to the shrine of Athena Pronaia, greater marvels still occurred to them than that which had happened before (ἐπίγινεταί σφι τέρεα ἔτι μέζονα τοῦ πρὶν γενομένου τέρεος). For it is indeed a great wonder that arms of war should appear of their own accord to be lying outside the temple (θῶμα μὲν γὰρ καὶ τοῦτο κάρτα ἐστί, ὅπλα ἀρήια αὐτόματα φανῆναι ἔξω προκείμενα τοῦ νηοῦ), yet those that came second after this are more deserving of wonder than all other apparitions (τὰ δὲ δὴ ἐπὶ τούτῳ δεύτερα ἐπιγενόμενα καὶ διὰ πάντων φασμάτων ἄξια θωμάσαι μάλιστα). For when the barbarians arrived at the shrine of Pronaia, at that moment thunderbolts fell on them from heaven (ἐκ μὲν τοῦ οὐρανοῦ κεραυνοὶ αὐτοῖσι ἐνέπιπτον), and from Parnessus two crags broke away and bore down on them with a great crashing noise and killed many of them, and from the shrine of Pronaia there came a shout and a war-cry. All these things mixing together, a panic had fallen upon the barbarians (φόβος τοῖσι βαρβάροισι ἐνεπεπτώκεε).

That Herodotus saw these apparitions (φασμάτα) as divine is revealed by his later remark that the fleeing Persians saw 'other divine things' (ἄλλα . . . θεῖα, 8. 38), two giant hoplites, identified by the Delphians as their heroes Phylacus and Autonous. Herodotus seems, together with the prophet Aceratus, to

[21] Cf. Xen. Hell. 6. 4. 30.

have assumed that since no one was permitted to touch the sacred arms, no one would have been so foolish as to have done so: this then constitutes proof that a divine hand was behind the marvel. The deduction that the thunder and the falling rocks were due to divine intervention is made partly perhaps on grounds of the unlikeliness of such events otherwise (albeit on this occasion the thunder does not emerge from a cloudless sky[22]), but perhaps mainly on the grounds of their timing as the Persians entered the shrine of Athena Pronaia, and of the coincidence of so many unlikely events.[23] The shouting and war-cry from the shrine of Athena is presumably not that of Delphians huddled within: it then (like the sound of the Eleusinian hymn heard by Demaratus and Dicaeus) is apparently judged divine on the grounds of its being inexplicable in any other terms.[24] All these events might be construed as in fulfilment of the god's response to the Delphians. Had the oracle never been solicited, however, or had it simply not been reported, the miracles would still most likely have been cast in very similar terms: the miracle of the arms might have been construed as a sign that the god intended to look after his own, or that (on the model of 9. 65. 2) the god did not wish to allow the Persians into Delphi; the deaths of the Persians that followed might easily, one senses, have been seen as vengeance for the attempt of the Persians to enter Delphi, or more generally for the transgression of crossing to Greece.

This is another important area of overlap. The outcome of the Cnidus miracle, discussed at the beginning of this chapter, with the inevitable submission of the plucky Cnidians to the Persian juggernaut, is apparently presented as being particularly unjust. However, the miracle at Plataea or the miraculous fulfilment of the wrath of Talthybius are in different ways clear

---

[22] Cf. 1. 87. 2, 7. 188. 2, 8. 12. 1.

[23] Cf. Masaracchia, ad loc. (viii. 174–5). Cf. the coincidence of a number of disasters occurring to the Chians, 6. 27.

[24] Contrast Lateiner's various verdicts on this passage: 'in this peculiar case the existence of the boulders seemingly moved from their former position . . . prevents Herodotus from scotching the report on the basis of his knowledge of physics' (1989: 98); Herodotus 'repeatedly distances himself from what he reports' (1989: 198); 'the mute boulders that broke off Mt. Parnassus . . . were an inadequate proof, of course, that gods were meddling in human affairs, and Herodotus does not here endorse that interpretation' (1989: 201).

instances of divine retribution; that of the jumping fish witnessed by Artayctes is also at least clear testament to his imminent punishment. Why some misfortunes are deemed instances of retribution and others to be omens or to reflect the mutability of fortune is a question that will be discussed further in the following chapter. In the cases at hand, however, it seems that it is the surrounding circumstances, the context or narrative frame of the story rather than any distinguishing features of the miracles themselves that determines the interpretation put upon them. The absence of any element of retribution from the miracles at Delphi may be merely an accident of reporting, but it is easy to see that any suggestion of retribution would be out of keeping with the tone and perspective of the miracle of the Cnidian ditch. Persians, on the other hand, are exemplary candidates for divine retribution.

There is no single pattern of the miracle then. A miracle may also be an omen; it may double as an instance of divine retribution. The miraculous element of an event may consist in its timing (a storm from a cloudless sky, for example, or the immediate fulfilment of an oracle) or in the unlikely coincidence of a number of factors; equally an event may be inherently impossible, like the resurrection of the fish being grilled by Artayctes' Athenian guards, or the sudden regrowth of Athena's olive tree. Miracles may often, like the coincidences between Plataea and Mycale, imply the moral that men should be mindful of the possibility of divine intervention in human affairs; but they may also suggest a more restricted lesson, for example (to take the story of Artayctes again) that the gods or heroes are capable of punishing wrongdoers.

The miraculous then should be seen not so much as a form of divine intervention as a criterion of intervention, and one that works alongside other criteria: that whereby, for example, a man's misfortune is deemed to be divine on the grounds of his having committed a crime worthy of punishment (discussed in Chapter 4), whereby an event or an utterance is deemed to have been divine on the grounds of its having been prophetic (discussed in Chapter 5), or whereby an event is judged divine simply on the grounds of its disproportionate consequences. On a number of occasions in the *Histories,* chance is said to be divine: so, for example, by a 'divine chance' (θείῃ τύχῃ) the

Samian Syloson gave the cloak he was wearing to the young
Darius (3. 139. 3), Cyrus was born (1. 126. 6), and the baby
Cypselus smiled at one of his would-be assassins (5. 92. γ3).[25]
None of these 'divine chances' is inherently impossible or
unlikely; what makes them divine is a retrospective judgement
of their outcome.[26] Cypselus' smile ensured his survival and his
subsequent tyranny: for 'it was necessary for evils to shoot up for
Corinth from the offspring of Aetion' (ἔδει δὲ ἐκ τοῦ Ἠετίωνος
γόνου Κορίνθῳ κακὰ ἀναβλαστεῖν, 5. 92. δ1).[27] Cyrus' survival at
birth, likewise, ensured his kingship and the overthrowal of the
Medes, and Syloson's chance encounter with Darius resulted in
the destruction of Samos.[28] The fact that Darius was an ordinary
officer in the Persian army at the time of their meeting is
evidence that Syloson's act could not have been cynical, that
the chance was authentic or divine.[29]

It is necessary also to consider the possibility that we should
distinguish a weaker class of miracles, the marvel. There are a
number of improbable events described in the *Histories,* often
apparently more frivolous than those we have seen so far, for
the divine origin of which Herodotus does not appear to vouch.
Unlike the miracles discussed earlier in this chapter, many of
which take place at crucial historical junctures, these appear
almost to be narrative non sequiturs, at best only loosely
attached to the surrounding events. A particularly marked
instance is the story of the priestess of Athena at Pedasa,
following directly on from the story of the Cnidian ditch,

[25] Contrast one other instance of 'divine chance', clearly miraculous, the
disappearance of Heracles' mares, 4. 8. 3. For Cyrus' birth, see further Ch. 9.

[26] Contrast Lateiner (1989: 200): the phrase θείη τύχη 'seems to mark
something humanly remarkable rather than divine and miraculous'; Lateiner
also finds it significant (1989: 218) that Herodotus allows no role to a deified
Fortune. For chance remarks that turn out in retrospect to be prophetic, e.g.
9. 91. 1, see also Ch. 5.

[27] Of course, in this case oracles provided advance warning also. The story
of Cypselus' miraculous escape is, according to Waters (1972: 142), an
example of a 'good tale being told for its own sake'.

[28] For Syloson, the nature of his cloak, and variant traditions of the story,
see Labarbe (1986), rationalizing the story as designed to absolve Syloson of
responsibility for the consequences of his attempt at power (pp. 24–5); see also
now van der Veen (1995).

[29] The same opposition of contrived and authentic (divine) chance can be
seen e.g. at 9. 91. 1.

leading only to the telegraphic report that the people of Pedasa were the only Carians to have attempted to withstand Harpagus' progress (1. 175):[30]

The Pedasians lived inland above Halicarnassus. Whenever anything unpleasant was about to happen to them or to their neighbours, the priestess of Athena grew a great beard. This happened three times.

Herodotus tells the story straight. Nevertheless, here are no grandiose judgements of the intentions of the divinity. Should we not label this episode a 'wonderful-but-true story', a marvel, rather than a miracle proper? Should we not accept that Herodotus has included such material simply for entertainment or relief?[31]

This formulation is misleading. We may recognize the need to distinguish between the (in our terms) historically more significant miracles of Plataea and Mycale, redolent of divine support for the Greek victory over Persia, and a less striking category of marvels never explicitly ascribed a divine cause, without then supposing that the second are devoid of *any* serious purpose. We have, moreover, no way of telling—save, that is, presumptions of the nature of history-writing projected back from our own day—what Herodotus deemed significant and what merely padding. We must surely then attach some significance even to those stories of which Herodotus is clearly sceptical *simply on the grounds of their inclusion.* To return to the words of the Proem, by telling such wonderful-but-true stories Herodotus is tracing the 'great and marvellous (θωμαστά) deeds of men';[32] he is tracing the margins of human experience, as his frequent use of superlatives—the first, the greatest and so on—suggests.[33]

[30] Cf. Pippidi's observations (1960: 78) on Herodotus' introduction ('sans sourciller') of the *terata* of 7. 57.

[31] See e.g. Murray (1980: 32): 'he also (and here perhaps the entertainer is most apparent) has a keen eye for marvels and strange customs.'

[32] For the importance of the marvellous, see the remarks of Hooker (1989: 145), Pembroke (1967: 16–18), and above all Redfield (1985). For a systematic description of the role of θωμάσια in ethnographic 'digressions', see Trüdinger (1918); see also Myres's table of the contents of ethnographic 'digressions' (1953: 73), or Lachenaud's (1978: 124). For a classification of θωμάσια, see Barth (1968).

[33] 1. 5. 3, 23, 94. 1, 105. 1, 163. 1; 2. 2–3, 14. 2, 40. 1, 77. 1, 83. 1, 157;

That is not to say, of course, that Herodotus believed all such
stories alike. In the case of Skyllias the diver (8. 8. 2),[34] who
travelled eighty stades under water, Herodotus appears to
express his disbelief frankly: 'I am amazed if what is said is
true' (θωμάζω δὲ εἰ τὰ λεγόμενά ἐστι ἀληθέα). (Herodotean
'wonder', as we have seen already, can suggest scepticism just
as it can reflect awe at a miracle.) The story of Arion, rescued
from drowning by a dolphin (1. 23–4),[35] he simply ascribes to
the Corinthians and the Lesbians, mentioning also the existence
of a statue of Arion at Taenarum (1. 23. 1, 24. 8).[36] Such
instances of scepticism or of reserve, however, should not be
thought in any way surprising. Neither scepticism nor credulity
needs to be argued or explained away but rather, as discussed in
Chapter 1, both need to be seen in relation to the other. The
remainder of this chapter will be an attempt to reveal a more
complex picture of Herodotus' beliefs by looking in turn at
three particular forms of divine intervention: the answering of
prayers, divine epiphanies, and finally natural miracles such as
earthquakes or storms. How could Herodotus and the Greeks
have sustained a belief in the possibility of the miraculous? How
was such a belief compatible with experience?

Prayers answered, like oracles fulfilled, constitute proof of
divine intervention. Herodotus makes no explicit statement
of belief in the miraculous fulfilment of prayer.[37] A number of
stories, however, are structured around the fulfilment of

3. 12. 3, 20. 1, 60. 3, 94. 2, 98. 2, 131. 3; 4. 5. 1, 48. 1, 50. 1, 58, 64. 3, 152. 3;
5. 3. 1, 119. 2; 6. 24. 1, 86. α2, 112. 3, 127. 3; 7. 70. 1; 8. 8. 1, 105. 1; 9. 35. 1,
37. 2, 64. 1, 78. 2.

[34] For Skyllias, see Paus. 10. 19. 1.

[35] See Bowra (1963) (for alternative versions of the story), Flory (1978a),
Munson (1986), and esp. Hooker (1989). According to Waters (1974: 6), the
story must have been introduced for 'literary' reasons as the 'historical
justification' for its insertion is 'extremely weak'. Fornara asserts (1971a:
19) that 'the adventure of Arion . . . is presented more for the magnificent
picture of his plight than for the miracle of his rescue'. Pritchett (1993: 16–
25), arguing against Fehling's scepticism concerning Herodotus' ascription of
the story to Corinthians and Lesbians (1989: 21–4), lists countless other
stories of the exploits of dolphins, or of the depictions of dolphins.

[36] For the process by which statues may give rise to stories (and then be
adduced as proof of those stories), see Ch. 2, n. 11.

[37] Linforth (1928: 213), Vandiver (1991: 103 n. 2) on 6. 61.

prayers. Rather than dwelling on questions of the degree of his detachment from such material, the topic will be addressed from a different angle: how might such stories reflect a working set of beliefs?

Croesus prays to Apollo, if ever the god had received a gift from him that deserved gratitude, to save him from death on the pyre (1. 87. 1): from a cloudless sky a storm then broke to quench the flames (1. 87. 2). The Pythian priestess later credits this intervention to Apollo (1. 91. 3). When the omens are unfavourable at Plataea, and a large number of Spartans are dying as a result, Pausanias looks towards the Plataean Heraion and calls upon the goddess 'not to disappoint them of their hope' (9. 61. 3). 'Immediately after the prayer of Pausanias, the omens as they sacrificed became favourable to the Lacedaimonians' (ἐγίνετο θυομένοισι τὰ σφάγια χρηστά, 9. 62). That they were not disappointed in their wider hope might also then be due (in some part) to Hera.[38] Ladice of Cyrene, unable to consummate her marriage to Amasis and threatened by him with death as a consequence, vows to Aphrodite 'in her mind'[39] or without speaking (εὔχεται ἐν τῷ νόῳ, 2. 181. 4) that, should Amasis succeed in having sex with her that night, she would dedicate a statue to the goddess in Cyrene. Immediately after the prayer, Amasis had sex with her. 'And from then on, whenever he came to her, he had sex with her and he loved her very dearly after this.'[40]

In all three of these cases it is the sudden and convenient

[38] As Pritchett remarks, i. 115 n. 24, '9. 33–37 reads like a battle on the level of omens.' Contrast Lateiner (1989: 131): 'the religious rigmarole about the omens . . . in fact crystallizes the secular, strategic dilemma on each side.' The omen of the seven crows that stiffens the resolve of the Persian conspirators against the Magus may perhaps also be in response to their prayer—as well as their dilemma, 3. 76.

[39] The fact that the prayer is unspoken may perhaps make its fulfilment more miraculous? See Versnel (1981: 26) on the association of silent prayer with evil; it can also, however (pp. 26 ff.), express intimacy with a god—or reflect sexual shame: van der Horst (1994: 5–6). See also, for silent prayer, Pulleyn (1997: 194–8, 186–7) putting Ladice's silence down to the presence of Amasis 'standing in front of her' (probably implicit).

[40] The relationship between Ladice and Amasis, we may guess, mirrors—if it is not actually a product of—that between Amasis and Cyrene. For the historical background to this marriage alliance, see Austin (1990: 293, 298 and n. 30).

timing—of the thunderstorm that saves Croesus, of the change of the Spartans' auspices or in Amasis' sex life—that suggests divine intervention in answer to prayer. Only in the case of Croesus is there an additional touch of the impossible in the detail that the storm broke from a cloudless sky. The retelling of such stories of the miraculous fulfilment of prayers must have served to bolster belief in the effectiveness of prayers. But an obvious problem arises: how—especially if fulfilment can be expected to take the form of storms from cloudless skies—can belief in the fulfilment of prayer be maintained in the face of evident non-fulfilment?[41]

The problem looks worse in the light of a number of passages suggesting that prayers or propitiation will necessarily be answered. Croesus asks Apollo whether it was the habit of Greek gods to be ungrateful (1. 90. 4; cf. 1. 90. 2); the Pythia's reply, that within the constraints of fate the god had done his best by first delaying Croesus' fate and then by saving him from death on the pyre (1. 91. 3), arguably accepts Croesus' conception of a crude relationship of *quid pro quo* between gods and men. There are similarly a number of instances in which the propitiation of a god is recommended by an oracle. The Amathousians are told by an oracle that if they bury the head of Onesilus and sacrifice to it every year, they should fare better (ἄμεινον συνοίσεσθαι, 5. 114. 2). The Spartans enquire which god they should propitiate in order that their fortunes should improve in their war against the Tegeans (1. 67. 2). When, as recommended, they recover the bones of Orestes from Tegean territory, their fortunes indeed improve dramatically (1. 68. 6): 'from this time', according to Herodotus (appearing implicitly to accept the effectiveness of the transferral of the bones), 'whenever there was a trial of arms between them, the Spartans were always much superior in the war, and now the vast part of the Peloponnese is subjected to them'. Conversely, the failure to propitiate a god or hero can be expected to result in the removal of his favour: Cleisthenes of Sicyon, refused permission to expel the Argive hero Adrastus from Sicyon, determines to starve Adrastus of sacrifices and festivals, transferring

---

[41] See here Pulleyn (1994: 18): 'If people thought they had tied the god down, what did they make of a phenomenon which one assumes must have been very common, namely unanswered prayer?' See also Mikalson (1989).

them to Dionysus or to Adrastus' enemy Melanippus, until
Adrastus should 'leave of his own accord' (ἐφρόντιζε μηχανὴν τῇ
αὐτὸς ὁ Ἄδρηστος ἀπαλλάξεται, 5. 67. 2).

Given this apparent certainty that prayer and propitiation
would have the required result, how then did such practices
survive? Even in the context of the *Histories*, such miraculous
fulfilment of prayer is rare. Prayer is mentioned as frequently
in the course of reports of different methods or customs of
sacrifice in Herodotus' descriptions of foreign peoples. When
in the course of sacrifice do a certain people pray (2. 40. 2),
when in the course of swearing an oath (3. 8. 1)? How do they
address the gods (2. 52. 1)? Which gods, heroes, or images do
they propitiate (e.g. 1. 131; 4. 7. 1, 26. 1, 188. 1)? What animals
or other objects do they consider suitable for sacrifice, which
unsuitable, either in general or for a particular god (e.g.
1. 216. 4; 2. 42, 45–7; 4. 63)? Who is permitted to make the
sacrifice (1. 132. 3; 6. 81)? Herodotus also occasionally reports
the different objects or formulae of prayer: the Persians pray,
he says, not for their own individual good fortune, but for that
of all Persians and of the King (1. 132. 2); from the time of
Marathon, the Athenian herald prays for good fortune for the
Plataeans as well as the Athenians (6. 111. 2).

Herodotus' accounts of differing practices and beliefs concerning prayer may give a more realistic picture of everyday
expectations than the stories of Croesus, Pausanias, and
Ladice: few men, we may suspect, lived in confidence of an
immediate answer to such specific injunctions. However,
though the object of prayer may in many cases have been
no more specific than a generalized good fortune, even such a
vague act of propitiation expresses the belief in the power of
the gods to intervene. Praying only for a generalized good
fortune, moreover, makes it easier to believe that that prayer
has been answered.[42] Even if no obvious piece of good fortune
comes one's way, the propitiation of a god may have saved one
from some much worse piece of ill-fortune. Characters often
pray to or propitiate the gods in response to an omen, a
success or a disaster (e.g. 1. 48. 1; 7. 192. 2; 8. 64. 2, 99. 1):
the intention behind such prayers is likewise surely either to

---

[42] Good fortune can embrace anything: Versnel (1981: 8).

maintain such good fortune or to preserve oneself from
further disasters.

There are other ways in which the belief that prayers are
answered may be sustained. In the cases of the prayers of
Croesus, Pausanias, or Ladice, or in the case of the prayer of
the mother of Cleobis and Biton, answered by their deaths
(1. 31. 4–5), the miraculous response follows almost instantly.
Fulfilment may also be delayed. The wife-to-be of the Spartan
king Ariston is cured of her ugliness by Helen (6. 61. 3–5), after
her nurse took her every day to Helen's shrine and prayed to
the goddess 'to release the child from her ugliness'. One day
Helen, or at least a mysterious woman, appeared to the pair
and, taking the child in her arms and touching her head,
pronounced that she would grow to be the most beautiful
woman in Sparta. From that day her appearance changed,
Herodotus says. But the full scale of this transformation was
delayed.

The reciprocal relationship between men and gods is also
never quite a simple matter of *quid pro quo*. As Simon Pulleyn
has put it, the τιμή or honour of the gods was 'not crudely
monetarist'.[43] This can be seen by looking further at the case of
Croesus.[44] Croesus expects that Apollo can be put under an
obligation by his gifts (ἐλπίζων τὸν θεὸν μᾶλλόν τι τούτοισι
ἀνακτήσεσθαι, 1. 50. 1). His prayer also, speaking of the *charis*
that his gifts might have engendered, has a markedly peremptory tone: he called out to Apollo 'if ever any of his gifts had
been received gratefully to protect and deliver him from the
present danger' (1. 87. 1).[45] However, as the Pythian priestess
tells him, Apollo's power is limited: even a god cannot bypass
fate (1. 91. 1). No number of dedications will necessarily secure
the fulfilment of a prayer. There are some signs, moreover, that

---

[43] Pulleyn (1997: 12–13); see also Parker (1998b: 118–21).

[44] The god Pan seems to imply that he would continue to help the
Athenians as he has in the past even if his affection were not requited;
arguably, however, the Athenians' propitiation cements the relationship,
6. 105. 2. For the nature of Pan's intervention, see now Parker (1996: 164),
with further refs. (n. 36).

[45] εἴ τί οἱ κεχαρισμένον ἐξ αὐτοῦ ἐδωρήθη, παραστῆναι καὶ ῥύσασθαί μιν ἐκ τοῦ
παρεόντος κακοῦ. The same formula (εἴ τι κεχαρισμένον) can be seen at e.g. Ar.
Pax. 385 ff. See Pulleyn (1997: ch. 2), Mikalson (1989: 94), Parker (1998b:
107).

Apollo saved Croesus for his piety and not simply the weight of his dedications. Herodotus earlier speculates that Cyrus had placed Croesus on the pyre in order to discover whether a god would save him on account of his piety (θεοσεβέα, 1. 86. 2). Apollo's rescue then confirms his piety and teaches Cyrus that Croesus was 'dear to the gods and a good man' (καὶ θεοφιλὴς καὶ ἀνὴρ ἀγαθός, 1. 87. 2). Unless piety is itself measured only in gold, then, it seems as if the *charis* that Croesus appealed to depended partly on the spirit, the sincerity, with which his dedications had been offered.[46]

This opens up a number of possible justifications for the non-fulfilment of prayers. Non-fulfilment might have been explained in terms of ritual impurity, though that is not reflected in the *Histories*.[47] Propitiation, however, may meet with a negative response simply on the grounds that, for quite extraneous reasons, it is not welcome. So, for example, the sacrifices and libations ordered by Xerxes at Troy are followed almost immediately by his camp suffering a sudden attack of panic (7. 43. 2). The entry of his army into the territory of Troy had been met with a storm that had killed a great number of his men (7. 42. 2). The implication of these passages must be that his entry into Troy, and then perhaps his attempt to legitimize his possession of Troy, if not somehow to legitimize his whole campaign by propitiating Athena and the Trojan heroes, in actual fact displeases them.[48] Conversely, the fulfilment of a prayer such as that of Pausanias to Hera suggests the goddess'

---

[46] For expressions of the virtue of offerings not lying exclusively in their size, or for propitiation as unwelcome, see Parker (1998*b*: 119–20 and n. 48).

[47] Cf. H. *Il*. 6. 266–7 (wash hands before libations), Hes. *Erga* 724–6 (wash hands before libations or gods will reject prayers). For the misdirection of a prayer to the wrong name as a let-out clause for non-fulfilment, see Xen. *Anab*. 7. 8. 1–6 with Pulleyn (1994: 18).

[48] Likewise, Datis' propitiation of Apollo Delios is followed closely by the Delos earthquake, 6. 97. 2–98, and Persian sacrifices in Athens are followed by a miracle suggesting Athenian recovery, 8. 54–5. A similar idea seems to lie behind the story of another milestone on the Persians' campaign: 'now let us pray to the gods who have allotted the Persians their territory and then cross', Xerxes pronounces by the Hellespont, 7. 53. 2, but if, as indeed the Persians are said to believe, Asia marks the limits of Persian empire, 1. 4. 4, 9. 116. 3, might not such a prayer be redundant, if not actually counter-productive? At the very least, it is an ironic signal of the inevitable failure of Xerxes' campaign.

approval of his broader project. Even the most deserving
candidates can, however, meet with no response to their
prayers. The Athenians, at the instigation of an oracle,
prayed to Boreas and Oreithyia, that they should come to
their assistance and destroy the ships of the barbarians as
they had at Mount Athos (7. 189). Herodotus clearly allows
for the possibility that it was for this reason that Boreas fell
upon the Persians (7. 189. 3), that the Athenians who subsequently set up a shrine to Boreas were correct in so doing, but
he professes that he cannot be certain.[49] There may be other
reasons, it seems, for any particular change in fortune which
outweigh the effectiveness of prayer. This final justification for
the non-fulfilment of prayer is also then the most universally
applicable: prayer and propitiation may habitually receive the
desired response, but do not always.

Divine epiphanies, those occasions on which gods or heroes
appear physically in the human world, constitute arguably the
purest, the most direct, form of divine intervention. Does
Herodotus believe in the possibility of divine epiphanies?
And if so, how? To the extent that he is sceptical, what is the
focus of his scepticism?

A number of examples of epiphanies do not tell very strongly
either for Herodotean belief or scepticism. So, for example, the
most notorious case of a divine epiphany in the *Histories*,
Philippides' encounter with Pan (6. 105):

This man then, as Philippides himself said and reported to the
Athenians, Pan met near Mount Parthenion above Tegea; and Pan,
calling out the name of Philippides, asked him to demand of the
Athenians why they paid no attention to him, even though he was well
disposed towards the Athenians and had often been useful to them,
and would be so in the future. And the Athenians, believing these

---

[49] Cf. the Persians' attempt to stop the winds by casting spells and
sacrificing to Thetis and the Nereids, 7. 191. They stopped the wind on the
fourth 'unless [or 'unless in some other way'] it [or 'he'?] stopped of its own
accord [or 'of its own will'?]': ἢ ἄλλως κως αὐτὸς ἐθέλων ἐκόπασε. 'At any rate',
Herodotus adds, 'on the fourth day it did stop.' Herodotus' slight reserve may
relate to the identification of Boreas, or to the efficacy of Persian sacrifices, but
not to the efficacy of any sacrifices. On this passage, see Linforth (1928: 214),
Legrand (1932: 133), vii. 207; cf. Xen. *Anab.* 4. 5. 4.

things to be true, when their affairs were on a better footing, set up a shrine of Pan under the Acropolis, and as a consequence of this message propitiate him with yearly sacrifices and a torch race.

The ascription of the story to Philippides himself need not imply scepticism,[50] but may indeed serve (in part, at least) as evidence of the story's authenticity: even if it were untrue, it was Philippides who dreamed it up rather than the Athenians. The only possible evidence that Herodotus doubts the story is his passing remark that the Athenians established a shrine and festival of Pan 'because they believed these things to be true' (ταῦτα . . . πιστεύσαντες εἶναι ἀληθέα, 6. 105. 3).

There are a number of cases of miraculous apparitions during battles.[51] Herodotus gives us three different versions of the manner in which the battle of Salamis began (8. 84). The first and least glamorous version, that of the Athenians, was that while all the other ships were backing water, Ameinias of Pallene led his ship out in a charge, but became entangled with an enemy ship, and so the others came to his rescue. The Aeginetans claimed that the ship which began the battle was that which had been sent to Aegina to collect the 'sons of Ajax'.[52]

[50] As e.g. Forrest (1979: 312), Müller (1981: 316), Lateiner (1989: 66)—'his implicit reluctance to accept the tale of Pan's encounter with Philippides provides a paradigm of his reserve'; Lateiner suggests also (1989: 33) that the Athenians' consecration of a shrine to Pan only after their victory at Marathon implies 'Herodotus' own desacralization of the past'. Fehling argues that the epiphany of Pan was a Herodotean fiction (1989: 117), a position successfully refuted by Pritchett (1993: 105–6), adducing evidence of the cult of Pan to suggest that the Athenians at least believed it true. For the cult of Pan at Athens, see also Borgeaud (1988: 133 ff.), Parker (1996: 163–8).

[51] All are apparitions of heroes rather than more major deities: Vandiver (1991: 109). Cf. the examples listed by Pritchett iii. 11–46, Speyer (1980: 60–9), Sinos (1993: 79–80). Diod. Sic., 5. 79. 4, seems to recognize a special class of ἥρωας ἐπιφανεῖς at least among the Cretans. For the Hellenistic Chian festival of θεοφάνεια as commemorating a divine apparition in battle, see Derow and Forrest (1982: 82) suggesting the Dioscuri, and (with ample parallels) Garbrah (1986).

[52] See Pritchett iii. 14 ff. for the question of whether the Aeacidae, 8. 64. 2, and the Tyndaridae, 5. 75. 2, were represented in an iconic form or were imagined to be actually present. The distinction is unreal, as they may have been envisaged as present through their images: Versnel (1987: 46–7), with further refs. For the conception of cult images, see also Gordon (1979), Gladigow (1985–6; 1990).

There is also this version (λέγεται δὲ καὶ τάδε), that an apparition (φάσμα) of a woman appeared, and doing so exhorted them, having shamed them first with the words: 'wretched men (Ὦ δαιμόνιοι), for how long will you back water?'

Herodotus expresses no judgement.[53] During Marathon, an Athenian, Epizelus, became suddenly blind, without receiving any other injury. The curious explanation that Herodotus gives is one, he says, that originates with Epizelus himself (6. 117. 3): a giant hoplite appeared opposite him with a beard that completely covered his shield, and then, passing by, killed the man standing alongside him. The final case of a battle apparition is that of the two giant hoplites who appeared to the Persians as they fled Delphi. Herodotus claims to have discovered that this was the story of the Persians themselves: 'as I discover, this is what the barbarians who returned said' (8. 38).[54] The Delphians then filled in the detail that these were the local heroes Phylacus and Autonous, whose shrines lay nearby (8. 39. 1).[55]

Two other miraculous apparitions occur to the same woman, the wife of Ariston and the mother of Demaratus. The first of these apparitions has been described already in this chapter, that of a mysterious woman who appears to Ariston's wife when she was a child (6. 65): the implication of the narrative is that the woman is Helen and that it was she who was responsible for removing the blight of the girl's ugliness.[56] A second apparition came to her as a woman, on the third night after her

---

[53] Shimron makes 8. 84. 2 emblematic of a class of 'obvious fictions' (1989: 37): it is unclear whether he supposes that Herodotus shared this classification. There are, of course, ample examples of apparitions during battle in other periods to assure us that it is possible for men to believe in such experiences: see Gould (1989: 36).

[54] ἔλεγον δὲ οἱ ἀπονοστήσαντες οὗτοι τῶν βαρβάρων, ὡς ἐγὼ πυνθάνομαι . . .

[55] Fehling's argument (1989: 12–16) that the story, being untrue, could only have had a single source, and that the Persian source is 'pure fiction', ignores 'the usual way out' that the Persian source was cited by the Delphians, and that Herodotus does not claim to have spoken to any such Persian source (see Pritchett 1993: 10), and also ignores the possibility that Greeks could have believed in miracles. See also now Dover (1998). Evans' suggestion (1992: 59) that a Persian apologetic source was responsible for the story of the epiphany is far-fetched.

[56] Cf. Versnel (1987: 45).

marriage to Ariston. As she later tells Demaratus (6. 69. 1–4), a figure (φάσμα) resembling Ariston came to her in the night, slept with her, and then placed garlands around her. A few minutes later Ariston himself arrived, and asked who it was who had given her the garlands. She said that it was he himself, but Ariston denied it. After both parties insisted upon the truth of their versions, Ariston 'realized that the event was divine' (ἔμαθε ὡς θεῖον εἴη τὸ πρῆγμα, 6. 69. 3). It then transpired that the garlands had come from the shrine of the hero Astraba-cus.[57] It is not stated how—perhaps simply the garlands were found to be missing at an appropriate time—but the story was then corroborated by prophets. Demaratus' mother concludes her story with the equivocal statement to her son: 'either you are born from this hero and your father is Astrabacus the hero, or your father is Ariston.'

Further evidence suggestive of a belief in the possibility of divine epiphany is provided by the story of the appearance of the Apis calf (ἐπιφανέος δὲ τούτου γενομένου, 3. 27. 1; cf. 2. 153).[58] Cambyses questioned the divinity of the calf (3. 29. 1–2):

When the priests brought Apis, Cambyses, like a man out of his senses, drawing his dagger and wishing to strike Apis' stomach hit his thigh. And laughing he said to the priests: 'wicked men, are there such gods as these, made of flesh and blood and sensitive to iron? This is a god worthy of the Egyptians!'

In the event, of course, Cambyses suffered for his scepticism. Much later in the *Histories,* in mounting his horse he wounded himself in the thigh, precisely the same spot in which he had earlier struck the Apis calf (3. 64. 3). That this coincidence proves that his death was retribution for his injury to Apis is only implied in this instance. On an earlier occasion, however, Herodotus makes plain that he considers Cambyses' treatment of Apis a sufficient explanation of divine vengeance (3. 33): 'in these ways Cambyses behaved madly towards his own nearest

---

[57] For the mythological background, see Burkert (1965).

[58] The Egyptians, according to Herodotus, claim that no gods had appeared in human form in 11,340 years, 2. 142. 3. For the truth behind these stories of Cambyses' reign, see now A. B. Lloyd (1988a), Kuhrt (1995: 661–4), Briant (1996: 66–72), though see also Depuydt (1995), arguing tentatively for Cambyses' guilt; contrast also Duchesne-Guillemin (1967/8: 4).

relations,[59] either due to Apis or some other reason: for many
misfortunes are likely to befall men' (ταῦτα μὲν ἐς τοὺς οἰκηιο-
τάτους ὁ Καμβύσης ἐξεμάνη, εἴτε δὴ διὰ τὸν ῍Απιν εἴτε καὶ ἄλλως, οἷα
πολλὰ ἔωθε ἀνθρώπους κακὰ καταλαμβάνειν).[60]

As the examples given so far illustrate, the idea that
epiphanies are the purest form of miracle is in many ways
unfounded. Divine presence is even here mediated. Astrabacus
takes the form of Ariston. Helen takes the form of a woman like
any other. The Apis calf is distinguished from all the other
calves born in Egypt by a number of identifying features
(3. 28. 3): 'it is black with a square spot of white on its forehead;
and on the back the figure of an eagle; and in the tail double
hairs; and on the tongue a beetle.' As Odysseus observes in the
Odyssey, it is hard to recognize gods.[61] In all these cases there is
room for interpretation that is crucial from the point of view of
sustaining belief in such epiphanies. This latitude for interpretation allows one to see a god behind a variety of phenomena. As Versnel has put it, rather starkly, 'ancient man could
never be sure whether the person he was talking with was not
actually a god in disguise'.[62] The Athenians believed that
Athena in some sense took the form of a snake on the Acropolis
(8. 41. 2–3):[63] when, during Xerxes' invasion, the food left out

---

[59] Rosén, however, emends to οἰκηίους.

[60] Herodotus continues to record another version that he suffered from
birth from a great disease 'which some name the sacred disease': his remarks
may reflect familiarity with ideas similar to those put forward by the author of
de morb. sacr. (at ch. 1), that the sacred disease was no more sacred than any
other. For the combination of natural and divine explanations of disease, see
esp. Parker (1983: 242–3), G. E. R. Lloyd (1979: 30 ff.); contrast the more
simplistic readings of Brown (1982), Munson (1991: esp. 46). For a more
conventionally historical perspective on the death of Cambyses, see Walser
(1983).

[61] H. Od. 13. 312–13; frequently there are giveaway signs, e.g. Od. 1. 322–
3, Il. 13. 68 ff.

[62] Versnel (1987: 46); cf. Mussies (1988: 2).

[63] The Acropolis snake is, of course, not seen: its presence is inferred from
the regular disappearance of honey cakes; when the honey cakes remain, the
snake (and the goddess) must have gone. Cf. also the (possibly miraculous)
disappearance of Hamilcar, 7. 166–7. There is no hint of anything miraculous
about the comparable disappearance of the body of Mardonius, 9. 84; we can
well imagine that the same story told from a different bias might have
contained such hints.

monthly for the snake one day appeared untouched, the conclusion was drawn that the goddess had deserted the Acropolis; the people, as a result, more readily evacuated the city. On seeing Xerxes' army cross the Hellespont, a Hellespontine man, presumably on the basis of the size of the Persian force, commented: 'Zeus, why, taking the form of a Persian man, and calling yourself Xerxes instead of Zeus, do you wish to depopulate Greece, taking with you the whole of mankind? For it would be possible to do this without these men' (7. 56. 2). Of course, we must draw a distinction between genuine identification of a god and the use of such language by way of analogy. Xerxes was subsequently proved to be no more than a man (7. 203. 2). But the fact that a man's excessive power could be expressed in such terms shows that the boundary between analogy and identification was a permeable one.

Epiphanies are capable of verification in a similar way to other miracles: the conclusion that an epiphany of god or hero has taken place is one that is based on deduction from evidence. In the case of the Apis calf, the identifying features are designed to prove beyond doubt the calf's divinity. Ariston reckons that 'the affair was divine' in order to explain his apparent presence in two places at the same time: the exact identity of the figure who had taken his form is then confirmed by the garland and by the authority of the prophets. Herodotus does on occasion reveal an explicit cynicism over stories of divine epiphanies. He appears, for example, to be openly sceptical of an apparition alleged to have appeared to Adeimantus and the Corinthians at Salamis (8. 94).[64] After the Corinthians had fled, they arrived at the shrine of Athena Sciras, where a light boat chanced to find them, 'sent by the divine' (θείη πομπῆ). As no one appeared to have sent the boat, and as the Corinthians to whom the boat came knew nothing of the remainder of the fleet, they 'conjectured that the affair was divine' (τῆδε συμβάλλονται εἶναι θεῖον τὸ πρῆγμα). A voice arose from those in the boat, accusing Adeimantus of the betrayal of Greece, and offering themselves as hostages to be put to death if the Greeks had not indeed been victorious in the battle. The

---

[64] See further Carrière (1988: 236 ff.).

Corinthians then returned to the site of the battle, but only after the victory had been won. The Corinthians, Herodotus concludes, deny the story, claiming that they played a full role in the battle—and 'the rest of Greece bears witness to what they say'. Herodotus' scepticism clearly here relates to the political convenience of the Athenians' story, not to the impossibility of the event itself: this is especially likely given his different response to the similar story of the apparition of the women said to have begun the battle (8. 84). The Corinthians' judgement that the 'affair was divine'—apparently on the basis of its impossibility—also parallels neatly the kind of process of deduction by which, as we have seen, other characters and Herodotus himself conclude that divine intervention has taken place.

A particular focus of Herodotus' scepticism appears to be the idea that gods may sleep with mortal women. The Chaldaean priests of Zeus Belus maintained that the god chose one of the local women who alone was allowed to spend the night in his temple (1. 181. 5). Herodotus' report of the rationale for this practice is brusque (1. 182):

These same men say—though what they say is not believable to me (ἐμοὶ μὲν οὐ πιστὰ λέγοντες)—that the god himself goes to the temple and rests upon the bed in the same manner as, the Egyptians say, happens in Thebes in Egypt: for a woman also lies in the temple of Theban Zeus, and both are said to avoid the company of men. In the same manner also the priestess who delivers the oracles at Patara in Lycia, when the god is there—for there is not an oracle there at all times—is shut up during the night in the temple with the god.

Herodotus' scepticism here is likely to be connected to his unwillingness to ascribe immortal parents to men, for example to Perseus (6. 53. 1).[65] He also professes doubt over the story

[65] For the Greek conception of the prophetess as a god's bride, and of sacred marriage as a 'foreign custom tinged with charlatanism', see Parker (1983: 92–4, esp. n. 77). For Herodotus' reticence concerning such genealogies, cf. Linforth (1928: 210), Darbo-Peschanski (1987: 26 ff.): Herodotus is not terribly concerned with the precise mechanism of the transition from divine to human generations. See also van Groningen (1953: 104) for a 'chronological no-man's land' of shadowy ancestors designed to 'conceal the transition' from human to divine; R. Thomas (1989: 106–7, 155 ff.) for the lack of proof required in genealogies. According to Lateiner (1989: 100)

that the parents of Targitaus were Zeus and the river Bor-
ysthenes (4. 5. 1), and refers—with apparent approval[66]—to the
rebuttal by the priests of Thebes of Hecataeus' claims to divine
ancestry (2. 143. 4): no man, they had told Hecataeus, was the
son of a god. Herodotus is almost consistent in giving the
names only of the mortal parents of heroes. On only one
occasion does he describe Perseus as the son of Zeus and
Danaë (7. 61. 3), on all others as the son of Danaë alone
(2. 91. 2, 6. 53. 1, 7. 150. 2).[67] Heracles likewise is the son
only of Amphitryon (2. 43–5, 146. 1; 6. 53. 2) or of Alcmene
(2. 145. 4), Helen the daughter of Tyndareus (2. 112. 2), Minos
and Sarpedon the sons of Europe (1. 173. 2).[68]

The consistency of this pattern suggests a fairly settled
unwillingness to accept the possibility of gods sleeping with
mortals. It also tallies with the evidence of other contemporaries, the incredulity or shock, for example, with which
Euripides' Ion or Heracles greet the same possibility.[69] It is
important, however, not to exaggerate the scope of Herodotus'
apparent distaste. If his objection is to the form of contact
possible between gods and men (based perhaps on the sense
that gods are likely to behave better than to take advantage of
their position), this need not preclude a belief in the possibility
of epiphanies such as that of Pan to Philippides,[70] let alone in
the possibility of more indirect contact—for example through
the miracles discussed earlier in this chapter, or through
dreams, effectively epiphanies at one remove.[71] Herodotus

Herodotus 'mocks the genealogies of Perseus . . . Finally he dismisses the
entire matter, explicitly because others have canvassed it, implicitly because
Heroic genealogy is not subject to his kind of critical investigation.' For this
question of the possibility of certain knowledge of the 'mythical period', see
Ch. 7.

[66] If not quite scorn or 'malicious joy', as supposed by Lloyd i. 127.
[67] Contrast Ion of Chios fr. 27 West.
[68] For Minos, cf. 3. 122. 2, discussed Ch. 7.
[69] E. *Ion* 338 ff., E. *Her.* 1340 ff.; cf. Ar. *Av.* 556 ff., Xenophanes DK 21 B
1. 21–4, B 11–12.
[70] See here Pearson (1941: 338–9 n. 15), criticizing Panitz (1935: 11, 18).
Darbo-Peschanski (1987: 38) claims too categorically that Herodotus 'refuse
catégoriquement d'admettre l'intrusion des dieux sous forme humaine dans le
monde des hommes'.
[71] See e.g. 2. 141. 3 (ἐν τῇ ὄψι ἐπιστάντα τὸν θεόν). Cf. Versnel (1987: 48),
Sinos (1993: 80).

may (depending on our reading of the text) consider that once
upon a time in Egypt gods and men lived alongside one another
(2. 144. 2).[72] At the same time the story of Astrabacus'
appearance to the wife of Ariston is reported by Herodotus at
least without any explicit demonstration of disapproval.[73]

Herodotus also conceives of the possibility of false or staged
epiphanies. Salmoxis, according to the Black Sea Greeks, hid
for three years in an underground chamber and then emerged
once more to his people, the Getae (4. 95. 4–5), so seeming to
prove the belief he had been espousing that his followers would
not die but would go to a place where they would enjoy every
luxury (4. 95. 3). Similarly, the Athenian tyrant Peisistratus
engineered his return to Athens by dressing a girl named Phye
as Athena, and riding alongside her in a chariot, while
messengers announced: 'Men of Athens, receive with good
will Peisistratus, whom Athena herself, having honoured above
all mankind, is bringing back from exile to her own Acropolis'
(1. 60. 4–5).[74] Herodotus is amazed that the Athenians, reputed
to be the cleverest of the Greeks, could have fallen for such a
trick, but he clearly believes that it happened as he describes.[75]
Such tales may suggest at first that Herodotus was writing from
the vantage point of an age where belief in the possibility of
such direct apparitions had withered away.[76] The reader may

[72] Depending on whether we read οἰκέοντας or (with Rosén now or
Vandiver 1991: 141) οὐκ ἐόντας.

[73] Contrast Legrand (1932: 131), seeing the apparent contradiction between
the story of the wife of Ariston and 6. 53 as characteristic of the untidiness of
Herodotus' thought. The story of Demaratus and Astrabacus shows, according to van Lieshout (1980: 23), the vague borderline 'between the passive type
of dreaming and the waking vision'.

[74] For the idea of this story as the distortion of a ritual procession or of cult
myth, see Delcourt (1944: 177–80), Gernet (1981: 300), Connor (1987), Stern
(1989: 13), Robertson (1992: 143). The historicity of the episode is challenged
more profoundly by Beloch (1890: 469–71; 1924: i/2. 288), Meyer (1892–9:
ii. 248–50), followed now by Schreiner (1981).

[75] Cf. also the plan of Tellias of Elis, who covered 600 Phocians in gypsum
before a night ambush on the Thessalians, 7. 27. 3–4: the Phocians were able
easily to identify their enemies, and the Thessalians, thinking that it was a
marvel (τέρας), were terrified. It is unclear that Tellias intended to mislead the
Thessalians.

[76] Linforth (1928: 213) sees this as evidence of Herodotus' disbelief in the
'direct intercourse of gods and men'.

begin to sense more generally that such evidence as exists for
Herodotus' belief in the possibility of divine epiphanies is
confined curiously to the fringes, chronological and geographical, of his world. Herodotus may—in the light of Cambyses'
end—not feel safe in doubting the divinity of the Apis calf; he
may make no explicit statement of disbelief in apparitions such
as that of Pan to Philippides. However, compared to his
forthright approval of some other miracle stories, that of the
distribution of the bodies at Plataea, for example (9. 65. 2), the
evidence for his belief in epiphanies is surely weak. Should we
not put two and two together and conclude that here at least we
have found a consistent pattern of Herodotean scepticism?

This misses an important point, however. Fifth- and fourth-
century Athenians, as Mikalson reminds us, 'did not see gods
popping up here and there'.[77] But men never do. There may be
many reasons why Pan appeared in Arcadia, but it is clear that
he could not very well have delivered his message direct to the
Athenian people in an assembly.[78] Belief in divine epiphanies
depends on their happening in some far-away place, to a friend
of a friend or a very long time ago.[79] In other words, the
evidence for Herodotus' belief in epiphanies is by its very
nature bound to look less compelling than the evidence for his
belief in other forms of intervention. For, unless gods appear
in disguise (as sometimes they do), it is obviously easier to
believe in less direct forms of divine intervention such as

[77] Mikalson (1991: 21; cf. 1983: 19). Likewise Connor (1987: esp. 49–50)
and Snodgrass (1980: 115) see the Phye episode as characteristically archaic,
unimaginable in the fifth century; Grote similarly commented (1888: 327 n. 1)
that Herodotus' 'criticism brings to our view the alteration and enlargement
which had taken place in the Greek mind during the century between
Peisistratus and Periklês'.

[78] The 'divine and the human come together in mountains': Buxton (1994:
91). See also Dodds (1951: 117), Borgeaud (1988: 134) on Paus. 8. 53. 11. For
the association of Pan and Arcadia, see also e.g. Pind. fr. 95 Snell, HHP 30;
for Pan and mountains, Soph. OT 1098–101, E. El. 699 ff.

[79] The epiphany is typical of the kind of miracle that is commonly believed
to have happened once but no longer (due for example to a lack of belief, or
moral decline): for parallels, see Herzfeld (1982: 171), Feeney (1998: 104–5).
For remote epiphanies, cf. 6. 127. 3 (the hospitality shown by Euphorion to
the Dioscuri), 2. 73. 1–2 (the phoenix), 2. 91. 3 (Perseus in Chemmis). See
also the observations of Sourvinou-Inwood (1997: 184) in the context of
tragedy, Mikalson (1991: 64 ff.) on the deus ex machina.

earthquakes. Earthquakes happen—although the question remains of how to interpret them—whereas divine epiphanies do not. Herodotus' belief in epiphanies is bound to be hypothetical and non-committal; his telling of stories of epiphanies is bound to lay special emphasis on the eyewitness nature of his sources; and the epiphanies are bound to have occurred in the more or less distant past. Herodotus' very concentration on stories of epiphanies, including dubious or fraudulent cases, reflects a belief, however, at least in their theoretical possibility.

The final form of divine intervention to be discussed in this chapter is the 'natural miracle', intervention through sudden storms, earthquakes, floodtides, or other natural phenomena. These are often treated as a class apart. For those who find Herodotus' ascription of events to divinity objectionable, natural miracles have a certain advantage: storms, earthquakes, eclipses do actually happen, and so, by supposing that the language of divine intervention is merely formulaic ('"the gods" (i.e. the weather)' in the words of one critic[80]), or by emphasizing the fact that an event really occurred, the divine can be ignored. As George Forrest commented on the storm at Aphetae—a storm (as we will see) explicitly ascribed to the god by Herodotus (8. 13)—'the adjustment was not brought about by an old man with a trident; it was made by a wind, a familiar enough natural phenomenon'.[81] Storms and eclipses have been described similarly as 'phenomena that for some reason are inexplicable by the state of knowledge at the time',[82] as if the explanation of natural events in terms of the divine served as no more than a stop-gap, until such time as a more satisfying way of thinking could be attained.

A number of points will become clear from a dispassionate analysis. Belief in natural miracles depends on reasoning parallel to that employed in the case of other miracles: though there may be other reasons for ascribing a divine

---

[80] Waters (1971: 70).   [81] Forrest (1979: 311).

[82] Shimron (1989: 38); Herodotus 'relatively rarely calls a natural event divine', he continues; cf. Vandiver (1991: 100 n. 2) for whom, while Herodotus is generally sceptical over miracles, in the case of natural phenomena he 'leaves the question of divine or heroic causation open'.

cause to a natural event, for example its prophetic or ominous character, it is often the impossible or improbable character of an event, or of its timing, that leads to this conclusion. We may distinguish between those miracles that happened and those which did not, we may detect a greater willingness on Herodotus' part to commit himself to natural miracles than to epiphanies, but such distinctions were not evident to Herodotus himself. Moreover, the explanation of such natural miracles in terms of divine intervention in no way precludes parallel explanation in scientific terms. As the example of the Cnidian ditch has already demonstrated, the belief in miracles does not require a suspension of any sense of probability; rather indeed the deduction that a miracle has taken place takes for granted a conception of what can normally be expected.

Herodotus makes explicit his belief in the divine origin of a number of natural miracles. When night came down on the Persian fleet at Aphetae, they were met by an 'endless rainstorm' and 'violent thunder' from the direction of Pelion (ὕδωρ . . . ἄπλετον,[83] . . . σκληραὶ βρονταί, 8. 12. 1). The bodies and the wrecks from the earlier storm at Pelion (7. 188. 2) drifted into the ships' oars, causing a panic among the men. They had not even recovered from that previous storm when they were forced to fight a sea battle, and now, fresh from that battle here were 'floods of rain, the rushing of swollen streams into the sea and a tremendous thunderstorm' (ὄμβρος τε λάβρος καὶ ῥεύματα ἰσχυρὰ ἐς θάλασσαν ὁρμημένα βρονταί τε σκληραί, 8. 12. 2).[84] The same storm and rain hit other Persians sailing around Euboea even more harshly: borne they knew not where by the wind, they were dashed against the rocks. Herodotus then remarks (8. 13):

All this was done by the god so that the Persian force should be made level to the Greek, or should not be much greater (ἐποιέετό τε πᾶν ὑπὸ τοῦ θεοῦ ὅκως ἂν ἐξισωθείη τῷ Ἑλληνικῷ τὸ Περσικὸν μηδὲ πολλῷ πλέον εἴη).

This remark appears at face value to embrace not only the most recent storm, but the whole sequence of misfortunes, the storm

---

[83] Poetic language: cf. Empedocles DK 31 B 17. 18, Pind. *Isthm.* 4. 11.

[84] The second storm, Bury (1895–6: 94) suggests, is a doublet, though see Lattimore (1939b).

at Pelion, the sea battle, this storm and the panic induced by it
and by the debris of Pelion. This sequence, this coincidence of
a number of misfortunes, appears to be one of the grounds for
Herodotus' deduction that there was a divine purpose behind
these events.[85] Another explanation is the unexpectedness of
the storms, an unexpectedness which shades into impossibility.
At Pelion, the storm, like that which saved Croesus from death
on his pyre (1. 87. 2), broke from a clear and cloudless sky (ἐξ
αἰθρίης τε καὶ νηνεμίης, 7. 188. 2).[86] The storm at Aphetae
happened both in quick succession to a sea battle and despite
the fact that it was the middle of summer (ἦν μὲν τῆς ὥρης μέσον
θέρος, 8. 12. 1).

That natural miracles are seen not as a special category but as
being of a kind with other miracles can be seen from the story
of the Persians' approach to Delphi. One of the miracles that
greets the Persians as they approach the temple of Athena
Pronaia at Delphi was the most wonderful of all 'apparitions'
(φάσματα), according to Herodotus (8. 37. 2–3). Thunderbolts
fell upon them from heaven, two rocks fell from Parnassus
(behind which, the cynic might note, the majority of the
Delphians were hiding, 8. 36. 2), and a great shouting and
battle-cry came from within the temple: 'all these things
mixing together, fear had fallen upon the barbarians'
(8. 38. 1). Herodotus judges these events as 'more worthy of
wonder than all other marvels' (διὰ πάντων φασμάτων ἄξια
θωμάσαι μάλιστα, 8. 37. 2), even than the miraculous displace-
ment of the untouchable sacred arms just described. Returning
Persian survivors, he later adds, reported that they saw 'other
divine things in addition to these' (ὡς πρὸς τούτοισι καὶ ἄλλα
ὥρων θεῖα, 8. 38): two giants, identified by the Delphians as
Phylacus and Autonous. The significant point here is the
coincidence of so many different forms of intervention: the
epiphanies of Phylacus and Autonous, the movement of the
arms, shouting from an empty shrine, rocks falling of their own

[85] As Immerwahr says (1954: 28), 'Herodotus does not say that all these
events were divine, but there is a certain compelling force in the repetitive
arrangement of the events'. Pelling makes the interesting observation (1991:
138 and n. 71) that the names of the 'Hellespontine' and the 'Strymonian'
winds, 7. 188. 2, 8. 118. 2, may not be quite coincidental.
[86] Cf. 1. 87. 2 (ἐκ δὲ αἰθρίης τε καὶ νηνεμίης); cf. Xen. Hell. 7. 1. 31.

accord, thunderbolts, and a panic attack. No one form of intervention is seen as being different in type: fear falls upon the Persians in the same way as thunderbolts. This combination, incidentally, is precisely that foreseen by Artabanus in his warning to Xerxes of the dangers of the campaign: the god in his envy sends down fear or thunder (7. 10.ε).[87]

Another passage in which Herodotus appears at first sight to accept the divine causation of natural phenomena is his discussion of the Peneius gorge (7. 129. 4):

Now the Thessalians themselves say that Poseidon made the gorge through which the Peneius flows, and they say so reasonably (οἰκότα λέγοντες). For whoever believes that Poseidon shakes the earth (ὅστις γὰρ νομίζει Ποσειδέωνα τὴν γῆν σείειν) and that the fissures caused by earthquakes are the works of this god would, seeing this, say that Poseidon had made it. For the division of the mountains is, it seems to me, the work of an earthquake.

This passage is an example, it has been claimed, of how 'supernatural events' in the *Histories* 'are more often "explained", doubted, or denied than admitted'.[88] The apparently euphemistic use of 'explanation' is unclear, but the reasoning appears to be that Herodotus is parodying the Thessalians' ascription of responsibility for the gorge to Poseidon: the Thessalians' explanation is reasonable, at least if you accept an absurd premise. The assumption underlying this view is that a natural explanation—that the gorge was the result of an earthquake—is somehow incompatible with an explanation in terms of the divine—that the earthquake was in turn caused by Poseidon.

This sceptical position is less likely in the light of some analogous passages. On the arrival of the Persian general Datis

[87] Cf. van der Veen (1996: 19 n. 55) for an alternative interpretation. Cf. the panic attack at Aphetae, 8. 12. 2, no sooner than they had recovered their breath from Pelion, or the panic of the Persians as they attempted to enter Cyrene, 4. 203. 3 (connected implicitly with their regret at obeying an earlier oracle, 4. 203. 1). For similar panic attacks, see Pritchett iii. 45–6; for a cult of Phobos at Sparta, Parker (1989: 162), Mactoux (1993).

[88] Lateiner (1989: 199). Contrast also apparently Linforth (1928: 217). Müller (1981: 316) uses 7. 129. 4 to show that Herodotus does not believe in divine intervention through nature. Fehling argues (1989: 31–3) that Herodotus 'has taken a single idea and composed variations on it, and attributed them to different people'.

in Eretria, 'Delos was moved, as the Delians themselves say, and this earthquake was the first and the last until my own day' (6. 98. 1).[89] Herodotus continues:

The god, it seems, showed this marvel to men as a sign of the evils that were to come (καὶ τοῦτο μέν κου τέρας ἀνθρώποισι τῶν μελλόντων ἔσεσθαι κακῶν ἔφηνε ὁ θεός). For in the generations of Darius, the son of Hystaspes, and Xerxes, the son of Darius, and Artaxerxes, the son of Xerxes, in these three generations together more evils occurred to Greece than in the twenty generations before Darius,[90] some of these brought upon her by the Persians, others by her own leaders fighting for control. So for Delos to have been moved, when it had never been moved before then, was in no way unreasonable (οὕτως οὐδὲν ἦν ἀεικὲς κινηθῆναι Δῆλον τὸ πρὶν ἐοῦσαν ἀκίνητον). And this was what was written in a prophecy about this: I will move even Delos though it has never been moved (κινήσω καὶ Δῆλον ἀκίνητόν περ ἐοῦσαν).

In this instance, the earthquake is explicitly said to be due to the god. It is also imagined to be in fulfilment of a prophecy: Herodotus' own words echo those of the prophecy as if to illustrate its fulfilment.[91] The earthquake itself, however, forebodes more evil. That the earthquake had a divine cause appears to Herodotus to be a reasonable deduction from the evidence of the evils that were to afflict Greece: the omen or marvel (τέρας) has, with hindsight, been fulfilled.

There are clear differences between this earthquake and the Thessalians' report of the Peneius gorge. In the case of the gorge, there are no suggestions that the original quake was in any way an omen capable of fulfilment; rather the discussion revolves around the proper way of understanding what is now an apparently immutable natural landscape. In the case of Delos, no direct suggestion is made of the god responsible.[92] That Herodotus thinks it possible to ascribe some natural phenomena to a particular god, in this case again Poseidon, is made clear, however, by his account of the sudden floodtide on

[89] For Thucydides' rival claim at 2. 8. 3, see Hornblower, ad loc.
[90] See Prakken (1940: 468–9), Raubitschek (1989: 41–2) for the suggestion that Herodotus intended the figure literally, and that on the basis of the genealogy of Leonidas, twenty generations would take us to the generation of Heracles.
[91] For textual variants, however, see now Rosén, ad loc.
[92] Cf. François (1957: 204–5).

the Strymon which killed a number of Persians (8. 129. 3).[93]
The Potidaeans say that the reason for the floodtide (αἴτιον δὲ
λέγουσι) was that the same Persians who were destroyed in this
disaster had earlier desecrated an image of Poseidon. He
concludes: 'in giving this explanation, they seem to me to
speak well' (αἴτιον δὲ τοῦτο λέγοντες εὖ λέγειν ἔμοιγε δοκέουσι).[94]
Here again is the element of surprise—at least for the Persians
(the Potidaeans were familiar with such floodtides): indeed the
way in which an initial low tide lures the Persians to their
deaths may suggest an element of divine entrapment. Further
proof of a divine cause is to be found in the very appropriate
coincidence that the victims were the same men who had
committed an act of sacrilege against—appropriately, if Herodotus believed in roughly conventional spheres of influences
for the gods—Poseidon. The fact that that sacrilege had been
against Poseidon confirms the identity of the god responsible
for the floodtide. To return to the Peneius gorge then, Herodotus' scepticism is directed very much more narrowly than
might, at first, appear to be the case. The only point necessarily
at issue, it would seem, is whether it is possible to ascribe
responsibility for one natural phenomenon, earthquakes, to one
god in particular. The dichotomy between a natural, scientific
explanation and explanation in terms of divine intervention can
be seen then to be a modern one.[95]

[93] Lloyd-Jones (1971: 64), comparing 7. 129. 4 and 8. 129. 3, sensibly
observes that the first of these two passages 'does not prove that he himself did
not believe it'. Macan vii. 1. 2. 557 makes the same comparison: 'perhaps the
direct intervention of the deity was more intelligible to him in a case of human
ἀσέβεια, than in the case of a natural object.'

[94] Forrest (1979: 312) cites this as an example of Herodotus coming 'near'
to giving his approval of a supernatural explanation, but translates εὖ λέγειν as
'to tell a good story'.

[95] See more judiciously Ferguson (1981: 2), 'his theory of earthquakes
mixes Poseidon and science'; G. E. R. Lloyd (1979: 30 n. 102), for whom
Herodotus 'endorses, but rationalises, the Thessalian story'; or Rhodes (1994:
158), according to whom Herodotus sounds 'agnostic'. As Lloyd says (1979:
52), 'to attribute earthquakes to Poseidon is, from the point of view of an
understanding of the nature of earthquakes, not to reduce the unknown to the
known, but to exchange one unknown for another'; since divine causation can
be imagined to operate in addition to natural causation, it is a very hard belief
to dispel (p. 55). Contrast Pythagoras' explanation of earthquakes as a
'concourse of the dead', DK 58 C 2 (thunder is to strike fear into those in

As well as these passages, there are a number of instances in which the divine cause of thunder, lightning and so on is not made so explicit, but is nevertheless implied by their narrative context and function, and by parallels with the instances referred to so far. The Persians come up against a number of natural obstacles in their progress to and through Greece. After the Persians entered the territory of Troy, 'thunder and lightning fell upon them,' killing large numbers (βρονταί τε καὶ πρηστῆρες ἐπεσπίπτουσι, 7. 42. 2). It appears from Xerxes' subsequent actions in Troy that he is attempting to take on the mantle of Priam as the champion of Asia in its perennial struggle against Europe. The timing of the thunder and lightning appear to express divine disapproval. This provides, of course, a close parallel to the reception the Persians receive at Delphi (8. 37. 3). Similarly, no sooner had the Persian bridge over the Hellespont been painstakingly constructed than a great storm broke it up (7. 34). In the course of the Marathon campaign too, a great wind had suddenly overwhelmed the Persians as they made their way around Athos (6. 44. 2). As in the examples of Delphi and of Aphetae, the disaster is overwhelming partly because of the coincidence of a number of misfortunes: those of the Persians who were not dashed onto rocks were eaten by sea monsters; others died from drowning; others still from cold.[96] The impression is of a relentless, and a complete, destruction.

All these examples tally closely with the wisdom put into the mouth of Xerxes' adviser Artabanus. The land and the sea are Xerxes' greatest enemies according to Artabanus (7. 49. 1): no harbours will be large enough for Xerxes' fleet to shelter from storms; the land also will beget a famine. Xerxes had imagined that extra men could make up for any difficulty (7. 48), but, as Artabanus has already warned, merely stoking up the scale of the expedition may actually attract disaster (7. 10. ε):

You see with living things how god strikes with thunder those which excel and does not allow them ostentation (ὁρᾷς τὰ ὑπερέχοντα ζῷα ὡς κεραυνοῖ ὁ θεὸς οὐδὲ ἐᾷ φαντάζεσθαι), whereas the small ones do not

Tartarus, 58 C 1). Cf. also the fourth-century controversy between Heraclides and Callisthenes over the cause of the earthquake which destroyed Helice (Gottschalk 1980: 94–5).

[96] For Persian swimming, see Hall (1994).

offend him. You see how it is at the greatest buildings and the tallest
trees that he always throws his bolts. For the god will cut down any
that excel (φιλέει γὰρ ὁ θεὸς τὰ ὑπερέχοντα πάντα κολούειν). So in this
manner even a great army is destroyed by a small one: whenever the
god through envy should throw fear or lightning at them, through
which they perish in a manner undeserving of themselves (ἐπεάν σφι ὁ
θεὸς φθονήσας φόβον ἐμβάλῃ ἢ βροντήν, δι᾽ ὧν ἐφθάρησαν ἀναξίως ἑωυτῶν).

The series of natural disasters that occur to the Persians on
their campaign seems almost to unfold in fulfilment of Artabanus' wisdom. The idea of the land and sea as Xerxes'
enemies can manifest itself even in an extraordinary detail:
white cliffs, for example, form themselves by an optical illusion
into ships to compound Persian fear (8. 107. 2).[97] The correlation here between what we might term Herodotus' news report
and his editorial suggests a degree of conscious design, as if he
were here providing a gloss on a recurrent feature of his
narrative. However, we should not therefore assume that the
pattern of natural miracles is purely a literary motif; rather, it
reflects the manner in which the traditions of the Persian wars
have developed around the assumption that the Persian defeat
was due to divine help.

The implication of some significance to natural phenomena
is often no more than a matter of narrative timing: in addition
to the well-timed thunder as Xerxes approached Troy (7. 43. 1),
one can cite the earthquake that heralds the beginning of the
battle of Salamis like some divine drumroll (8. 64),[98] the
thunder that seems to confirm the sovereignty of Darius
(3. 86. 2),[99] the thunder and earthquake that coincide to trigger
a fit of madness in a group of Athenians so that they kill one
another—or which alternatively coincide with the attack of
some Argives on the same Athenians, confirming the justice
of their deaths (5. 85. 2, 86. 4). Then there are the sudden
winds that bury armies (3. 26. 3; 4. 173), or the fateful gusts

[97] For this land and sea imagery, see Lachenaud (1978: 136 ff.), but
especially now Pelling (1991: 136 ff.; 1997: 7–8); see further Harrison (forthcoming).

[98] Cf. H. Il. 17. 593–6, Od. 21. 413.

[99] At the same time as his horse has been artificially induced to neigh. For
the Persian background to Oebares' trick, see J. M. Cook (1983: 54–5), with
further refs.

which cause a fire in Miletus to burn down the temple of
Athena (1. 19. 1), send Paris to Egypt (2. 113. 1), so precipitat-
ing a completely futile Trojan war (2. 120. 5), Corobius to
Platea, resulting in the foundation of Cyrene (4. 151. 2),
Colaeus and the Samians 'with divine guidance' to Tartessus
(θείῃ πομπῇ χρεώμενοι, 4. 152. 2), thus producing the biggest
profit ever made from the cargo of one ship, or Jason to Libya,
a voyage which promises to result—by a circuitous route—in
the foundation of one hundred Greek cities on the shores of
Lake Triton (4. 179). The winds in such episodes are certainly
not central characters as in the disaster at Athos, but bit-
players who all contribute to a loosely destined end.[100] Like
the divine chances discussed above, there is nothing intrinsi-
cally impossible about the appearance of such winds; the
judgement that they were divine, in so far as it is ever
expressed, is one that is arrived at in retrospect in the light
of their disproportionate consequences. Such chance events
reflect, nonetheless, a belief in the possibility of divine intervention in human life, no matter how unselfconscious that
belief may be: the presence of the prosaic historical figure of
Colaeus amongst those carried by fateful winds is perhaps
enough to show that the possibility of such intervention was
not restricted to any heroic past.

What makes a miracle, finally, may differ from place to place.
In Scythia, Herodotus tells us, thunder is considered to be a
marvel (τέρας) during the winter, whereas in the summer it is
the norm; earthquakes are considered to be marvels whatever
the season (4. 28. 3). In Egyptian Thebes, on the other hand,
rainfall is considered the greatest φάσμα or apparition
(3. 10. 3).[101] Such inversions of ordinary (Greek) conditions
bring out a contradiction at the heart of belief in miracles.
Whilst by definition they break the rules of ordinary expectations, ultimately they operate according to principles which are

---

[100] The idea of the divine causation of winds is inverted in the story of
Miltiades and Lemnos, 6. 139. 4–40: Miltiades manages to sail from Attica to
Lemnos with a northerly wind in a single day by treating the Athenian
territory of the Chersonese as Attica.

[101] The Egyptians, 2. 82. 2, record more *terata* than any other people;
contrast Lloyd ii. 345–6.

predictable. This can be illustrated most clearly by returning once more to the miracle of the jumping fish that appear to the Persian Artayctes (9. 120). The Athenian guards who witnessed the scene were astonished—but only because they did not understand it. Once the miracle has been satisfactorily decoded and, happily for them, has been shown to relate not to them but to their prisoner, there is no cause for fear or even amazement. There is in this sense then nothing miraculous about miracles: they only seem to be so due to man's inadequate understanding of the world.

4

Divine Retribution

Pheretime, however, did not end her life well (Οὐ μὲν οὐδὲ ἡ Φερετίμη εὖ τὴν ζόην κατέπλεξε). For, after having taken vengeance on the Barcaeans, as soon as she had returned to Egypt from Libya, she died a terrible death: for she swarmed with worms while she was still alive. So the over-harsh vengeances of men are abominated by the gods (ὡς ἄρα ἀνθρώποισι αἱ λίην ἰσχυραὶ τιμωρίαι πρὸς θεῶν ἐπίφθονοι γίνονται). Such and so great was the vengeance of Pheretime, the daughter of Battus, against the Barcaeans (4. 205).[1]

The crime of Pheretime against the people of Barca had been to impale its leading men, and then to cut off the breasts of their wives and use them to dress the walls of the city. Her story is a peculiarly garish one. Its moral, however, is little different to that of a number of comparable passages in Herodotus' *Histories*: that if you behave as Pheretime behaves, you will be punished as she was punished. That Herodotus believed in the possibility of divine retribution is, in the light of such passages, irrefutable.[2] This chapter will address two main questions: first, that of the nature of Herodotus' belief in divine retribution (its significance in the *Histories*, the actions which receive retribution, the means by which the conclusion

---

[1] An earlier version of the main argument of this chapter appeared, with additional observations, as Harrison (1997). For similar deaths by worms, see Dawson (with notes by D. Harvey) (1986: 95 n. 43), Africa (1982).

[2] But see Lateiner (1980) who, on the basis of the expression *dikas didonai* argues (p. 32) that 'by using direct and reported speech for all but one example of this metaphor, Herodotus frees himself from any responsibility for believing in or promulgating the moral universe which its use implies'. To take the phrase *dikas didonai* in isolation presupposes, however, that it was chosen very consciously. Contrast also Shimron (1989: 55), adducing the unjust fate of Mycerinus, 2. 133, as evidence that Herodotus was unlikely to have believed in the principle of 'divine justice'.

of divine retribution is drawn); and secondly, the question of
how Herodotus could have believed such a thing, how (to use a
piece of modern jargon) such a belief was 'sustainable' in the
light of experience.[3]

Herodotus believes that certain actions will inevitably
receive retribution from the gods. (How those actions can be
defined is a question to which we will return.) This is a rule, in
theory at least, without exceptions. When on one occasion
Athenians and Spartans both commit identical crimes—the
murder of Persian ambassadors—but only the Spartans are
known to have been punished for it, Herodotus is sufficiently
puzzled to look for an appropriate punishment (7. 133. 2).
'What undesirable thing happened to the Athenians for what
they had done to the heralds I cannot say, except that their
country and city were ravaged, but this I think did not happen
for this reason.' The Athenians, Herodotus assumes, must have
been punished somehow.[4]

The same assumption that certain actions will inevitably
attract retribution can also be seen ascribed, unchallenged, to
characters in the *Histories*.[5] The Ethiopian king of Egypt,
Sabacus, sees in his dream a man who tells him to gather
together all the priests in Egypt and cut them in half (2. 139. 1).
He remembers, however, a prophecy which stated that he was
destined to rule Egypt only for fifty years, and so he recognizes
the dream as a divine trap: the gods had shown him the dream
'so that, having committed an act of sacrilege, he might suffer
some evil from either gods or men' (ἵνα ἀσεβήσας περὶ τὰ ἱρὰ
κακόν τι πρὸς θεῶν ἢ πρὸς ἀνθρώπων λάβοι, 2. 139. 2). Punishment

---

[3] Contrast Starr (1968*a*: 140–1), according to whom Herodotus is 'too
empirical a historian to view [the hand of the gods in human affairs] as directly
ethical in motivation'.

[4] Cf. Parker (1983: 188), Wéry (1966: 482); Shimron (1989: 69) sees 'bitter
humour' on Herodotus' part here. Pausanias reports, 3. 12. 7, that Talthybius'
wrath fell in Athens on Miltiades, Plutarch, *Them*. 6, that only the heralds'
interpreter had been killed on the proposal of Themistocles. For the
inviolability of heralds, see Wéry (1966: esp. 479–86), Ducrey (1968: 301–
4), Parker (1983: 188). See also Palli Bonet (1956) for Talthybius, Sealey
(1976) for an attempted historical rationalization.

[5] A similar assumption appears to lie behind the odd case of the Chians,
1. 160. 5, who having gained Atarneus in exchange for giving up a suppliant,
try apparently to avert vengeance by excluding the produce of Atarneus from
their temples (closing the stable door after the horse has bolted?).

would—had Sabacus not been able, as it were, to sidestep
fate—have been automatic. Recognizing that his time was up,
however, Sabacus took himself back to Ethiopia. The story of
Sabacus has been seen as evidence that 'in Egypt the gods move
in mysterious ways indeed'.[6] An unequivocally Greek parallel
is provided, however, by the case of Aristodicus of Cyme
(1. 158–9). Aristodicus had been granted permission by the
god at Branchidae to expel a suppliant. But this was something
for which he should never have asked. Why then had the god
said yes? 'So that, committing an act of impiety, you might
more quickly come to your end, and never again come to the
oracle to enquire about the expulsion of suppliants' (1. 159. 4).[7]

The idea that crimes will inevitably be punished also constitutes the moral implicit in a number of stories, such as that
of Pheretime quoted above. Time and again characters suppose
that they are immune from divine vengeance, commit a crime,
and fall foul of a god.[8] Alexander (Paris) resolved to take a wife
from Greece by force, supposing that he would not be made to
pay for it (ἐπιστάμενον πάντως ὅτι οὐ δώσει δίκας, 1. 3. 1).[9] He is,

---

[6] This suggestion of West (1987: 264) seems to me exaggerated: the
parallels with, for example, the deceptive dreams that appear to Artabanus
and Xerxes, 7. 12–18, or with the story of Aristodicus, suggest that Sabacus'
dream has become to a significant extent Hellenized. West (pp. 264–5) does
not believe that the dreams of Xerxes and Artabanus are intended to deceive.
See further Ch. 5.

[7] ἵνα γε ἀσεβήσαντες θᾶσσον ἀπόλησθε, ὡς μὴ τὸ λοιπὸν περὶ ἱκετέων ἐκδόσιος
ἔλθητε ἐπὶ τὸ χρηστήριον. Herodotus also reports that peoples other than Greeks
or Egyptians argue, in support of their practice of having sex in temples, that
animals and birds have sex in temples, and that if it was not 'acceptable to the
god, the animals would not do it' (εἰ ὦν εἶναι τῷ θεῷ τοῦτο μὴ φίλον, οὐκ ἂν οὐδὲ
τὰ κτήνεα ποιέειν, 2. 64. 2). The ability of the gods to punish or prevent such
behaviour is taken for granted. Herodotus finds this position objectionable:
possibly, however, what he objects to is the analogy between men and other
animals (2. 64. 1), rather than the logic of the argument.

[8] Cf. Cambyses' death, 3. 64. 3, for which see Ch. 3, 'the goddess''
punishment of the Sythians by inflicting on them the 'female disease',
1. 105. 2–4. For the female disease, see Halliday (1910–11); cf. Hipp. Airs,
Waters, Places 22; for the divine cause of disease, see Demont (1988).

[9] It seems to be human vengeance that Paris has in mind (the Greeks, after
all, had not paid for their seizure of Medea): but this is just another way in
which he was mistaken. For the pattern whereby men do not expect divine
retribution for their crimes, see also Ch. 9; cf. H. Od. 22. 39–40, Pind. Ol.
1. 102–3, Theogn. 203 ff. (delay in retribution deceives men).

of course, mistaken. The destruction of the Trojans in the Trojan war was engineered by the divine (τοῦ δαιμονίου παρα-σκευάζοντος, 2. 120. 5) in order to make it clear to men that 'great injustices meet also with great vengeances from the gods' (ὡς τῶν μεγάλων ἀδικημάτων μεγάλαι εἰσὶ καὶ αἱ τιμωρίαι παρὰ τῶν θεῶν). Herodotus makes it clear that this is his own interpreta-tion.[10] Then there is the case of Hermotimus and Panionius. Hermotimus was captured by enemies, bought, castrated, and sold on by Panionius.[11] He then, however, earned the favour of Xerxes, and so was able to have his revenge. It was, according to Herodotus, 'the greatest revenge of anyone who has been wronged of all the men we know' (τῷ μεγίστη τίσις ἤδη ἀδικηθέντι ἐγένετο πάντων τῶν ἡμεῖς ἴδμεν, 8. 105. 1). The gods, in Hermotimus' words, brought Panionius into his hands (8. 106. 3). That is also the impression given by the concluding sentence of Herodotus' account (8. 106. 4): 'thus vengeance (τίσις) and Hermotimus overtook Panionius.'

Complementary to the principle of retribution inevitably following a crime is a second principle: that, if some misfortune occurs, it must be in retribution for an earlier action; the question is then asked 'what action?'. If a misfortune can be traced back not simply to an action of a type likely to incur retribution but to an action hostile to a particular deity—as, for example, the miracle of the distribution of the Persian bodies around the shrine of Demeter can be related to the victims' desecration of her shrine at Eleusis (9. 65. 2), or the Potidaea floodtide to its victims' sacrilege against Poseidon (7. 129. 3)—this may help to identify the deity responsible for the mis-fortune.[12] This 'moral' explanation of human suffering is not the only form of divine explanation adopted by Herodotus—other 'amoral' explanations for misfortunes, that they are

---

[10] ὡς μὲν ἐγὼ γνώμην ἀποφαίνομαι . . ., καὶ ταῦτα μὲν τῇ ἐμοὶ δοκέει εἴρηται. Contrast Shimron (1989: 20), for whom the story of Helen's stay in Troy is 'laughed off'—'although here as elsewhere Herodotus adds some serious considerations'.

[11] The stigma attached to such activities is also reflected in the trouble taken by the Samians, 3. 48. 2–4, to save some Corcyraean children from this fate by e.g. the invention of a festival: see here Ducat (1995). Hermotimus describes his castration as transforming him from a man into a nothing, 8. 106. 3: cf. the attitude to childlessness and to the murder of children, Ch. 2.

[12] For these questions, see Ch. 6.

omens or that the divinity is capricious, are also available. When, however, the selection of this 'moral explanation' has been made it is presented as quite the only option, or at least as the only divine option.

So, for example, Cleomenes' madness and subsequent death by self-mutilation provoke Herodotus to speculate on what might have been the cause. Although he reports one possible non-divine explanation (ἐκ δαιμονίου . . . οὐδενὸς μανῆναι Κλεομένεα, 6. 84. 1) for Cleomenes' madness, that it was caused by an alcoholism learnt from Scythian ambassadors, in the event Herodotus chooses one of three explanations that imply a divine origin, though one might not suppose so from many modern interpretations of this passage:[13] was Cleomenes' madness caused by his act of sacrilege in Argos, as predictably the Argives thought (6. 75. 3, 84. 1), by his act of sacrilege at Eleusis, as in the Athenians' version (6. 75. 3), or by his bribery of the Pythia to ensure the deposition of Demaratus (6. 66, 75. 3), the view, Herodotus says, of most Greeks?[14] He opts for the majority view: 'I think that Cleomenes suffered this retribution on account of Demaratus' (ἐμοὶ δὲ δοκέει τίσιν ταύτην ὁ Κλεομένης Δημαρήτῳ ἐκτεῖσαι, 6. 84. 3). Herodotus' reasoning on this occasion runs in the reverse direction to his thought on the question of the retribution for the Athenians' killing of the Persian envoys. There a clear act of impiety or injustice leads him to suppose that they must have received

---

[13] See e.g. the puzzling interpretations of de Romilly (1977: 45–6), who, acknowledging that Herodotus accepts 'this trend of thought', insinuates that 'he is careful to mention . . . another and more realistic explanation', or of Lateiner (1989: 203–4), that Herodotus 'positions himself somewhere in between, endorsing the concept that Cleomenes "got what he deserved" . . . but not endorsing the hypothesis of divine interference'. De Romilly pursues a similarly Delphic approach to this passage elsewhere (1971: 316): 'ce flottement et cette incertitude révèlent plus de piété que de théologie, et plus de curiosité que de foi résolue.' (Why must Herodotus' beliefs be inflexible and dogmatic?) Lang maintains oddly (1984b: 98) that 'here he maintains the majority opinion, less because it was the majority opinion than because he shared the majority *need* to respect and reverence the oracle and Delphi' (my italics). Van der Veen likewise (1996: 62) describes the bribery of Delphi simply as the 'most popular explanation'.

[14] For the traditions concerning Cleomenes, see the excellent A. Griffiths (1989); for the suggestion that 'perhaps this was not a case of madness, but of delirium tremens', see Dawson (1986: 94).

some sort of divine retribution: the question is what form that might have taken. In this case, Cleomenes' death and madness are presumed to be in retribution for some act of impiety or injustice: the question is what that might have been. That Herodotus offers, even if only to reject, a non-divine explanation for Cleomenes' end in parallel to the divine causes still has important implications: the conclusion that a vengeful deity lies behind a particular misfortune is made as a result of a process of deduction that could just as easily have ended in an exclusively human cause; a disaster that is divinely motivated looks no different from one that is not.[15]

The idea that a misfortune is explicable in terms of an earlier misdemeanour is again one that can be seen ascribed almost incidentally by Herodotus to characters in his *Histories*. The Sybarites are anxious to prove that the Spartan Dorieus, on his way to found a colony in the territory of Eryx, had helped the Crotoniates to capture Sybaris (5. 45. 1). The 'greatest piece of evidence' ($\mu\alpha\rho\tau\acute{\upsilon}\rho\iota\upsilon\nu$ $\mu\acute{\epsilon}\gamma\iota\sigma\tau\upsilon\nu$)[16] presented by the Sybarites in support of their claim was Dorieus' death: he had been given a mandate by the god to found a colony; he must in some way have overstepped this mandate, or else the colony would have been successful and he would not have died.[17] The Sybarites naturally do not consider the possibility that Dorieus might have committed some other transgression: their own suffering was the only possible cause. Herodotus' choice of the words 'greatest piece of evidence', and his failure to rebut their argument, suggest surely that he felt the Sybarites' case to be at least no less respectable than the argument put forward by the Crotoniates (5. 45. 2) that, had Dorieus helped them, his family would have been granted property in their territory. He concludes with a statement of neutrality.

What are the actions which provoke retribution? Their range

---

[15] As Parker observes (1983: 267), 'Disaster was constantly traced back to those maleficent but invisible powers, bribery and treachery' just as to divine causes.

[16] For the meaning of $\mu\alpha\rho\tau\acute{\upsilon}\rho\iota\upsilon\nu$, see R. Thomas (1997: 137–8).

[17] Cf. Andoc. 1. 137–9 (safe journeys are proof that one has committed no offence). This passage also has important implications for belief in oracles: see Ch. 6.

in the *Histories* is broader than might at first appear to be the case.[18] Certainly, a majority of such actions are what we might describe as specifically 'religious' crimes: the ravaging or burning of temples, stealing money from temples, and having sex with women in temples,[19] the neglect of the instructions of an oracle, the request for permission to expel a suppliant, and even, of course (surely the most comically overdrawn act of sacrilege), that recommended to Sabacus, cutting priests in half.[20] Alexander's action in stealing Helen and money from Menelaus, described repeatedly by Egyptian characters as unholy or impious (2. 114. 2, 115. 4–5), may seem at first sight a relatively 'secular' offence, but Alexander's impiety most likely consists chiefly in its being a 'breach of guest-friendship'.[21] These unequivocally 'religious' crimes, however, form only the majority of the actions that attract divine retribution, not the sum.[22] Panionius' crime was to gain his living from the 'most unholy deeds' (ἔργων ἀνοσιωτάτων, 8. 105. 1), the castration and sale of children. Herodotus' verdict on the Trojan war is that it provides an example of how 'great injustices' (μεγάλων ἀδικη-μάτων, 2. 120. 5) receive great vengeances.[23] While it is still

---

[18] For the similar pattern of the crimes which attract punishment in tragedy, see Mikalson (1991: ch. 4).

[19] For the taboo against stealing money, see esp. Parker (1983: 171), 'disrespect for sacred money was a mark of extreme social decay, the behaviour of a tyrant or a barbarian'; cf. 1. 187 (Nitocris' tomb), Solon fr. 4. 12–13 West, Xen. *Hieron* 4. 11, Diod. Sic. 14. 63. 1, 67. 4, 70. 4, 76. 3–4. For the taboos concerning sex, see Parker (1983: 74 ff.), 'sexual activity is in some sense incompatible with the sacred'; cf. 1. 198 (shameful Babylonian custom of temple prostitution), 2. 64 (barbarian justification for temple sex: animals do it), 2. 111. 4–5 (a chaste woman's urine cures Pherus of blindness). For the Persian defeat as divine retribution for Persian sacrilege, cf. 8. 33, 53. 2, 109. 3, 143. 2.

[20] See Masson (1950), West (1987: 265–6), for near-eastern parallels for Sabacus' 'sacrilege' (or for the punishment of Pythius' son: 7. 39. 3).

[21] See here Herman (1987: 125–6).

[22] Contrast de Romilly (1971: 316, 332).

[23] The overlap of the unjust and the unholy is also reflected at 2. 154. 2 (Clearchus' co-opting of Themison for the murder of his daughter), 3. 16. 2–3 (Cambyses' burning of Amasis unjust and unholy), 3. 65. 5 (Cambyses' murder of Smerdis), 3. 120. 1 (Oroites' murder of Polycrates), 4. 146. 1 (the Minyae's claim to a share of the Spartan kingship). For Herodotus' idea of justice (and sophistic overtones), see now Coulet (1992). A similar equation or overlap can be seen in a range of other writers: cf. Theogn. 145–6, Aesch. *Suppl.* 395–6,

possible for a formally pious act also to be unjust (so, for
example, the common motif of the manipulation of oaths to
unjust ends[24]), there is then at least a good deal of confusion or
overlap between the ideas of the unholy and of the unjust.[25] The
category of actions likely to receive retribution is broader
(potentially, at least) than just the narrow class of acts of
sacrilege.

As the gods punish injustice, so their retribution is envisaged
as being just. The divine response to Alexander's theft of
Helen, the destruction of Troy, is (whatever we might think)

Soph. *Ant.* 743–5, Cleoboulus DK 10. 3 (ἀδικίαν μισεῖν, εὐσέβειαν φυλάσσειν).
There is an expectation that gods should behave justly: so, if an unjust man is
unfortunate, this is seen as evidence of the existence, the justice of the gods, or
that the gods deserve reverence: H. *Od.* 24. 351–2, Aesch. *Ag.* 1577 ff., E.
Suppl. 731–3, *Hipp.* 1169, *Tro.* 82–6, *Andr.* 439; see also Dover (1974: 20–1) on
Men. *Dysk.* 639–47. Cf. also Soph. *Ant.* 288 (gods don't honour *kakous*), E.
Hec. 798 ff. (gods support justice), and (obscurely) Heraclitus DK 22 B 102
(gods have only good and unjust; men have taken just and unjust). Conversely,
if unjust men go unpunished, the gods are said not to exist, not to be just, or not
to deserve reverence: Ar. *Nub.* 398 ff., Soph. *El.* 245–50, *OT* 883–910, E. *El.*
583–4. For complaints against injustice of gods, however, cf. Theogn. 149–50,
373–82, 743 ff., Soph. *Phil.* 446 ff.; that villains prosper is the joke of Aristophanes' *Ploutos* (e.g. 32 ff.); the Eumenides complain unfairly, Aesch. *Eum.*
153–4, 162–3, of the injustice of the younger gods.

[24] See esp. the story of Etearchus who, persuaded by his second wife to
commit the 'unholy deed' (ἔργον οὐκ ὅσιον) of killing his daughter Phronime,
induces his friend Themison to swear an oath to do whatever he asks, and then
asks him to drown his daughter (4. 154. 2–3). Themison is 'angry at the deceit
of the oath', but devises a means of 'discharging the oath' (ἀποσιεύμενος τὴν
ἐξόρκωσιν) without killing the girl (4. 154. 4): he ties ropes to her feet, dips her
into the water and pulls her out again. There is interestingly no implication
that oaths should not be used for unjust ends: the narrative is rather shaped
around Themison's ingenious fulfilment of the oath. Cf. 3. 132–3 (Democedes
and Atossa), 4. 201 (Amasis' trick at Barca), 6. 62 (Ariston and Agetus),
9. 109. 2 (Xerxes and Artaynte); in the last case, however, Artaynte has not
stage-managed the oath merely for the purpose of extracting the cloak. For
such rash promises, see Braund (1998). Cf. Aesch. *Eum.* 432: Athena tells the
Eumenides not to win an unjust victory through oaths; but there is nothing to
stop them doing so. Contrast, however, Xen. *Hell.* 4. 7. 2–3.

[25] Cf. the observations of Dover (1974: 252), Rudhardt (1981: 25), Connor
(1988: 181); contrast here A. B. Lloyd (1988a: 58), envisaging in my view too
simple an equation of piety and justice, and Mikalson (1991: 178–9): his
verdict that every impious act is unjust, but that not every unjust act is
impious, is again rather too tidy: the impious is not merely a subset of a larger
category of the unjust, nor are they equivalent categories.

envisaged apparently by Herodotus as a proportional response: 'great injustices' receive 'great vengeances'. That is also the implication of Hermotimus' appropriate vengeance on Panionius, judged by Herodotus to be the 'greatest act of vengeance' within his knowledge (8. 105. 1), forcing the man who had castrated him to do the same to all four of his sons, before they in turn castrate him (8. 106. 4); as Hermotimus tells Panionius, the gods led Panionius, who had committed 'unholy deeds' (ἀνόσια), into his hands, 'in accordance with a just law' (νόμῳ δικαίῳ χρεώμενοι, 8. 106. 3). That divine retribution is just is the implication also of the vengeance wrought by Talthybius upon the Spartans (7. 137. 1–2):

This appears to me to have been most divine (τοῦτό μοι ἐν τοῖσι θειότατον φαίνεται γενέσθαι). For that the anger of Talthybius fell upon the ambassadors and that it did not cease until it found its fulfilment, so much was just (τὸ δίκαιον οὕτω ἔφερε). But that it should have fallen on the sons of the same men who had gone up to the King on account of [Talthybius'] anger, that is on Nicolaus son of Boulis and on Aneristus son of Sperthias . . ., makes it clear to me that the affair was divine (δῆλον ὦν μοι ὅτι θεῖον ἐγένετο τὸ πρῆγμα [ἐκ τῆς μήνιος]).

There seems to be a sliding scale in operation here: the more coincidental the retribution, the more just; justice as miraculously appropriate as this must be divine.[26] Clearly the element of delay makes the eventual fulfilment of Talthybius' wrath more miraculous.

Herodotus' belief in divine retribution appears then to constitute a complete moral system: unjust actions meet without fail with a just, proportional response. There are clear difficulties with this conclusion, however. In the real world, how could anyone believe this? A morality based entirely on the expectation of direct divine retribution would soon, surely, become impractically liberal. The belief in the certainty of divine retribution is sustained, however, by means of a number of 'let-out clauses'.

---

[26] That divine retribution for the sins of fathers could be delayed to subsequent generations was also in antiquity viewed as unjust (see below, n. 34). This need not, however, affect the association of 'the just' and 'the divine' in this passage: why the punishment of Spartan heralds (as opposed to Sparta in general) should be deemed just is also not immediately evident.

First, divine retribution can operate through human agency.[27] So, for example, Sabacus would have taken his punishment for cutting the priests in half 'either from gods or men' (2. 139. 2). Hermotimus similarly (before taking his coolly calculated revenge) tells Panionius not to complain of the punishment he was about to receive from him, as the gods themselves had led him into his hands (8. 106. 3); the same idea of divine vengeance being worked out through human actions may be reflected also in Herodotus' judgement on this episode that 'vengeance and Hermotimus' caught up with Panionius (8. 106. 4). Divine retribution can also serve as a corrective to human vengeance. Oroites' action in plotting the death of the Samian tyrant Polycrates was 'unholy' in so far as he had never suffered any harm from Polycrates (3. 120. 1). (The idea enshrined, for example, in Solon's law that 'anyone who wished' could prosecute a crime rather than just the victim or his family, or the belief that killing a tyrant was a good in itself, have noticeably made no dent here.[28]) The crime of the Athenians against the Persian ambassadors is surely *in part* that their aggression was unprovoked. Pheretime dies in quite such a grisly fashion because her acts of vengeance against others had been excessive (4. 205).[29] The way in which the belief in divine vengeance depends on a pattern of human vengeance is

[27] De Romilly (1971: 317, 332–3) seems to see this as a sign of untidy thought. Boedeker (1988: 46–7) comments similarly that 'the capture and execution of Artayktes . . . is credited to Protesilaos' power by the victim himself, yet is ostensibly carried out by the Athenians at the insistence of the Elaiousians, with the agreement of Xanthippos.' Why should this be surprising? Starr (1968: 95), in saying that 'divine retribution more often now operated through the actions of men themselves', seems to imagine a time when gods were able to intervene directly. For human vengeance in the *Histories,* see also Sealey (1957), Gould (1991), Fisher (1992: 343 ff.), Mossman (1995: 174–6), Darbo-Peschanski (1987: 43 ff.).

[28] [Arist.] *Ath. Pol.* 9. 1; Theogn. 1181–2 (no nemesis for man who kills demos-eating tyrant).

[29] Other excessive acts of vengeance include that of Astyages against Harpagus, 1. 118–19, for which see Mossman (1995: 174), Darbo-Peschanski (1987: 59), and the Corcyraeans' unprovoked killing of Periander's son Lycophron, 3. 53. 7, described by Herodotus as a πρῆγμα ἀτάσθαλον, 3. 49. 2. Mossman suggests (1995: 175) that Pheretime by her excessive vengeance had 'usurped divine authority' in that 'lack of discrimination in punishment is usually a characteristic of divine vengeance'.

also perhaps reflected in the ethos of revenge as a religious duty disclosed in tragedy.[30]

There are, however, fixed limits imposed to the pattern of human vengeance other than just the principle of proportionality. Lampon, in the course of what Herodotus describes as a 'most unholy speech' (ἀνοσιώτατον . . . λόγον, 9. 78. 1), proposes that Pausanias should put the finishing touches to the great glory he has won at Plataea by submitting the body of Mardonius to the same indignities as Leonidas had suffered at the hands of Xerxes and Mardonius (9. 78).[31] Pausanias, however, rebukes him (9. 79):

Such behaviour is more appropriate for barbarians than for Greeks; we find it a cause of blame, moreover, even in them. May I never find favour with the Aeginetans on this account nor with any who approve of such behaviour. But it is enough for me to please the Spartans by doing and speaking piously (ἀποχρᾷ δέ μοι Σπαρτιήτῃσι ἀρεσκόμενον ὅσια μὲν ποιέειν, ὅσια δὲ καὶ λέγειν).

The gods act then as a kind of outside regulatory body of human attempts at justice: when they scent an irregularity, either an excessively disproportionate response or one that violates certain fixed rules, they step in and compensate.[32]

Another let-out clause for belief in retribution is that retribution, though often it follows immediately upon a crime (e.g. 3. 126. 1), can also be delayed—even for a number of generations. As Robert Parker has written, the idea of inherited guilt 'protects the belief in divine justice from crude empirical refutation'.[33] So, as we have seen, Talthybius' vengeance was

[30] See e.g. Aesch. *Choeph.* 122–3, Soph. *OT* 106–7, E. *El.* 976. When the Athenians accuse Alexander, 7. 143. 3, of encouraging them to do ἀθέμιστα, ἀθέμιστα may be the failure to avenge the Persians?

[31] Xerxes, Herodotus adds, must have hated Leonidas more than any man alive in order to have defiled his corpse, for the Persians were in general accustomed to give great honour to those brave in war, 7. 238. 1. For the mistreatment of corpses as unholy, cf. 3. 16. 2, H. *Il.* 22. 395–400, *Od.* 11. 71 ff., 22. 412, Soph. *Ant.* 72–4, *Aj.* 1129 ff., E. *Phoen.* 1663, *Suppl.* 18–19, *El.* 893 ff.

[32] Cf. esp. Darbo-Peschanski (1987: 56), Fornara (1990: 42).

[33] Parker (1983: 201–2); cf. Theogn. 203 ff. (delay deceives men), H. *Il.* 158 ff., Hes. *Erga* 217–8, E. *Or.* 419. Darbo-Peschanski argues (1987: 59) that two differences between divine and human vengeance are the extension of culpability to the descendants of the offender and delay. The killing (or

wrought upon the sons of the heralds who had volunteered to
die in expiation of the hero's wrath (7. 137): the delay, and the
fact that punishment fell on the sons of the very same men,
indeed make that punishment especially divine. Croesus
famously paid the price for his ancestor Gyges (1. 91. 1).
There is no statute of limitations for divine retribution: something unfortunate is bound to happen sooner or later. For the
sins of the fathers to be visited on the sons may today be seen
(and was indeed seen by some in antiquity[34]) as fundamentally
unjust. One might equally, however, see attractions in the idea
of delayed retribution: it is better perhaps for one's own
misfortune to be put down to the actions of a silent ancestor
than one's own misbehaviour.[35]

The final let-out clause for the belief in the certainty of
divine retribution is provided by the existence of an alternative
explanation of human suffering. As we have seen, for example
in the story of Cleomenes, certain misfortunes are interpreted
as evidence of retribution quite as if it were the only possible
explanation. Clearly, however, this is not so; elsewhere Herodotus explains similar events without recourse to the idea of
divine retribution. The earthquake at Delos, for example,
which occurred just after the departure of the Persian commander Datis from the island, is seen purely as an omen of
further misfortunes to come (6. 98). Other misfortunes are
interpreted only as illustrations of the mixed and unpredictable
nature of human fortune.[36] The question, in short, of how to

'destruction' through castration: 8. 106. 4) of the children of one's enemy is,
however, a common form of human vengeance: 3. 15. 1, 35. 1–4; 9. 120. 4.
The vengeance of Hermotimus against Panionius, 8. 105–6, is also delayed,
moreover (although the greatness, in Herodotus' eyes, of Hermotimus'
vengeance may be due in part to its mimicking the vengeance of gods).

[34] See Parker (1983: 200), Asheri (1998: 75) on the human vengeance of
9. 88; cf. Theogn. 731 ff., E. *Hipp.* 1379–83. See Dover (1974: 261 ff.; 1972:
208–9), for the idea that inherited punishment was displaced by an idea of the
afterlife.

[35] Cf. Dover (1972: 209).

[36] The combination of 'moral' and 'amoral' strands in Herodotus' causation
has been recognized by e.g. Legrand (1932: 135–6), De Sanctis (1936: 4–5),
Hooker (1989: 142); de Ste Croix (1977: 140) distinguishes three strands
(moral, immoral and amoral), Lateiner (arbitrarily) five 'systems of explanation' (1989: 196 ff.); see also the excellent discussion of Pippidi (1960).

account for instances of patently unfair suffering already has an
answer: men do not always get their just deserts.[37]

The criteria by which any one explanation—the amoral
Solonian explanation or the 'moral' explanation of retribution—is attached to any misfortune are clearly matters of
which Herodotus is not entirely conscious.[38] Only on one
occasion—in seeking to understand the mad actions of Cambyses towards his family—does he explicitly apply a choice of
these two explanations: Cambyses did these things, Herodotus
says, 'either due to Apis or for some other reason: for many
misfortunes tend to befall men' (3. 33). Both of these main
explanations can operate simultaneously, moreover: the phrase
used of Pheretime that she 'did not end her life well' (4. 205),
or of Leutychidas that 'he did not grow old in Sparta' (6. 72. 1),
are both markedly redolent of the language of Solon in Book 1;
yet both their deaths are also instances of retribution.[39] What
might seem to us, moreover, to be the kind of actions likely to
provoke retribution are often presented as misfortunes: the
event that disrupted the prosperity of Ameinocles the Magnesian was the death of his son at his own hands (7. 190).[40] In the
same way, the murder of his wife Melissa is the first of two
misfortunes to strike Periander, the second being the conse-
quent estrangement and death of his son Lycophron (συμφορὴν,
3. 50. 1). In certain cases, however, where one explanation is
clearly predominant, we may make some assessment as to why
that should be. An omen like that of the Delos earthquake
(6. 98) might perhaps have been seen as an instance of
retribution, had there been any clear victim. The Potidaea
floodtide (8. 129. 3), a comparable natural disaster, does have
victims, and is indeed seen as retribution. Conveniently, the
victims are also Persian: we might surely wonder whether the
Potidaeans would have been so quick to connect the floodtide
to an act of sacrilege against Poseidon had they themselves been

---

[37] Contrast Dover (1974: 80), according to whom the idea of an impersonal
fate 'made it easier to think of the gods as good'; cf. also J. G. Griffiths (1991:
70) for the idea of the divine will as 'inscrutable or even capricious' as 'an
outlook which cannot evade the charge of obscurantism for it defies explanation or consistency'.   [38] Cf. G. E. R. Lloyd (1990: 27).

[39] Maddalena notes the contradiction that death can be interpreted either as
a punishment or reward (1950: 77).   [40] See further Ch. 2.

the chief (or only) casualties.[41] Two disasters befall the Chians, both with very clear victims (6. 27), the collapse of a school building killing all but one of one hundred and twenty children, and the death by plague of all but two of one hundred young men sent to Delphi, yet there is no suggestion that these disasters should be construed as instances of retribution; they are seen—surely in part because of the unblemished lives of their victims (what could such young men have done to deserve this?)—simply as omens. It is important, however, not to overemphasize such 'guidelines'. The traditions surrounding Cleomenes in the *Histories* dwell on his acts of sacrilege: his death, we might suppose, is simply part of the package.[42] The same might have been said, however, of the notoriously sacrilegious Cambyses: yet, in that case, Herodotus appears to countenance an amoral explanation of misfortune. Such apparent inconsistency might be thought problematic. It is precisely this, however, the potential for two contradictory but parallel forms of explanation, that allows for the belief in the possibility of divine intervention to be maintained.

The proposition that Herodotus could have believed in the possibility (and, in certain circumstances, in the certainty) of divine retribution is itself eminently believable then. Indeed, as Kenneth Dover has written, with a delightful air of menace, even today 'action in the absolute certainty of "escaping the notice of gods and men" . . . is not just an experience which rarely comes our way, but a purely hypothetical experience which we cannot have'.[43] So long as there is suffering or

[41] As Parker observes (1983: 168 n. 133), 'one's own side burns temples by accident only' while one's enemy does so intentionally: see esp. 5. 102. 1. Alyattes is allowed to burn the temple of Athena accidentally, 1. 19, but this does not absolve him of the responsibility for repairing it. Cf. Diod. Sic. 16. 58. 6.

[42] An interesting case is the death and madness of the Athenians sent to recover the sacred olive wood images of Damias and Auxesia from Aegina, 5. 82–7. We might have expected the Argives to have attributed the Athenians' death to divine retribution for an act of sacrilege. It is the Athenians, however, who ascribe their men's death to the divine (τοῦ δαιμονίου, 5. 87. 2): is divine retribution more palatable than military defeat?

[43] Dover (1974: 223); cf. pp. 259–60, 'Belief of this kind . . . is hard to reconcile with experience, even when hedged about with reservations and exceptions'.

misfortune, as Godfrey Lienhardt remarked of the Dinka, 'there is always evidence, for those who wish to refer to it, of divine justice'.[44]

However, though Herodotus' *Histories* repeatedly reflect a number of assumptions regarding divine retribution, and while certain aspects of his belief in retribution—most prominently, the story of Artayctes and Protesilaus with its moral that men should be mindful of the gods—have an evangelizing tone, it should be underlined again that Herodotus is not setting forth a consciously refined philosophy of history; his belief in retribution, like the belief in the mutability of fortune that runs parallel to it, is rather an engrained habit of understanding the world, an attitude of mind that has both shaped and been shaped by the events that Herodotus records. The selection of one of a number of divine explanations of a misfortune takes place, as we have seen, subliminally. In the story of Sabacus, he appears to take for granted that an act of sacrilege would incur some punishment. It is very doubtful then whether we can describe Herodotus' beliefs in divine retribution as a 'cosmic system of justice',[45] still less assert (with Peter Derow) that he 'subscribed to what might be called the conflict, or retributive, theory of world order of Anaximander'.[46] Certainly there are affinities between Herodotus' belief in divine retribution and the extant fragment of Anaximander, affinities revealed most clearly by Herodotus' judgement on the 'divine foresight' that ensures a balance of power between different animal species (3. 108. 2).[47] But Herodotus' religious thought is simply too untidy, too responsive, too live, too far from being a simple creed or set of dogmas (and our knowledge of Anaximander is surely too scanty), for us to be able to describe his beliefs as 'theories', or to imagine that they were susceptible to anything more than the most intangible, indirect form of 'intellectual influence'.

One other important question remains. Herodotus may believe that Paris or Pheretime were liable to divine retribution,

---

[44] Lienhardt (1961: 47).   [45] Fornara (1990: 41).

[46] Derow (1994: 78); see also here e.g. Maddalena (1950: 77–8), Immerwahr (1966: 215), Plescia (1972: 310–11) on the 'equilibratory function of the gods', A. B. Lloyd (1990: 233).

[47] For the idea of divine foresight, see Parker (1992); see also Ch. 9.

but what of less exotic figures? Was his own life similarly overshadowed by the fear of a vengeful deity? Or do such stories, projected into the more or less distant past and onto uniquely powerful or notorious figures, operate on a separate level from ordinary life?

The question is brought into particularly sharp relief by the story of Glaucus, put into the mouth of the Spartan king Leutychidas. Glaucus was not extraordinarily powerful, but had a great reputation for honesty. It is as a result of this that he is asked by a Milesian visitor to look after a sum of money on his behalf (6. 86. α2–5): for Ionia was always a risky place, whereas the Peloponnese was 'safely established' (ἀσφαλέως ἱδρυμένη, 6. 86. α4). Glaucus agrees (6. 86. β1) but when, much later, the man's sons come to collect the money, he denies all knowledge of the compact (6. 86. β2). If their story is true, he agrees, their claim is just. In three months, he tells them, he will have decided his course of action. In the meantime he goes to Delphi to consult the god as to 'whether he should steal the money by an oath' (εἰ ὅρκῳ τὰ χρήματα ληίσηται, 6. 86. γ1). The priestess replies that he can do what he wants: death awaits even the 'man who abides by his oaths' (εὔορκον, 6. 86. γ2). But there are other hidden consequences:

But the child of Oath has no name, nor does he have hands or feet (ἀλλ' Ὅρκου πάϊς ἐστὶν ἀνώνυμος, οὐδ' ἔπι χεῖρες οὐδὲ πόδες). He pursues swiftly until, having seized, he destroys the whole family and all the house. But the family of a man who abides by his oath is afterwards more blessed (ἀνδρὸς δ' εὐόρκου γενεὴ μετόπισθεν ἀμείνων).[48]

Glaucus asks for pardon, but the oracle replies that to 'ask the god and to commit the deed are equivalent' (τὸ πειρηθῆναι τοῦ θεοῦ καὶ τὸ ποιῆσαι ἴσον δύνασθαι, 6. 86. γ2).[49] That is then proved by the outcome, for although Glaucus returns the money, by the time of the narrator, the Spartan king Leutychidas, no descendant of Glaucus and no hearth bearing his name survives (6. 86. δ); Glaucus, Leutychidas adds in language echoing the fate of Solon's happy man (1. 32. 9), had

[48] Cf. Hes. Erg. 285.
[49] Contrast Mikalson (1991: 130), arguing that thoughts (in tragedy) are not punishable on the grounds of the crude dogma that 'in Greek religion what mattered was the action, not the intent and frame of mind'.

'been removed root and branch from Sparta' (ἐκτέτριπταί τε πρόρριζος ἐκ Σπάρτης, 6. 86. δ).[50]

The matter is apparently straightforward: even thinking about breaking one's oath will lead to the direst consequences. The story is told by Leutychidas in the context of his attempt to persuade the Athenians to release some Aeginetan hostages. The Athenians, not wanting to give them up, had made excuses (6. 86): they did not think it just to return the hostages to one king alone when they had been left by both. Glaucus, then, provides an example of what would happen to them should they refuse. The moral weight of the story of Glaucus is rather undermined, however, by the Athenians' response, reported by Herodotus in one abrupt sentence: 'Leutychidas, when he had said these things, and when the Athenians did not listen even then, departed' (6. 87). The moral of the story may then be precisely that moralizing is useless. Leutychidas himself, as the reader already knows, would eventually come to a bad end himself for another form of corruption: caught on campaign, red-handed with a glove full of silver, he was exiled, and his house (echoing the fate of Glaucus?) razed to the ground (6. 72).[51]

More significant, however, for the status of the Glaucus story is that the Athenians' perjury appears to go unpunished. Unlike the case of the Persian heralds—in which Herodotus assumes that the Athenians must have been punished in some way, albeit undiscoverable—in this case their oath-breaking is simply forgotten. The full story of the conflict between Aegina and Athens is very much more complex.[52] In the

---

[50] Lateiner (1989: 144): 'the historian's character Leutychides here offers what the author Herodotus shrinks from; he tells us what to make of his fable', i.e. the moral of the story that oath-breaking is punished. Havelock (1978: 300–2) manages the extraordinary feat of discussing this passage at length as if the gods played no part. For the view of childlessness or the extinction of one's *genos* as a peculiarly dreadful punishment, see Ch. 2. For the destruction of the *genos* invoked in oaths, see Parker (1983: 186–7 and n. 234). For oaths in general, see Plescia (1970), Burkert (1985a: 250–4), Aubriot (1991).

[51] For razing of houses as a remedy for pollution, see the fascinating article of Connor (1985); for the historical implications of Leutychidas' house being razed to the ground, see Connor's Appendix I (pp. 99 ff.).

[52] The Aeginetans, Herodotus' narrative continues, had not yet 'paid the punishment for their previous injustices against the Athenians' (τῶν πρότερον ἀδικημάτων δοῦναι δίκας τῶν ἐς 'Αθηναίους ὕβρισαν, 6. 87)—a gratuitous raid on Phaleron and the coast of Attica designed to please the Thebans, 5. 81—but

great confusion of reciprocal vengeance between the Aeginetans and Athenians it is just possible that the punishment
theoretically incurred by the Athenians has become lost.[53]
The Athenians' perjury, however, is far from unique.[54]
Indeed, unless one counts the eccentric conception of perjury
among the Scythians—in which the perjurer is punished only
after a lengthy process of identification through divination,
itself enormously costly in human life (4. 68–9)[55]—there are
no cases of the divine punishment of perjury in the *Histories*.
This is no reason, however, to doubt the sincerity with which
Herodotus retells the cautionary tale of Glaucus. For while
perjury may have been considered a crime liable to incur
divine wrath—and while stories such as that of Glaucus
illustrated this truth[56]—in everyday life, in a world in which
the use of oaths was taken for granted, it was neither a

now, 'thinking that they themselves had been dealt an injustice' (ἀξιοῦντες
ἀδικέεσθαι), they prepared immediately to avenge the Athenians: they seized at
Sounium an Athenian theoric ship full of the leading men of Athens. Does the
Aeginetans' own unjust behaviour in some sense mitigate the Athenians'
apparent perjury?

[53] An alternative, rather fanciful, solution would be that a great punishment
was still in store for the Athenians: so Immerwahr suggests (1966: 214),
linking this passage to 5. 89. 2, and 7. 133. 2, that 'it was an important
observation of the historian that Athens was not punished in his own lifetime
for her religious crimes'.

[54] See esp. the Phocaeans' heaping of 'strong curses' (ἰσχυρὰς κατάρας,
1. 165. 2) on any of their number who might choose to return to their city;
as they were sailing away, longing and pity seized half of them, and so,
'breaking their oaths' (ψευδόρκιοι . . . γενόμενοι), they returned home. Herodotus reports no particular hardships suffered by the Phocaeans who
remained at home: those, on the other hand, who remained true to their
oaths, went through a series of trials until they seemed, at least, to settle
successfully at Vela (1. 166–7). In the tradition of the Phocaeans' flight, their
oath is perhaps primarily important as a sign of the emotional tear involved in
their departure, or as a dramatic explanation of the split between those who
stayed and those who left. Possibly also, the fact that the Phocaeans are
breaking a promise to themselves rather than to others to some extent
mitigates their oath-breaking.

[55] Any illness suffered by the king is taken as evidence of perjury by one of
his citizens, 4. 68. See further Hartog (1988: 112 ff.).

[56] Aphorisms over oaths are common: cf. e.g. Hes. *Erga* 219 ff., *Th.* 231–2,
Theogn. 1195–6, Empedocles DK 31 B 115, Heraclitus DK 22 B 28, Soph. fr.
472, E. *Med.* 168–72, Xen. *Anab.* 2. 5. 7.

sufficiently outstanding nor, we may suspect, a sufficiently unusual offence for any single example to be related to a particular misfortune. To abide by one's oaths was simply the action of a pious man; the pious man would be rewarded with good fortune. Herodotus' *Histories* also, however, provide ample evidence of the expectation of perjury.[57]

That Herodotus believed divine retribution in general to have been a possibility in his own day is elsewhere clearly implied. The moral of the story of Artayctes and Protesilaus is precisely that the past is never simply the past (9. 120):[58] though Protesilaus may be dead and dry like the fish that spring into life in front of Artayctes, he still has the power to punish wrongdoers (9. 120. 2). Artayctes is executed by being nailed to a plank, overlooking the Hellespont, while his son is stoned before his eyes (9. 120. 4). Protesilaus—the first Greek to disembark in Asia, and immediately to die, in the course of the Trojan war[59]—points back to an earlier conflict between Greece and Asia. At the same time the identity of the Athenian commander responsible for Artayctes' notably barbaric[60] punishment—Xanthippus the father of Pericles—points forward to

[57] See esp. 1. 74. 4, 6. 23. 3–4; cf. 3. 19. 3 (Cambyses respects the oaths of the Phoenicians not to march against the Carthaginians, but only on pragmatic grounds). For relatively casual statements of the abuse of oaths, cf. P. *Leg.* 948 b-d, Xen. *Mem.* 1. 1. 19. Strepsiades shamelessly swears false oaths, Ar. *Nub.* 1232–6. Cyrus thought false oaths characteristically Greek, 1. 153. 3. For the Persian obsession with avoiding falsehood, see 1. 138. 1, 3. 27, 3. 65. 6, 3. 72. 3–5; this aspect of Persian ideology is also arguably reflected at ML 12 lines 28–9.

[58] In the words of Edith Hall (1989: 37), 'the mythical time of the "then and there", the world of heroes, exists parallel to and constantly illuminates the discourse of the "here and now"'. See further Ch. 7.

[59] Cf. H. *Il.* 2. 698–702.

[60] Hanging up a human body, either alive or dead (or displaying a human head), appears to be characteristic of barbarians, especially Persians: see 2. 121. γ2, 3. 125. 4, 4. 103. 2, 6. 30. 1, 7. 194. 1–2, 7. 238. 1, 9. 78. 3. For the association of barbarians with excessive punishment and the mistreatment of corpses, see Hall (1989: 25–7, 103–5, 158–9); for the mutilation of corpses as impious, see also e.g. 3. 16. 2, H. *Il.* 22. 395–400, *Od.* 11. 71 ff., 22. 412, Soph. *Ant.* 72–4, *Aj.* 1129 ff., E. *Phoen.* 1663, *Suppl.* 18–19, *El.* 893 ff. The killing of one's enemy's children is, however, a common Greek trait, as is stoning (1. 167. 1, 5. 38. 1, 9. 5. 2–3): see Mossman (1995: 188–90). Mossman argues (1995: 175–6) for Herodotus' approval of Artayctes' punishment on the basis of the shape of the narrative. Certainly the moral of the miracle of the

the excesses of another expansionist empire, that of the Athenians.[61] As Deborah Boedeker and others have shown, it is no accident that the story of Artayctes is positioned at the end of the final book.[62] This positioning, with the last chapters of the *Histories* echoing in various ways their opening (by the pair of references, for example, to the Persian belief that all of Asia belonged to them, 1. 4. 4, 9. 116. 3), lends an extra weight to the moral of this story. The moral of divine retribution is indeed a moral of the *Histories* as a whole. Even Herodotus' own activity in writing is itself potentially subject to divine retribution. In conclusion to his argument for the existence of two Heracles, one god and one man, he asks for kindness from gods and heroes: a safety provision apparently in the event that he might be mistaken (2. 45. 3).[63]

fish is that crimes such as his will not go unpunished; however, the fact that his punishment was in some sense divinely sanctioned need not imply that the means of it were similarly sanctioned, or that a certain stigma could not attach to the human agents of this retribution: in this way, the cycle of retribution for excessive acts of vengeance is allowed to continue.

[61] See here Fornara (1971a: ch. 3); for an argument against the suggestion that the story of Artayctes was a 'tribute' to the father of Pericles (1971a: 55–6).

[62] See esp. Boedeker (1988); also Immerwahr (1954: 26; 1966: 43), Fisher (1992: 351–2), Mossman (1995: 175–6), Moles (1996: 271–7), Dewald (1997), Griffiths (1999).

[63] See further Ch. 7. Contrast here Vandiver (1991: 139) for whom Herodotus 'appears to indicate that he recognises a certain heterodoxy in his own reason which could perhaps be offensive to traditional religious sensibilities', i.e. not his own.

5

Oracles and Divination

Divination is often seen in modern discussions as primarily a political matter, as a source of guidance for human action, a focus for decision-making, rather than a simple exercise in fortune-telling.[1] Such practical uses as divination undeniably had, however, rested upon a conviction that divination was a form of divine intervention: the means through which divinity indicated morals or the shape of future events to men. Rather than being concerned with the historical authenticity of particular oracles and prophecies,[2] or with questions of the procedure for consulting an oracle such as Delphi—Herodotus appears to take for granted knowledge of Delphic procedure (7. 111. 2)[3]—this chapter will focus instead on those areas where Herodotus provides the richest evidence: attitudes to oracles and divination, the distinctions drawn between different types of divination, and the mechanisms by which belief in divination was sustained and reinforced.

Oracles and other forms of divination—dreams, omens, or the prophecies of individuals such as Bacis or Musaeus[4]—will

---

[1] See e.g. Bremmer (1993: 153; 1994: 33); see also, in the context of Nuer prophets, D. H. Johnson's justification of the term 'mantic' in preference to 'prophecy' (1994: 35). For the political dimension of Greek divination, see esp. Parker (1985).

[2] See esp. Fontenrose (1978), Crahay (1956), Malkin (1987) on colonization oracles. See also Elayi (1979b: 67 ff.).

[3] Parke and Wormell (1956: 17–8), Parke (1967b: 42). For Delphic procedure, see Amandry (1950), Parke and Wormell (1956: ch. 3), Fontenrose (1978: ch. 7); for spirit possession, Maurizio (1995); in less depth, Lloyd-Jones (1976), Lachenaud (1978: 249 ff.), Price (1985).

[4] One form of divination that will scarcely be mentioned is necromancy, for which see 5. 92. η2–4 with Will (1953), Stern (1989), or (from a very different perspective) Pellizer (1993). For other relatively obscure forms of divination, e.g. Scythian rhabdomancy (4. 67 ff.), or for Hippias' sneeze (6. 107. 3–4), see Pritchett iii. 47 ff.

all be discussed together, the justification for this being that
they are parallel phenomena.[5] All are ways of the gods
'showing' or 'indicating' coming events, a recommended
course of action, or other lessons to men.[6] A dream came to
Croesus which 'showed him the truth of all the future evils
that would come to his son' (1. 34. 1).[7] Cyrus tells Darius'
father that 'the daimon forecast' (προέφαινε, 1. 210. 1) to him
that he would die, again through a dream.[8] By speaking of
wooden walls, the Athenians ask themselves, was the god of
Delphi indicating the ships (σημαίνειν, 7. 142. 2)? The god,
the Magi tell Xerxes in interpretation of an eclipse of the sun,
is showing the eclipse of their cities (προδεικνύει, 7. 37. 3)—for
the sun is the 'symbol' (προδέκτορα)[9] of the Greeks and the
moon of the Persians. Omens such as those inflicted on Chios,
the death by disease of all but two of a hundred young men
sent as a chorus to Delphi, the death of all but one of one
hundred and twenty children when the roof of their school
collapsed, though also disasters in their own right, are seen as
signals given by god to men—tokens of further misfortunes
(6. 27): 'there tends to be some sign in advance when great
misfortunes are about to occur to a city or a people . . . These
signs the god showed them of what was to come.'[10] The omen
is fulfilled, as oracles are fulfilled, through the future evils
that it presages. So similarly the earthquake at Delos is
fulfilled, and made comprehensible for Herodotus—there is
'nothing unreasonable', he says, in the fact that Delos was
shaken for the first time in these circumstances—by the fact
that in the generations of Darius, Xerxes, and Artaxerxes,

[5] This is recognized by Crahay (1956). For the unusual respect shown by
Herodotus towards prophets such as Bacis, see Asheri (1993: 63).

[6] Fornara (1990: 39). Cf. H. *Il*. 1. 62–3, Aesch. *PV* 484 ff., Soph. *El*. 498–
50, E. *IT* 570 ff., Xen. *Hipp*. 9. 9. Shimron (1989: 39) claims that oracles 'are
not supernatural occurrences in the strict sense, but rather human experiences
based on belief'. What then are supernatural occurrences? The vocabulary of
divine intervention is illustrated in a number of tables by Lachenaud (1978:
182 ff.).

[7] οἱ τὴν ἀληθείην ἔφαινε τῶν μελλόντων γενέσθαι κακῶν κατὰ τὸν παῖδα.

[8] See also 3. 65. 4: it was the Magus Smerdis whom the daimon had
indicated to Cambyses in his dream (προέφαινε).

[9] A word coined from προδείκνυμι: see How and Wells, ad loc.

[10] φιλέει δέ κως προσημαίνειν, εὖτ' ἂν μέλλῃ μεγάλα κακὰ ἢ πόλι ἢ ἔθνεϊ ἔσεσθαι . . .
ταῦτα μέν σφι σημήια ὁ θεὸς προέδεξε.

there was more suffering in Greece than in the twenty
preceding generations (6. 98. 2).[11]

No form of divination is seen by Herodotus as in its essence
suspect. Although he observes that the Egyptians believe that
the gift or skill of prophecy (μαντική) belongs only to gods, never
to men (2. 83), he draws no such distinction himself, either
implicitly or explicitly.[12] Indeed his clearest statement of his
belief in divination is made in the context of a prophecy of Bacis
(8. 77). Though omens or dreams may not be corruptible at
source, as it were, in the same sense as oracles or prophecies, the
possibility of corruption exists, as we will see, at least in their
interpretation. All forms of divination also require interpretation. The question of whether man or god is responsible for
misinterpretation is asked equally whether it be in the context of
dreams or oracles. 'You are not responsible' (αἴτιος), Croesus
tells Adrastus of his son Atys' death, 'except in so far as you
committed the act unwillingly, but one of the gods [is respons-
ible] who long ago forecast to me what would happen'—through
a dream (προεσήμαινε τὰ μέλλοντα ἔσεσθαι, 1. 45. 2). Later he
explains to Cyrus why he had started a war against him. 'I did
these things for your good fortune and my own bad fortune: the
god of the Greeks was responsible for these things by encouraging me to go to war' (αἴτιος, 1. 87. 3). The god had, of course,
encouraged him on this occasion through the oracle at Delphi.

Never, moreover, does Herodotus draw any distinction
between consciously solicited (or 'besought') and unsolicited
forms of divination. It is a distinction at any rate often
confounded in practice. Dreams might be said to be the
archetypally unsolicited form of divination, but the Nasamonians sleep by the tombs of their ancestors in the expectation of
a dream: this is their regular form of divination (4. 172. 3).[13]

---

[11] Such fulfilment might be thought rather vague, but so are the terms of
many oracles, e.g. 5. 90. 2.

[12] The distinction between human and divine μαντική is a common one, e.g.
Soph. *Ajax* 1418–20, *OT* 497–503, 707–9, E. *El.* 399–400, *Phoen.* 958–9.
Often criticisms of human μαντική are contradicted by the course of events,
e.g. Soph. *OT*, E. *Phoen.*; however, these occasions involve the prophet
Tiresias, the only man, *OT* 298–9, in whom the truth is implanted. For the
Egyptian distinction of human and divine μαντική, see Lloyd ii. 346 ff.

[13] For techniques of inducing dreams, Dodds (1951: 110 ff.), van Lieshout
(1970: 231–2). Nasamonian incubation was still practised in the same area of

Conversely, even the Delphic oracle frequently gives answers which are apparently irrelevant to any question posed to it.[14] Spartans are told to liberate Athens, regardless of their purpose in consultation, regardless also of whether they had come on private or public business (5. 63. 1). Grinnus is told to found a colony after asking 'about other matters' (περὶ ἄλλων, 4. 150. 3).[15] Battus asks about his stammer, and when in response he is told to colonize Libya, complains of the irrelevance of Apollo's answer (4. 155. 3–4): 'Lord, I came to ask you about my voice, but you tell me other impossible things, ordering me to colonize Libya.'[16] Lycurgus is told that he is a god before he has apparently even opened his mouth (1. 65. 2–3). When Herodotus records an oracular response without any question,[17] or when enquiries—like the Spartans' enquiry 'about the war' (7. 120. 3)—are so vague as to be essentially open-ended, the point is reinforced: when a man consults an oracle, he must be open-minded about the consequences. It may very well be, of course, that in practice there was a much greater degree of correlation between questions and answers, that on many occasions oracles followed the promptings of their consultants.[18] Had all responses been so dangerously unpredictable, an oracle may well have alienated its clientèle.[19] Such a gap

---

Africa in the nineteenth century: Pritchett iii. 92 ff., Camps (1985: 55). For incubation at the shrine of Amphiaraus, forbidden to Thebans, cf. 8. 34.

[14] See also here Parke (1962) on αὐτοματίζω.

[15] Malkin (1987: 27–8, 64–5) suggests that the theme of the 'surprise oikist' originates in an attempt to improve the leader's authority: 'a leader malgré lui always appears more credible.'

[16] See also 9. 33. 2 (Teisamenus), 6. 19. 2, 77. 2 (the common oracle to the Argives and Milesians). In this last case, the Milesians had not even consulted the oracle on any question: Parker (1985: 318 n. 72) suggests mitigating circumstances; see also Bury's solution (1902) to the problem of the Pythia's digression into irrelevant affairs, 'something quite outside the range of probability'.

[17] e.g. 2. 133. 1 (Mycerinus), 5. 90. 2 (Cleomenes' prophecies concerning Athenians).

[18] N. D. Smith (1989: 154). For the suggestion that the oracle of the wooden walls was the result of a well-formulated question of Themistocles, see Burn (1962: 357), Labarbe (1957: 119), Hands (1965: 60).

[19] Parker (1985: 299): 'it was obviously hazardous to consult the Pythia even about crop-failure if she was liable to respond with a demand, for instance, to "recall all exiles".'

between the myth and the reality of Delphi may arguably have
served a useful function, however: of feeding its authority and
reputation for independence.[20]

Different forms of divination are also interchangeable in so
far as they provide motivation for men. The Persian general
Otanes decided to repopulate Samos after a dream and after
contracting a disease of the genitals (3. 149). The Athenians
hurry to evacuate the city both out of a desire to obey the
oracle given them and because of the ill omen of the desertion
of the snake from the Acropolis (8. 41. 2–3). Polycrates goes to
meet the satrap Oroites and his death—despite the discouragement of his 'prophets' (μαντίων), his friends, and his daughter's
dream of his impending execution (3. 124. 1). Dreams, oracles
and omens may reinforce or complement each other. Just as
the Corinthian Bacchiads only grasp the necessity of their
killing Cypselus when they put two oracles together
(5. 92. β3–γ1), so the Ethiopian king Sabacus puts a dream
and an oracle together (2. 139). Sabacus receives a dream
tempting him to commit an act of sacrilege, which, if committed, would inevitably be punished. But he then remembers
an oracle which he had received in Ethiopia 'that he was
destined to be king of Egypt for fifty years' (ὡς δέοι αὐτὸν
Αἰγύπτου βασιλεῦσαι ἔτεα πεντήκοντα): sidestepping fate apparently, he leaves Egypt. Herodotus defends his view that there
was nothing unreasonable or unlikely in an earthquake taking
place on Delos for the first time by citing an oracle that
predicted an earthquake there (6. 98. 3).[21] Often an oracle is
consulted as a consequence, even as a means of interpretation,
of an omen. The Cnidians' response to the miraculous number
of injuries incurred in digging a canal across the Isthmus
connecting their city to the mainland was to consult Delphi
as to what it was that was obstructing them: the god told

---

[20] Parker (1985: 300): 'divination fails of its function if its objectivity is not
effectively demonstrated. Though clients seldom go away with an answer that
is unsatisfactory, the possibility must always be present. Divination is a drama
that leads through many a perilous reversal to a satisfactory dénouement.' The
authority of an oracular response must also have been enhanced if it was
solicited (Parker 1985: 298, followed by Morgan 1990: 154)—and also if it was
as hoped or expected.

[21] Cf. 9. 93–4: the gods announce through Delphi that they mean to grant
Euenius the gift of prophecy.

them—unequivocally—to stop digging (1. 174. 3–5).[22] The
omen of the injuries to the Cnidians and the consultation of
Delphi together constitute a single episode. There are similarly
a number of cases of the consultation of an oracle following
plagues, the sudden failure of harvests, or the failure of
animals or women to reproduce.[23]

Oracles also operate in tandem with what one might
describe as 'accidental prophecies'. An oracle is given to the
Spartans advising them to ask Xerxes for justice for the death
of their king Leonidas (8. 114. 1). This oracle is then diverted,
as it were, through a whimsical remark of Xerxes' that turns
out to be prophetic. Xerxes, when asked by Spartan ambassadors for some compensation, laughed in their faces, and as
Mardonius chanced to be standing next to him, told them that
Mardonius would 'pay whatever price was fitting' (δίκας δώσει
τοιαύτας οἵας ἐκείνοισι πρέπει, 8. 114. 2). Xerxes presumably
had no intention that Mardonius should indeed pay the price
for Leonidas' death with his own at Plataea: 'so justice for the
death of Leonidas was according to the oracle satisfied for the
Spartans by Mardonius' (ἐνθαῦτα ἥ τε δίκη τοῦ φόνου τοῦ
Λεωνίδεω κατὰ τὸ χρηστήριον τοῖσι Σπαρτιήτῃσι ἐκ Μαρδονίου
ἐπετελέετο, 9. 64. 1).[24]

The distinction between institutionalized prophecies and
random omens can be seen to be broken down still further in
the traditional, local account recorded by Herodotus of the
origins of the oracle at Dodona (2. 55. 1–2). Two black doves

---

[22] See Ch. 3. For the genuineness of the oracle, see Kebric (1983: Appendix 1).

[23] e.g. 1. 167. 1–2; 4. 149. 2, 151. 1; 5. 82. 1; 6. 139; 9. 93. 3–4; cf. Soph. *OT*
22 ff.

[24] On this passage see Solmsen (1944: 243), Lateiner (1980: 31–2), but esp.
now the excellent Asheri (1998). Cf. the case of the Pelasgians, 6. 138–40: in
punishment for the Pelasgians' killing of their Attic wives and children, their
land bore no fruit, their women and flocks no offspring. They are ordered by
Delphi to pay whatever price the Athenians demand. But when the Athenians
lay out a sumptuous banquet in their *prytaneion* and ask the Pelasgians to
hand over their land in a similar state, the Pelasgians promise to do so only
when a ship travels from Athenian territory to Lemnos with a northerly wind.
Miltiades contrives the fulfilment of this accidental prophecy by treating the
Athenian Chersonese as Attica. He has to remind the Pelasgians of the oracle.
The Hephaistians accept his interpretation, the people of Myrina do not and
so he captures their town by seige.

came from Egyptian Thebes, one to Libya, the other to Dodona (2. 55. 1) . . .[25]

and this one, sitting on an oak tree, proclaimed in a human voice that it was necessary for an oracle of Zeus to be there (ὡς χρεὸν εἴη μαντήιον αὐτόθι Διὸς γενέσθαι); and the people believed that this message to them was divine (αὐτοὺς ὑπολαβεῖν θεῖον εἶναι τὸ ἐπαγγελλόμενον αὐτοῖσι) and so acted accordingly (2. 55. 2).[26]

How does an oracle become an oracle except by its first utterance being deduced to be divine? Oracles are merely customary, long-established sources of insight into the divine.[27]

Any flippant, accidental remark may indeed turn out in retrospect to be prophetic.[28] When Darius, for example, arrives to lay siege to Babylon, the Babylonians come out onto their walls to taunt him, and one of the Babylonians 'made this remark' (εἶπε τοῦτο τὸ ἔπος, 3. 151. 2): 'why do you sit here, Persians? why don't you go away? When mules give birth to foals, then you'll capture us.' The anonymous Babylonian said this, of course, 'in no way imagining that a mule would give birth to a foal' (οὐδαμὰ ἐλπίζων ἂν ἡμίονον τεκεῖν). But nineteen months later, when Darius' army and every possible stratagem seemed to be exhausted (3. 152), a mule did indeed give birth to a foal (3. 153). Zopyrus saw it and deduced that Babylon would be captured—for he realized that 'that man had spoken with divine inspiration' (σὺν γὰρ θεῷ ἐκεῖνον . . . εἰπεῖν)—and devised a sophisticated plan, enormously costly in the lives of Darius' own men, whereby Babylon was eventually captured. Similarly the Spartan king Leutychidas asks a Samian commander with whom he is contracting a treaty for his name, and on discover-

[25] For a modern rationalization of Herodotus' own rationalization, see Parke (1967a: 52 ff.).

[26] For the association of birds, foreign women, and prophecy, cf. Aesch. *Ag.* 1050–2, Soph. *Trach.* 1060, *Ant.* 1002, E. *Bacch.* 1034–5, Ar. *Av.* 199–200, *Ran.* 679–82, *Pax* 681; see further Harrison (1998a).

[27] The fact that Delphi lent its stamp of approval to the prophetic powers of Euenius, 9. 93–4, suggests, however, that Delphi did not consider itself in competition with individual prophets, but that there was a difference of kind. See also Suarez de la Torre (1992) for the origins of Melampus' powers of prophecy (Apollodorus 1. 9. 11).

[28] Cf. Liebeschütz (1979: 25–6) for similar chance words and deeds in Roman republican divination.

ing it—he is Hegesistratus or 'Army-leader'—accepts it as an omen (οἰωνὸν, 9. 91). Herodotus questions in passing whether Leutychidas had asked for the Samian's name in conscious search of an omen (κληδόνος εἴνεκεν) or whether the 'accident was of a god's making' (κατὰ συντυχίην θεοῦ ποιεῦντος, 9. 91. 1):[29] there is perhaps an implication that an omen is devalued if so contrived. Either way, however, what such stories reveal is that, just as any chance event may turn out with hindsight to have been divine, so any chance remark too may do so: potential omens and prophecies are everywhere.[30]

Human wisdom too may be prophetic.[31] Croesus initially dismissed Solon's advice (1. 33), but on the pyre he realizes that Solon had spoken 'with divine inspiration' (σὺν θεῷ, 1. 86. 3).[32] Here is a pattern common to all types of prophecy or divination: rejection, forgetfulness, or mistaken interpretation are followed by surprise fulfilment and repentance.[33] Solon's advice to Croesus is fulfilled in detail through the fulfilment of the oracle concerning his dumb son (1. 85. 2): his son would speak for the first time on an 'unfortunate day'. His first words were spoken to save his father Croesus' life (1. 85. 4)— just as he seemed to have realized the truth of what Solon had told him that death was better than life (1. 85. 3, 1. 31. 3).[34] On

---

[29] Even a sigh may be an omen: 2. 175. 5. For parallel cases of the phenomenon of the *nomen omen* which 'hides mysterious workings in the scheme of things', see Bowra (1964: 211 ff.), Pritchett iii. 135, Somville (1989), and further below, Appendix 2. The term κληδών is used also of the (more conventionally oracular) order given by the priestess of Athena to Cleomenes, 5. 72. 4, an omen fulfilled by the expulsion of Cleomenes: for this incident, see now Parker (1998a).

[30] A good illustration of this is Xen. *Anab.* 3. 2. 9.

[31] Cf. also Nitocris, 1. 187, on whom see now Dillery (1992), Chilon's prophecy concerning Cythera, 7. 235. 2 (with Fornara 1981: 151), and Dicaeus and Demaratus, 8. 65 (discussed Ch. 3). Cf. Soph. *OC* 1516–7 (Oedipus a prophet), H. *Od.* 1. 200 ff. (Athena in mortal disguise prophesies—while warning that she is not a prophet), Pindar fr. 150 Snell (μαντεύο, Μοῖσα, προφατεύσω δ'ἐγώ). There is a grey line on occasions between the oath or curse and the prophecy, in so far as oaths and curses also are capable of fulfilment: see e.g. 1. 165. 2–3, 3. 75. 3; cf. H. *Il.* 233 ff.

[32] Stahl (1975: 13): 'the phrase . . . εἰρημένον σὺν θεῷ raises his warning to the rank of a prophecy.' Cf. Aesch. *Ag.* 1084 with Fraenkel, ad loc.

[33] Cf. Ariston's casual comment on his paternity of Demaratus, 6. 63.

[34] Parke and Wormell (1956: i. 138): 'The story . . . is true to nature, in that some forms of dumbness can be overcome by a sudden nervous shock.'

this occasion, the fulfilment of the oracle given to Croesus is, in a sense, subordinate to the fulfilment of Solon's wisdom. The wise adviser indeed, the figure whose advice, like prophecies, is usually neglected until too late, is himself akin to a prophet. As Xerxes tells another such figure, Demaratus, 'everything has turned out as you said' (ὅσα γὰρ εἶπας, ἅπαντα ἀπέβη οὕτω, 7. 234. 1).

All forms of divination—oracles, dreams, prophecies, accidental prophecies and omens—need then to be discussed in parallel. A central question awaits. How did Herodotus sustain a belief in the validity of divination, that is in the belief that divination provided a genuine means of eliciting knowledge from the gods?

The answer that Herodotus himself gives—at least in the context of prophecies—is a very simple one: prophecies are worth taking seriously because they are true (8. 77):

I am not able to speak against prophecies as not being true (Χρησμοῖσι δὲ οὐκ ἔχω ἀντιλέγειν ὡς οὐκ εἰσὶ ἀληθέες), not wishing to impugn those that speak clearly (ἐναργέως λέγοντας) . . . Looking on such things and seeing that Bacis speaks so clearly (οὕτω ἐναργέως λέγοντι Βάκιδι), I do not dare myself to say anything in contradiction of prophecies, nor allow others to do so (ἀντιλογίας χρησμῶν πέρι οὔτε αὐτὸς λέγειν τολμέω οὔτε παρ' ἄλλων ἐνδέκομαι).[35]

There is a clear sense here that, if some prophecies speak 'so clearly', it is necessary to give the benefit of the doubt to prophecies as a whole. There is perhaps even an element of religious dread in his last words, a sense that those who deny the truth of all prophecies are not to be listened to. But in what sense do prophecies speak 'clearly'? The word is clearly in some sense limiting. Herodotus acknowledges by implication

---

[35] For an argument against the deletion of this chapter from the text, see Asheri (1993: 65 ff.). Asheri demonstrates brilliantly that the prophecy refers metaphorically to a bridge of ships across the bay of Marathon (1993: 66 ff.), suggesting (p. 71) that the prophecy had been recycled by the addition of the word περσάντες with the result that it was appropriate only to Salamis. That Herodotus is aware of the possibility of oracles being recycled is clear from 9. 43, for which see below, this chapter. See also here Darbo-Peschanski (1987: 81). For the process by which Bacis, Musaeus, etc. became canonized, see Prandi (1993).

the possibility of scepticism towards such prophecies,[36] that some are more 'clear' than others, and indeed that some prophecies are untrue. Essentially there are two possibilities: does Bacis speak clearly in the sense that the outcome of the war, the meaning of his prophecy, could easily have been understood at the time of its being given, in other words that the prophecy was unambiguous,[37] or in the sense that (in retrospect) the outcome was clearly foretold?[38]

Nowhere else is the impression given that clarity is a desirable characteristic in a prophecy; it is very possible indeed, as we will see, that a degree of obscurity is demanded.[39] It is the clear fulfilment of prophecy then that is the chief ground for belief in its validity. Indeed, just as individual miracles imply the moral that men should believe in the intervention of the gods in human affairs, so the fulfilment of divination makes a similar point: that men should give at least the benefit of the doubt to divination, and that the gods are present in human affairs. Another illustration of this is a prophecy of Lysistratus fulfilled through the battle of Salamis. Salamis saw apparently a whole body of prophecies fulfilled, so

[36] Possibly Herodotus had the sophists in his sights here (Radermacher 1898: 501). For the implications of this passage see also Müller (1981: 317), Darbo-Peschanski (1987: 83), Masaracchia, ad loc. (p. 196).

[37] See e.g. Shimron (1989: 39): '8. 77 cannot be applied to oracles which for some reason are not "clear" or "unambiguous"'; cf. Asheri (1993: 65 ff.), arguing that Herodotus is polemical not only against those who believe in no prophecies, but also against those who believe in all prophecies indiscriminately (p. 72). Van Lieshout takes the view (1980: 50 n. 24) that ἐνάργεια refers here narrowly to the topographical indications of the prophecy; the term in general describes the vivid nature of the vision rather than the clarity of its meaning (1980: 18–19). The same question mark hangs over the description as 'very clear' of Hipparchus' dream the day before his death (ἐναργεστάτην, 5. 55). The text here can be emended to fit one's preferred meaning: see van Lieshout (1980: 49 n. 23). When Xerxes asks Artabanus whether he would still have given the same advice had the vision not appeared so clearly to him (ἐναργὴς, 7. 47. 1), it can only be the dream itself that is vivid, as it has not been fulfilled.

[38] Cf. Legrand (1937: 282–3), criticizing Panitz (1935): 'Le chapitre 77 n'exprime pas une velléité de concession d'un esprit fort à une opinion qu'il juge superstitieuse; c'est une profession de foi.' Elayi similarly (1978: 95) sees it as a passionate profession of faith.

[39] See below, this chapter, for interpretation.

many that Herodotus specifies this one alone by way of illustration (8. 96. 2):[40]

But a west wind carrying away many of the wrecks drove them on the shore of Attica which is called Colias, so as to fulfil both all the other prophecies delivered by Bacis and Musaeus concerning this sea battle and also that relating to the wrecks carried onto this shore, a prophecy delivered many years earlier by Lysistratus, an Athenian man and a prophet, which had not been understood by any of the Greeks (ὥστε ἀποπλησθῆναι τὸν χρησμὸν τόν τε ἄλλον πάντα τὸν περὶ τῆς ναυμαχίης ταύτης εἰρημένον Βάκιδι καὶ Μουσαίῳ, καὶ δὴ καὶ κατὰ τὰ ναυήγια τὰ ταύτῃ ἐξενειχθέντα τὸ εἰρημένον πολλοῖσι ἔτεσι πρότερον τούτων ἐν χρησμῷ Λυσιστράτῳ Ἀθηναίῳ ἀνδρὶ χρησμολόγῳ, τὸ ἐλελήθεε πάντας τοὺς Ἕλληνας): 'the Colian women shall do their roasting with oars'. This was to happen after the departure of the King.

The fact of Lysistratus' prophecy being given so many years before the battle is particular proof of its truth. It stands especially well then as an example of the others.[41]

A similar 'profession of faith'[42] in the possibility of divination through dreams is implicit in the story of the dreams that visit Xerxes and Artabanus at the beginning of Book 7. Herodotus never makes any explicit judgement, but the length of the episode and its crucial position in the *Histories,* immediately before the launching of Xerxes' expedition, suggest as with the encounter of Solon and Croesus in Book 1 that it is serving some programmatic function. Xerxes is persuaded—by a coalition of Mardonius, the Thessalian Aleuadae, the Peisistratids and the seer Onomacritus—to undertake a campaign against Greece (7. 5–7. 1), and summons the leading Persians to tell them so (7. 8): 'the god leads us on', he tells them, from conquest to conquest; 'it is by remaining constantly active that our fortune increases' (7. 8. α1). Artabanus advises against the campaign (7. 10). Xerxes tells Artabanus off for his 'foolish words' (7. 11. 1); he, Xerxes, 'well understands' (εὖ ἐπιστάμενος, 7. 11. 2) that he

---

[40] Carrière argues convincingly (1988: 242) that this prophecy has been recycled from a sixth-century context.

[41] Cf. Soph. *OT* 461–2, where Tiresias makes one prophecy the test of his prophetic powers in general, and Soph. *El.* 495–501 where the chorus announces that prophecy is impossible through dreams or oracles if Clytemnestra's dream is not fulfilled. The logic here is similar to that of the idea that successful retribution for injustice proves the existence of the gods: see Ch. 4.

[42] See Legrand, quoted above, n. 38.

has no choice, that if he does not attack the Greeks, they will surely attack him and take all that he possesses. When night falls, however, Artabanus' opinion begins to play on his mind, and he changes his view (7. 12. 1). A dream comes to him warning him against this change of mind (7. 12. 2),[43] but in the light of day he takes 'no account of the dream' (7. 13. 1); he summons the Persians in order to cancel the campaign and to apologize to Artabanus. That night the dream comes again, however, reprimanding him for making light of his first dream, and warning him that, if he fails to undertake the campaign, just as he became great in a short time, so equally quickly he will become wretched (7. 14). Xerxes confides in Artabanus, and suggests a plan to him: Artabanus should put on the King's clothes, sit on the throne and sleep in his bed, and then if it was indeed God who sent the dream, and if it was pleasing to God that they should invade Greece, the dream would come to Artabanus (7. 14. 3). Artabanus, however, has an altogether different explanation of dreams (7. 16. β1–γ1):

Now, however, after you have changed your mind for the better, you say that, since you have given up the expedition against the Greeks, a dream has come to you, sent by some god (θεοῦ τινος πομπῇ), which forbids you to abandon the enterprise. But these things, my boy, are not divine (θεῖα). I am many years older than you, and dreams that wander among men are such as I will explain to you. These visions of dreams that hover around men more often than not concern things which worry us during the day; in the last few days, we have been much busied about this expedition. If, however, this is not such as I judge, but has something divine in it (τι τοῦ θείου μετέχον), you have correctly summed up the whole in few words: then let it appear and give the same injunction to me as to you.[44]

[43] This 'passive type' of dream is most frequent in Herodotus and Homer (van Lieshout 1980: 14). There is certainly a Homeric flavour to the story of Artabanus and Xerxes (see also Stein, ad loc.), but this need not undermine the passage as evidence for Herodotus' beliefs. Fehling uses the Homeric tone of the passage to support the case for its invention (1989: 204): 'No Persians— with or without quotation marks—dreamt up this story. It was Greeks, Greeks who knew their Aeschylus and their Homer.' Van Lieshout (1970: 225–7) finds, I think, an implausible degree of subtlety behind the terminology of this passage. For dreams (purportedly in Greek literature in general, but primarily in Homer), see also Kessels (1978).

[44] Fornara (1990: 36 ff.): Herodotus 'gives every indication that he understands both sides of the question'. How and Wells, ad loc., judge this 'the

Artabanus too leaves room for doubt: even if the dream did not
appear to him, if it were to appear to Xerxes this would still be
something to take notice of; if it were to appear repeatedly to
Xerxes, even he 'would say that this was divine' (φαίην ἂν καὶ
αὐτὸς θεῖον εἶναι, 7. 16. γ2).[45]
   Artabanus protests against the charade of dressing in Xerxes'
clothes (7. 16. γ) and then does so (7. 17. 1).[46] The dream then
comes to him, the same dream that had come twice to Xerxes.
The dream tells Artabanus that he will not escape punishment
for his attempt to 'turn aside what was necessary' (ἀποτρέπων τὸ
χρεὸν γενέσθαι, 7. 17. 2). The dream was on the point of putting
hot irons into Artabanus' eyes when he leapt up and ran to
Xerxes (7. 18. 1).[47] Even now Artabanus (or Herodotus) cannot
resist reciting the solid Solonian grounds on which he had
discouraged Xerxes from the campaign (7. 18. 2–3). Artabanus
concludes, however, with a clear misreading of the dream
(7. 18. 3):

But since some divine impulse has sprung up (δαιμονίη τις γίνεται
ὁρμή), and some heaven-sent destruction, as it seems, is overtaking
the Greeks (Ἕλληνας, ὡς οἶκε, φθορή τις καταλαμβάνει θεήλατος), I
myself am converted and my opinion is changed. Make known then
to the Persians those messages from the god, and command them to

best explanation' of dreams, 'however insufficient'. See also Björk's comparison of ancient and modern dreams (1946: 306): 'les hommes du temps jadis
ne rêvaient pas qu'ils montaient en avion, qu'ils prenaient un verre de café
noir ou qu'ils assistaient à la conférence de Dumbarton Oaks. Mais je ne
vois aucune raison pour supposer que leur manière même de rêver, leurs
accessoires matériels mis à part, ait différé sensiblement de la nôtre.'

[45] Van Lieshout (1970: 229–30) suggests that the truth of the dream
depends on its repetition and ἐνάργεια.

[46] For echoes of a Near-Eastern 'rite of substitution', see Germain (1956),
but see now Köhnken (1988: esp. 38–9); for Homeric parallels, Gärtner
(1983). Immerwahr (1954: 35) makes the nice suggestion that this garment
exchange, like Croesus' testing of the Delphic and other oracles, 1. 46. 2 ff., or
Polycrates' 'attempt to change fate', was bound to be futile. See, however,
now Christ (1994: 189–97), arguing against the notion that Herodotus
disapproves of Croesus' test. Herodotus' attitude is not so much one of
disapproval as of wry detachment: Croesus was trying to attain an impossible
degree of certainty.

[47] This blinding is a symbol of castration according to Maxwell-Stuart
(1976: 358–9); contrast, however, van Lieshout (1970: 228 n. 1).

follow the orders first given by you for the preparations, and act so that, since the god commands it, nothing on your part may be wanting.

Artabanus' 'rationalist' explanation of dreams is introduced for the sole purpose of being contradicted.[48] Just as Croesus had tested the oracles, so Artabanus and Xerxes test their dream to discover that it is divine. But the attempt to attain certainty just as certainly fails. Artabanus and Xerxes indeed make just the same mistake as Croesus in supposing that it is the Greeks rather than they themselves who are destined for destruction.[49] Whether Herodotus believed that Artabanus' rationalization of dreams applied to only a handful or the majority of dreams is a question on which speculation is fruitless: a belief that all dreams came from the gods—that none were, as it were, blanks—seems substantially harder to sustain.[50] What is

[48] 'What [the reader] learns here . . . is that Xerxes' decision was preordained', Fornara (1990: 44). (See also Fornara's treatment (1990: 35–6) of Atys, 'a typical rationalist', 1. 39.) 7. 12–18 shows (Immerwahr 1954: 33) that 'a necessity does indeed exist for Xerxes'. Shimron (1989: 52) fights a rearguard action on the dreams of Artabanus and Xerxes: 'at least it must be admitted that he does not call it divine and indicates doubts.'

[49] On a later occasion, Xerxes and Artabanus come very close to seeing the truth, 7. 47. Shimron's attempt (1989: 51–3) to show Herodotus to be keen in these chapters to dissociate himself from a belief in dreams is extremely unconvincing: Herodotus' use of the term λέγεται may not even reflect doubts about the historicity of the episode, let alone doubts over the divine nature of dreams; Shimron's idea that the fact that the apparition is 'a big man who is never named or called divine' shows 'some mental—perhaps unconscious—reservation', or that what Herodotus presents is a 'historical and political exposition' with the supernatural element 'reduced . . . as much as possible' are hard to dispute—as they are sheer prejudice.

[50] Cf. West's remark (1987: 264) that Herodotus 'may be assumed to have shared with prudent Penelope (Od. 19. 560–9) and his own wise Artabanus . . . the belief that many dreams are without significance'; she does allow that Herodotus thinks that some dreams (e.g. that of Sabacus, 2. 139) are more than random. Van Lieshout (1980: 6) holds that Artabanus' speech, 7. 16. β1–γ1, probably represents Herodotus' own opinion, and again (p. 41) that 'the very mention of this theory in its generality—admittedly to give a dramatic turn to the story—can well betray that for Herodotus dreams were taken to be significant only in exceptional cases.' Elsewhere van Lieshout (1970: 245) argues on the basis of the story of Artabanus that 'in exceptional cases, in which the dream repeats itself and possesses a special ἐνάργεια, he acknowledges the divine origin of the dream'. It is surely likely that Herodotus would

clear, however, is that divine intervention through dreams can
occur—even (or especially?) at crucial historical intersections
such as the Persian debate on the expedition to Greece. As the
evidence of Xenophon's *Anabasis* suggests, moreover, the
belief in the divine origin of dreams was not one projected
back into a world of larger-than-life figures: dreams could
provide a regular source of everyday guidance.[51]

The dreams sent to Xerxes and Artabanus are clearly
intended to deceive.[52] It could not fairly be said then that
they have been misinterpreted in the same way as Croesus
misinterpreted his dream concerning Atys. Though a subsequent dream in which Xerxes wore a garland of olive
branches that reached out over the whole earth and then
suddenly vanished (7. 19) might be said to offer Xerxes a
final chance to see where his campaign was leading,[53] it is
harder to see any way in which Xerxes and Artabanus could be
responsible for their misinterpretation, unless proper interpretation can take the form of brazen—and, in the case of
Artabanus, brave—disregard. Full discussion of these problems will be deferred until the discussion of 'Fate and Human
Responsibility' in Chapter 9. However, one final problem
emerges with the dreams of Xerxes and Artabanus. In the

not have interpreted all dreams alike as significant (as apparently imagined by
Frisch (1968: 60–1)—compare the idea, *Od.* 2. 181–2, that birds' flight cannot
always be construed as providing an omen—but this should not obscure the
positive programmatic nature of the story of Xerxes and Artabanus. For other
explanations of dreams in supernatural terms, even in ancient philosophical
texts, see van Lieshout (1980: 140–1).

[51] Xen. *Anab.* 3. 1. 1, 3. 1. 11–14, 4. 3. 8–9, 6. 1. 22.

[52] That the dreams are *intended* to deceive seems to me self-evident, as to
e.g. Lloyd-Jones (1971: 61), despite the assertions of Immerwahr (1954: 34–
5), von Fritz (1967: i. 249), van Lieshout (1970: 227) and West (1987: 264–5).
Parallels for divine deception can be seen in the cases of Sabacus, 2. 139, and
(on my interpretation, Ch. 9) Miltiades, 6. 134–5. (Christ's argument that the
cases of Sabacus and Artabanus are distinct in so far as Sabacus' dream 'makes
no provision for punishment should he disobey' (1994: 196) misses the point
that Sabacus obeys the *original* oracle.) The idea that gods do lie through
dreams or other forms of divination can be seen at e.g. H. *Il.* 2. 6, *Od.* 16. 194–
5, Aesch. *Ag.* 477–8, E. *Ion* 1536–7, *IT* 570 ff., *Hel.* 744 ff., *Rhes.* 65–7. The
threat made in Artabanus' dream (7. 17. 2) of disaster in the event of their
failure to invade Europe is the heart of the lie: this is, of course, what will
happen if they do go ahead.

[53] Marinatos (1982: 262).

case of Croesus' dream of Atys, the dream is fulfilled—despite all Croesus' precautions—by Atys' death. In the case of another deceptive dream, Sabacus' vision of cutting all the priests of Egypt in half, the fulfilment of the dream is avoided by Sabacus' failing to fulfil the necessary condition: he realizes that the gods had shown him the dream 'as a pretext so that, committing an impiety, he should receive some evil from gods or men' (2. 139. 2),[54] and so he refuses to respond to the dream's promptings. In what sense, however, are the dreams of Xerxes and Artabanus capable of fulfilment? Would terrible consequences *really* have followed had Xerxes disregarded the dreams and stayed at home?[55] Or are those consequences— Xerxes being made small as quickly as he had come to great- ness—ironically fulfilled by his obedience to the god's warning?

No such problems arise in the case of Herodotus' belief in omens. The omen of the Delos earthquake (6. 98), for example, may only be fulfilled in vague terms but it is precisely on the grounds that the earthquake is fulfilled—through the concen- tration of misfortunes in the reigns of Darius, Xerxes, and Artaxerxes—that Herodotus judges that there was 'nothing unreasonable' in Delos being shaken for the first time. Simi- larly, the misfortunes that occur to the Chians are 'classified' as omens by Herodotus on the grounds that they forebode further impending evils (6. 27), on the grounds, in other words, that further misfortunes took place. (Had those further evils not occurred, we may speculate, they would very probably have been seen simply as large blots on the otherwise uninterrupted record of Chian prosperity.) It is indeed the potential for fulfilment that distinguishes an omen from a pure miracle.[56]

As such omens demonstrate, however, fulfilment may take a

[54] Van Lieshout's description of Sabacus' dream as 'an order to kill political opponents' (1980: 11) does not inspire confidence. For Sabacus, see Ch. 4.

[55] There is certainly no evidence of a threat of civil unrest: the Persians are, in fact, extremely unhappy about Xerxes' plans (7. 10. α1) and delighted at his temporary abandonment of them (7. 13. 3).

[56] A miracle that promises a more precise fulfilment arguably is the epiphany of Pan (6. 105), itself perhaps a form of largely unmediated prophecy. Pan, through Philippides, sends a message to the Athenians, a message that, like an oracle, recommends a certain course of action and, implicitly at least, promises fulfilment: should the Athenians continue to propitiate the god, he would continue to give them his support.

number of forms. The Chian omens are fulfilled through events which are not remotely divine in their own right: their sufferings during the Ionian revolt. As the Magi tell Astyages—admittedly in the context of their mistaken interpretation of Astyages' dreams—prophecies and dreams are often fulfilled in undramatic ways (1. 120. 3).[57] They are always, it is implied, fulfilled somehow. But, on the other hand, divination may also be fulfilled through miracles. Apollo's proud statement that he could look after his own possessions against the Persians (8. 36. 1) is fulfilled, as we have seen, by a whole stream of miracles (8. 37–9). In a sense, however, even if the events by which divination is fulfilled would otherwise have appeared quite ordinary, all fulfilment is miraculous (except perhaps the very vague fulfilment of omens) by virtue of its detailed echoes of the original message. For unlike omens such as the Delos earthquake, where the coincidence of later misfortunes suggests—but does not perhaps prove beyond doubt—that the original event was prophetic, the detail in which some prophecies and dreams are fulfilled makes it impossible that this fulfilment could have occurred except by divine intervention.[58]

A good example of this is the fulfilment of the oracle given to the Spartans to help them discover the bones of Orestes (1. 67. 4):

In the level plain of Arcadia lies Tegea,
where two winds by hard compulsion blow,
and strike answers to strike, and suffering lies upon suffering.
There life-engendering earth contains Agamemnon's son:
carry him home and you will be victorious over Tegea.

There is nothing clear about such an oracle. Liches, however, one of the Spartan *agathoergoi* (or 'do-gooders'), the men—five a year—who on their release from the cavalry are sent out to serve Spartan interests in the wider world (1. 67. 5), found the

[57] παρὰ σμικρὰ γὰρ καὶ τῶν λογίων ἡμῖν ἔνια κεχώρηκε, καὶ τά γε τῶν ὀνειράτων ἐχόμενα τελέως ἐς ἀσθενὲς ἔρχεται. How and Wells, ad loc., find this remark 'curious in so strong a believer in oracles as H.'.

[58] Just as the precise coincidence that the men punished by Talthybius for the Spartan killing of Persian ambassadors were the sons of the men who originally volunteered for death proves to Herodotus that the matter was divine, 7. 137. 2: see above, Chs. 3–4. Another form of detailed fulfilment is fulfilment by means of a pun, e.g. 5. 1. 3, for which see Powell (1937).

bones by a 'mixture of chance and ingenuity' (καὶ συντυχίῃ χρησάμενος καὶ σοφίῃ, 1. 68. 1).[59] He happened to go into a smith's workshop where he was amazed at the sight of the smith forging iron. Seeing his astonishment, the smith stopped what he was doing to talk to him (1. 68. 2): if he was amazed at that, he would certainly be amazed to know that he had discovered a corpse seven cubits long. At this point Liches discovers his ingenuity (1. 68. 3–4):

Reflecting on what he had been told, he conjectured (συνεβάλλετο) from the words of the oracle that this must be the body of Orestes, conjecturing (συμβαλλόμενος) in this way: seeing the two bellows he discerned the two winds, and in the anvil and hammer the strike answering strike, and in the iron being forged suffering lying upon suffering, reckoning (εἰκάζων) in this way that iron was invented to the harm of man.

Far from the source of the fulfilment having been clear from the original oracle, it is only the element of chance that allows for the bones' discovery.[60] Similarly, when a detail of an oracle or dream is misunderstood, as when Cambyses thought that he would die an old man in Median Ecbatana rather than a Syrian village of the same name (3. 64. 3–4), this adds an additional authority to its fulfilment: 'there', Cambyses called aloud, 'Cambyses, son of Cyrus, is destined to die' (ἐστὶ πεπρωμένον τελευτᾶν, 3. 64. 5)[61]

The clear fulfilment of prophecies may be the explanation that Herodotus would have employed had one questioned his belief in divination. Clearly, however, there are a number of other,

[59] For the historical and geographical context of the bones, see Huxley (1979), arguing (following Forrest 1968: 74), that the bones were the remains of a prehistoric monster of Pleistocene date; contrast now Pritchett (1982: 45–6). For the mythological background, see Singor (1987), Vandiver (1991: 34 ff.), seeing the episode as 'skilfully and carefully constructed to recall the myth of the lost Heroic Age before the discovery of iron' (p. 38), but above all the admirable Boedeker (1993).

[60] For other cases of fulfilment spelled out, cf. 3. 125. 4, 6. 19. 3, 8. 53. 1.

[61] Very similar is Cleomenes' accidental fulfilment of the prophecy that he would 'take Argos', 6. 76. 1, 80–82, when he takes the sacred grove of the same name: he asks the name and then decides to wind up his campaign and return home. His enemies in Sparta doubted his piety. See Fontenrose (1978: 58–62) for similar 'Jerusalem Chamber' oracles.

less conscious means by which a belief in divination may have
been protected from 'empirical refutation'. Fulfilment may be a
long time postponed: so, for example, the prophecy of Lysistratus fulfilled through the battle of Salamis (8. 96. 2).[62] It may
also be very circuitous, as in the case of the oracle which
advised the Spartans to ask Xerxes for justice for the death of
Leonidas (8. 114. 1).[63] The expectation of fulfilment is indeed
so ingrained that it may simply be insinuated rather than made
explicit. Pericles' mother dreamed that she gave birth to a lion
and a few days later gave birth to Pericles (6. 131. 2), who
clearly, in one sense or another, turned out to be a lion.[64] Delay
in fulfilment clearly provides an infinitely flexible justification
for apparent non-fulfilment: the truth would come out in the
end. At the same time we may surely speculate whether
unfulfilled prophecies were not quite simply forgotten while
they awaited fulfilment.[65] One such dormant oracle is apparently mentioned by Herodotus in the context of the island of
Phla off Libya: an oracle told the Spartans to establish a colony
there (4. 178; cf. 4. 179), an opportunity presumably that still
lay open to them.

A number of other explanations for the non-fulfilment of
divination may appear at first sight simply to be evidence of
scepticism on Herodotus' part. Prophets may be corrupt.[66]
Deiphon may not, Herodotus reports, have been the son of
Euenius, but another man altogether trading on his name

[62] Cf. the delayed fulfilment of the prophecies of Ngungdeng: D. H
Johnson (1994: 324).

[63] The motif of oracles ordering men to ask for retribution is a common
one: e.g. the Pelasgians, 6. 139–40, Euenius, 9. 93–4.

[64] The comparison with a lion was 'not a safe compliment', as Momigliano
remarked (1984: 72). For the significance of this passage, see Strasburger
(1955: 16 ff.), Harvey (1966: 254–5), Fornara (1971a: 53–4), R. Thomas (1989:
270 ff.); the fullest discussion is still Dyson (1929). Develin (1985: 133) sees
the dream as 'merely a graphic detail'. Cf. the lion-parable at Aesch. Ag. 717–
36, for which see Knox (1952).

[65] Cf. Whittaker (1965: 28–9), Liebeschütz (1979: 28).

[66] For accusations of bribery, dishonesty, or treachery, see e.g. H. Od.
2. 184–6, Soph. OT 330–1, 380 ff., Ant. 1033 ff., E. IA 520–1, 956 ff. The
friction between Tiresias and Oedipus and Tiresias and Creon is (dramatically, at least) constructive in so far as it induces Tiresias to say more than he
otherwise would.

(9. 95).[67] Onomacritus is almost the model of the corrupt seer (7. 6. 3–4):[68]

The Peisistratids brought with them Onomacritus, an Athenian and a prophet (χρησμολόγον) and the editor of the prophecies of Musaeus, having patched up their quarrel. For Onomacritus had been expelled from Athens by Hipparchus the son of Peisistratus, having been caught red-handed by Lasus of Hermione while introducing a prophecy amongst those of Musaeus to the effect that the islands off Lemnos would disappear under the sea. For this reason Hipparchus expelled him, though before that they had been particular friends. But later, having gone up with them, whenever he came into the sight of the King, with the Peisistratids talking him up solemnly (λεγόντων τῶν Πεισιστρατιδέων περὶ αὐτοῦ σεμνοὺς λόγους), he gave a recital of prophecies (κατέλεγε τῶν χρησμῶν): if there was something in the collection that portended harm to the barbarian (εἰ μέν τι ἐνέοι σφάλμα φέρον τῷ βαρβάρῳ) he said nothing of this, but he selected those parts that were most favourable (εὐτυχέστατα ἐκλεγόμενος), saying that the Hellespont was bound to be be yoked by a Persian man (τόν τε Ἑλλήσποντον ὡς ζευχθῆναι χρεὸν εἴη ὑπ' ἀνδρὸς Πέρσεω), and describing the march.

Herodotus also retells stories of the bribery of Delphi. Cleomenes had liberated Athens from tyranny only after every Spartan visitor to the oracle at Delphi, whether on private business or public, had been given the same instruction 'to free Athens' (5. 63. 1). When he later regrets his action and decides to reimpose Hippias on Athens (5. 91. 1), he does so on the grounds of his having uncovered Alcmeonid bribery of the oracle, and also of his discovery of a number of prophecies which had formerly been in the possession of the Peisistratids and which Cleomenes had taken home with him from the Athenian Acropolis.[69] Herodotus sees Cleomenes as driven

---

[67] This is evidence that prophecy was to some extent seen as an inherited skill: Burkert (1985a: 112 and n. 17); see also e.g. 7. 221, H. *Od.* 15. 224, E. *Hel.* 15.

[68] Legrand (1937: 277–8): 'la fraude d'Onomacrite . . . est présentée . . . non pas comme une peccadille dont on puisse rire, mais comme une véritable profanation.'

[69] Knowledge of oracles and the possession of collections can constitute a powerful political prerogative (as well as an opportunity for corruption). One of the privileges or responsibilities of the Spartan kings was the safeguarding of prophecies, 6. 57. 4; although they were overseen in this by the Pythioi,

partly by political motives (5. 90. 1, 91. 1). However, except for one slight expression of reservation in a different context (6. 123. 2), he appears relatively trusting in the story of Alcmeonid bribery.[70] He tells the story of Cleomenes' own bribery of Delphi without any such sign of doubt.

None of these cases of abuse, or possible abuse, cut to the bone of belief in prophecy, however.[71] Indeed, the possibility of corruption offers another convenient 'let-out clause' by which belief in divination is sustained.[72] Aristodicus is so surprised on the Cymeans' receiving an oracle advising them to expel a suppliant that he suspects the ambassadors sent to consult the oracle of having doctored its response (1. 158. 2). Such 'mistrust even of their oracles and messengers is characteristic of the Greeks', commented A. H. Sayce.[73] To distrust the messenger, however, preserves the imagined integrity of the message. False prophets too, like false oracles, presuppose true ones. Despite what he knows of Onomacritus' work on Musaeus' *corpus,* Herodotus believes in the fulfilment of the prophecies of Musaeus concerning the Persian war. It should be noted also that he never challenges the truth of the

these officials were their own appointees, 6. 57. 2. Hippias likewise forecast misfortunes for the Corinthians from Athens as the man 'who understood the oracles most accurately of all' (οἷά τε τοὺς χρησμοὺς ἀτρεκέστατα ἀνδρῶν ἐξεπιστάμενος, 5. 93. 2). Periander forewarns his friend Thrasybulus of Miletus of an oracle given to Alyattes almost as if it were an industrial secret, 1. 20.

[70] It is easy to speculate on a more innocent explanation of this account: i.e. that the Alcmeonids' extravagant refacing of the temple, 5. 62. 3, was construed as bribery. See here Parke and Wormell (1956: i. 146–7). The newly found prophecies from the Acropolis might also arouse suspicion by their judicious mix of vagueness and certainty, 5. 90. 2. When the Corinthians later resist Cleomenes' attempt to reimpose Hippias, Hippias warns them in similarly vague terms, 5. 93. 1. On the Alcmeonid liberation of Athens, see Forrest (1969), Rhodes (1981: 190–2), and now R. Thomas (1989: ch. 5) and Lavelle (1993).

[71] Contrast, however, Nock (1942: 474): 'These facts . . . were utilized by critics of the oracle'—citing Cicero, *de div*. 2. 118.

[72] Parker (1985: 302); Forrest (1982: 309). See also K. Thomas (1971: 401) on astrology in early modern England, quoted also by G. E. R. Lloyd (1979: 19), 'The paradox was that the mistakes of any one astrologer only served to buttress the status of the system as a whole'; Lienhardt (1961: 69), 'the experience of a false diviner, far from calling into doubt the abilities of all, reminded them of many others who really did have the insight which this man claimed'.   [73] Sayce, ad loc.

prophecies from which Onomacritus garners his selection for Xerxes. Indeed, his description of Onomacritus' technique rather implies a belief in the authenticity of Musaeus' prophecies. The Hellespont was indeed yoked by a Persian; only the same Persian was subsequently defeated by the Greeks. The prophecies bandied about by Cleomenes or by Hippias might also themselves be authentic—the Corinthians do indeed come to suffer distress from the Athenians—but it is the use, the presentation, of these prophecies that is suspect.[74] The Alcmeonids' bribery of Delphi, or Cleomenes' subsequent bribery to ensure the deposition of Demaratus (6. 66. 2–3), likewise need not have had any effect on the credibility of the oracle itself.[75] The priestess Perialla serves as a scapegoat, deposed from her post (6. 66. 3).[76] Cobon, Cleomenes' intermediary, fled from Delphi. Cleomenes' madness and death, Herodotus later reveals, were the price for his bribery of Delphi (6. 75. 3, 84. 3).[77] No stigma is attached to the institution itself.

Herodotus is clearly aware of the possibility of oracles being 'recycled'.[78] The oracle, known to Mardonius, which prophesied that the Persians would sack Delphi and be destroyed, referred in actual fact, Herodotus says, to the Illyrians and Encheleans (9. 43). Whether the recycling was cynical or a matter of accident, Herodotus does not mention. Either way,

---

[74] Cf. Themistocles' presentation of the wooden wall oracle as an unequivocal promise of victory, 8. 60. γ.

[75] Contrast, however, Whittaker (1965: 29): 'private intrigues like that of the Alcmaeonidae . . . may have helped to crack the facade of infallibility.'

[76] Price (1985: 142). Cf. Aesch. *Eum.* 33 (μαντεύομαι γὰρ ὡς ἂν ἡγῆται θεός). Whittaker (1965: 34–5) sees the idea of the Pythia's possession as intended both to endow the priestess with authority and to exonerate her of responsibility: 'if public opinion maintained that the Pythia was possessed by Apollo, the responsibility and moral judgements of Delphi were those of society itself.'

[77] By contrast to Cleomenes, the Alcmeonids seem to suffer no loss in reputation as a result of their bribery of Delphi. Herodotus uses the story of their corruption of Delphi as evidence of their hatred of tyranny, that they would never have raised a shield to the Persians at Marathon, 6. 123. 2: does the end justify the means?

[78] The phrase is Asheri's (1993: 71). For the 'tesaurizzazione delle profezie' and its consequences, see Prandi (1993). For the gradual collection of an established body of sayings in an oral culture, see D. H. Johnson (1994: 332–3).

one can well see why such a convenient oracle—essentially threatening destruction for whoever dared attack Delphi—might have been reused. Herodotus also envisages the possibility of *post-eventum* fabrication.[79] The Telmessian seers who interpreted an omen as prophesying Croesus' defeat by Cyrus knew nothing, Herodotus makes clear, of the events at Sardis when they gave their verdict (1. 78. 3).[80] Similarly, Thersander of Orchomenus, to whom a Persian confided the secret of their imminent defeat at Plataea, assured Herodotus, he says, that he had made the Persian's wisdom known to a number of people before the battle (9. 16. 5)—presumably an assurance again that he had not invented the 'prophecy' in the light of the miraculous outcome of the battle.[81] Such qualifications are in neither case intended to cast doubt on these 'prophecies', the interpretation of the seers or the quasi-prophecy of Thersander. Rather they serve as assurances of their truth, an automatic response to an anticipated cynicism. Such phenomena as the selection and misrepresentation of collections of prophecies, or *post eventum* forgery, must, of course, also depend upon the belief of those on whom they are perpetrated for their effect; they may even depend upon the conviction of those responsible.[82]

As well as corrupt oracles, there are also those which are simply not so good. Croesus searches for and finds what he considers 'the only two oracles of men' (τάδε μαντήια εἶναι μοῦνα ἐν ἀνθρώποισι, 1. 53. 2). Amasis fancied he knew which oracles were truthful: those which did not flatter him but called him a

---

[79] See Legrand (1937: 276–7), Klees (1964: 73). Cf. Ar. *Pax* 1085, with Carey (1982: 466). Aeschines accuses Demosthenes of saying that he had received his knowledge of the death of Philip from the gods in a dream, when in fact he had received advance information, Aeschin. 3. 77. At 2. 18. 1, Herodotus is keen to stress that he had formed his judgement on the extent of Egypt before discovering an oracle that confirmed this: this illustrates (obliquely) his trust in the authority of the oracle.

[80] For the 'less interesting' question of the location of this Telmessos, see Harvey (1991).

[81] Cf. Hipparchus' dream, which he confides to the dream-interpreters on the morning of his death, 5. 56. 2.

[82] Cf. medieval forgery of charters, for which see Clanchy (1993: 318 ff.). Forgery can be the wrong deed for the right reason: see also Southern (1990: 359 ff.) on the 'Lanfranc forgeries' driven by the desire to prove Canterbury's claim to primacy.

thief (2. 174. 2).[83] Though Herodotus knows of a number of oracles in Egypt, the oracle of Leto in Buto, he says, is that held in the greatest honour (1. 83). There, he later observes, is the Egyptians' 'most unlying oracle' (μαντήιον ἀψευδέστατον, 2. 152. 3).[84] Although Herodotus never explicitly draws a distinction between more and less established sources of prophecy, let alone between Delphi and the rest, the prominence of Delphi in the *Histories* must, surely, reflect an especial interest and respect.[85]

Some prophets or interpreters too are better than others. Although prophecy can still be seen as a god-given art (9. 93. 4, 94. 3), expertise is clearly relative. Melampus, the man responsible, in Herodotus' view, for bringing the cult of Dionysus to Greece, was 'a wise man who had acquired the art of prophecy' (2. 49. 2).[86] The prophet Kallias, who ran away from Sybaris when the omens for their attack against Croton were unfavourable, at least had trust in his own work (5. 44. 2).[87] The dream-interpreters who told Astyages that his dream of Cyrus as king had already been fulfilled by his acting the king with other children were clearly wrong: and so Astyages had them impaled (1. 128. 2). Enthusiasm too may make a difference to the outcome of divination. Hegesistratus sacrificed eagerly 'because of his hatred of the Spartans and out of desire for profit' (9. 38. 1).[88] Hegesistratus' profit-motive does not, it should be said, necessarily devalue the results of his divination: despite his eagerness, the omens were still unfavourable, and Mardonius eventually decided to obey the Persian custom and ignore them (9. 41. 4). The Magi had reassured Astyages of their reliability by reminding him that it was in their interests too that the Medes should not lose their

[83] For Egyptian traditions behind this passage, see de Meulenaere (1949).

[84] Oracles are very often said to be unlying (ἀψευδές) rather than truthful: 1. 49, 2. 174. 2; Mycerinus tries to show the oracle of Buto to be lying by making his nights into days and his six years of life into twelve, 2. 133. 5.

[85] Cf. Forrest (1984: 7), Kirchberg (1965: 11–29), Schwabl (1969: 258 ff.); contrast Bowden (1991: 21, 52).

[86] Herodotus does not specify how: see Suarez de la Torre (1992).

[87] Although he was rewarded *after* his defection, 5. 45. 2.

[88] Cf. Ar. *Eq.* 1097 (the wisest seer is the one who flatters most), E. *Phoen.* 954–9 (Phoebus should be the only prophet because he fears no man), Xen. *Anab.* 5. 6. 18 (financial interests of Silanus).

power to the Persians (1. 120. 6). This is not an acknowledgement that they are charlatans, but an attempt to reassure
the king that they will not be careless, that they will make sure
to report promptly every sign of danger.[89] But at the same time
it is easy to imagine how a lack of eagerness—and in some
instances also an excessive enthusiasm—might have been used
to explain unsatisfactory results.

It is possible also that different forms of divination might
have been seen as inherently more or less reliable than others.
Herodotus, as has been said already, draws no such distinctions
himself, but he does ascribe them to foreign peoples. The
Atlantes never have dreams—clearly then there was no scope
for interpreting them (4. 184. 4).[90] The Egyptians believe that
prophecy ($\mu\alpha\nu\tau\iota\kappa\dot\eta$) is a skill that belongs to gods but to no man
(2. 83).[91] Like corruption or the belief that certain oracles are
more truthful than others, the distinction of whole categories of
divination as inherently (if not unfailingly) unreliable would
surely have been a convenient position in the event of dis-
satisfaction. Indeed a range of forms of divination, leading to
an imagined variety in the standards of reliability offered by
these different forms, may very well have been essential for
belief in divination in general to have been maintained.[92] It is

---

[89] The father of the elder Cyrus is said to have taught his son $\mu\alpha\nu\tau\iota\kappa\dot\eta$ so that
he should not be at the mercy of seers, Xen. *Cyr.* 1. 6. 2. Cf. the accusation or
suspicion that an oracle or dream had been misrepresented out of self-interest,
1. 158. 2, Soph. *OT* 603–4, Hyp. 4. 15. Prophecies obviously might never be
revealed at all, although the statement in tragedy of unwillingness to reveal
prophecies, e.g. Soph. *OT* 316 ff., *Ant.* 1060, E. *Phoen.* 865–7, is inevitably a
prelude to their being revealed.

[90] Or, at least, they are said not to see dreams: $\dot\epsilon\nu\dot\upsilon\pi\nu\iota\alpha$ $\dot o\rho\hat\alpha\nu$. For foreign
divination in the *Histories*, see further Klees (1964: 16 ff.), Kirchberg (1965:
43 ff.); on Egyptian prophecies, Mora (1985), Lachenaud (1978: 229 ff.).

[91] A common Greek distinction: see above, this chapter. On the other hand,
$\mu\alpha\nu\tau\iota\kappa\dot\eta$ from victims is said to originate in Egypt, 2. 57. 3. It is unclear
whether Herodotus believes that the individual Greek prophets to whom he
refers, and whose prophecies he clearly trusts to be true, derive their power of
prophecy from gods, that it is somehow innate, or merely vaguely 'sharing in
the divine'. The vague boundary between human wisdom and divine know-
ledge shown by the way in which Solon, for example, speaks $\sigma\dot\upsilon\nu$ $\theta\epsilon\hat\omega$, perhaps
supports the final possibility.

[92] Cf. Ngungdeng's distinction of his own divinity from others' magic
(D. H. Johnson 1994: 96–101); for the various reputations of Dinka diviners,
see Lienhardt (1961: 73–80).

perhaps not a coincidence that those peoples whom Herodotus describes as envisaging only a single form of divination—the Nasamonians (4. 172. 3) or the Getae (4. 94. 2–3)[93]—are also amongst the most distant, one might almost say mythical, of his foreign peoples. It is a vital point, however, that the distinctions between different types of divination or between different oracular shrines could not have been too black-and-white. Again it is perhaps significant that the firmest distinctions between types of divination are drawn by the Atlantes and the Egyptians. In Greece, on the other hand (in a working system of divination, in other words), any attempt to draw too rigid a line between the reliable and unreliable tends to be confounded: Croesus discovered sources of reliable oracles and then misinterpreted them; Oedipus categorically rejects all human prophecy only to see Tiresias vindicated; and, perhaps the most striking example, Themistocles proved through his interpretation of the oracle of the wooden walls that amateurs could do better than professionals (7. 142–3).[94] The reason why this fluidity was necessary is simple. If everyone had known which oracles were reliable and which not, if all prophets had been deemed charlatans, or if expertise in interpretation had been thought to be the exclusive prerogative of a body of accredited professionals, the business of eliciting reliable answers to one's questions would have been too easy—and, the cynic might add, divination in general would have been revealed to be unreliable.

Another possible explanation for an unsatisfactory oracle is a fault in the procedure by which the oracle is consulted. Aristodicus was right to distrust the prophecy he received from the oracle at Branchidae advising him to expel the Persian suppliant Pactyes. But he failed to see the reason for this false oracle in the Cymeans' own misconduct (1. 158–9). When told a second time to expel Pactyes, Aristodicus goes around the temple disturbing the nests of all the birds that lived under its eaves. A voice came from inside the sanctuary, calling Aristodicus the 'most unholy

[93] The divination practised by the Getae can hardly perhaps be called divination given that it is weighted always to give the same response. It is seen primarily, moreover, as a form of communication *from* the Getae *to* their god.

[94] Cf. Xen. *Anab.* 6. 1. 31: some omens can be interpreted without particular expertise.

of men' and asking why it was that he was turning out the god's suppliants from his temple. Not at a loss for an answer (οὐκ ἀπορήσαντα), Aristodicus pointed out the irony: the god was looking after his own suppliants but ordering the Cymeans to expel theirs. The god, however, also had an answer (1. 159. 4):

Indeed I order it, so that by committing an impiety you will more quickly come to your end (ἵνα γε ἀσεβήσαντες θᾶσσον ἀπόλησθε) and never again come to the oracle to ask about the expulsion of suppliants.[95]

By asking the god to sanction an impious act, the Cymeans invited their own deception.[96] Glaucus similarly asks an impious question, whether he might commit perjury. Unlike in the case of Aristodicus, the god is never anything less than straightforward to Glaucus, but his answer is no more comforting. Perjurers are invariably punished—for the child of Oath destroys the perjurer's house and his family—and Glaucus cannot even take back his question, for 'to test the god and to do the deed are the same', the Pythia tells him (6. 86. γ2).[97] If one can displease the god by an impious question, in how many other ways, we may ask, is it possible for the enquirer unknowingly to invalidate the expected response?[98] Before

[95] See here (in rather vague terms) Morgan (1990: 160–1), and Parker (1985: 313), who like Herodotus seems to express some sympathy for the Cymeans: 'one can well see how attractive it might have been to hope that the god might somehow see this as a special case.' For a political rationalization, see Brown (1978: esp. 70 ff.), Parke (1985: 16–17); see also Fontenrose (1988: 10–11). Shimron (1989: 51) claims that 'it remains unexplained why Apollo acts differently in similar cases'; in the case of Aristodicus (1989: 50) he feels that the oracle 'could have achieved its "educational" purpose by direct admonition'.

[96] Cf. Diod. Sic. 15. 2. See here Parker (1985: 299). Parker comments also, however, that 'it seems that consultants do not ask about moral questions': this is, surely, contradicted by Xen. *Hell.* 4. 7. 2 which he cites himself (p. 300). Rules as to (in)appropriate topics for consultation may change at short notice, e.g. Xen. *Hell.* 3. 2. 22, although they are not conceived, of course, as changes. You cannot compel the god to tell the whole truth: e.g. Soph. *OT* 280–1, E. *Ion* 390–1.

[97] See Ch. 4. The connection between Aristodicus and Glaucus is also made by Brown (1978: 72).

[98] It is noticeable, however, that the excuses for faulty responses or for no response in the *Histories* are either very memorable (e.g. the insistence that Alyattes should rebuild the temple of Athena in Miletus, 1. 19. 3), or imply at

the Pythian priestess delivered the oracle to the Athenians advising them to 'flee to the ends of the earth', Herodotus thinks to mention that the Athenians 'had performed the customary actions about the temple' (σφι ποιήσασι περὶ τὸ ἱρὸν τὰ νομιζόμενα, 7. 140. 1):[99] this is perhaps to discount the possibility that they had by some omission attracted the prophecy themselves. The convenient potential for explaining away unfavourable prophecies by such taboos is obvious.[100]

Arguably the most common justification for the non-fulfilment of divination—the most common, at least, to emerge in the *Histories*—is the possibility of misinterpretation. The Ethiopians, Herodotus reports, obey their oracle to the letter and march wherever and whenever their god tells (2. 29. 7). How, we may wonder again, could any system of belief so inflexible be sustained? Greek oracles and prophecies, by contrast, are frequently equivocal—and so require interpretation.[101] It is clearly easier to believe in the fulfilment of a prophecy if its terms are sufficiently equivocal to allow a number of interpretations.[102] Only hindsight decides which

least a serious moral (Glaucus, 6. 86). No faulty oracle is clearly explained on a technicality; Dorieus' failure to consult *at all* is rather more than a technicality. We may suspect that explanation in these terms was more common in everyday life.

[99] Cf. Dorieus, 5. 42. 2: οὔτε τῷ ἐν Δελφοῖσι χρηστηρίῳ χρησάμενος ἐς ἥντινα γῆν κτίσων ἴῃ, οὔτε ποιήσας οὐδὲν τῶν νομιζομένων. Cf. also the story of the fall of Sardis, 1. 84, for a rationalization of which see Bunnens (1969).

[100] See Evans-Pritchard (1976: 132, 156 ff., 172), for similar let-out clauses for Zande belief, e.g. (p. 172): 'they say that a sincere man who wished to keep his oracle potent would not use it for two or three days after having had sexual intercourse. They attribute much of the error in the oracle's judgements to slackness in this respect.' A range of taboos, more and less purely 'religious' is given by Hes. *Erga* 724–828.

[101] The idea that oracles are unclear and require careful interpretation is common: e.g. Theogn. 805–10, Pind. *Ol.* 12. 10–18, Aesch. *Ag.* 1255, E. *Med.* 674 ff., *Suppl.* 138, Heraclitus DK 22 B 93; see on this Asheri (1993: 74). The idea, E. *Or.* 591–3, that everyone obeys Delphi blindly is unusual and probably represents an ideal pattern of behaviour in cases (of unequivocal prophecy) where absolute obedience is possible.

[102] Whittaker (1965: 33). See also van Groningen (1956) and den Boer (1957), who interpret two particular oracles (4. 159. 3 and 5. 92. β2 respectively) as intentionally ambiguous. Xenophon's observation, *Anab.* 3. 5. 3, of the unanimity of *manteis* in the interpretation of a prophecy raises the possibility that divided verdicts were useful in sustaining belief in fulfilment.

was the right interpretation, that the wooden walls, for example, were the Athenians' ships and not the Acropolis—as a beleaguered few continued to maintain (7. 142. 1, 8. 51. 2).[103] In the case of an omen such as the Delos earthquake, presaging only a great number of future evils, fulfilment is obviously easier still. At the same time, it is sometimes precisely the detail of a prophecy, an implied condition for example, that allows a legalistic loophole for non-fulfilment. So Mardonius asks his men whether they have heard of a prophecy to the effect that the Persians would sack Delphi and then be expelled from Greece. They murmur that they have indeed. But since they have not sacked Delphi, he reassures them, they would not be expelled (9. 42).[104] The Spartans similarly had heard of a prophecy that the Dorians would be expelled from the Peloponnese by the Athenians and Persians—hence their eagerness to prevent any alliance between the two, to defuse the prophecy (8. 141. 1).

The equivocal nature of many prophecies and the interpretation that this necessitates are not merely suffered as necessary evils: they are considered apparently to be of the essence of prophecy.[105] There is evidence at times even of an ethos of resistance towards oracles. Herodotus reveals perhaps a sneaking admiration for Aristodicus of Cyme, at least for the speed of his wit (1. 159. 4), but he quite openly applauds the

---

[103] Contrast, however, Shimron (1989: 50): 'the ἐκκλησία decreed what the divine plan was . . . the fact that the Athenians had a choice and did choose contradicts the assumption of a divine plan . . .' The assembly did not decree what the divine plan was, but what they *thought* the divine plan was: the course of events revealed that they were right.

[104] But, of course, they at least tried to do so, 8. 36–9, and contemplation of a crime, according to the reply to Glaucus, is equivalent to the crime itself, 6. 86. γ2. See here the curious parallel to this prophecy at E. *Bacch.* 1330 ff. with Dodds (1960) ad loc. Cf. Calchas' prophecy concerning Ajax, Soph. *Aj.* 749 ff., Aesch. *Ag.* 338–42.

[105] Parker (1985: 301–2). See also the Satrian oracle of Dionysus, 'no more complicated' or 'no more elaborate' than Delphi, 7. 111. 2 (οὐδὲν ποικιλώτερον): in what sense it is complex or elaborate, it is hard to say. Legrand uses this passage to show that Herodotus thought the functioning of the Delphic oracle simple, 7. 117 n. 3: 'Les modernes voudraient bien en être aussi assurées . . .' Contrast here Fontenrose (1978: 236): 'Herodotus quotes ambiguous and obscure oracles, but never says that ambiguity was a Delphic characteristic.'

Athenians before Salamis for keeping their nerve in the face of
the first oracle they received from Delphi (7. 139. 6): 'The
alarming oracles that came from Delphi and threw them into a
terror did not persuade them to desert Greece, but, standing
their ground, they had the courage to receive the invader of
their country.' The first oracle they received had told them
'leaving your homes to flee to the ends of the earth' (λιπὼν φεῦγ᾽
ἔσχατα γαίης / δώματα, 7. 140. 2). But then, on the advice of a
leading Delphian, Timon son of Androboulus, they entered the
sanctuary once more, but as suppliants, and begged the god for
a more favourable response (7. 141. 1): the second oracle, that
advising the Athenians to take to their wooden walls, was
'gentler' than the first (ἠπιώτερα, 7. 142. 1), and by virtue of
offering constructive advice—albeit advice requiring interpretation—showed the way to their deliverance.[106]

It is hard initially to see how Herodotus could have understood the second 'wooden walls' oracle as merely a refinement
of the first: it seems at first sight as though Herodotus is in
favour in this instance of outright disobedience towards the
oracle, that he has apparently no difficulties with a god who is
capable of such swift self-contradiction.[107] Yet the two oracles
are in fact perfectly consistent so long as the first is understood
correctly. The land which the Athenians are told to flee was—
in their view and in retrospect—the land that they did indeed
flee, that of Attica rather than the earth as a whole.[108] As

[106] For Delphi's strategy during the Persian wars, i.e. 'one of confirming
the consultants in their own inclinations', see the comments of Parker (1985:
317–18).

[107] See Maddalena (1950: 63–4); Parke and Wormell (1956: i. 170), 'no
forger would have perpetrated such a mistake as to show Apollo induced to
change his mind'; Shimron (1989: 50), 'they compelled Apollo to change his
first oracle'; Shapiro (1990: 345), speculating that the status of oracles and
oracle-mongers seems never to have recovered fully from this blow (Delphi's
alleged medism).

[108] Elayi (1979a: 229), followed by Corcella (1984: 161). There is a good
Solonian precedent, of course, Solon frag. 4a West: πρεσβυτάτην γαῖαν Ἰαονίης.
Robertson accepts (1987: 9) that the second oracle reflects the same outlook as
the first; he argues, however (pp. 7–8), in support of his theory that the
'wooden walls' were a wall across the Isthmus, that the phrase means
'withdraw to the Peloponnesus, the furthest part of peninsular Greece'. See
also Evans (1988a), arguing against Robertson (p. 30) that the Isthmus wall
was 'insufficiently ligneous to serve as a wooden wall'.

Herodotus later makes explicit, the first oracle prophesies the evacuation and destruction of Athens in exemplary detail: 'it was necessary according to the oracle for the whole of mainland Attica to come under the Persians' (8. 53. 1). There is no reason to suppose that Herodotus or the Athenians saw any contradiction between the two oracles. What Herodotus is applauding then is not outright disobedience of an oracle, but the courage and the composure with which the Athenians (unlike Croesus?) sought to check their first oracle.[109]

Herodotus is clearly aware of the possibility of a conflict between the advice of an oracle and a consultant's estimate of his self-interest. The Spartans, in expelling their friends the Peisistratids from Athens, 'gave the affairs of the god priority over those of men' (τὰ γὰρ τοῦ θεοῦ πρεσβύτερα ἐποιεῦντο ἢ τὰ τῶν ἀνδρῶν, 5. 63. 2).[110] Mardonius, conversely, advises the Persians before Plataea to ignore their unfavourable omens, and not to try to force them to be favourable. This rejection of divination is meant to be in keeping with a Persian custom (9. 41. 4), and contrasts with the exemplary behaviour of

---

[109] Cf. 6. 35. 3–36. 1 (Miltiades checks as to whether he should obey the oracle given to the Dolonkians), Soph. *OT* 1438 ff. (Creon plans to confirm fate of Oedipus), E. *Hipp.* 1055–6 (Hippolytus complains at being banished without appeal to an oracle). Like Croesus, 1. 75. 2, the Spartans too 'relied on an ambiguous oracle' (χρησμῷ κιβδήλῳ πίσυνοι, 1. 66. 3). The term need not, I think be pejorative, as Flower asserts (1991: 71), unless we follow Shimron (on 8. 77, discussed above) in supposing that Herodotus thought clarity to be a necessary or desirable characteristic in a prophecy. Of the three uses of the word κίβδηλος, only in one does it appear to mean 'dud' or false (as supposed by Asheri 1993: 73): it is used of the oracles given to the Spartans as a result of Alcmeonid bribery, 5. 91. 2; the oracles given to the Spartans concerning Tegea and to Croesus concerning his planned attack on Cyrus are both fulfilled in unexpected ways, 1. 66. 3, 75. 2. Shimron (1989: 34) defines κίβδηλος as ' "deceptive", but with the undertone, at least, of "fraudulent" '. Used to describe currency, as e.g. Ar. *Ran.* 721, Theogn. 119, E. *Med.* 516, κιβδήλος must be taken to mean 'dud', but women—except perhaps in so far as their wretchedness is not immediately evident—can surely only be said to constitute a κίβδηλον κακὸν, E. *Hipp.* 616, in so far as they deceive men.

[110] The Spartans, moreover, subsequently 'discover' that the oracle had been bribed by the Alcmeonids: I do not imagine, however, that the story is a cautionary tale of the hazards encountered if you stray from the path of self-interest. For the peculiar nature of Spartan religiosity, see Parker (1989). Cf. E. *Suppl.* 155 ff., 229 ff., Aesch. *Choeph.* 900 ff. (Orestes must obey Apollo and his own oaths and kill his mother—despite some reluctance).

Pausanias and the Spartans who continue to incur casualties until the omens turn in their favour (9. 61. 3–62. 1):

But as the victims were not favourable to them, many of them fell in this time and many more were wounded; for the Persians, making a barricade of their shields, let fly many arrows unsparingly, so that the Spartans, being hard pressed, and the victims remaining unfavourable, Pausanias, looking towards the Heraion of the Plataeans, called upon the goddess, requesting that they might not be disappointed of their hopes (ἐπικαλέσασθαι τὴν θεόν, χρηίζοντα μηδαμῶς σφέας ψευσθῆναι τῆς ἐλπίδος). While he was calling upon her, the Tegeans, starting forward, attacked the barbarians, and immediately after the prayer of Pausanias the victims became favourable to the Lacedaimonians as they sacrificed (τοῖσι Λακεδαιμονίοισι αὐτίκα μετὰ τὴν εὐχὴν τὴν Παυσανίεω ἐγίνετο θυομένοισι τὰ σφάγια χρηστά).

Such cases of obedience to divination in spite of one's obvious interests are certainly few and far between.[111] Such stories must surely, however, have served as models for the proper reaction to such dilemmas.

Cases of the neglect of oracles or of disobedience must similarly have reinforced a proper pattern of response.[112] The Euboeans had made light of the oracle of Bacis commanding them to evacuate their island, nor had they moved their possessions into their strongholds as they would had they imagined (on practical grounds) that war was imminent. It was because of their neglect of the oracle, Herodotus says, that their prospects now were so bleak (8. 20. 2): 'as they paid no attention to these verses in the calamities then present and those that impended they fell into the greatest distress.'[113]

---

[111] Pritchett remarks, i. 112–13, that this is the only instance of a battle being held up by unsatisfactory σφάγια with the exception of Aesch. Sept. 377–9. See also, however, E. Rhes. 63–9. For other instances of generals obeying omens against their own judgement, see Pritchett iii. 78 ff.

[112] For neglect or forgetfulness of oracles, cf. 1. 13. 2, 4. 164. 1. A fascinating case of reluctance to obey oracles is Herodotus' story of the Theran foundation of Cyrene, 4. 150 ff.: twice they are punished for their failure to comply with an oracle, 4. 151. 1, 156. 1; the punishments serve, however, as a further inducement to go ahead with the colony. See here Darbo-Peschanski (1987: 76); for the religious dimension of the colony of Cyrene, see now Cawkwell (1992: esp. 292).

[113] τούτοισι [δὲ] οὐδὲν τοῖσι ἔπεσι χρησαμένοισι ἐν τοῖσι τότε παρεοῦσί τε καὶ προσδοκίμοισι κακοῖσι παρῆν σφι συμφορῇ χρᾶσθαι πρὸς τὰ μέγιστα.

Though, as the Athenians' behaviour at the time of Salamis
illustrates, men should never be slaves to divination, they
should also never neglect it.[114] Even failure to consult an
oracle can be considered an offence. Before setting off on the
colonizing expedition on which he died, the Spartan Dorieus
had made another abortive attempt at a colony (5. 42).
'Neither did he consult the god at Delphi as to which land
he should go to found a colony, nor did he do any of the
other customary things' (τῶν νομιζομένων, 5. 42. 2). It is at
least strongly implied by Herodotus' narrative that Dorieus'
failure to consult Delphi and the failure of his expedition are
related.

Dorieus' later history has even more interesting implications, however. He sought and obtained the approval of Delphi
to reclaim the territory of Eryx that had once belonged to his
ancestor Heracles (5. 43). His subsequent death, according to
the Sybarites, was the greatest proof of their claim that he had
supported the Crotoniates in their war against Sybaris: for,
'had he done nothing contrary, but only that for which he was
sent, he would have taken and held the Erycian territory, and
neither he nor his army would have been destroyed' (εἰ γὰρ δὴ
μὴ παρέπρηξε μηδέν, ἐπ' ὃ δὲ ἐστάλη ἐποίεε, εἷλε ἂν τὴν Ἐρυκίνην

---

[114] Cf., however, the Argives' contemplation of an alliance with the
Persians, in contravention of an oracle, 7. 148–9; in the event the Argives
do not join in the war, but it is Spartan arrogance (in refusing to cede their
leadership) rather than religious scruples that prevent them. Parker (1985: 298
and n. 3) suggests that this is not an exception to his rule that 'no clear case of
disobedience to a specifically solicited oracle is recorded' on the grounds that
it is 'probably apologetic fiction': even so it is still important that the Argives
were imagined to have been prepared to disobey an oracle. The explanation
for the fact that they receive no punishment for their neglect of the oracle is
perhaps that they take no actual action—beyond their offer to the Spartans.
(In this case, the principle espoused by Delphi in the case of Glaucus, 6. 86. γ2,
that the contemplation of a crime is as good as the crime itself, does not
apparently apply.) But there are also perhaps, as in the case of Leonidas'
'contrived fulfilment' of an oracle, mitigating circumstances: they wanted to
do the brave thing *even so*. They never deny that obedience to an oracle is
necessary and desirable: they are 'fearful' of the oracle (see Price 1985: 151),
but they balance this fear against another practical necessity, that of allowing
their children to grow into men. Cf. the Aeginetans' choice, 5. 89. 2, to attack
the Athenians despite threatened consequences; the necessity of vengeance
proved greater than the necessity of obedience to Delphi (5. 89. 3). For
ingenious rationalizations, see Parke and Wormell (1956: i. 149–50).

χώρην καὶ ἑλὼν κατέσχε, οὐδ᾽ ἂν αὐτός τε καὶ ἡ στρατιὴ διεφθάρη,
5. 45. 1–2).[115] The initial impression here seems to be that it
was simply Dorieus' failure to fulfil the instructions of the
oracle that resulted in his death.[116] There is perhaps a further
implication, however, that Dorieus should have limited himself
only to those actions positively prescribed by the oracle. If this
is so, if actions quite unrelated to the terms of an oracle or the
manner of its procedure may jeopardize the chances of its
fulfilment, this opens up another large pool of potential
justifications for the non-fulfilment of divination.[117] This idea
is supported by a passing remark concerning the Lydian king
Alyattes. The priestess tells Alyattes that he will receive no
answer until he has rebuilt the temple of Athena in Miletus
(1. 19. 3).[118] Of course, one might reasonably argue that this
was itself an answer: by rebuilding the temple of Athena, and
building a second for good measure, Alyattes recovered from
the illness which had been the cause of his initial consultation
(1. 21. 4). However, there is again—in theory at least—the
possibility that consultation may be jeopardized by an action
apparently quite unrelated.

In addition to all the let-out clauses that have been detailed so
far, one other ingredient crucial to the belief in the validity of
divination needs to be mentioned. This might be described as a
degree of wishful thinking, but perhaps more accurately as an
inherited assumption of the validity of divination.[119] Herodotus
may, as we have seen, in declaring his belief in the truth of
prophecies (8. 77), acknowledge the possibility that others
might adopt a more sceptical stance, but it is important to
emphasize that the various turns of argument by which belief

[115] For this passage, cf. Kukofka (1991).
[116] Cf. Cleisthenes of Sicyon who circumvents the clear message of Delphi
that he should not expel Adrastus by ensuring that he left of his own accord,
5. 67. 2, or Cleomenes' bypassing of the river Erasinus, 6. 76.
[117] Cf. Crahay (1956: 145): 'la responsabilité du sanctuaire se limite à l'objet
précis de la consultation.'
[118] Parker (1985: 415) comments that the Pythia was here 'perhaps being a
little tendentious'. Was such imperious handling of enquiries restricted to
barbarians?
[119] Cf. D. H. Johnson (1994: 35): 'In any society with a developed or
developing prophetic tradition, prophecy takes on a life of its own.'

in the fulfilment of oracles and other forms of divination is maintained do not constitute a consciously developed system but rather a set of *ad hoc* strategies for answering the questions that a belief in divination inevitably threw up. Divination, in the words of Liebeschütz, was 'to a considerable extent . . . protected by the vagueness of its theoretical principles'.[120] Any attempt to excavate the network of such principles will tend to lend them an artificial impression of coherence.

One final point needs to be raised. The anecdotes recorded by Herodotus may tell us much about the mechanisms by which the Greeks sustained their belief in divination. On a number of levels, however, there is clearly a dislocation between these anecdotes and the reality, the practice, of Greek divination. Mistakes in interpretation, for example, are so common in the *Histories* as to constitute the rule rather than the exception.[121] It may well, however, have been the case *in practice* that the majority of oracles were relatively unequivocal responses to clear questions. There are indeed some hints of this more everyday divination in the *Histories*: Dorieus, for example, on consulting Delphi as to whether he should undertake a colony to Eryx (a plan inspired by some prophecies of Laius), is told simply that he should (5. 43);[122] the Cnidians are

---

[120] Leibeschütz (1979: 24), of Roman divination.

[121] The expectation of misinterpretation in Herodotus' narrative is so ingrained that it is frequently implied rather than spelled out: Xerxes dreams that he has been crowned with olive-branches, and that these branches reach out to cover the whole world, when suddenly the garland vanishes, 7. 19. 1. The Magi interpret the dream as meaning that all men would become the slaves of the King. Herodotus' audience or readers can hardly have failed to think of a more likely reading. On the Magi see Bickermann and Tadmor (1978): 'the Greeks used it ("Magus") for a sham diviner' (p. 251). For another clear case of misinterpretation, cf. 7. 37. 2.

[122] Usually such unequivocal answers seem to follow yes-or-no questions: e.g. 2. 18. 1, 52. 3; 5. 43, 66. 3, 67. 2; 6. 35. 3; 7. 169. 2. Even the oracle given to Gyges, with its proviso of vengeance in the fifth generation, was perceived as being unequivocal, 1. 13. Clear oracles are sometimes in response to less clear questions, however: when the Epidaurians consult about a famine, Delphi tells them to set up images of Damias and Auxesia. When they follow up this response by enquiring whether they should make these images of bronze or of stone, the Pythia allowed neither of these, but ordered them to use olive wood, 5. 82. 2. Two oracles order the Cnidians and the Egyptians to stop their construction of canals, 1. 174. 5, 2. 158. 5—both times in response to general enquiries about the injuries or casualties incurred.

told to stop digging. If all oracles had been subject to such disastrous misinterpretation, if misinterpretation had indeed constituted the rule rather than the exception, Delphi would surely very quickly have alienated its clientèle. The dislocation, however, is in one sense more apparent than real. For the tales of Herodotus, with their implicit messages of the proper response to divination and reminders of the miraculous fulfilment of earlier prophecies, themselves serve to reinforce belief in divination. Glamorous incidents of misinterpretation such as that of Croesus essentially constitute Delphic charter myths. Not only do such instances of mistaken interpretation reinforce the very rightness, the fated nature, of the eventual outcome, but at the same time they supply their audience with the tools to explain apparent non-fulfilment: the story of Croesus serves to illustrate both the possibility of fulfilment against one's expectations and—through the oracle given to Gyges prophesying vengeance in the fifth generation (1. 13. 2)—that of dormant oracles, long forgotten, being fulfilled nonetheless. The very glamour and status of the protagonists in such cautionary tales serve a function: if even Croesus—proverbial for his wealth—could have fallen foul of the oracle, others could rest assured that all men were indeed equal before the god.

Lachenaud classifies clear and ambiguous oracles (1978: 270 ff.). Versnel (1981: 4) sees Delphi as too exalted to attract questions on 'man's daily cares'; cf. Georges (1986: 31), assuming apparently that the collections of Fontenrose or Parke and Wormell are representative.

6

The Unity and Multiplicity of the Divine

After having now examined the main forms of divine intervention in the *Histories* it is necessary to stand back and examine a
number of questions that intersect them. The first is the question
of the nature of the divine itself, and the character of the language
used by Herodotus to describe divine intervention. 'It would be
ingenuity misspent', Charles Fornara has written, 'to seek for
real distinctions within the broad range of his terminology.'[1] It is
important to state at the outset that no clear patterns or distinctions are possible; no imposed theology can be detected or
distilled from the pages of the *Histories*. The purpose of this
chapter is to describe the contradictions in Herodotus' thought,
rather than to attempt to rationalize or to reconcile them.

We begin with relatively simple matters. What distinctions
are drawn between different varieties of divinity? How do
heroes or daimones differ from one another or from gods?

The term 'hero' itself clearly includes a range of disparate
figures. Enoch Powell in his *Lexicon* divided Herodotus' heroes
into two categories: 'denizen(s) of the heroic age' and 'mortal(s)
worshipped after death'. In the first category are the Argonauts
(4. 145. 3) and the heroes of Troy (7. 43. 2). In the latter category
of mortals are, for example, Cyrnus, the son of Heracles
(1. 167. 4), Heracles himself (2. 44. 5), Ajax and the other nine
heroes of the Athenian tribes (and by implication the sons of Ion
whom they usurped) (5. 66. 2), as well as, in our terms, more
historical individuals, such as Onesilus[2] and Artachaies, from
the times respectively of the Ionian Revolt and the Persian Wars
(5. 114. 2, 7. 117. 2). It is hard to imagine that Powell meant to

[1] Fornara (1983: 78 n. 36).
[2] For the pattern whereby cities pay heroic honours to their (usually
defeated) enemies, see esp. Visser (1982); cf. 1. 167. 1–2, 4. 103. 3, 5. 47.
For speculation that Herodotus' burial in the agora of Thurii reflects his own
heroization, see Ghimadeyev (1986).

imply the historicity of all those in his second category; but it is equally hard to see any other rationale behind the distinction.[3] The heroes of Troy are mentioned only in the context of Xerxes' order to the Magi to propitiate them. Heracles must surely be a denizen of the 'heroic age' no matter how that time period is defined. It is as well then to state at the outset that the fact that Herodotus uses the same word of both Powell's categories, of Heracles and of Onesilus alike, must reflect the fact that he believed them both, to a significant degree, to be of one type. There is no reason to suppose that he drew any of the distinctions customarily made between heroes in modern scholarship.[4]

In certain contexts, Herodotus appears to operate with a firm distinction between heroes and gods. The Egyptians do not worship heroes (νομίζουσι, 2. 50. 3), he observes. His conclusion to his lengthy theological inquiry into the status of Heracles, that those men are correct who 'sacrifice' to one immortal Heracles, but 'make offerings' (ἐναγίζουσι) to another Heracles, the hero (2. 44. 5), is not only predicated on a firm distinction between the classes of hero and god but also suggests a distinction in the proper manner of their propitiation.[5] However, in less self-consciously theological contexts, the distinction appears rather

[3] Possibly Powell believed that Herodotus used the word to describe some mythological figures who did not receive cult: the classification is still misleading.

[4] Rudhardt (1992a: 129–30). Farnell's classification of heroes into seven categories (1921: 19) does not, by contrast, purport to be based on ancient categories of thought. See Brelich (1958) (and comments of Kearns 1989: 2) for an attempt to see features common to heroes; Nock (1944: 142–3) sees minimal unity. Vandiver (1991: 16–19), in her discussion of alternative definitions, accepts (p. 19) that Powell's two categories overlap but chooses only to examine the hero as the 'denizen of the heroic age'.

[5] The only other use of the word ἐναγίζω in Herodotus is to describe the expiation that the Agyllaioi are ordered to undertake for the murder of a group of Phocaeans, 1. 167. 2: if these Phocaeans are not explicitly called heroes, they are at any rate men propitiated after their death. For the association of this word with heroes, see Rudhardt (1992a: 238–9), but also the qualifications of Nock (1944), Kearns (1989: 5). The Magi sacrifice to Athena, pour libations to the heroes (7. 43. 2). On other occasions, however, heroes do receive sacrifices (5. 47. 2, 67. 3, 114. 2; 7. 117. 2) (although gods never receive ἐναγισμός). The Acanthians sacrifice to Artachaies, and the Amathousians are ordered to sacrifice to Onesilus, 'as to a hero' (ὡς ἥρωι, 5. 114. 2, 7. 117. 2), possibly again reflecting the different character of the sacrifices offered to gods and heroes.

less well focused. The story of Cleisthenes' hatred of the Argive hero Adrastus (5. 67. 5), for example, appears to suggest that sacrificial honours can be transferred from god to hero or vice versa regardless of any strict ritual distinction of status: before the time of their tyrant Cleisthenes, the Sicyonians had honoured Adrastus with tragic choruses; Cleisthenes then gave Adrastus' choruses to Dionysus and the rest of the sacrifices to Melanippus, Adrastus' legendary rival. It was the 'gods and the heroes', according to Themistocles, who begrudged Xerxes the rule of Asia and Europe (8. 109. 3).[6] But the formula on one occasion slips with 'daimones' taking the place of 'heroes' (9. 76. 2). It is also misapplied: the priests at Thebes connected none of their predecessors to any god or hero (2. 143. 4), Herodotus reports, forgetting apparently that the Egyptians did not worship heroes (2. 50. 3).[7]

Clearer evidence of confusion can be seen by looking at the status of a number of individual divinities.[8] Protesilaus receives his power to inflict retribution 'from the gods' (9. 120. 2), but Artayctes, the victim of this retribution, speaks of Protesilaus in his next sentence as a god in his own right (9. 120. 3). There appears to be no reason why Artayctes should have been put up to this apparent contradiction on dramatic grounds—as there had been earlier for his presenting Protesilaus as a living man (9. 116. 3).[9] Herodotus appears to speak of Ajax as one of the gods (8. 121. 1)[10]—casually so, but suggestive again of a degree of casualness in his thought. He also describes Helen as a goddess (6. 61. 3). He does not feel the need to rationalize the

---

[6] Cf. 8. 143. 2: Xerxes paid no regard to the gods and the heroes on whom they rely, the Athenians tell Alexander. For the expression (paralleled also at 9. 76. 2) θεῶν ὄπιν οὐκ ἀλέγοντες, see Burkert (1981).

[7] This is, at least, an oversimplification: see Sourdille (1910: 55 n. 4), Lloyd ii. 238–9, Mora (1985: 203).

[8] As well as those treated below, Vandiver cites Trophonius and Amphiaraus as 'clear examples of characters whose natures fluctuate between god and hero' (1991: 93–4). Herodotus, however, as she acknowledges, 'does not choose to comment upon their status'; their oracles are never distinguished from the oracles of gods. The only evidence contained in the *Histories* that Amphiaraus was, in Herodotus' view, anything less than a god, is the report of Amphiaraus' offer to the Thebans that they could have him either as their prophet or their ally, 8. 134. 2, hardly conclusive.

[9] For evidence of the cult of Protesilaus, see Boedeker (1988: 34–5).

[10] Cf. also 6. 80, where Argos is less certainly described as a god.

fact that she also plays an apparently historical part in the 'heroic age' or that (with the exception of her brothers[11]) Helen's contemporaries were heroes.[12] This classification of Helen as a goddess may be merely a reflection of the fact that, as Isocrates mentions, she received divine rather than heroic honours at Sparta. But Isocrates himself also describes Helen as semi-divine, and as a 'human rendered immortal', and the Dioscuri as raised up to immortality by Helen.[13] The confusion over Helen's status—not only a matter, it seems, of correct ritual observance—seems to have been universal.[14]

What are the characteristics of the hero? Heroes—with the exception of Heracles—are clearly more localized in their spheres of influence than gods.[15] They are perhaps more

[11] Herodotus clearly classes the Dioscuri as gods (2. 43. 2, 50. 2), but, at the same time, he retells stories of how they sailed on the Argo (4. 145. 5), rescued Helen from Theseus (9. 73), and were entertained by a historical individual, Euphorion (6. 127. 3). Vandiver appears to treat Herodotus' terming of the Dioscuri as Tyndaridae as a sign of confusion on his part as regards their status (1991: 95). As is evident from his treatment of Helen, however (2. 112. 2), Herodotus was clearly not aware that there was any contradiction involved in this. This double-think too seems to have been common: see *CEG* 373, where the Dioscuri are called both Dioscuri and Tyndaridae in successive lines.

[12] Vandiver (1991: 103); later, however (pp. 128–9), Vandiver seems to imply that she thinks that Herodotus was conscious of a difference between the historical Helen (or the Helen of 'heroic legend') of Book 2 and the character of folklore of Book 6, where he can 'allow more rein to fabulous elements'.

[13] Divine honours: Isoc. 10. 63 (for dedications to Helen and Menelaus, see Catling and Cavanagh (1976)); for a semi-divine status, however, see Isoc. 10. 16, 60–1 (for Helen raising up her brothers, 10. 61). Cf. also E. *Or.* 1629 ff., where Helen is saved from death at the hands of Orestes by Apollo at Zeus' instruction, and joins the Dioscuri in the aether. It is just possible that Herodotus' classification of Helen as a goddess is the result of a personal theory of his own: he supports his revisionist version of the Trojan war (that Helen spent the duration of the war in Egypt) by the association of Helen and the cult in Memphis of Aphrodite Xeinie, a unique epithet, 2. 112. 2. If Herodotus had made a mental connection between these two passages, it is likely that he would have made it explicit, however.

[14] The divine status of Helen may be connected to the fact that the boundaries of heroic status appear generally more fluid for heroines than for heroes: see Kearns (1989: 22, 126–7).

[15] For this, see esp. Kearns (1990*a*), Rusten (1983); for the immediacy of heroes' motivation, Kearns (1990*b*: 327). Heroes are described as local (5. 66. 2, 8. 39. 1), apparently suggesting that they could be universal. When Cleisthenes, however, is said to have chosen (with the sole exception of

inclined to appear on earth than gods.[16] They are physically large: Phylacus and Autonous, the heroes who made an appearance at Delphi were 'bigger than is natural for men' (μέζονας ἢ κατὰ ἀνθρώπων φύσιν, 8. 38), the body of Orestes seven cubits in length (1. 68. 3). And they are not immortal (2. 44. 5). Indeed, as the case of Protesilaus shows, they are actually conceived of as being mortal (τεθνεὼς, 9. 120. 2): Protesilaus has power in spite of his death.[17]

But at the same time, the distinction of gods and heroes is in many ways a relative one. Heroes share in the divine. Astrabacus' twilight visit to the mother of Demaratus was, her husband deduced, a 'divine matter' (6. 69. 3),[18] the apparitions of Phylacus and Autonous are classed by Herodotus as 'other divine things' (8. 38), the fulfilment of the wrath of Talthybius as a 'divine matter' and as 'most divine' (7. 137. 1–2). The propitiation of heroes will result in improved fortunes just like the propitiation of gods (5. 114. 2; cf. 6. 105. 2),[19] and conversely heroes like gods may begrudge men good fortune (8. 109. 3). Heroes (if Protesilaus is a hero) can point moral lessons through miracles; they have the power (even if they borrow that power from the gods) to punish injustices (9. 120. 1–2).

Men too can break through the barriers that separate them from heroes and gods and share in the divine. Height and

Ajax) local heroes for his new tribes, presumably what is meant is not local as opposed to Panhellenic, but local to Athens as opposed to local to, for example, Salamis (5. 66. 2): Ajax was a 'neighbour'. For local gods, 5. 102. 1, 9. 119. 1, see Ch. 8.

[16] See Ch. 3.

[17] A defining characteristic of heroes: see Kearns (1989: 128–9), Rudhardt (1992a: 129). But heroes are also described as escaping death: see e.g. PMG 894 (φίλταθ' Ἁρμόδιε, οὔ τί πω τέθνηκας), discussed by Kearns. Cf. also Paus. 6. 9. 8 (where the Delphic oracle pronounces Kleomedes a hero on the grounds that he is 'no longer mortal', μηκέτι θνητὸν), Soph. Trach. 1109–11 (Heracles continues to avenge kakoi after death). For the immortality of the Getae, 4. 94. 1, see Ch. 8.

[18] Admittedly before he knew the identity of the god or hero responsible.

[19] As Kearns remarks, then (1989: 10), 'like gods, heroes may concern themselves with almost any aspect of an individual's life'. Cf. also 1. 67. 2: the Spartans ask which god they should propitiate for their fortunes to improve in their war against Tegea, and are told to look for the bones of Orestes. It is presumably in the expectation of some return that the Acanthians call on Artachaies by name, 7. 117. 2.

beauty are both divine characteristics.[20] It was because of her exceptional size—three fingers short of four cubits—and beauty that the humble Phye was chosen to impersonate Athena (1. 60. 4; cf. 4. 180. 3). Phye's divinity is false. However, if divinity is defined essentially in human terms, this has the consequence that humans are capable of attaining—at least in part—to divinity. Artachaies, heroized by the Acanthians, was the tallest of all the Persians at four fingers short of five royal cubits—8 feet 2 inches (nearly 2.5m.), in Rawlinson's estimate—and had the strongest voice of any man (7. 117; cf. 4. 141). What made Philip the son of Boutacides worthy of heroization was his beauty (5. 47. 2).[21] The story of the Spartan Lycurgus' visit to Delphi appears to have similar implications, that outstanding human characteristics elevate some men above others, though the criteria of divinity in this case are never expressed: 'I wonder if you to whom I prophesy are god or man', the Pythia told him, 'but I think rather that you are a god' (1. 65. 3).[22] At the same time, of course, by imitating the divine too closely, men can themselves incur divine envy. As discussed above in Chapter 2, the behaviour recommended by Thrasybulus to Periander, to cut down all those men in Corinth who stand out above the ordinary

[20] For the physical characteristics of heroes, see esp. Mussies (1988: 4–5). Beauty is given miraculously, apparently, by Helen to the wife of Ariston, the mother of Demaratus, 6. 61. 2–5 (for which see the excellent discussion of Boedeker 1987: esp. 188–9). Dreams are good-looking, e.g. 7. 12. 1. For beauty as in the gift of a goddess in Homer, cf. H. *Od.* 6. 224 ff., 18. 190 ff., 23. 156 ff. Beauty is seen as the prerogative of goddesses: it is not seemly for mortals to rival them, H. *Od.* 5. 212–3; Helen recognizes Aphrodite by her beauty even when she is in disguise, H. *Il.* 3. 395 ff.

[21] Fontenrose (1968) and Bohringer (1979) discuss a number of athletes paid heroic honours, but (unlike Visser 1982: 410) the frequent references to beauty do not strike them. Isocrates, 10. 60, remarks that more mortals were rendered immortal as a result of their beauty than for any other virtue. Vandiver sees the size of Orestes' bones only as an 'iconic metaphor for a hero' (1991: 37). For other good-looking individuals (and hints of a heroic ideal applying to Persians as well as Greeks), cf. 4. 91. 2; 6. 127. 4; 7. 187. 2; 9. 25. 1, 72. 1, 96. 2. For the beauty and strength of Persian kings, cf. Briant (1996: 237–9). In Homer similarly the heroic ideal of beauty applies equally to Greeks and Trojans: Hall (1989: 40).

[22] Other individuals, never explicitly termed heroes, may have heroic overtones: see Boedeker (1987: 190) of Demaratus, suggesting that he 'reverberates with potential for disaster which is not fully realized'.

(5. 92. ζ2), mimics the character of the divine as described by Artabanus to Xerxes (7. 10. ε). The garish punishment of Pheretime for her excessive punishment of the people of Barca might be interpreted as due to her having usurped a divine prerogative.[23] Tyrants or potential tyrants have a virtual monopoly over another divine characteristic also—envy itself (3. 52. 5, 80. 4, 146. 1; 7. 236. 1, 237. 2; 8. 69. 1).

A similar pattern of uncertainty and contradiction can be seen in Herodotus' distinction of the 'daimon'. Herodotus uses 'daimon' for the most part interchangeably with 'god'.[24] Poseidon and the Dioscuri are both termed daimones by Herodotus while in both the surrounding sentences they are gods (2. 43. 3). The Borysthenites describe Dionysus in the same sentence as a daimon and a god (4. 79. 4). Isis is the daimon whom the Egyptians consider the greatest (2. 40. 1). Apollo too is arguably referred to as a daimon. Cyrus puts Croesus on the pyre to see if one of the daimones would save him (1. 86. 2). When subsequently explaining his actions to Cyrus, Croesus remarks that the 'god of the Greeks' had encouraged him to go to war. No one would make war gratuitously, 'but a daimon wished these things to happen thus' (1. 87. 4).[25] 'Daimon' and 'God' are also apparently interchangeable in a number of passing Herodotean expressions. When Artabanus remarks, for example, that a 'daemonic impulse' (δαιμονίη ὁρμή) had sprung up and a 'god-sent destruction' (φθορή . . . θεήλατος), no theological distinction seems intended (7. 18. 3).[26] Again, as we have seen, when a woman deserter tells Pausanias that Xerxes had no respect for 'gods or daimones' rather than, in Themistocles' formulation,

[23] Mossman (1995: 175).

[24] François (1957: 334–6); see also Page, *SLG* 387. 4, Richardson, *HHD* 300. François develops a theory of the evolution of the word from a primitive sense that excluded the Olympian gods (1957: 328–9, 334). In the light of the fact that the first uses of daimon to describe the Olympian gods are from Homer, and given the prolonged coexistence of the multiple senses of the word (catalogued by François) for the centuries after Homer, it seems an act only of wishful thinking to project back a pure sense of the word. Similar speculations on the origins of the term can be seen in the tortuous account of Dietrich (1965: 14–58), or in Usener's idea of 'Söndergotter' (1896), criticized sensibly by Farnell (1921: 76–94). Two more sensible accounts of the evolution of the term are Burkert (1985a: 179–81, 329–32), and Detienne (1963: 169–70).

[25] But see François's suggestion of the alternative reading δαιμόσι (1957: 202 n. 2), accepted by Rosén.   [26] Linforth (1928: 233).

'gods and heroes' (8. 109. 3; cf. 8. 143. 2), the point is simply to
emphasize how the King was scornful of *all* Greek divinities.[27]
At the same time, the term 'daimon' can describe individuals
whom we might expect to have been called heroes, such as
Iphigenia[28] or lesser divinities such as Damias and Auxesia
(4. 103. 2, 5. 83. 3).[29] Two ideas seem to coexist, unchallenged
and unrationalized: one that Iphigenia, say, is somehow of a
type with Poseidon, the other that there is a second (if not also a
third[30]) division of divinities.[31]

[27] Gods and daimones are differentiated by this formula e.g. at E. *El.* 1234,
Med. 1391, P. *Crat.* 438c, Ar. *Pl.* 81, Is. *Men.* 47, Andoc. *Myst.* 97 (describing
an oath prescribed by law to consider all tyrannicides pure before the gods and
daimones).

[28] For the ambiguous status of Iphigenia, see Farnell (1921: 55–8), but esp.
Kearns (1989: 27–35).

[29] Evidence for the confusion of heroes and daimones can be seen e.g. in
Hesiod's use of the word (*Erga* 122–6) to describe the men of the Golden Age
(*contra* François 1957: 338 n. 1), their function as 'guardians' is reminiscent of
the intermediary function of heroes), and in Plato's application of the term to
those who are brave in battle, *Resp.* 469a–b, 540c (although Plato, following
Hesiod, *Crat.* 398b–c, also argues that good men should be considered
daimones in their lifetimes). Diotima's daimon Eros has similar intermediary
functions, P. *Symp.* 202d–203a. Other cases of men as daimones (cited by
François 1957: 340): Theogn. 1348, Aesch. *Pers* 620, 641 (though see below,
n. 31), E. *Alc.* 1003, Isoc. *Ev.* 72, *Paneg.* 151 (although there is some
confusion between daimones and gods in these last two instances). Cf. also
E. *Rhes.* 971, Theogn. 991. François also gives a more extensive list of uses of
daimon to describe 'un être surnaturel secondaire' (1957: 337–9).

[30] For the series gods–daimones–heroes, see P. *Leg.* 738b, 818c, *Resp.* 427b,
Epin. 984b–985b, but compare e.g. *Leg.* 799a (the gods, their children and
daimones), 909e–910a (the gods, daimones and the gods' children), 848d (the
gods and the daimones that follow them). The formula gods—daimones—
heroes can also be found in inscriptions from Dodona, *GDI* 1566, 1582a, and
1585b (on the basis of which Burkert suggests a ritual background to the
formula (1972: 74 n. 132)), but see *GDI* 1582b and 1587 for the alternative
formula 'gods and heroes'. More sensibly Detienne explains the formula by a
desire not to omit from prayer any possible source of helpful intervention
(1963: 40). Dietrich (1965: 26) wrongly talks of a clear hierarchy or 'system' of
gods, daimones and heroes in philosophy. Vernant (1980: 107–8) also gives an
oversimplified picture of a clear hierarchy, but then blurs it: the gods are more
distant in philosophy, in Vernant's view, but the intermediary class of heroes
(which has expanded to take in daimones) gives men a kind of stepping stone to
divinity, thus more immediate at the same time as distant.

[31] As Kearns remarks of the ambivalent status of heroes, 'when the group of
three is reduced to two, as not infrequently happens in such a series, heroes

There are other shades to the definition of the daimon, however, than simply that of a vaguely subordinate divinity.[32] It may in some contexts have pejorative overtones.[33] The Ionians, suffering—as they think—under the slavery of the naval training of Dionysius of Phocaea, ask which daimon they have offended (6. 12. 3). Croesus, after his defeat by Cyrus, is clearly scornful of Apollo, even after the god has saved his life (1. 87. 3–4, 90. 2, 4): just as he belittles Apollo as the 'god of the Greeks', terming the god a daimon may be intended to diminish him. Cyrus was at least unsure of the effectiveness of the daimones revered by Croesus when he chose to test them by placing Croesus on the pyre (1. 86. 2). The Borysthenite, who taunts the Scythians with his report of how their king is possessed by Dionysus (4. 79. 4), possibly switches from describing Dionysus as a god to describing him as a daimon

may move either towards gods or men' (1989: 125). Cf. Mikalson (1991: 45): 'what emerges is a complex structure in which terms such as "god", "the gods", *daimon,* and "hero" move into or apart from from one another.' In this Herodotus is not unusual: see e.g. Aeschylus' various descriptions of Darius in the *Persae*, 155–8 (θεοῦ—Chorus), 632 (μόνος . . . θνητῶν—Ch.), 634 (ἰσοδαίμων βασιλεὺς—Ch.), 641–3 (δαίμονα, Σουσιγενῆ θεόν—Ch.), 647 (φίλος ἀνήρ), 711 (Πέρσαις ὡς θεὸς—Queen), 857 (ἰσόθεος—Ch.).

[32] There is no evidence, however, of the 'distributive' definition of the word (see Burkert (1985*a*: 420 n. 3), Dietrich (1965: 14 and n. 1), Wilamowitz (1931: 362–9); contrast François (1957: 9)), the sense of daimon as a spirit or genie (François 1957: 333–4), as a variety of monstrous animals (Dietrich 1965: 18–20) or as a man's personal fortune (it is the gods who look out for Cyrus, 1. 124. 1, 209. 4, even if then the daimon sends him a dream, 1. 210. 1), nor is there any strong evidence of the use of 'daimon' in the collective sense of François as 'une Puissance suprême' (François 1957: 207–8).

[33] Cf. e.g. Aesch. *Ag.* 769, 1175, 1468, 1482, 1660, *Pers.* 345, 354, 472, 515, 724–5, 911, 921, *Sept.* 705, E. *Hel.* 201, P. *Epist.* vii. 336b. Cf. also Hippocr. viii. 466 Littré (evil daimones drive women to suicide). For the evolution of daimones into evil 'demons', see Burkert (1985*a*: 179–81, 329–32). See also Detienne (1963: 32 ff., 46 ff., 48 ff.) for the association of daimones with (respectively) agricultural afflictions, diseases, and vengeance. Brunius-Nilsson (1955: 132–3) is right to insist, however (on the basis of Herodotus' juxtaposition of εὐδαιμονίη and κακοδαιμονίη, 1. 87. 3) that the daimonic is not necessarily either good or evil in itself. Cf. also the use of δαιμόνιος as an insult, 4. 126, 7. 48, 8. 84. 2 (on which see Brunius-Nilsson 1955: esp. 80–2). Burkert (1985*a*: 180) uses this expression (in epic, at least) as evidence that daimon and theos are 'never simply interchangeable': the expression evidences a belief in daimon as 'occult power, a force that drives man forward where no agent can be named'. This kind of reconstruction of beliefs on the

in order to remind the Scythians sarcastically of their low estimation of the god (4. 79. 3):[34]

'You mock us, Scythians, because we become frenzied and the god possesses us. But now this daimon has possessed even your king, and he too is in a frenzy and is made mad by the god. If you do not trust me, follow me, and I will show you.'

Similar pejorative associations may underlie Herodotus' use of the word to describe the god of the Getai, Salmoxis (4. 94–6). The Getai believed, he says, that when they died they went 'to their daimon Salmoxis' (παρὰ Σάλμοξιν δαίμονα, 4. 94. 1),[35] and that no other god existed but their own (4. 94. 4). The Greeks, however, told a story that Salmoxis was a slave of Pythagoras who hid himself in an underground chamber and then re-emerged four years later—a stunt designed to convince the Getai of his immortality (4. 95).[36] This version, Herodotus says, he neither doubts nor 'trusts too much' (4. 96. 1).[37] Whether Salmoxis had been a man or was a 'local daimon' of the Getae, the matter should be let be (4. 96. 2). That Herodotus should use the term 'daimon' rather than 'god' in the context of an individual whose divinity was so clearly

basis of etymology is difficult to prove, however. Less convincing still, for example, is Burkert's attempt (1985a: 181) to see a belief in a man's personal daimon behind words such as *eudaimon* (although this can more legitimately be seen in earlier sources, e.g. Theogn. 653–4, cited by Wilamowitz (1931: 369)). An expression such as δαιμόνιος may be more significant for its epic than its theological overtones (as suggested of 8. 84. 2 by Brunius-Nilsson 1955: 82).

[34] Cf. Aesch. *Suppl.* 921–2: Greek gods are gods, Egyptian gods daimones.

[35] For Getan immortality, see Coman (1981), Guthrie (1962: 158–9) for its un-Greek character; for the meaning of the word ἀθανατίζουσι see Linforth (1918).

[36] For the association of daimones and Pythagoreanism, see Burkert (1972: 73 ff.), Detienne (1963), Alexandrescu (1980); for the story of Salmoxis' underground chamber as a misunderstanding of Thracian myth and ritual, see Burkert (1972: 157 ff.), Eliade (1972: 24–7), Pfister (1953). It is possible that Herodotus' description of Salmoxis as a daimon is an allusion to, or (more likely) indirectly influenced by, this association of daimones and Pythagoreans. Alexandrescu possibly sees too much significance in Herodotus' choice of the word. See also Pritchett (1993: 115) for a defence of the Salmoxis story against the charge of fabrication. For Salmoxis, see further Ch. 8.

[37] Cf. Soph. *El.* 884 (πιστεύεις ἄγαν). Cf. also the two alternative versions of the fate of the Tyndaridae, immortality or death, E. *Hel.* 137 ff.

suspect, and to whom (even if he were not a fraud) he is willing only to ascribe the status of a local divinity, may not be accidental.[38] The same association of a merely regional influence is, of course, common to Croesus' remarks about Apollo (1. 90. 2, 4).

One further distinguishing feature of the daimon must be discussed: that is, precisely its lack of clear character. In the almost mystically beautiful words of Walter Burkert,

> Daimon does not designate a specific class of divine beings, but a peculiar mode of activity . . . Daimon is occult power, a force that drives man forward where no agent can be named . . . Every god can act as a daimon; not every act of his reveals the god. Daimon is the veiled countenance of divine activity. There is no image of a daimon and there is no cult. Daimon is thus the necessary complement to the Homeric view of the gods as individuals with personal characteristics; it covers that embarrassing remainder which eludes characterization and naming.[39]

It can be stated straight away that such a characterization will not possibly cover all the term's usages. Poseidon, the Dioscuri, Salmoxis, Isis, Iphigenia are all named as daimones (2. 40. 1, 43. 3; 4. 94. 1, 96. 2, 103. 2). Though these disparate figures may not constitute a clear 'class of divine beings', equally clearly they suggest no distinctly daimonic 'mode of activity'. When Amasis transforms a golden footbath into the image of a daimon—implying, of course, the possibility that daimones might be the object of cult[40]—there is no question, similarly, that the term is meant to suggest any characteristics, such as anonymity or the impersonal, distinct from those of a god (2. 172. 3). Some expressions employed by Herodotus—

---

[38] Cf. Hartog (1978: 18–19).

[39] Burkert (1985a: 180). See also Brunius-Nilsson (1955: 126); Else (1949: 29–30), 'It is not a religious word and the daimôn as such is not a personality; one does not pray to a, or the, daimôn'; Chantraine (1952: 51); Detienne (1963: 13, 20, 27, 131, 52), 'Le δαίμων est la traduction dans le langage de la pensée religieuse de certains phénomènes de la vie humaine . . .' Contrast Rudhardt (1992a: 55–6, 104, 319), for whom a daimon may be either a minor divinity ('plus ou moins nettement individualisées') or an anonymous, impersonal divinity, Brunius-Nilsson's sensible survey of daimon in Homer (1955: 115–34), or François (1957: 9–10, 327–43), who envisages an even broader range of definitions.

[40] Cf. also P. Resp. 427b, Leg. 828a–b, 909e–910a.

'according to some daimon' (κατὰ δαίμονα, 1. 111. 1), 'if a daimon wishes it' (εἰ δαίμων ἐθέλει, 3. 119. 6), or 'it was a daimon's wish that this should happen' (ἀλλὰ ταῦτα δαίμονί κου φίλον ἦν οὕτω γενέσθαι, 1. 87. 4)[41]—seem initially to support this conception of daimonic intervention.[42] However, such expressions can all be paralleled by others in the *Histories*. 'According to some daimon' (κατὰ δαίμονα, 1. 111. 1) seems no different in meaning, for example, from 'by divine chance' (θείῃ τύχῃ, e.g. 5. 92. γ3).[43] As mentioned above, a 'daimonic impulse' (δαιμονίη ὁρμή) and a 'god-sent destruction' (φθορή θεήλατος) threaten the Greeks in tandem (7. 18. 3). Such parallels could be multiplied.[44] Herodotus indeed has ample ways of covering the 'embarrassing remainder' which individuated, Homeric gods cannot reach. As Ivan Linforth remarked, 'when he is speaking with the deepest conviction of the divine government of the world, the words which come most naturally to his lips are οἱ θεοί, ὁ θεός, or τὸ θεῖον.'[45]

Indeed it is often claimed that such 'vague designations' were adopted by Herodotus not simply as a complement but as an *alternative* to individuated, Homeric gods. Such expressions indicate, it has been said, the 'desire to avoid predicating

[41] Although, in this last case, the daimon is possibly identifiable as Apollo.
[42] When the Ionians ask which of the daimones they have offended, their question is surely rhetorical (6. 12. 3).
[43] See further Ch. 3.
[44] The daimon warned Cyrus that he would die among the Massagetai to be succeeded by Darius (1. 210. 1; cf. 3. 65. 4), just as the god was said by the Magi to have forewarned the Greeks of the eclipse of their cities by an eclipse of the sun (7. 37. 2–3); cf. also 1. 31. 3; 6. 27. 3, 98. 1; 9. 120. 2. (For the association of dreams and daimones, see esp. Detienne (1963: 43–6); however, gods also send dreams, 7. 15. 3, 16. β1, 18. 3.) The remark of Croesus that the course of events was δαίμονί . . . φίλον (1. 87. 4) can be paralleled by the judgement (ascribed by Herodotus to the majority of barbarians) that animals would not copulate in temples were it 'not dear to the god' (τῷ θεῷ . . . μὴ φίλον, 2. 64. 2); cf. also 7. 10. ε, 6. 27. 1. Intaphernes' wife's remark that she could have another husband εἰ δαίμων ἐθέλοι, but never another brother, 3. 119. 6, can perhaps be paralleled by Themistocles saying that if men fail to deliberate reasonably 'the god does not wish' to help them (οὐκ ἐθέλει . . . ὁ θεὸς, 8. 60. γ). Themistocles' remark is perhaps, however, a less casual piece of theology than that of Intaphernes' wife: 3. 119. 6 can better be compared then with expressions such as κατὰ δαίμονα and θείῃ τύχῃ, 1. 111. 1, 5. 92. γ3.
[45] Linforth (1924: 287).

anything of the divine as far as possible'.[46] The expression οἱ θεοί
clearly in one sense assumes the existence of a plurality of gods.
Expressions such as 'one of the gods' or 'none of the gods',[47]
'alone of' or 'fastest of the gods',[48] or references to the temples of
the gods or the worship they deserve[49] clearly emphasize this
plurality. But in those cases in which some form of (actual or
potential) intervention is ascribed to 'the gods', the number of
the gods seems to make little or no difference. The formulaic
expression θεῶν τὰ ἴσα νεμόντων, or 'if the gods are impartial',
used in advance of both the battles of Lade and Marathon by the
respective Greek commanders (6. 11. 3, 109. 5), can be paralleled
by Herodotus' more conscious judgement on the storms that hit
the Persian fleet at Aphetae that 'all this was done by the god so
that the Persian force should be made level (ἐξισωθείη) to the
Greek' (8. 13). The gods gave Croesus as a slave to Cyrus,
Croesus asserts (1. 89. 1); they overlook and protect Cyrus
(1. 124. 1, 209. 4); they led Panionius into the hands of his
nemesis (8. 106. 3). But Croesus, it should be noted, also ascribes
his mistaken attack on Cyrus (shortly before) to the 'god of the
Greeks'—to be understood, from the context, to be Apollo—and
to his own 'ill fortune and Cyrus' good fortune' (1. 87. 3). Cyrus'
survival from death as a child was 'by divine chance' (1. 126. 6),
'according to a daimon' (1. 111. 1), was made out to be 'more
divine' than it was by his parents (θειοτέρως, 1. 122. 3), and was
'according to the gods and [Harpagus]' (1. 124. 1).[50] 'Tisis and
Hermotimus' caught up with Panionius (8. 106. 4). Except
perhaps in so far as the last two expressions emphasize the
'dual determination' of the events in question,[51] no significant

---

[46] Lloyd ii. 18–9; cf. A. B. Lloyd (1990: 249). See also Linforth (1928: 238),
Lachenaud (1978: 644), Boedeker (1988: 46). Pötscher (1958: 8) suggests that
Herodotus uses θεῖον and θεός on different levels, without clearly indicating the
differences; he sees τὸ θεῖον (p. 29) as Herodotus' way of making history
comprehensible in terms of the divine.

[47] 1. 45. 2, 67. 2, 86. 2; 2. 52. 1, 82. 1; 6. 80.

[48] 1. 90. 2, 216. 4; 2. 29. 7; 3. 8. 3; 5. 7.

[49] 1. 118. 2; 2. 133. 2; 4. 78. 4; 8. 144. 2.

[50] κατὰ θεούς τε καὶ ἐμέ. Harpagus could have used a formulation such as 'by
divine chance and his own ingenuity' (cf. 1. 68. 1) without any significant
change in meaning.

[51] For similar expressions suggestive of 'dual determination', cf. 4. 136. 4,
7. 139. 5, 8. 106. 4.

distinction could be drawn between such expressions. Pheretime's death showed how excessive vengeances were begrudged by
the gods (ἐπίφθονοι, 4. 205), but the divine can also be grudging or
envious (1. 32. 1, 3. 40. 2; cf. 7. 46. 3, 8. 109. 3); the very
comparable vengeance that falls upon Alexander and the Trojans, revealing how great injustices receive great vengeances, is
ascribed by Herodotus both to the gods and to τὸ δαιμόνιον
(2. 120. 5).[52] Possibly the only passage in which divine intervention is ascribed to 'the gods' where the term suggests any, even
casual, theological distinction is that, already cited in this
chapter, in which Protesilaus is said to receive his power to
exact vengeance from the gods (9. 120. 2).[53]

The expression ὁ θεός is more problematic. It can undoubtedly in some instances refer to a particular divinity.
When, in the course of tracing the genealogy of Perseus, for
example, Herodotus announces that he is omitting 'the god',
the partner of Danaë, the god can be supposed safely to be Zeus
(6. 53. 1). The god of Delphi can be assumed to be Apollo
(1. 50. 1, 7. 132. 2, 9. 81. 1).[54] In some cases, it is clear also that
ὁ θεός may serve as a shorthand for 'the god in question'.[55]
Animals, most foreign peoples reason, would not copulate in
temples 'if it were not dear to the god' (2. 64. 2): just as
Demeter or Poseidon punished the violators of their temples
(9. 65. 2; 8. 129. 3), so the gods in question would have

---

[52] For other uses of τὸ δαιμόνιον, cf. 5. 87. 2, 6. 84. 1 (both interestingly in
the context of madness: cf. Parker (1983: 247–8) on the verb δαιμονιῶ); for the
expression δαιμονίη . . . ὁρμή (7. 18. 3), see above, this chapter.

[53] For other uses of οἱ θεοί, see 8. 109. 3, 143. 2; 9. 76. 2 ('gods and heroes'
or 'gods and daimones'), 1. 27. 3, 1. 71. 4; 3. 21. 3 (gods introduce foolish or
bad ideas of external expansion into men's minds), 2. 139. 2 (Sabacus avoids
evil 'from gods or men'), 8. 65. 5 (the gods will take care of Xerxes' army,
according to Demaratus).

[54] See Linforth (1928: 219–20) for more of these unambiguous cases.
Attribution to a particular god on the basis of traditional characteristics
cannot, however, be taken for granted in the light of e.g. 7. 129. 4 (discussed
above, Ch. 3). See below for 7. 10. ε. Cf. also the destruction of the palace of
Scyles by lightning, 4. 79. 2, ascribed by Linforth to Zeus (1928: 219), though
Scyles was also on the verge of initiation into the rites of Dionysus.

[55] Linforth (1928: 223). I do not discuss certain relatively uncontroversial
passages treated by Linforth or François, for example those where 'the god' is
used as shorthand for the advice of an oracle, 5. 1, 7. 170. 1 (for which see
Linforth (1928: 223–4); on 7. 170. 1 see also François (1957: 206)).

protected theirs. But in other instances, it is clear that ὁ θεός must stand for divinity in general.[56] Most obvious perhaps are the remarks of Solon in Book 1, where 'the god' appears to be interchangeable with 'the divine', and where no particular divinity is available to be supplied (1. 32. 1, 9; cf. 1. 31. 3).[57] Similar are the remarks of Artabanus to Xerxes (7. 46. 3–4) or of an anonymous Persian to Thersander (9. 16. 4).[58] In both cases ὁ θεός is opposed to ὁ ἄνθρωπος,[59] suggesting that ὁ θεός stands for 'god-kind' as opposed to mankind (e.g. 7. 46. 4):

So death, life being burdensome, becomes the most desirable refuge for man, and the deity, having given us a taste of the sweetness of life, is discovered to be jealous in his gift (οὕτως ὁ μὲν θάνατος μοχθηρῆς ἐούσης τῆς ζόης καταφυγὴ αἱρετωτάτη τῷ ἀνθρώπῳ γέγονε, ὁ δὲ θεὸς γλυκὺν γεύσας τὸν αἰῶνα φθονερὸς ἐν αὐτῷ εὑρίσκεται ἐών).

Herodotus in such instances is presenting generalizations about the nature of divinity. To suppose that he intended the reader to understand 'the particular god active in a particular course of events' is surely unduly legalistic.[60] Herodotus' remark that 'the god showed these signs' to the Chians (6. 27. 3) is made again in the context of what appears to be a generalizing statement of the behaviour of divinity in general (6. 27. 1):

Whenever great evils are about to occur to a city or a people, there tend to be [or: the god tends to give?[61]] signs in advance (φιλέει δέ κως προσημαίνειν εὖτ' ἂν μέλλῃ μεγάλα κακὰ ἢ πόλι ἢ ἔθνεϊ ἔσεσθαι). And the signs given to the Chians in advance of these events were great.

[56] For the collective sense, see Linforth (1928: 222–3), comparing 1. 69. 2 (τὸν Ἕλληνα), 1. 80. 2 (τῇ καμήλῳ), or the expression 'send for the doctor': 'The singular form does not mean that there is only one doctor in the world, nor does it mean that all doctors are somehow merged in one'; cf. Else (1949: 31) on ὁ ἄνθρωπος. See also the distinction of François (1957: 17) between the collective and the generic sense. Legrand (1932: 131) divides the instances of ὁ θεός in Herodotus into three categories: those in which the phrase is to be taken in 'une valeur collective', taken to mean 'la puissance suprême regnant sur les dieux de second rang', and those where a particular god is intended.

[57] Rather than seeing the divine and the god as equivalent in meaning here, Linforth believes (1928: 230) that 'one god is typical of the conduct of all the gods'.   [58] Cf. also 8. 60. γ.

[59] In 9. 16. 4, there is no article before ἀνθρώπῳ, but there is still the same sense of two opposing spheres: ὅ τι δεῖ γενέσθαι ἐκ τοῦ θεοῦ, ἀμήχανον ἀποτρέψαι ἀνθρώπῳ.   [60] Linforth (1928: 231).

[61] Linforth (1928: 227–8): 'no doubt ὁ θεός is to be understood'; he then

It is hard here also to imagine substituting any particular god for 'the god' without the sentence losing some of its sense: can Herodotus really be saying that the 'god in question' or 'the particular god who sent the signs' has a tendency to send signs?[62]

The possibility of such a generalizing use of ὁ θεός should prompt us to be more cautious in 'reading in' the identity of particular divinities. In cases of the use of ὁ θεός where no particular divinity is implied—either by the context or (less certainly) by the god's action matching the traditional attributes of a specific divinity—we cannot really be sure that the reading 'the god in question' is the correct one. When Prexaspes remarks to Cambyses, for example, after Cambyses had shot his son dead with an arrow, that 'not even the god could shoot so well' (3. 35. 4), to supply, as Linforth does, 'the god who has special skill with the bow' is surely to fill out Herodotus' thought unjustifiably.[63] Linforth may well be right in saying that 'no Greek, reading this, could take "the god" to be the unified divine power', but this is perhaps to establish an unnecessarily harsh opposition. The use of ὁ θεός to mean divinity in general need not entail a conception of a 'unified divine power'; it need not, in fact, imply any theological reflection at all.[64]

says that a belief in signs 'has no theistic implications'. Macan, ad loc. (iv. 1. 289), suggests that ὁ θεός here is Zeus.

[62] Contrast François' acknowledgement (1957: 204–5) that 6. 27. 3 and 6. 98. 1 (and more cautiously 7. 18. 3) may refer to particular gods.

[63] Linforth (1928: 226); he adds, however, that a Greek 'would probably think of Apollo, as a Persian would think of Mithra'. The same objection can be made to Linforth's interpretation of another passage. The Persian fleet was wrecked ὑπὸ τοῦ θεοῦ in order that the two forces should be reduced to the same level (8. 13). Linforth says that to supply Boreas, Zeus, or Poseidon, is 'to know more than Herodotus knew in the matter'; τοῦ θεοῦ is merely 'the god who caused the storm'. But the word must, surely, embrace the possibility that not one but all of these gods could have been responsible. This position is, of course, not very different from Linforth's suggestion of the 'collective singular': it is important to stress, though, that Herodotus' words in a case such as this were probably not carefully weighed. François interprets τοῦ θεοῦ here as 'la Puissance divine' (1957: 202, 204), comparing it with 2. 120. 5.

[64] Cf. Linforth (1928: 226–7) on 1. 210. 1, supposing that the daimon who sent a dream to Cyrus should be taken to mean 'the god who sends the dream and who has the affair in hand'. Cyrus' remark follows closely after his saying that 'the gods' look after him, 1. 209. 4: it is at least as possible that 'the gods' and 'the daimon' have the same sense then. For the omission of the article, e.g.

Indeed, there are at least two passages in which Herodotus can be shown to alternate suddenly from the usage of 'divinity in general' to speaking of a particular divinity. The reason why we can be certain of this is that the divinity in question is female, in both cases Hera. So, the mother of Cleobis and Biton prays—in front of the image of Hera—for the goddess (τὴν θεὸν) to grant her sons the best fortune possible for man (1. 31. 4). Herodotus' gloss on the passage—or rather Solon's—while echoing the words of the woman's prayer, attributes the whole episode to 'the god', a masculine god (1. 31. 3): 'the god showed through these things that death is better than life for men' (ὁ θεὸς). Similar is the story of the Spartan Cleomenes' sacrifice to Hera. After burning a grove sacred to the hero Argos, Cleomenes reckoned (or claimed that he reckoned, 6. 82. 1) that 'the oracle of the god' (that is, Apollo) which prophesied that he would capture Argos had been fulfilled. He then offered sacrifice to Hera in order to see whether the god (ὁ θεὸς) was favourable to his advancing further or not (6. 82. 2). A flame shone out of the head of the image, showing him that he had done 'everything that the god wished' (ὅσον ὁ θεὸς ἐβούλετο γενέσθαι). In both cases, we could indulge in elaborate theological justifications of Herodotus' terminology. In the case of Cleobis and Biton, we could follow Linforth in supposing that the 'generalizing masculine represents Hera as typical of divine opinion' or that his use of ὁ θεὸς to describe even a goddess shows how well established was this idiom for 'the particular god in question'.[65] In the case of Cleomenes, we might suppose that 'conduct of the affair' had passed to Hera, or that Cleomenes had resorted to Hera 'as the nearest representative of god-kind, to learn the will of Apollo'; but, as Linforth himself concluded, this is precisely the 'kind of theological question that Herodotus and Greeks in general did not raise'.[66] The precise relationship between ὁ θεὸς and Hera—what

at 1. 209. 4, see François (1957: 205, 305 n. 2). François (1957: 207) sees this as an instance of the collective sense of daimon.

[65] Linforth (1928: 232–3). Cf. 2. 133. 2, 1. 105. 4. In the second of these cases Rosén now accepts the variant reading of ἡ θεός, though ὁ θεός must surely be the *lectio difficilior*.

[66] Linforth (1928: 224–5). Cf. Legrand, ad loc. (6. 89 n. 3): 'le dieu suprême, dont Héra serait l'interprète'.

answer Herodotus might have given had he been presented with the inconsistency—is in neither case knowable. In both cases, all that can be safely told is that Herodotus swings from a generalizing divinity to talking of a specific one.

This quick alternation of a generalizing and a specific divinity raises further obstacles to any attempt to pin down the meaning of particular passages. We cannot assume a consistency of usage even from one sentence to another, let alone throughout an entire *logos*, or through the *Histories* as a whole.[67] One example out of many is Artabanus' speech to Xerxes advising him against undertaking the campaign to Greece (7. 10. ε). The god, according to Artabanus, 'strikes the tallest creatures with lightning' and does not allow them to 'vaunt themselves'; he throws his bolts always against the biggest houses and tallest trees; 'for the god loves always to cut down those that excel'; out of envy the god inflicts fear or thunder on men, for he does not allow anyone other than himself to 'think big thoughts'. If we were to judge on the basis of the traditional attributes of the gods, the mentions of thunder and lightning might suggest that we should identify Artabanus' god as Zeus. However, other features of the passage, the generalizing tone of the remark that 'the god loves always to cut down those that excel', or the mention of the envy of the god suggest that Artabanus is speaking of divinity in general: 'the god' is envious here as 'the divine' is, or the gods are, elsewhere (1. 32. 1, 3. 40. 2, 4. 205. 1).[68] It cannot clearly then be said whether a generalizing divinity is intended consistently throughout the passage, or whether Herodotus' usage constantly alternates. All that can be told, as Linforth comments in another context, is that 'Herodotus did not write Ζεύς and did write θεός, both words of four letters'.[69]

<hr/>

[67] See e.g. Linforth (1928: 231) on 1. 34. 1, implying on the basis of 1. 45. 2 that a particular god is intended; 1. 34. 1 equally follows hard on remarks of Solon in which 'the divine' appears to be interchangeable with 'the god' (1. 32. 1, 9). François makes the equally speculative suggestion (1957: 206) that Herodotus may have meant to distinguish his own interpretation of 1. 34. 1 from Croesus' of 1. 45. 2. Contrast Linforth (1928: 231) on the uncertainty of language and thought of 1. 87 ff.   [68] Cf. François (1957: 203–4).

[69] Linforth (1928: 228) (cf. pp. 220–1). See Linforth himself on 7. 10. ε (1928: 232): 'The first ὁ θεός is Zeus; the second is undetermined; in the third

If we move on to the last 'vague designation' for divinity in the *Histories*, τὸ θεῖον, some interesting differences become apparent. The most characteristic use of the expression 'the divine' is in the context of a deduction, by a character or by Herodotus himself, that a certain event is the result of miraculous intervention: the Cnidians calculate that the many injuries they had incurred by digging the canal across their isthmus were 'more divine than was reasonable' (1. 174. 4–5); the people of Dodona, when they saw a black dove speaking, understood that its pronouncements were divine (2. 55. 2); Polycrates realizes, when the ring that he discarded as a symbol of his good fortune resurfaces in the belly of a fish, that the matter was divine (θεῖον εἶναι τὸ πρῆγμα, 3. 42. 4); on hearing his wife swear that she had just been visited by a man who was his own double, Ariston realized that the 'affair was divine' (6. 69. 3); the vengeance wrought by Talthybius is judged 'most divine' and a 'matter divine' on the grounds of the coincidence that vengeance was visited on the sons of the same men who had previously escaped it; the coincidence of the battles of Plataea and Mycale, and the coincidences between the battles, convince Herodotus of 'the divine nature of affairs' (τὰ θεῖα τῶν πρηγμάτων, 9. 100. 2). Two other passages show the same process of deduction from different positions. Artabanus and Xerxes devise a test to discover whether or not dreams 'share in any way in the divine' (τι τοῦ θείου μετέχον, 7. 16. β2, γ1–2): because Xerxes' dream comes also to Artabanus, its divine origin is deemed proved. Cyrus' natural parents also put about that his foster mother Kyno (or 'bitch') had indeed been a dog so that the manner of his survival should seem 'more divine' (θειοτέρως, 1. 122. 3): they staged—at least in part—a miraculous escape from death. A piece of chance may be divine, similarly, depending on the significance of its outcome (1. 126. 6, 3. 139. 3, 4. 8. 3, 5. 92. γ3); ships are borne on, Smerdis' guards allow the conspirators past, the seer Amphilytus addresses Peisistratus, and a phantom boat appears to the Corinthian Adeimantus 'to have been sent by the divine' (θείῃ πομπῇ, 4. 152. 2; 3. 77. 1; 1. 62. 4; 8. 94. 2).[70]

the Zeus-motif sounds again . . .; in the fourth there is no limitation to any one god . . . Herodotus . . . really leaves the god undetermined throughout.'

[70] The same idea seems to lie behind the peculiar story of the divine

As the use of comparatives and superlatives,[71] or expressions such as 'sharing somewhat in the divine' make clear,[72] where τὸ θεῖον is used there is a much sharper sense of the judgement that divine intervention has taken place as a considered and rational deduction from events. Whereas ὁ θεός may be used for generalizing statements on the behaviour of divinity, and while ὁ θεός and οἱ θεοί are used to describe divine actions—could Herodotus have said so comfortably that 'the divine gave Croesus as a slave' into Cyrus' hands or that the 'divine fought alongside the Athenians'?—τὸ θεῖον is a term applied to the diagnosis of divine intervention in the world. There is a good deal of validity to such a sketch, but it is only a sketch. τὸ θεῖον may, in fact, exercise a surprising degree of initiative. The divine is prone to envy, Polycrates and Solon discover (1. 32. 1, 3. 40. 2), in exactly the same way as the god, gods or gods and heroes (although never any single named god) (4. 205; 7. 10. ε, 46. 4; 8. 109. 3). The 'foresight of the divine' (τοῦ θείου ἡ προνοίη, 3. 108. 1) engineers things so that fierce animals reproduce less easily than the weak.[73] τὸ δαιμόνιον, a term apparently largely synonymous with 'the divine',[74] engineered

possession of Egyptian cats (θεῖα πρήγματα, 2. 66. 3): see Ch. 2. Salamis is deduced to be divine—in a different sense, presumably, of being looked over by, or belonging to a god or gods—because of the good that will occur to the Greeks there, 7. 141. 4, 142. 2, 143. 1.

[71] Linforth (1928: 234–5) finds it 'somewhat curious' to find θεῖος used in the comparative and superlative degrees, 1. 122. 3, 174. 4; 7. 137. 2: 'there can hardly be degrees of divine agency'; the 'degrees of comparison are mere matters of language'. This overlooks the way in which the divine nature of miracles is deduced from the evidence of the impossibility of the event (see Ch. 3): the more miraculous, the more divine. This is something Linforth nearly recognizes in his actual analysis of the passages in question: e.g. on 1. 174. 4, 'as the injuries increased beyond this normal number, the probability of divine intervention became greater'; and on 7. 137. 2, 'this', says Herodotus, 'seems to me to have been a most certain instance of divine activity . . .'

[72] Cf. also 'more than human': 1. 204. 2, 2. 90. 2, 8. 140. β2.

[73] This is the first time, Pippidi (1960: 80), Parker (1992: 87), that (in Parker's words) 'divine *pronoia* is revealed in the permanent conditions of existence established by the gods'. Falus (1977) finds the idea of a natural equilibrium 'géniale' but sees its ascription to divine foresight as regrettable.

[74] There are no differences in meaning between θεῖον and δαιμόνιον (Linforth (1928: 233, 236); Rudhardt (1992a: 105))—unless possibly there are negative connotations to δαιμόνιον (as suggested above).

the Trojan wars as an example to men that great crimes receive great vengeances (2. 120. 5).

Another point needs to be underlined. The ascription of responsibility for an event to 'the divine' in no sense precludes in Herodotus' mind the responsibility of an individual divinity.[75] This is revealed most clearly in the case of the wrath of Talthybius, but individual divinities lurk close beneath the surface in many other instances.[76] Investigation reassured Ariston that his wife's visitor had been the hero Astrabacus (6. 69. 3). There were shrines of Demeter at the sites both of Plataea and of Mycale: if Herodotus makes the deduction of the 'divine nature of affairs' *on this basis*, this in no way excludes his ascribing some responsibility for the victories to Demeter in particular (9. 100. 2). Cleomenes' madness and death were, according to the Spartans, due to 'no divine cause' (ἐκ δαιμονίου . . . οὐδενὸς[77]) but alchoholism (6. 84. 1): as all the alternative explanations for his death take the form of vengence for particular acts of sacrilege against particular gods, it appears

---

[75] Herodotus speaks of τὸ ἀνθρώπινον, 1. 86. 5, neither to deny the plurality of men, nor out of a desire to predicate as little as possible of the human. See François (1957: 201–2) on the collective sense of τὸ θεῖον; cf. also Lloyd-Jones (1971: 64): the use of abstract terms does not prove him to be a 'disbeliever in the personal gods of legend'.

[76] The Cnidians were told by Delphi that if Zeus had wished Cnidos to be an island he would have made it one, 1. 174. 4–5. The black dove had just told the people of Dodona that it was necessary for them to establish there an oracle of Zeus, 2. 55. 2. That divine πομπή can, in some cases, be traced to an individual divinity is supported by the fact that Artabanus (while he still believes that dreams are not divine) speaks of a dream coming θεοῦ τινος πομπῇ or 'sent by some god' (7. 16. β1; cf. 7. 15. 3, 18. 3). That 'divine chance' is in theory traceable to a particular divinity is perhaps supported by 9. 91. 1: Leutychidas asks for the name of the Samian commander Hegesistratus, either in a conscious search for an omen, or 'by chance, (a) god contriving it' (εἴτε καὶ κατὰ συντυχίην θεοῦ ποιεῦντος).

[77] Linforth (1928: 237) believes that the addition of οὐδενὸς in this passage 'makes it almost certain that δαιμονίου is not a divine agent but a divine act. It is neither divine power in general . . . nor a particular god.' While it is still significant that Herodotus chooses to express himself in these abstract terms, it is impossible (given the alternative explanations of Cleomenes' death that this expression is intended to encapsulate) that Herodotus could have excluded the possibility of the responsibility of a particular god. François (1957: 203) follows Linforth's interpretation here, and more tentatively for 5. 87. 2.

that τὸ δαιμόνιον too can embrace the actions of individual divinities.[78]

Herodotus was no closet monotheist then.[79] The use of singular nouns, as Jean Rudhardt has observed, no more reflects a resolute monotheism than plurals would suggest a radical polytheism.[80] Indeed, as his portrayal of the Pelasgians before their discovery of the names of the gods reveals—their addressing the gods simply as 'gods' (2. 52. 1)[81]—Herodotus' polytheism was a rooted assumption. The use of ὁ θεός to describe divinity in general can be paralleled throughout early Greek literature:[82] there is no just cause then to think of this phenomenon as revolutionary,[83] or to talk of the fifth century as a time when 'the old polytheism was beginning to decline in Greece'.[84] His use of τὸ θεῖον is perhaps more original[85] but may in large part be the reflection of his historical subject

---

[78] Cf. 2. 120. 5: the lesson of Troy, engineered by τὸ δαιμόνιον was that great injustices met with great vengeances from the gods. See Linforth (1928: 233), François (1957: 202).

[79] Linforth (1928: 220). Lachenaud gives the same cautions (1978: 193, 204). Both Jones (1913: 252) and François (1957: 7) claim at first to have believed that the expression was a reflection of monotheism.

[80] Rudhardt (1981: 22).

[81] Though see Burkert (1985b: 130) for the curious description of the Pelasgian gods as an 'ungeschiedenen Einheit'; for this passage, see further below, Appendix 2.

[82] For similar terminology in other authors, see Jones (1913), but above all François (1957). In a passage of Aeschylus' Persae, for example, Darius manages to speak of Zeus, the gods and a god in the space of four lines without any particular reason for distinguishing them, 739–42. See now, in a Roman context, the comments of Feeney (1998: 80–1).

[83] Cf. Lachenaud (1978: 198). As Jones pointed out (1913: 254), 'it is therefore misleading to speak' of 'the vague use of θεός in tragedy'.

[84] Lloyd ii. 244. Lloyd admits that 'vague designations of the gods' were common in earlier times, but seems to envisage that they served a different function: 'when the worshipper felt a divine power at work which he could not identify.' The influence of pre-Socratic philosophy (as suggested also by Else 1949: 35) on this aspect of Herodotus' thought can be exaggerated. Xenophanes' paradoxical expression 'one god, greatest of gods and men', DK 21 B 23—if it is indeed genuine (see the compelling arguments of Edwards (1991) for its interpolation)—is no more than the epitome of a common strand of thought in Greek polytheism.

[85] For θεῖον in other authors, see François' 'index des mots grecs' s.v. θεῖον (1957: 362). The closest parallels are: Aesch. Cho. 958, Ag. 1084 (with Fraenkel, ad loc.), Soph. Phil. 1326, OC 1585.

matter:[86] in describing an everyday world in which divine intervention is not patent, in which gods do not—by and large—make direct appearances, insight into the divine is necessarily elusive; the conclusion that divine intervention has taken place depends inevitably on a process of 'diagnosis'.

Where the evidence is available, moreover, that diagnosis may proceed a step further: Herodotus not only deduces that the event was divine, but can speculate as to the particular god responsible. There is no evidence of a general unwillingness on Herodotus' part to ascribe intervention to named divinities.[87] So, for example, in the case of the Potidaea floodtide, the fact that the victims were the same men who had earlier committed acts of sacrilege against Poseidon, together perhaps with an assumption regarding the traditional attributes of Poseidon, suggests to the Potidaeans and to Herodotus that that god was responsible (8. 129. 3).[88] At Plataea similarly, the fact that of the Persians who died none lay within the sanctuary of Demeter can be explained, Herodotus speculates, by the information that the same Persians had earlier committed sacrilege at another shrine of Demeter (9. 65. 2):[89]

I think, if it is possible to speculate concerning divine affairs, that the goddess did not receive those who had burnt her shrine at Eleusis (δοκέω δέ, εἴ τι περὶ τῶν θείων πρηγμάτων δοκέειν δεῖ, ἡ θεὸς αὐτή σφεας οὐκ ἐδέκετο ἐμπρήσαντας [τὸ ἱρὸν] τὸ ἐν Ἐλευσῖνι ἀνάκτορον).

This final passage raises problems, however. Herodotus' apparent caution in speculating 'concerning divine matters'

---

[86] Cf. Pötscher (1958: 29). Contrast Immerwahr's idea of individual gods as local, the divine as transcending any locality (1966: 314).

[87] Contrast Linforth (1928: 218, 238–9); see also Lachenaud (1978: 208). There may be only a small number of cases in which such an attribution is certain (cf. Linforth 1928: 217), but this is to overlook those cases, discussed above in chs. 3–5, in which such an attribution is implicit.

[88] Cf. Herodotus' ascription of responsibility for the female disease of the Scythians who ravaged the temple of Aphrodite at Ascalon either to the goddess (Aphrodite) or to the god, 1. 105. 4, depending on one's reading of the text (see above, n. 65).

[89] Boedeker has suggested (1988: 46) that Demeter is particularly associated with vengeance by Herodotus. The evidence is limited, resting mainly (though cf. 6. 91, 134–6) on the coincidence that the (allegedly simultaneous) battles of Plataea and Mycale both took place by shrines of Demeter, 9. 101. 1. The victory at Plataea is also, implicitly at least, associated with Hera, 9. 61. 3–62.

has frequently been interpreted as evidence that he considers such matters incapable of proof, unsuitable material for history. Herodotus 'prefers', it has been said, 'not to explain what seemed to him inexplicable' but 'under pressure . . . threw out a *merely* divine explanation'.[90] The precise nature of Herodotus' reserve here, the extent to which he believed that knowledge of the divine was attainable, the distinctions that he drew between the knowable and the unknowable: these will be the focus of the following chapter.

[90] Lateiner (1989: 67).

7

The Limits of Knowledge and Inquiry

Herodotus' Egypt is a vast reservoir of knowledge of the gods. It was the Egyptians, for example, who first used the names of the twelve gods, and from whom the Greeks then took them on, who first established altars and images and temples to the gods (2. 4. 2), or from whom the phallic procession in honour of Dionysus was brought to Greece (2. 49). It was from an Egyptian story that Aeschylus learnt to make Artemis the daughter of Demeter (2. 156. 6), and from Egypt that some Greeks—Herodotus omits to name them—took the theory of the transmigration of the soul and pretended that it was their own (2. 123. 2–3).[1] But close to the outset of his account of Egypt Herodotus makes a surprising statement (2. 3. 2):

Those parts of what I heard them relate which concern the divine I am not eager to relate, with the exception only of their names, considering that all men know equally about such things. What I recall of such matters I will do because I am compelled by my narrative. (τὰ μέν νυν θεῖα τῶν ἀπηγημάτων οἷα ἤκουον, οὐκ εἰμὶ πρόθυμος ἐξηγέεσθαι, ἔξω ἢ τὰ οὐνόματα αὐτῶν μοῦνον, νομίζων πάντας ἀνθρώπους ἴσον περὶ αὐτῶν ἐπίστασθαι· τὰ δ' ἂν ἐπιμνησθέω αὐτῶν, ὑπὸ τοῦ λόγου ἐξαναγκαζόμενος ἐπιμνησθήσομαι.)

He then announces his intention to turn to 'human matters' (ἀνθρωπήια πρήγματα, 2. 4. 1). A similar remark—reassuring us that Herodotus' original remark was not 'written thoughtlessly'—follows later in Book 2.[2] All animals in Egypt are considered sacred (2. 65. 2):

But if I were to say for what reasons they are considered sacred, I would be delving in my narrative into divine affairs, which I especially mean to avoid. When I have touched upon them, I have

---

[1] For the truth of such borrowings, see now Zographou (1995); Herodotus is also central to Bernal's thesis of Egyptian influence on classical civilization (1987: ch. 1, esp. 75, 98–101).　　　　[2] Linforth (1924: 270).

spoken because constrained by necessity. (τῶν δὲ εἵνεκεν ἀνεῖται τὰ ἱρὰ
εἰ λέγοιμι, καταβαίην ἂν τῷ λόγῳ ἐς τὰ θεῖα πρήγματα, τὰ ἐγὼ φεύγω
μάλιστα ἀπηγέεσθαι. τὰ δὲ καὶ εἴρηκα αὐτῶν ἐπιψαύσας, ἀναγκαίῃ κατα-
λαμβανόμενος εἶπον.)

Even at a very basic level Herodotus' meaning here is difficult
to establish. Given the attention paid in Book 2 to the names of
the gods, and in particular to their distribution, it must surely
be 'the divine' in general that all men understand equally.[3]
There are difficulties even so. What does Herodotus mean to
exclude and why? Given Egypt's status as a source of knowledge of the gods how can all men possess equal knowledge of
the gods?[4]

Herodotus' 'policy of exclusion' is one that is limited to Egypt.
It is the divine things that he was told (or claimed to have been
told[5]) by the priests of Thebes, Memphis, and Heliopolis that he
is not eager to report. This narrow focus is confirmed by his
practice within Book 2. Immediately after he has announced his
intention of turning to 'human affairs', Herodotus reports that
the Egyptians were the first men to use the names of the twelve
gods, to establish altars and images and temples, and to carve
figures in stone (2. 4. 2). Herodotus' subsequent descriptions of
the Egyptians' worship of the gods, of their religious scruples or
their manner of sacrifice (e.g. 2. 37–42), must then, in the terms
of his initial distinction, fall outside the heading of 'the divine'.[6]
There are a number of other passages also in which Herodotus
appears to be referring back to his distinction: his discussions of
the nature of Heracles, god or hero or both (2. 43–5), of the

[3] Cf. Stein, ad loc., How and Wells, ad loc. (p. 157), Linforth (1924: 276–
7), Lloyd ii. 17.

[4] The most important contributions to this question are those of Linforth
(1924), Sourdille (1925), Lloyd ii. 17–19, Gould (1994: 92–4); see also Mora,
esp. (1981), Darbo-Peschanski (1987: 35–8). Some appear to take for granted
the meaning of Herodotus' distinction: Lloyd, ii. 17, pronounces that the
'distinction is, in fact, that between the metaphysical . . . and the physical
worlds'; Lateiner (1989: 247 n. 19) appears certain of the two chief exceptions
to the rule.

[5] See, however, for scepticism concerning Herodotus' Egyptian priests,
Heidel (1935), Fehling (1989: esp. 71 ff.) and West (1991). For attempts to
vindicate Herodotus, see Brown (1965), Wilson (1970), and more adequately
Lloyd (1988b: 25 ff.), Pritchett (1993) passim.

[6] Linforth (1924: 271), Sourdille (1925: 290), Lloyd ii. 17.

introduction of Dionysus to Greece (2. 49), of the nature of the
Pelasgians' worship of the gods before they learnt of the names
of the gods from Egypt (2. 50–53), or of the Egyptian chronology
of the gods and the Greek belief that Pan and Dionysus had lived
and grown old in Greece (2. 146), are all framed in terms of the
'names of the gods'.[7]

There are also clear traces of a pattern of deliberate omission
in Book 2, a pattern that is quite unparalleled in the *Histories*
more generally.[8]

1. The Mendesians portray Pan as a goat: 'for what reason they
portray him in this fashion it is not pleasing for me to say' (ὅτευ δὲ
εἵνεκα τοιοῦτον γράφουσι αὐτόν, οὔ μοι ἥδιόν ἐστι λέγειν, 2. 46. 2).

2. The Egyptians only sacrifice pigs to the moon and to Dionysus,
and only at the full moon: 'as to why they abominate pigs in all other
festivals but sacrifice them in this there is a story told about this by
the Egyptians but, though I know it, I find it unbecoming to mention
it' (δι' ὅ τι δὲ τοὺς ῦς ἐν μὲν τῆσι ἄλλῃσι ὁρτῆσι ἀπεστυγήκασι, ἐν δὲ ταύτῃ
θύουσι, ἔστι μὲν λόγος περὶ αὐτοῦ ὑπ' Αἰγυπτίων λεγόμενος, ἐμοὶ μέντοι
ἐπισταμένῳ οὐκ εὐπρεπέστερός ἐστι λέγεσθαι, 2. 47. 2).[9]

3. At the festival of Dionysus, instead of processing with phalluses,
the Egyptians hold images with outsized penises ('in size not much
less than the body'): 'as to why it has such large genitals and why only
this part of the body moves there is a sacred story told about this' (δι' ὅ
τι δὲ μέζον τε ἔχει τὸ αἰδοῖον καὶ κινέει μοῦνον τοῦ σώματος, ἔστι λόγος περὶ
αὐτοῦ ἱρὸς λεγόμενος, 2. 48. 3).

[7] For a lengthy discussion of the meaning of this phrase, see Appendix 2.

[8] Everyone's list of announced omissions is different (see e.g. Lateiner
1989: 247 n. 19): mine attempts to be comprehensive. Lloyd, ii. 18, compares
1. 51, 1. 193, 3. 125, 4. 43 with the ἱροὶ λόγοι that Herodotus is inclined to
omit. However, 1. 51. 4 and 4. 43 appear to reflect an aversion to blackening
other men's reputations, 3. 125. 3 a disinclination to report the unfitting
manner of death of Polycrates, and 1. 193. 4 the feeling that his audience will
not believe the height to which sesame and millet grow in Babylon. The only
nearly comparable case outside Book 2 is his passing reference to Epidaurian
secret rites (ἄρρητοι ἱροργίαι, 5. 83. 3). At 2. 123. 3, Herodotus omits to
mention the names of the Greek men who 'use' the Egyptian idea of the
transmigration of the soul without acknowledging that it is not their own. Cf.
also 7. 214. 3 and 2. 128 (in which, respectively, Herodotus records the name
of Ephialtes precisely to blacken it, and conversely, the Egyptians damn the
memory of a man through consciously not naming him).

[9] For the pig as an Egyptian sacred animal, see Newberry (1928: 213–14),
with delightful illustrations.

4. The Athenians were the first Greeks to adorn their statues of Hermes with an erect penis, having learnt this from the Pelasgians: 'the Pelasgians told a sacred story about this, which is revealed in the Samothracian mysteries' (οἱ δὲ Πελασγοὶ ἱρόν τινα λόγον περὶ αὐτοῦ ἔλεξαν, τὰ ἐν τοῖσι ἐν Σαμοθρηίκῃ μυστηρίοισι δεδήλωται, 2. 51. 4).

5. At the festival of Isis at Busiris all the men and women beat their breasts in lament: 'why they strike themselves it is not holy for me to say' (τὸν δὲ τύπτονται, οὔ μοι ὅσιόν ἐστι λέγειν, 2. 61. 1).[10]

6. At the festival of Athena in Sais, and elsewhere in Egypt on the same night, lamps are burnt: 'as to the reason why this night receives this light and honour there is a sacred story told about this' (ὅτευ δὲ εἵνεκα φῶς ἔλαχε καὶ τιμὴν ἡ νὺξ αὕτη, ἐστι ἱρὸς περὶ αὐτοῦ λόγος λεγόμενος, 2. 62. 2).

7. The Egyptians do not wear wool in temples, for it is 'not holy' (οὐ γὰρ ὅσιον); in this they agree with the 'Orphic things' and the 'Bacchic things', for it is not holy for those who share in these rites to be buried in woollen clothes: 'there is a sacred story told about such things' (ἔστι δὲ περὶ αὐτῶν ἱρὸς λόγος λεγόμενος, 2. 81. 2).

8. The most perfect of the wooden pictures of corpses is said to be that of 'him whose name I do not consider it holy to name in such a connection' (τοῦ οὐκ ὅσιον ποιεῦμαι τὸ οὔνομα ἐπὶ τοιούτῳ πρήγματι ὀνομάζειν, 2. 86. 2).

9. The Egyptians annually bring out the cow in which the daughter of Mycerinus is buried into the light; this is done at the time of year when the Egyptians beat themselves in honour of the 'god whom I do not name in connection with such a matter' (τὸν οὐκ ὀνομαζόμενον θεὸν ὑπ' ἐμεῦ ἐπὶ τοιούτῳ πρήγματι, 2. 132. 2).

10. At Sais is the tomb of 'him whose name I do not consider it holy to mention in such a connection' (τοῦ οὐκ ὅσιον ποιεῦμαι ἐπὶ τοιούτῳ πρήγματι ἐξαγορεύειν τοὔνομα, 2. 170. 1).

11. On the round pond of Sais the people hold a demonstration of the sufferings of the god, which the Egyptians call 'mysteries': 'now about these things, although I know more about the details of them, let me hold my peace' (περὶ μέν νυν τούτων εἰδότι μοι ἐπὶ πλέον ὡς ἕκαστα αὐτῶν ἔχει, εὔστομα κείσθω, 2. 171. 1).

12. The same principle applies to the mysteries of Demeter which the Greeks call the Thesmophoria (2. 171. 2): 'and about this let me hold my peace, except in as much as it is inoffensive to speak of' (καὶ ταύτης

[10] As a ritual re-enactment of the myth of Osiris: Lloyd ii. 277–9. Xenophanes finds it absurd to mourn a god: DK 21 A 13. See here Mora (1985: 188–9).

μοι πέρι εὔστομα κείσθω, πλὴν ὅσον αὐτῆς ὁσίη ἐστὶ λέγειν). What it is apparently acceptable to say is that the daughters of Danaus brought the Thesmophoria to Greece and taught them to the Pelasgian women (2. 171. 3).

Herodotus' omissions fall into three (overlapping) categories: omissions of stories explaining religious iconography (1, 3, 4), of stories explaining particular ritual practices (2, 3, 5, 6, 7, 11, 12), and the omission to mention the name of Osiris (5, 8, 9, 10). Of course, it cannot be ascertained for certain that Herodotus only holds back material on those occasions on which he tells us,[11] but the sudden appearance of such a rash of reticence in close proximity to his statement at 2. 3. 2 makes it surely highly probable that the two are connected. The omissions of the name of Osiris fall superficially into a class of their own: the names of the gods, after all, were specifically exempted from Herodotus' policy of exclusion. It is possible also to drive a number of other wedges between these examples of omission: to claim, with Ivan Linforth, that it is only in five cases that genuine religious scruples, as opposed to a sense of propriety, are revealed,[12] that the phrase 'I am not eager' (οὐκ εἰμὶ πρόθυμος, 2. 3. 2) is of less 'definite religious import' than 'let me hold my peace' (εὔστομα κείσθω, 2. 171. 2, 3), that Herodotus might then have used an expression such as 'it is not holy' (οὐκ ὅσιόν μοι) at 2. 3. 2 to make his meaning more plain.[13] Herodotus, however, was not anticipating Linforth's legalism.[14] On the whole, the similarities are greater than the differences. There are a number of repeated phrases, most obviously 'there is a sacred story told' (ἐστι ἱρὸς. . . . λόγος

---

[11] Linforth (1924: 278–9).

[12] Linforth (1924: 281), highlighting the expressions οὔ ἥδιόν (2. 46. 2) or οὐκ εὐπρεπέστερός (2. 47. 3) as weaker than οὔ ὅσιόν. Linforth is followed by Legrand (1932: 132), refuted by Sourdille (1925: 293–4), with counter examples of less proper material included without any apparent embarrassment. See here also Mora (1985: 134–6), who first agrees that these 'weaker' expressions reflect the same concept but then suggests that they indicate a more subjective aversion (cf. Mora 1981: 214).

[13] Linforth (1924: 279–80).

[14] Mora (1985: 130–9) is also chiefly concerned to classify Herodotus' religious silences—even into subgroups of one or two examples. Mora (1981) follows very similar lines, esp. at pp. 218 ff.

λεγόμενος) or 'it is not holy'. It is 'not holy' to name Osiris (in 5, 8, and 10) just as it is not holy for him to divulge other information (in 13).[15]

That Herodotus' policy of reticence was limited in this way is suggested by the context in which he restates his remark at 2. 65. 2, to justify his failure to explain the reasons why the Egyptians treated animals as sacred. It is also suggested precisely by his inclusion of other 'divine' material in the course of Book 2: Herodotus acknowledges that he may be compelled on occasion to disregard his 'ban'; a handful of passages match the impression given by his 'announced omissions' neatly. So, for example, that Zeus once disguised himself as a ram in order to see Heracles explains why some Egyptians sacrifice sheep instead of goats (2. 42. 2–4); that Ares once fought his way through to sleeping with his mother explains a fight that takes place during the festival at Papremis (2. 64. 1); the Chemmites tell how Perseus had instructed them to establish a gymnastic contest in his honour (2. 91. 2–6).[16] Perhaps the greatest infringement, however, of Herodotus' own rule of the exclusion of τὰ θεῖα is his digression on the nature of Heracles (2. 43–5): for, while it may proceed from the bare observation that the Greeks took the name of Heracles from the Egyptians and gave it to Heracles son of Amphitryon, and while much of the discussion may be taken up with questions of chronology, his conclusion—that there are two Heracles, one to whom one should sacrifice as a god and another whom one should propitiate as a hero—reveals that it is not only the 'dire chronological repercussions' of the contradictions between Egyptian and Greek belief[17] that concern him

---

[15] Herodotus does name the god Osiris on other occasions, 2. 42. 4, 144. 2 (*bis*), 156. 4, leading Lateiner (1989: 246 n. 16) to suppose that Herodotus' piety was a pretence. But, in three of the four instances of the omission of the name of Osiris, 2. 86. 2, 132. 2, 170. 1, Herodotus is clear that he only cannot mention the name of the god 'in connection with such a matter', suggesting a distinct reason for omission (albeit we cannot tell what it may have been). Mora (1985: 137; 1981: 216) criticizes the 'sceptical interpretation' of the religious silences—on insufficient grounds.

[16] Cf. 2. 156. 2–6 (the aetiology of the floating island of Chemmis).

[17] Lloyd ii. 18; see also Lateiner (1989: 66) and Linforth (1924: 291) on 2. 142–6 (Herodotus was 'reclaiming for human history vast tracts of time'). Lloyd also finds a justification other than 'extreme compulsion' for the

but the chronology of the gods themselves. It is no coincidence then that Herodotus' digression on the nature of Heracles concludes with his most emphatic expression of pious caution (2. 45. 2):[18]

And though I have spoken to such an extent about these matters may the gods and heroes be well-disposed to me (καὶ περὶ μὲν τούτων τοσαῦτα ἡμῖν εἰποῦσι καὶ παρὰ τῶν θεῶν καὶ παρὰ τῶν ἡρώων εὐμένεια εἴη).

The clear conclusion then is that—though Herodotus' omissions are announced with an element of showmanship, though they provide the opportunity for the advertisement of his knowledge[19]—his reticence is motivated by piety.[20] This reverent attitude of discretion seems to be triggered either in the face of the aetiologies for certain ritual practices[21] or by an imagined taboo over the naming of a god. His discretion concerning

Heracles excursus in the argument that Herodotus' rule does not cover heroes who 'were historical personages and could be discussed'. This seems rather legalistic given that Herodotus' concern in the excursus is to distinguish the status of Heracles. Linforth allows the occasional suspension of his 'rule requiring the exclusion of θεῖα' in order to 'provide a place for a report of the results obtained by such investigation' (1924: 289).

[18] Linforth (1924: 281–2) distinguishes this, his fifth case of religious scruples, from 2. 3. 2 by the argument that it is not in this case the information that he had derived from the priests so much as the use to which he had then put it that 'seems to him to border on indiscretion'. Lateiner (1989: 66–7) calls this request for favour formulaic; Vandiver also (1991: 139) sees Herodotus as nodding to 'traditional religious sensibilities', i.e. not his own?

[19] See Sourdille (1910: 1), suggesting that 2. 65. 2 was motivated partly by a desire not to seem ignorant; Darbo-Peschanski (1987: 42), 'Le silence que s'impose l'enquêteur est à la fois rigoreux et ostentateur'. Contrast, however, Linforth (1924: 280 n. 13): his doubt over Herodotus' motivation is probably related to his belief (p. 288) that Herodotus was the master of a vast body of Egyptian mythology, but chose only to 'allow himself the pleasure of telling now and then one of the countless local divine myths which were to be heard everywhere in Egypt'.

[20] Cf. Müller (1981: 315–16), 2. 3. 2 'zeugt wohl nicht allein von religiöser Scheu, sondern auch von einem gewissen Agnostizismus göttlichen Dingen gegenüber', and more straightforwardly Macan vii. i. 2 (pp. 734–5), 'this reserve . . . seems to arise rather from a belief in the vindictive nature of the gods, an apprehension that such speculations might be visited with a nemesis'.

[21] As Mora defines ἱροὶ λόγοι (1985: 133): 'discorsi sacri, cioè miti o tradizioni sacerdotali intese a spiegare il motivo di singoli aspetti di culto.' See also Sourdille (1925: 290–1).

aetiologies seems to have been formed to a large extent by analogy to Greek mysteries: the Pelasgian 'sacred story' explaining the erect penis of Hermes was revealed to Herodotus through the Samothracian mysteries of which he was presumably an initiate[22] (2. 51. 4); he is discrete concerning the Thesmophoria just as he is also concerning what the Egyptians call 'mysteries' (2. 171).[23] His reluctance to name Osiris may also have its roots in a Greek taboo concerning the naming of gods in certain contexts.[24] At the same time, even if the form of Herodotus' discretion may be largely the product of Greek attitudes, its concentration in Book 2 must surely reflect the privileged status that he accorded Egypt as the origin of so much of Greek theology and religious practice.

Herodotus' statement that 'all men understand equally about these things' (νομίζων πάντας ἀνθρώπους ἴσον περὶ αὐτῶν ἐπίστασθαι, 2. 3. 2), that is about τὰ θεῖα, has a broader significance, however. This knowledge clearly cannot be of the names of the gods: though the Greek names of the gods, he believes, derived from Egypt, he surely cannot imagine that the process of the dissemination of these names had, by his own day, been completed. It is difficult to imagine that this knowledge can be knowledge of the sacred stories omitted by Herodotus in the course of Book 2—the reason for his silence cannot really be that his audience knows already—or that it is the knowledge of all initiates the world over.[25] The level at which Herodotus'

---

[22] Gould (1994: 92).

[23] See Mora (1987: 47; 1981: 210–11), speculating that the connection had been made long before Herodotus by the Greeks in Egypt with the encouragement of the Egyptian priests. For the difficult question of whether (and if so when) there were ever Egyptian mysteries, see Sourdille (1925: 302 n. 2), Bleeker (1965: esp. 53–4), Bianchi (1980).

[24] See e.g. E. *Hel.* 1307, P. *Menex* 238b, Dem. 60. 30; for a taboo surrounding Persephone see Clinton (1986: esp. 44); see now also Pulleyn (1994: 23–4).

[25] As maintained by Sourdille (1910: 12–13): wherever mysteries were celebrated, initiation had the same object. In defence (1925: 304 n. 1), Sourdille draws the analogy of an assertion of Demosthenes that Philip had done wrong to the whole world. Exaggeration in that context is more natural, however: a circle of initiates is *by definition* a closed, exclusive one, something Sourdille himself acknowledges by opposing the religion of the mysteries to vulgar or popular mythology (1910: 17), or in supposing that the mysteries were—like the names of the gods—diffused (1910: 13). Sayce hazards an extraordinary translation of this phrase (p. 126 n. 9) as 'considering that all

idea of equal knowledge operates can be gleaned rather by looking again at the miracle of the distribution of Persian bodies at Plataea (9. 65. 2):[26]

I think, if one may speculate about divine matters (δοκέω δέ, εἴ τι περὶ τῶν θείων πρηγμάτων δοκέειν δεῖ), that the goddess refused to receive the men who had burnt her temple in Eleusis.

Herodotus speculates over 'divine matters' in the same breath as he expresses concern over the validity of such speculation. It is not then that Herodotus considers any attempt to venture an opinion concerning the divine worthless[27]—there is evidence, in this instance, for Herodotus' speculation in the distribution of the bodies of the Persians outside, but not within, the precinct of Demeter—only that such an opinion requires some accompanying statement of reservation, that speculation should be attempted in the sure belief that certain knowledge is impossible. A similar caution is reflected elsewhere: in his conclusion to the discussion of the true dates of Heracles, Pan, and Dionysus that anyone may 'use' whichever version they prefer (2. 146. 1),[28] or in his observation that Cambyses must have been mad to mock the 'sacred things' and the customs of the Egyptians (ἱροῖσί τε καὶ νομαίοισι, 3. 38. 1); arguably, too, it informs his belief that the benefit of the doubt should be given to prophecy (8. 77).[29] Solon does on one

people are convinced that they ought not to be talked about'. Mora's remark (1985: 137) that this phrase springs from an 'idea of the common religious experience of humanity' does little more than to restate the problem; his longer definition (1987: 44 n. 7) is extremely obscure.

[26] Lateiner (1989: 67) sees Herodotus' 'stated reluctance about delving into the *thoma* of 9. 65 as 'the exception that proves the rule' (whatever that may mean): 'he prefers not to explain what seemed to him inexplicable; under pressure he threw out a *merely* divine explanation.' See similarly Shimron's 'Polybian rule' 'to fall back on supernatural explanations only when all rational ones fail (1989: 12 n. 22). Contrast the splendid remarks of Sourdille (1925: 301 n. 1).

[27] As asserted by Stein (on 2. 3. 2), Müller (1981: 315); contrast Sourdille (1910: 6 ff.), Linforth (1924: 280).   [28] Cf. 2. 123. 1, 3; 4. 96. 2.

[29] Cf. also Herodotus' judgements on the Magi's killing of animals and on Salmoxis, 1. 140. 3, 4. 96. 2 (with Lateiner's comment (1990: 243) that 'Herodotus here dismisses the whole matter, presumably as a question beyond the scope of his historiography'). Cf. 2. 28. 1 for a similar remark in conclusion to Herodotus' geographical speculations.

occasion make a claim to knowledge of the divine, but his knowledge is of the jealousy of the divine and the unpredictable consequences of this for the affairs of men (ἐπιστάμενόν με τὸ θεῖον πᾶν ἐὸν φθονερόν τε καὶ ταραχῶδες, 1. 32. 1): indeed the story of Solon and Croesus illustrates—through Croesus' repeated misinterpretation of prophetic signals—precisely the impossibility of certain knowlege.

This group of ideas could be taken together with Herodotus' use of 'vague designations' to suggest an agnosticism or a 'vague deism' on Herodotus' part.[30] The impossibility of certain knowledge concerning the gods is a common sentiment, however, both in 'sceptical' pre-Socratic philosophy and in more conventionally religious literature.[31] It would be more accurate to see both phenomena—that is, both Herodotus' 'vague designations' and what John Gould has christened the 'uncertainty principle' of Greek religion[32]—as necessary complements rather than qualifications to a traditional model of Greek religion. 'Zeus, whoever Zeus may be, if this name is pleasing to him, by this name I address him. I can compare with him, measuring all things against him, none but Zeus.'[33] It is precisely by means of the fall-back that the classification of

[30] Pearson (1939: 20–1). This imagined agnosticism appears to make Herodotus easier company for some modern critics: see e.g. Forrest (1979: 312).

[31] See e.g. Xenophanes DK 21 B 34, Heraclitus 22 B 86, Protagoras 80 B 4, Pindar fr. 61 Snell, H. Od. 23. 81–2, Aesch. Ag. 160 ff., E. Hel. 711–12, 1137, Bacch. 200, Or. 418, Tro. 884–8. See also Masaracchia on 9. 65. 2 (pp. 185–6). Muir, by contrast (1985: 199), sees the 'nagging suspicion that nothing in the world . . . can be fairly and certainly established' as new to the 'New Education'. Clearly there is a difference between uncertainty concerning the divine and Protagoras' uncertainty concerning the existence of the gods, 80 B 4; but see Barnes (1982: 450), emphasizing the gulf between agnosticism and atheism.

[32] Gould (1994: 94): 'Herodotus' acknowledgements of the same necessary uncertainty are not based on specific "historiographical principle" but on the nature of Greek religion.' See also esp. Rudhardt (1981: 22–3; 1992a: 103–6, 88; 1992b: 233–4), Sourvinou-Inwood (1997: 162) on the principle of 'unknowability'; cf., in Dinka religion, Lienhardt (1961: 53–4).

[33] Aesch. Ag. 160 ff. (tr. Lloyd-Jones). For similar formulae, see Lloyd-Jones (1956: 61–2), Versnel (1981: 13), Pulleyn (1994); for Roman religion, Alvar (1985), Feeney (1998: 87), 'Such phrasing is a token of a quirky recognition that the net which humans try to throw over the creatures swimming in that other medium is a net of human manufacture which we can never be entirely confident has the right-sized mesh.' See further Appendix 2 (n. 29).

individual gods is traditional, even arbitrary, that such distinctions (and their reflection in cult action) are maintained.[34] It was Homer and Hesiod, according to Herodotus, who 'gave the gods their titles, chose their honours and skills, and pointed out their forms' (2. 53. 2),[35] but this seems in no way to devalue those traditional sets of attributes: indeed, as we have seen, in his conclusion to his discussion of the nature of Heracles, Herodotus feels able even to recommend a particular course of ritual action (2. 44. 5).

It is necessary here to confront an apparent contradiction. Despite this 'uncertainty principle', the idea of the 'unknowability' of the divine, neither knowledge of the divine nor knowledge derived from the divine are envisaged as being in any way of a different order to what we might call ordinary human knowledge.[36] Though divination is of course subject to interpretation, it can (in retrospect, at least) be the source of knowledge quite as concrete as the evidence of men's eyes. So at Thermopylae, the Greeks discovered their impending death first from their prophet Megistias, second from deserters, and finally from scouts (7. 219. 1).[37] The knowledge derived from the divine may indeed form the model for human wisdom.[38]

---

[34] Contrast, however, Bremmer (1982: 52), seeing unknowability as *correlative* to the Greek lack of a priesthood or scriptures. For 'unity in diversity' in Greek religion, see Rudhardt (1991: 59); cf. the summary of views of François (1957: 13 ff., 307), or the famous formulation of Vernant (1980: 98). For the same theme in other polytheistic religions, cf. Evans-Pritchard (1956), Lienhardt (1961: 94–6), Skorupski (1973; 1976: 219–20).

[35] Echoing Hes. *Theog.* 112.

[36] Cf. the modern distinction between different forms of knowledge, symbolic, encyclopaedic, semantic, advanced by Sperber (1975), summarized by B. Morris (1987: 234–5), and applied by Price (1984: 8).

[37] Cf. also 8. 20 (the Euboeans might have known of their impending misfortunes from an oracle rather than first-hand), 1. 78. 3 (the Telmessian seers knew nothing (οὐδὲν . . . εἰδότες) of the the capture of Sardis at the time at which they prophesied it).

[38] Cf. H. *Il.* 17. 152 ff., Theogn. 543–6, Bacchyl. fr. 57, Soph. *OT* 298–9, *Ant.* 631, Alkmaion DK 24 B 1, Philolaos DK 44 B 6; as Starr remarks (1968b: 349), 'thinkers had a cankering fear that only the gods could really know the truth'. Cf. Gould (1985: 23), observing that 'the notion of ambiguity in divine communication, of a divine language of signs rather than words, seems deeply rooted in the Greek imagination, so that when, in Herodotus, for example, men aspire to divinity and claim the power to predict the future, it is in such language that they speak.' It is not only, however, when men aspire to divinity

So, for example, the Scythian chiefs sent a messenger to the invading Persians with presents for their king Darius: a bird, a mouse, a frog, and five arrows (4. 131–2). The messenger refused to tell them the meaning of these gifts, and so they too held a council to discuss the matter. Darius' opinion was that the Scythians intended surrender of their earth and water: the mouse inhabited the earth and the frog the water; the bird resembled a horse; and the arrows stood for their power. Gobryas then offered a less optimistic interpretation (4. 132. 3):

Unless, Persians, you become birds and fly away into the sky, or become mice and burrow under the ground, or become frogs and leap into the lakes, you will not return back home but will be shot down by these arrows.[39]

Croesus likewise threatens to wipe out the Lampsacenes like a pine tree if they do not return their hostage Miltiades safely (6. 37. 1). Just as Themistocles and the Athenians confer in assembly over the interpretation of the 'wooden walls' oracle, so the Lampsacenes put their heads together to discover the meaning of Croesus' threat (6. 37. 2):

The Lampsacenes being uncertain in their discussions as to the meaning of the remark (τὸ θέλει τὸ ἔπος εἶπαι) with which Croesus threatened them—that he would rub them out like a pine tree (πίτυος τρόπον ἐκτρίψειν)—eventually with difficulty one of the elders discovered it

or prophetic powers that they use oracular language: prophecies can, as we have seen, be accidental. Conversely, for Delphic proverbs, see Fontenrose (1978: 83 ff.).

[39] For this passage, see now West (1988) who argues on the basis of a wealth of parallels that Herodotus has preserved an authentic detail of a practice 'widely attested among illiterate peoples'. For the interpretation of objects, see Dewald (1993). Cf. 1. 141. 1–2 (Cyrus and dancing fish), 5. 92. ζ (Thrasybulus and ears of corn), 6. 1. 2 (Artaphernes and the shoe). Another comparable passage is that in which Gelon tells the Greek ambassadors that the spring has been taken out of their year (7. 162. 1). For this expression and its associations with Pericles, see Treves (1941), more satisfactorily Fornara (1971a: 83–4). The subsequent interpretation (as the spring was the finest season of the year, so were his troops the finest in the Greek army) need not be interpolated: cf. 4. 131. 2, 9. 98. 4; the slightly laboured interpretation is comparable to 1. 68. 3–4, 4. 132, 6. 37. 2.

and spoke the truth (εἶπε τὸ ἐόν), that alone of all trees the pine when it is chopped down produces no shoots but is completely destroyed and annihilated.[40]

The old man, the outsider, coming forward with the correct interpretation is almost a cliché of the interpretation of oracles.[41] One difference, it has been suggested, between these 'human attempts to speak the language of divinity' and the real thing is that the human approximations can 'be so easily read and their messages falsified' or 'rendered harmless'.[42] The messages of divinity, however—the dream, for example, that told Sabacus to slice the priests of Egypt in half (2. 139)—can also be disarmed in the same way. A number of prophecies, as we saw in Chapter 5—that, for example, which told that the Persians would sack Delphi and be destroyed (9. 42)—depend on a condition for their fulfilment. By returning Miltiades the Lampsacenes similarly remove the condition essential for the fulfilment of Croesus' threat.

Such quasi-oracular pieces of diplomacy may, of course, be a function of Herodotus' oral sources: to survive, such stories of international diplomacy must first be epitomized, encapsulated in a proverbial form. But it is possible also that such stories were believed to be true, that the certain knowledge that can be derived from the gods forms the model of all knowledge. Far from being seen as a means of managing or taming the unseen powers of chance,[43] the interpretation of oracles and prophecies is envisaged in fact as being no different in nature from the solution of any other practical question.[44] After recounting the

[40] The story is built around a pun: Pityusa was an old name of Lampsacus (see Macan or How and Wells, ad loc.). 'No adult Lampsakene could have been at a loss for an explanation for the bitter jest of Kroisos'—at least if he had read Charon of Lampsacus: Macan iv. 1. 297.

[41] Cf. 5. 79. 2 (anonymous Theban), 6. 52. 5–7 (Messenian Panites), 7. 143. 1 (little known Themistocles). The phrase τὸ θέλει τὸ ἔπος εἶπαι echoes expressions such as τὸ θέλει προφαίνειν τὸ φάσμα or τὸ θέλει σημαίνειν τὸ τέρας (1. 78. 2, 7. 37. 2).   [42] Gould (1985: 23–4).

[43] Contrast Whittaker (1965: 43), Flacelière (1965: 87); see, however, Burkert (1985a: 112), describing the interpretation of omens as 'quasi-rational'.

[44] As Evans-Pritchard comments of the Azande (1976: 121): 'in many situations where we seek to base a verdict upon evidence or try to regulate our conduct by weighing of probabilities the Zande consults, without hesitation, the poison oracle.' Statements that there is no need of *manteis* in

story of Themistocles' interpretation of the wooden wall oracle, Herodotus passes on to the Athenian's 'other judgement' (ἑτέρη . . . γνώμη): on the most expedient use of the windfall from the Laureion silver mines (7. 144. 1).[45] Of course, these rational interpretations of prophecy are founded on presuppositions very different from our own. Herodotus, in the dramatic words of Catherine Darbo-Peschanski, was the 'prisoner of a religious logic'.[46] When an oracle tells the Thebans to ask for their neighbours' help in their war of vengeance against Athens, it is quite natural for one of them (again in the context of an assembly-meeting, 5. 79. 2) to interpret this command in the light of mythical precedent (5. 80). There is nothing, however, to suggest that the interpretation of oracles is seen as a different department of political life.

Herodotus also applies precisely the same criteria of truth to questions of the nature of divinity as to any other matter. The divine nature of events is 'clear by many proofs' (δῆλα δὴ πολλοῖσι τεκμηρίοισί, 9. 100. 2): that the battles of Plataea and Mycale occurred on the same day, yet that a rumour of the victory at Plataea reached Mycale to cheer the Greeks fighting there, and that both battles were fought by shrines of Demeter. His investigation into the age and nature of Heracles (and the proper form of his worship[47]) is also peppered with his most scientific historical vocabulary.[48] Herodotus is concerned to

this case, e.g. E. *Rhes.* 952–3, or the idea of consulting an oracle to confirm a decision, as a court of last instance, E. *Hipp.* 1055–6, suggest similarly that divination was applied not to different questions but to difficult questions. Cf. also Oedipus' boast, Soph. *OT* 396–8, that he interpreted the riddle of the sphinx by his own *gnome* rather than by birds.

[45] Lonis (1979: 79) sees Themistocles as an exceptional innovator in the interpretation of oracles (with only Cleomenes comparable). He was not alone, however, in his view of the 'wooden walls', 7. 142. 2, only in his reading of 'divine Salamis': Themistocles merely excelled on one occasion at a game that all Athenians were apparently accustomed to play.

[46] Darbo-Peschanski (1987: 82), 'prisonnier d'une logique religieuse'.

[47] It would be possible, of course, to see the Heracles digression as concerned exclusively with human worship, to interpret his conclusion that 'Heracles is an ancient god' as spoken (in Linforth's phrase) in the 'manner of the taxonomist'. Herodotus' engagement in the question and his concluding statement of pious reservation suggest that it is a more than academic matter for him.

[48] Cf. Hunter (1982: 68), Gould (1989: 11), Zographou (1995: esp. 197); see

prove that the Greeks derived the name of Heracles from the Egyptians (rather than the other way around) and that they then gave it to Heracles the son of Amphitryon. There are, he says, 'many pieces of evidence' (πολλά . . . τεκμήριά, 2. 43. 2) for this:[49] for example, that the Egyptians are ignorant of the names of Poseidon and the Dioscuri, for if they had taken the name of any daimon from the Greeks, it would surely have been these, given that both they and the Greeks—'as I suppose and is my judgement' (γνώμη)—practised navigation at that time (2. 43. 3). 'Wishing then to know clearly about these things' (καὶ θέλων δὲ τούτων πέρι σαφές τι εἰδέναι, 2. 44. 1), Herodotus then travelled to Tyre in Phoenicia, having heard that there was a temple of Heracles there, and having discovered from the priests that it dated from the foundation of Tyre two thousand three hundred years before their day (2. 44. 3). He also saw there a temple of Heracles the Thasian on the basis of which he travelled to Thasos and discovered a temple founded five generations before the birth of Heracles the son of Amphitryon (2. 44. 4). Finally he concludes that 'these researches of mine indicate clearly that Heracles is an ancient god' (τὰ μέν νυν ἱστορημένα δηλοῖ σαφέως παλαιὸν θεὸν Ἡρακλέα ἐόντα, 2. 44. 5).

The proposition that Herodotus applies the same criteria of proof to such mythical questions as to other matters may be found surprising. For it is well known that it was Herodotus—building on the first clumsy steps of Hecataeus[50]—who liber-

---

also, more generally, Nickau (1990). Cf. 2. 112–120 (with Connor 1993: 11–12), 2. 145–6. Such scientific language arouses the suspicion of Fehling, of course (1989: 59–65). Cf. also R. Thomas's sophisticated argument (1997) that 'Herodotus stresses that he has evidence or proof in precisely those contexts where . . . the security of his evidence is dubious' (p. 135) or the matter discussed is controversial. Thomas appears to take for granted that arguments concerning the divine would have been considered dubious (135–6 on 9. 100. 2, 146 on 2. 43–5).

[49] For the meaning of τεκμήριον as somewhere between evidence and proof, see R. Thomas (1997: esp. 134–5).

[50] See e.g. Fornara (1983: 4–5) (with qualifications, pp. 6–7), Lloyd i. 136, Derow (1994: 73), or now Fowler (1996: 71–2) on Herodotus' predecessors in general: 'It is one thing to develop a revolutionary new method; it is another to realize all its possibilities and to think instinctively of applying it at every opportunity.'

ated history from myth.[51] 'Both Herodotus and Thucydides', we may read, 'held the view that myth was unsatisfactory.'[52] 'For Herodotus myths lacked a "truth function".'[53] Herodotus 'has freed himself from myth and mythical speculations; supernatural wisdom is irrelevant to him'.[54] 'Decked out in the brand new garb of the Ionian "scientific" historian', Herodotus 'can chuck "myth" on the rubbish-heap'.[55] A very similar interpretation of Herodotus' statement at 2. 3. 2 has also been advanced, that Herodotus holds that τὰ θεῖα cannot be the 'objects of certain knowledge';[56] 'Herodotus chose', it has been written, 'not to tell a myriad of fictions about Greek and alien gods because there was no rational way to control these stories, no tangible evidence, no system to distinguish true from false . . .'[57]

One counter-example such as Herodotus' investigation into Heracles should perhaps be enough to undermine such grandiose statements fatally. Such triumphalism, however, is as tenacious as it is vague. A little active dismantling may be needed. It is unclear, to begin with, what it is that Herodotus is renouncing. A number of overlapping definitions seem to be in operation. The definition of a myth as 'a story in which some of the chief characters are gods' (in Northrop Frye's formulation[58]) is jostling, it seems, with the everyday sense of a myth as an untrue story.[59] (The now conventional modern definition of

[51] Cf. Fornara (1983: 7): 'Herodotus' insistence on the separation of the age of myth from the age of history is well-known.'

[52] Wardman (1960: 403).

[53] Hornblower (1987: 21); cf. (1987: 18; 1983: 268).

[54] van Groningen (1953: 25).

[55] Detienne, cited by Cartledge in Bruit Zaidman and Schmitt Pantel (1992: 148): 'but without renouncing any of the traditional tales, let alone the genealogies of the divine powers', he continues. Cf. also Momigliano (1966: 114), White (1969: 45).

[56] Lloyd ii. 17; see also Linforth (1924: 291–2).

[57] Lateiner (1989: 65); cf. Dover (1974: 13), commenting on 9. 65. 2 that it 'does not imply that unquestioning acceptance of traditions about divine intervention is virtuous, but that once the possibility of such divine intervention is admitted the standards of probability upon which rational opinion about past events is based lose their validity'.

[58] Cited by Kirk (1970: 10), 'Northrop Frye states baldly, if rather emptily'.

[59] See esp. Wardman (1960: 404–5), Lang (1984b: 101) defining myths 'in

myth as 'traditional tale' is at best only dimly present.[60])
Underpinning many of the expressions quoted above, however,
is a chronological definition of myth, the belief that Herodotus
drew a distinction between mythical and historical time. It is
with this last definition, the extraordinary mirage of the
spatium mythicum, that it is necessary to begin.[61]

The chief evidence for this distinction is to be found in
Herodotus' conclusion to his opening chapters retelling the
reciprocal thefts of Io, Europe, Medea, and Helen (1. 5. 3–6. 2).

I will not say about these matters that it happened in this way or in
that. Rather, indicating the man whom I know to have been the first
to initiate unjust deeds against the Greeks (τὸν δὲ οἶδα αὐτὸς πρῶτον
ὑπάρξαντα ἀδίκων ἔργων ἐς τοὺς Ἕλληνας), I will proceed with my
account, touching as I do so on both small and great cities of men
alike. This Croesus was the first barbarian we know to subdue some
Greeks so that they paid him tribute, and to make others his friends
(οὗτος ὁ Κροῖσος βαρβάρων πρῶτος τῶν ἡμεῖς ἴδμεν τοὺς μὲν κατεστρέψατο
Ἑλλήνων ἐς φόρου ἀπαγωγήν, τοὺς δὲ φίλους προσεποιήσατο).

Up until the time of Croesus, the story goes, everything is
shifting and uncertain; with Croesus at last we reach historical dry land. The first five chapters of myth are revealed as a

the modern sense' extraordinarily as 'lies and propaganda'. For excellent
discussions of the difficulties of defining myth, see Kirk (1970; 1973), Buxton
(1994: 13 ff.); cf. also Bremmer (1987), Dowden (1992).

[60] See Bremmer (1987: 1), 'a traditional tale with secondary, partial
reference to something of collective importance' (the phrasing of Burkert);
p. 7, 'traditional tales relevant to society' (Bremmer's own words); the
presence of gods and heroes, he continues (p. 7), is 'only to be expected
when religion is embedded in society'.

[61] See above all Shimron (1973) on the phrase πρῶτος τῶν ἡμεῖς ἴδμεν,
foreshadowed or approved (with inevitably varying nuance) also by e.g.
Krischer (1965: 160), Forrest (1969: 95 n. 4), Müller (1981: 316), Lang
(1984a: 3), Darbo-Peschanski (1987), Lateiner (1989: 35–8), Flower (1991:
59–61), Pritchett (1993: 56), Vannicelli (1993: 15), and Rhodes (1994: 159).
For a much less brittle or more restricted (but in some cases more confused)
distinction of myth and history, see e.g. van Groningen (1953: 31); Wardman
(1960); Hunter (1982: 86–8, 103 ff.); Parke (1984: 223 n. 19); Murray (1987:
96), remarking delphically that *spatium mythicum* and *historicum* are 'concepts
which possess more resonance than power'; R. Thomas (1989: 181 n. 64–5),
cf. (1992: 112, 116); Brillante (1990: 93, 102), cf. p. 95; Evans (1991: 105–7);
Vandiver (1991: 8–9, 97, 132, 237). For a more forthright denial of the
distinction, see Macan (1927: 409), Raubitschek (1989: 43), Nickau (1990).

false start. An apparent difficulty is that it subsequently emerges from Herodotus' narrative that Croesus was not the first to perpetrate unjust deeds against the Greeks:[62] Gyges attacked Miletus and Smyrna and took possession of Colophon (1. 14. 1); Ardyes took Priene and attacked Miletus (1. 15); Alyattes took Smyrna, attacked Clazomenae (1. 16. 2), and was engaged in a more or less continuous war against the Milesians (1. 17–22). Herodotus, however, 'ascribed a higher degree of reliability' to the period after Croesus than that before: Croesus was 'the first man *we know*' to have perpetrated unjust deeds against the Greeks. Croesus' predecessors, in other words, do not count as they lived and died before the beginning of the historical period. 'Herodotus takes as his starting-date roughly 546 BC.'[63]

Other evidence is also adduced. Polycrates, Herodotus tells us, is the 'first Greek we know (πρῶτος τῶν ἡμεῖς ἴδμεν Ἑλλήνων) to aim at the rule of the sea, except Minos of Knossos and anyone who may have ruled the sea before this man; Polycrates is the first of what we might call[64] the human generation' or the 'human era' (τῆς δὲ ἀνθρωπηίης λεγομένης γενεῆς, 3. 122. 2). Herodotus' comparison of Xerxes' expedition with previous campaigns (7. 20. 2), that of Darius against the Scythians, the Scythians against the Cimmerians, the sons of Atreus against Troy, or that of the Mysians and Teucrians into Europe, has also been used to show that Herodotus 'obviously divides history into three parts, each indicated by a notable military expedition'. The 'mythical period is'—by the use of the phrase

---

[62] First observed by Jacoby (1913: 338).

[63] Hornblower (1987: 21). Shimron is more cautious (1973: 47): Herodotus' 'continuous historical narrative begins approximately with the generation of Croesus, that is about 550–530 BC'; see also Myres (1953: 61), White (1969: 45), Ayo (1984: 32), Carbonell (1985: 139), Brown (1989: 1), Flower (1991: 59).

[64] If λεγόμενης were to imply scepticism, it is hard to see what the object of that scepticism might be: he could hardly be insinuating that the human generation does not exist; and this would be at very least an oblique way of suggesting the non-existence or the uncertain existence of the divine (or pre-human) generation. λεγόμενης might then be only a way of introducing his own neologism: 'at any rate he was the first of *what one might call* the human generation'. It may be no stronger in sense than our inverted commas: cf. 1. 1; 2. 145. 1, 156. 4; 3. 23. 4; 6. 127. 1; 7. 114. 2 (for which, see Ch. 8).

'according to what is said' of the Trojan war (κατὰ τὰ λεγόμενα)—'distinctly separated from later times as one on which
there is no certain information'.[65]

There are first some general objections to this thesis. We
should have some concern surely for the effect of this reading
on the opening chapters of the *Histories*. These chapters may
have a virtuoso pace to them, they may even be intended to be
humorous,[66] but with their Homeric echoes, and with their
introduction of a number of the 'explanatory models' employed
through the *Histories*—in particular the idea of reciprocal
vengeance between Asia and Europe[67]—they are also serious.
Many aspects of these opening chapters are recalled at the close
of Book 9, for example by the story of Artayctes.[68] Was the
opening of his *Histories* really a likely moment for Herodotus to
play such a curious game of cat and mouse with his audience?
For Herodotus to deny in passing that the stories of Io, Medea,
Europe, and Helen are verifiable is one thing; for him to
dismiss such stories in so far as they are characteristic of a
category of material *in essence unverifiable* is quite another.[69]

[65] Shimron (1973: 46–7), followed by Vandiver (1991: 208).
[66] Ar. *Ach* 523 ff. might possibly be intended in turn as a parody of
Herodotus; although see Fornara (1971b: 28), Sansone (1985).
[67] See here Raubitschek (1989: 43), Immerwahr (1966: 18 n. 6). See,
however, Myres (1953: 135–6), followed by Neville (1977: 3) and in a more
nuanced fashion by Nickau (1990: 92 ff.), envisaging Herodotus as disposing
of the '*cherchez la femme* theory, and the *east-and-west* theory'; Shimron
(1989: 8) confusingly asserts that 'by smiling at the hallowed tradition that the
Trojan war started because of a woman . . . he possibly paved his way for the
story of Atossa's role in the preliminaries of the Persian war'. Moles's
Herodotus (1993: 96) 'has it all possible ways: he uses the sandwiched material
to begin his work in great style, to maintain the association between his work
and Homer's *Iliad*, to entertain his readers, to suggest ideas dear to himself—
yet he also distances himself from it and makes a distinction between myth
and solid, verifiable history'.
[68] For the story of Artayctes, see Ch. 4. For the last chapter, 9. 122, see
Bischoff (1932: 78 ff.), Immerwahr (1954: 26; 1966: 43), Avery (1972b: 534–5),
Krischer (1974), Redfield (1985: 114), Fisher (1992: 351–2), Mossman (1995:
175–6), less adequately Waters (1971: 53) or Ayo (1984). The stories of
Candaules and Masistes may also balance one another: Wolff (1964), Gammie
(1986: 185–7), Lateiner (1989: 36, 141), A. Griffiths (1999). For Lateiner (1989:
38 n. 74) the parody of 1. 1–5 is 'formally distinguished from the rest of the
Histories' by the opening and closing references to the Trojan war.
[69] Fowler (1996: 83).

Why then would he make such a fundamental statement of historical principle in such a flippant, peremptory fashion?[70] If Croesus indeed marked the boundary between historical and mythical time, it is strange that Herodotus should revert immediately to 'mythical' time through his account of Croesus' predecessors.[71] The expression on which so much weight is placed in this argument, 'the first man whom we know', is one, moreover, that is used of a number of figures, many of whom lived and died before Croesus: Arion was the first dithyrambic poet, half a century before Croesus (1. 23); the Lydians were the first to mint gold or silver coins (1. 94. 1); the city of Azotus held out under seige by the Egyptian Psammetichus for the longest time of all the cities we know (2. 57); the Egyptian king Necos was the first man we know to demonstrate that it was possible to circumnavigate Libya (4. 42. 2); Gyges was the 'first barbarian we know—after Midas' to make dedications at Delphi (1. 14. 2). Even in his opening chapters of supposed myth, Herodotus had found one 'first': according to the Persians, the theft of Io was the first act of injustice (τῶν ἀδικημάτων πρῶτον τοῦτο ἄρξαι, 1. 2. 1). Exceptional causes can be found, of course, for any number of exceptions: Herodotus found Egyptian history more reliable than Greek;[72] Gyges' dedications were tangible evidence, but there was no such evidence for his other exploits;[73] 'it is probable that Herodotus attended dithyrambs ascribed to Arion; these, together with the small statue that Herodotus saw in Taenarum, would constitute visible evidence for him.'[74] A catch-all defence is also sometimes hinted at: that though Herodotus may not have succeeded in every detail, that does not devalue his attempt.[75]

There is a simpler solution, however. Herodotus' apparent

[70] Fornara (1983: 7).

[71] M. Lloyd (1984). Cf. Shimron's weak glossing over of this problem (1989: 42): '26. 1 marks a recommencement of the *Histories*' promised narrative after a rapid survey . . . of obscure earlier times.'

[72] Shimron (1973: 49).

[73] Shimron (1973: 50–1), Lydian coins, pp. 48–9.

[74] Shimron (1973: 48). West observes (1985: 303 and n. 113) that Herodotus 'explicitly argues from epigraphical evidence' only in the period before the Trojan war.

[75] Collingwood (1946: 18), Fornara (1983: 9), Hornblower (1987: 19).

contradiction—his statement that Croesus was the 'first man we know' to perpetrate unjust actions against the Greeks despite his knowledge that his predecessors committed similar deeds— can be explained, as Michael Lloyd has shown, as a function of Herodotus' paratactic style, typical of the way in which Herodotus makes a general claim and then progressively qualifies that claim without introducing a 'but' or 'except'.[76] Herodotus qualifies his initial claim by saying that this Croesus was 'the first man we know' to subdue the Greeks to the point where they paid him tribute (1. 6. 2). In maintaining this distinction between Croesus' *systematic* injustice and the hit-and-run aggression of his predecessors, he is entirely consistent.[77] He distinguishes Croesus' conquests from the Cimmerian conquest of Ionia on the grounds that it was 'not a subjugation of the cities, but a plundering raid' (οὐ καταστροφὴ ἐγένετο τῶν πολίων, ἀλλ' ἐξ ἐπιδρομῆς ἁρπαγή, 1. 6. 3): the purpose of this distinction is to explain why it was that Croesus was the first to subdue the Greeks despite the fact that the Cimmerian expedition predated Croesus. 'After the Greeks in Asia had been reduced by him to the payment of tribute' (ὡς δὲ ἄρα οἱ ἐν τῇ Ἀσίῃ Ἕλληνες κατεστράφατο ἐς φόρου ἀπαγωγήν), Herodotus adds later, Croesus prepared to attack the islanders (1. 27. 1).[78]

Herodotus clearly envisages the past as a continuous whole.[79]

[76] M. Lloyd (1984); Lloyd believes, however, that Herodotus 'does indeed distinguish between myth and history in the way suggested by Shimron', but that he 'does not tacitly exclude myth when making general statements'. Cf. Flory (1987: 15); Fehling (1989: 58–9), seeing 1. 5. 3 as a 'common kind of transitional formula'; Wardman (1961: 138–45), demonstrating that Herodotus' use of the word οἶδα of one account is not *necessarily* intended to demonstrate the falsity of the account preceding or opposed to it, envisaging a distinction between the important or political and the unimportant or personal.

[77] Hellmann (1934: 25 ff.); Maddalena (1942: 15–16, ch. 1 *passim*); Pohlenz (1937: 10–11), followed by Immerwahr (1966: 82 n. 13); Wardman (1961: 135–6). Shimron is undoubtedly right in saying (1973: 45) that Herodotus does not 'say that the *adikia* of Croesus' *adika erga* consisted in imposing tribute upon all the Ionians'. An easy retort, however, is that he also (more surprisingly) never spells out his distinction of the time before and after Croesus.

[78] Cf. 2. 182. 2 (εἷλε δὲ Κύπρον πρῶτος ἀνθρώπων καὶ κατεστρέψατο ἐς φόρου ἀπαγωγήν). Shimron (1973: 45) suggests that the early Lydian kings 'most probably subjected them (the Greeks of Asia Minor) to tribute'—irrelevant even if true.

[79] A point stressed above all by von Leyden (1949–50: 92 ff.), but acknowledged surprisingly by Shimron (1989: 22); see also Shimron's observation

His comparison of Xerxes' campaign with previous expeditions, far from suggesting that history is split into three or more units,[80] relies upon the fact that those earlier expeditions are *comparable* (7. 20. 2).[81] Like the pattern by which Herodotus seeks out the 'first inventor' of any phenomenon, the first language, the first dithyrambic poet, it reveals an instinct always to look back to the past.[82] Whether that past is, in our terms, historical or mythical is immaterial. In conclusion to Cleomenes' abortive campaign against Athens Herodotus notes that that this was the fourth time that the Dorians had invaded Attica: the first was contemporary with the foundation of Megara, during the reign of Codrus (5. 76). The oracle advising the Cretans to take no part in the Persian wars prompts a lengthy footnote on Minos and the Cretans' part in the Trojan war (7. 170–1).[83] Similarly, after recording the bravery of Sophanes of Decelea during the battle of Plataea, Herodotus digresses in order to retell Decelea's other great contribution 'in all time' (ἐς τὸν πάντα χρόνον), the help they gave to the Tyndaridae in recovering Helen from Theseus (9. 73).[84]

Herodotus, of course, was able also to distinguish between men and gods. That is probably the clearest distinction that emerges from his remarks on the thalassocracy of Polycrates

(p. 19) that 'the argument that he saw in mythological personnages historical figures is irrelevant: so did Thucydides'.

[80] Why Herodotus' categorization should be merely tripartite according to Shimron is not immediately evident: see further (1973: 49–50).

[81] Cf. M. Lloyd (1984).

[82] Van Groningen (1953: 27): 'Herodotus always wants to lead back to the past.' For the idea of the first inventor, see van Groningen (1953: 33–4), Kleingünther (1933: 46 ff.), Nisbet and Hubbard (1970: 49–50), on Horace *Odes* 1. 3. 12, Fowler (1996: 73–4). Herodotean firsts: 1. 5. 3, 6. 2, 23, 94. 1, 163. 1; 2. 188. 2; 6. 112. 3; for other superlatives, see Ch. 3.

[83] Evans (1991: 106) notes Herodotus' digression on Minos as an exception to the rule of the exclusion of myth. On the evolution of this legend, see Dunbabin (1948), Bérard (1941: 417 ff.).

[84] See Vandiver's interesting interpretation of this passage in the light of Decelea's role in the Peloponnesian war (1991: 70–1). Von Leyden (1949–50) gives a number of other examples of the long historical perspective of Herodotus: e.g. 2. 15, 49. 2, 53. 1, 154; 5. 9. 3. A similar long perspective is revealed by characters: esp. 7. 161. 3, 9. 26–7 (on which, however, see Evans (1991: 83), Vandiver (1991: 65)).

—that Polycrates unlike Minos was human (3. 122. 2).[85] These remarks have frequently been translated or paraphrased in such a way as to suggest a firm distinction in Herodotus' mind between a mythical and historical period[86]—as if Herodotus was referring back to his distinction of a *spatium mythicum* and *spatium historicum* at the time of Croesus.[87] It is certainly possible that Herodotus' two 'qualifiers'—that Polycrates was the 'first Greek we know' to aim at the rule of the sea, and that he was the first 'of what we might call the human generation' to do so—are equivalent,[88] that there is a weak and unconscious feeling on Herodotus' part that pre-human history was inherently unverifiable.[89] Such a statement, however, cannot be seen

[85] Vandiver (1991: 146); cf. Brillante's discussion of Herodotus' thought here in relation to Hesiod (1990: 102), or Hunter's in relation to Thucydides (1982: 106 ff.).

[86] So e.g. von Leyden (1949–50: 95), the 'so-called historical age'; Vidal-Naquet (1960: 67; = 1986: 45), 'L'histoire humaine s'oppose ainsi à la mythologie'; Finley (1975: 18), 'the first in historical, as distinct from mythical times'; M. Lloyd (1984), Polycrates was 'the first historical figure to do so'; Flory (1987: 50), 'he also consigns Minos . . . to the world of myth'; Lattimore (1958: 20 n. 6), Minos was 'prehistoric, really prehuman'; Lateiner (1989: 118), 'in ordinary human history'; 'the gods . . . and semi–legendary beings such as Minos are beyond the evidence that history can deliver or explain. They are generally obscure in their workings and not part of the "human epoch"'; Asheri ad loc. (iii. 338), 'è una chiara distinzione polemica tra età mitica ed età storica'.

[87] See e.g. Evans' remark (1991: 106) that Polycrates belonged to 'a span of time beginning a little more than three generations earlier in the Greek world' (implicitly equating the time of Polycrates to that of Croesus). The oral memory of different cities may, of course, have dried up at a similar period: see White (1969: 45), Starr (1968b: 358), Lateiner (1989: 117), for the limits of oral memory R. Thomas (1989: esp. 122–31); it is the object of Vannicelli (1993) to demonstrate that Herodotus limited himself to the period of three generations leading up to the Persian wars. For Herodotus' chronology, see Mitchel (1956), den Boer (1967), Strasburger (1956), Hammond (1955), Miller (1965), Lloyd i. 171 ff., Burkert (1995).

[88] Fowler (1996: 83). It is possible also that the second statement qualifies or refines the first.

[89] It is open to question whether any rigid chronological distinction of myth and history reflects as well on Herodotus as its proponents suppose. Fornara expresses amazement (1983: 7) that Jacoby expressed only an 'unconscious and very weak feeling that historical recollections and epic traditions are incommensurable qualities' (1909: 99 n. 2; = 1956: 37 n. 63). Better, however, a weak feeling than a high principle from which Herodotus only lapses.

in isolation. As we have seen, Minos is elsewhere treated straightforwardly as a historical figure (7. 170–1).[90] A similarly literal-minded approach to the 'mythical past' is revealed elsewhere. Herodotus apparently envisages a time at which gods ruled Egypt one by one (2. 144. 2), living side by side with men (or before them).[91] He also claims to have seen, and to have been able easily to read, examples of 'Cadmeian letters' inscribed in the temple of Apollo Ismenias in Thebes (5. 59–61); these inscriptions, in immaculate Greek verse, he believed to have been inscribed by contemporaries of Oedipus and his father Laius.[92]

This is not to say that he was not also critical of certain traditions concerning the early history of gods and heroes. As we saw in Chapter 3, Herodotus is wary of attributing divine parents to mortals (e.g. 6. 53. 1). The Greeks, he says, retell many things uncritically ($\dot{a}\nu\epsilon\pi\iota\sigma\kappa\dot{\epsilon}\pi\tau\omega\varsigma$, 2. 45. 1), for example a story of how the Egyptians attempted to sacrifice Heracles (2. 45. 1): how would the Egyptians, he counters, so squeamish in their choice of sacrificial victims, have sacrificed a man? how could Heracles, a single man, have slain thousands to make good his escape (2. 45. 2–3)?[93] Similar instances of the fabulous—Thucydides' *to mythodes* (1. 22. 4)—are, as we have seen, erased from the story of Io (1. 1–2. 1).[94] But 'demythologisation', as Paul Veyne has written, is not the same thing as irreligion.[95] Such rationalizations or revisions—the scholarly caution, for example, with which he refrains from introducing

[90] Cf. Darbo-Peschanski (1987: 25 ff.), e.g. (p. 33) 'pour écarter Minos et ses prédécesseurs, il faut en poser l'existence'.

[91] According to whether we read $o\dot{\iota}\kappa\dot{\epsilon}o\nu\tau a\varsigma$ or (with Rosén now, or Vandiver 1991: 141) $o\dot{v}\kappa$ $\dot{\epsilon}\acute{o}\nu\tau a\varsigma$. Benardete (1969: 61) seems here to confuse his own scepticism with that of Herodotus.

[92] West (1985: 290–5); cf. Herodotus' investigations into the history of the Gephyraioi, 5. 57.

[93] Cf. esp. Helen's stay in Egypt (2. 113–20—see further Ch. 8), the cult of Heracles (2. 43–5—see above, this chapter), or the black doves of Dodona (2. 55–7). Shimron (1989: 23), reclassifying the Dodona myth as 'not mythical but semi-historical', claims that Herodotus 'does not rationalize myths'. Fehling believes this myth to be Herodotus' own invention (1989: 65–70), but the association of Dodona with Egypt predates him: see Parke (1967a: 207–8), Pritchett (1993: 71–5).

[94] See Ch. 2.

[95] Veyne (1988: 98). Cf. Hunter (1982: 111–12), Brillante (1990: 97).

divine parents—far from reflecting any sense of the inherent unreliability of such early history reveal only its potential truth.

In what sense then can we talk of myth in the *Histories*? 'Etymology', as Kirk remarked, 'is a traditional point of departure, but in this case an unhelpful one.'[96] Herodotus' uses of the word μῦθος cannot safely be taken as 'implying disbelief'—as Powell puts it in his *Lexicon*.[97] The person who wrote about the Ocean, Herodotus says, 'by carrying the μῦθος to where it can no longer be seen' (ἐς ἀφανὲς τὸν μῦθον ἀνενείκας) defies any possible refutation (οὐκ ἔχει ἔλεγχον, 2. 23): it is what is done to the μῦθος that makes it impossible to falsify; there is nothing inherently impossible about the story itself. Herodotus' second use of the word, although it follows immediately after the remark that the 'the Greeks tell many things thoughtlessly' (λέγουσι δὲ πολλὰ καὶ ἄλλα ἀνεπισκέπτως οἱ Ἕλληνες,[98] 2. 45. 1), is again inconclusive. The story that it heralds of Heracles on the rampage is forcefully dismissed by Herodotus, but arguably no differently from many Herodotean *logoi*. (Of course, if the word μῦθος were a sufficiently clear indication of Herodotus' scepticism, there would be no need for him to distance himself so forcefully from the story.)

At any rate the word is only used twice: no one, I imagine,

[96] Kirk (1970: 8); 'for the Greeks', he continues, '*muthos* just meant a tale, or something one uttered, in a wide range of senses: a statement, a story, the plot of a play'. Contrast Edmunds (1990: 4), Dowden (1992: 4–5), Bremmer (1982: 43). See now, however, the less casual history of the term of Nickau (1990), envisaging the sense of *mythos* as untrue story involving the gods as new to the 420s.

[97] As supposed by Wardman (1960: 403–4); Detienne (1986: 49–51), Herodotus 'censures' two 'myths'; Murray (1987: 99–100), *mythos* 'designates *logoi* which Herodotus believes to be ridiculous as well as false'—'a category', however, which Herodotus 'usually seems to have ignored'; apparently G. E. R. Lloyd (1990: 23); Evans (1991: 105); Marincola (1997: 118 n. 285). Contrast Nickau (1990: 84–7), connecting Herodotus' use of *mythos* to his following in these passages of Hecataeus (see the following note). Wardman acknowledges, however, that it was easy for later writers to forget Herodotus' attitude to myth in these two passages (1960: 405): see e.g. Diod. Sic. 11. 37. 6, where Diodorus observes that the *Histories* began before the Trojan war.

[98] Echoing Hecataeus, *FGH* 1 F 1: 'the stories of the Greeks are many and foolish as they appear to me' (οἱ γὰρ Ἑλλήνων λόγοι πολλοί τε καὶ γελοῖοι, ὡς ἐμοὶ φαίνονται, εἰσίν); Hecataeus uses μυθέομαι of his own words.

would seriously maintain that there are only two myths, in any sense of the word, in the *Histories*.[99] If we adopt, on the other hand, the definition of myth as a 'traditional tale relevant to society'—not surely a definition to which Herodotus might himself have subscribed—how much of the *Histories* might qualify?[100] Herodotus clearly can (in some sense) distinguish true from false. He can also—as the story of the Ocean shows—distinguish a story on the grounds that it is not falsifiable.[101] However, though he may apply the tests of falsifiability or of verifiability to some 'stories in which the chief characters are gods', there is no reason to suppose that this category, or that of 'stories of the distant past', were coterminous with (or subsets of) a category of stories *by definition* unverifiable, by definition unfalsifiable. Quite simply, the Herodotean conception and rejection of 'myth' are of modern construction, built upon sand and held together with wishful thinking.

[99] Vandiver (1991: 7); contrast the curious remark of J. Z. Smith (1978: 248) that 'he only relates seven myths'.

[100] Cf. van Groningen (1953: 102), Finley (1975: 13).

[101] See here Fowler (1996: 79); for *to aphanes* in Herodotus, see also the wanderings of Corcella (1984). For geographical limits to knowledge and Herodotus' partial demythologization of 'mythic geography' see Romm (1989; 1992: esp. 32 ff.), for Ocean and its possible connection with the *apeiron* of Anaximander (pp. 22 ff.). For geographical symmetry, see Lachenaud (1978: 209 ff.), Lateiner (1985b), Redfield (1985), Gianotti (1988), Hartog (1988); for modern parallels of monstrous peoples on the fringes of the earth, see McCartney (1941).

8

Foreign Gods and Foreign Religion

The Getae have a particularly cunning way of discovering the disposition of their god Salmoxis (4. 94. 3). They select a man by lot to send as a messenger to Salmoxis; then, holding him by the hands and feet, they swing him onto the points of three javelins. If he should die, the god is deemed to be favourable towards them; if he should survive, he is said to be wicked and another man is tried. Similar mental tricks, it might be said, are employed to justify and maintain Greek belief in divination. What is different about many of the beliefs and practices projected onto foreign peoples by the Greeks is that they are so clearly unworkable.[1] The story illustrates well just how remote Herodotus—the 'Father of the History of Religions', as well as of History, Anthropology, and Lies[2]—may be from the reality of foreign religious experience. The veracity of his 'accounts' of foreign religion, however, the manner in which details have been distorted or in which they must be handled in the reconstruction of non-Greek religions, are not at issue here.[3] This chapter will focus rather on Greek religion as it is reflected in Herodotus' accounts of foreign peoples.

Herodotus' accounts of foreign religion provide some of our most valuable insights into the nature of Greek religious assumptions. The Persians require one of the Magi to be present at every sacrifice (1. 132. 3), Herodotus reports with apparent amazement.[4] On the other hand, they use no altars, temples or images, the reason being, Herodotus suggests, that they 'do not believe the gods to be human in form as the Greeks do' (οὐκ ἀνθρωποφυέας ἐνόμισαν τοὺς θεοὺς κατά περ οἱ Ἕλληνες εἶναι, 1. 131. 1)—an oddity again, but not apparently an

---

[1] Cf. Ethiopian divination, 2. 29. 7.
[2] J. Z. Smith (1978: 245 and n. 16).
[3] For these questions, see esp. Mora (1985), Burkert (1990).
[4] Burkert (1985a: 95).

inconceivable one.[5] Foreign religions, however, do not serve only as a 'mirror' in which Greek preconceptions are inverted. Direct comparison can be made, as if between two Greek cities—so, for example, between the funerals of the Spartan and Persian kings (6. 58. 2).[6] At the same time, Herodotus employs another model for understanding the religions of foreign peoples: that of diffusion. As we saw in Chapter 7, Egypt is characterized as a privileged source of religious wisdom, the origin of the greatest part of Greek religious beliefs and practices. At times, for example in his discussion of the origins of the names of the gods (discussed below in Appendix 2), Herodotus seems to take for granted the foreign origins of Greek religion, to be looking only for the most likely country of origin for a given god.

It is questionable indeed whether it is legitimate to talk of foreign religion at all.[7] 'Herodotus, of course', as Robert Parker has written, 'tends to suppose that Greek and foreign gods can be translated into one another, like Greek and foreign words. Indeed it seems that for him the gods themselves are the same everywhere.'[8] The Assyrians, Herodotus says, for example, call (καλέουσι) Aphrodite 'Mylitta', the Arabians call her 'Alilat', and the Persians 'Mitra'[9] (1. 131. 3); the Arabians name

[5] As Legrand observes (1932: 131), Herodotus passes no pejorative comment. Burkert suggests indeed (1990: 21) that this passage is a reflection of contemporary Greek ideas, and speculates that Herodotus has introduced his own reproach of Greek beliefs into the Persians' mouths. For the Greek opposition to anthropomorphic deities, see famously Xenophanes DK 21 B 14–16. For the simultaneously zoomorphic and anthropomorphic nature of Greek divinities, see Sourvinou-Inwood (1997: 166).

[6] Cf. the Scythian custom whereby sons honour the gilded skulls of their fathers with sacrifices, compared to the Greeks' celebration of their fathers' deaths, 4. 26. 2. Herodotus here must intend to shock.

[7] Rudhardt (1992b: 230).

[8] Parker (1996: 159); see also Gould (1994: 103), Rudhardt (1992b: 224 ff.), Hall (1989: 5, 183–4), Parke (1967a: 52–3). See also the Table of Herodotus' equations of Greek and foreign gods (here, or see Linforth 1926: 6–7). In the fanciful theology he ascribes to Herodotus, Immerwahr (1966: 314) seems not to have observed the equation of Greek and foreign gods.

[9] Mitra is in fact the male Mithras, one of Herodotus' greater mistakes: see Burkert (1990: 18), Mora (1985: 32 ff.). Herodotus (or a predecessor) may have been misled by the resemblance of Μίτρα and Μήτρα or mother: Merkelbach (1984: 10 n. 1). (If the mistake were Herodotus' own, this would appear to sit uncomfortably with the Persian belief in non-anthro-

TABLE: *Herodotus' equations of Greek and foreign gods*

	ARABS	ASSYRIANS	EGYPTIANS	ETHIOP.	LIBYANS	MASSAG.	PERSIANS	PHOEN.	SCYTHIANS	TAURIANS	THRAC.
APHRODITE (Ouranie)	Alilat 1. *131*, 3. 8	Mylitta 1. *131*, 1. 199	2. 41, 112[a]				Mitra 1. 131		Argimpasa 4. 59		
APOLLO			Horus 2. 83, *144*, *155*, *156*						Goitosyrus 4. 59		
ARES			2. 59, 63, 83								
ARTEMIS			Bubastis 2. 59, 83, *137*, 155						4. 59		5. 7
ATHENA			2. 28, 59, 83, 169, 170		4. *180*, 188						
CABIRI			3. 37								
DEMETER			Isis 2. 41, *42*, 59, 61, 122–3, *156*, 171, 176, 4. 186								
DIONYSUS	Orotalt 3. 8		Osiris 2. 42, 47, 48–9, 52, 123, *144–5*, 156	2. 29, 3. 97							5. 7, 7. 111
EPAPHUS			Apis 2. 38, *153*, 3. *27–8, 64*								
GE (Earth)							1. 131				
HELIOS[b] (Sun)			2. 59, 63, 73, 111			1. 216	1. 131		Api 4. 59		

HEPHAESTUS	2. 2, 99, 101, 108, 110, 112, 121, 136, 141, 142, 147, 151, 153, 176, 3. 37			
HERACLES	2. 42–5, 83, 113, 145–6	2. 44		4. 59
HERMES	2. 67, 138			
HESTIA			Tabiti 4. 59	
IPHIGENIA				4. 103[c]
LETO	2. 59, 83, 152, 155–6			
PAN	Mendes 2. 42, 46, 145			
PERSEUS	2. 91			
POSEIDON	2. 52, 4. 188		Thagimasadas 4. 59	
SELENE (Moon)	2. 47			
TRITON	4. 188			
TYPHON	2. 144, 156, 3. 5			
ZEUS	Amon 1. 182, 2. 42, 45, 54, 57, 74, 83, 136, 143	2. 29	1. 131 Papaios 4. 59	

NOTES:

Bold type (used of a people) signifies that the gods listed represent all those, in Herodotus' view, known by a given people.
Italic type (of references) signifies the passage at which an equation between a Greek and a foreign name has been made.
Two identifications do not appear on this table. The Barcaeans respect Isis (4. 186). The Ammonians have a temple resembling Theban Zeus (4. 181).

a Herodotus identifies the shrine of Aphrodite Xeinie as a shrine of Helen.
b The Persians also worship water, wind, and fire; certain Libyans likewise, 4. 188, sacrifice only to the sun and moon. For the ambiguous Greek attitude to such natural phenomena as deities, reflected e.g. by the observation at Ar. Pax 406 ff. that barbarians all sacrifice to sun and moon, see Mikalson (1989: 97–8).
c The identification of their daimon with Iphigenia is one ascribed by Herodotus to the Taurians.

Dionysus 'Orotalt' (ὀνομάζουσι, 3. 8. 3); Hestia is named 'Tabiti' 'in Scythian' (Σκυθιστὶ, 4. 59. 2).[10] Another common formula reveals this universalism even more starkly. 'The people there revere Zeus and Dionysus alone of the gods' (οἱ δ' ἐν ταύτῃ Δία θεῶν καὶ Διόνυσον μούνους σέβονται, 2. 29. 7; cf. 1. 216. 4, 3. 8. 3, 5. 7).[11] Herodotus appears to conceive of a finite number of deities, revealed to different peoples rather in the manner of an advent calendar: any given people has knowledge of a number of these deities; none has knowledge of all.[12] Parallel to this process of identification is the moral, expressed most clearly in Herodotus' judgement on Cambyses that men should respect the gods revered by others: 'it was clear in every way that Cambsyes was greatly insane'—for he would not otherwise have attempted to mock the sacred customs of the Egyptians (3. 38. 1).[13] Cambyses later died in Ecbatana in Syria from a self-inflicted wound in exactly the same spot as that in which he had wounded the Egyptian Apis-calf (3. 64. 3), whom he had earlier mocked as a preposterous god fit only for the Egyptians.[14]

Herodotus' gods know no frontiers then. It is only in the forms of worship employed, in the choice of the gods worshipped, or the characteristics attributed to the gods that peoples differ. When the Athenians give their reasons for standing fast against the Persians, they talk of the the 'shrines

pomorphic gods.) For an alternative 'justification' of Herodotus, an association of Venus, Mithras, and the Morning Star, see Edwards (1990).

[10] For the name of Orotalt, see Cumont (1902), Mora (1985: 76). For Papaios and Api (e.g. as father and mother), see Macan ad loc. (iv. 1. 40 n. 8), Meuli (1935: 141), Zgusta (1953; 1955: 303–4), Mora (1985: 51). For Tabiti, Macan iv. 1. 40 n. 3, Corcella ad loc. (pp. 279 ff.). For Argimpasa and Oitosorus, Ferguson (1981: 7); cf. CIG 6013–4. For variant readings of their names, see further Rosén ad loc. (p. 384). For the Scythian gods, see further Mora (1985: 49 ff.); for Herodotus' account of Scythian religion generally, see Diesner (1961).

[11] As Asheri remarks of 3. 8. 3 (ad loc., p. 222) and other Greeks' summaries of Arab religion, 'sono semplificazioni greche di scarso valore'. For Thracian religion (and further bib.), see Nenci on 5. 7 (pp. 162–3).

[12] See Rudhardt (1992b: 228).

[13] Cf. Hes. Erga 755–6 (do not mock unfamiliar rites).

[14] For the truth of Cambyses' crimes in Egypt, see Ch. 3. For Xerxes' comparable destruction of Babylonian temples, see Kuhrt and Sherwin-White (1987).

of the gods that we have in common', of 'common sacrifices' and customs, not of common gods (8. 144. 2).[15] The Scythian Scyles is said to have propitiated the gods 'according to the customs of the Greeks' (κατὰ νόμους τοὺς Ἑλλήνων, 4. 78. 4) as if the same gods were being approached merely by different means. The same distinction is evident in Herodotus' own practice in his descriptions of foreign peoples. As he travels from people to people, travels in the imagination if not in reality, he details in very spare terms both the religious customs—the form of sacrifice or of divination, the animals sacrificed, the nature of a people's taboos and so on—and the names of the gods worshipped, differences in their representation.[16]

The identification of gods takes place, as a result, in spite of what seem extraordinary obstacles.[17] The Persians call the whole circle of the sky Zeus (1. 131. 2); they have, as we have seen, no temples, no altars, no images, and their gods do not take human form (1. 131. 1). At the same time, however, identifications seem to be rooted precisely in coincidences between the myths or rituals of the gods in question. So, for example, it is the association of Zeus with the sky that presumably leads to his identification with the Persian sky-god (1. 131. 2), the association of Mendes with a goat—or the fact that in Egyptian the same word denotes the god Mendes and a goat—that leads to the identification of Mendes with Pan

---

[15] For this passage, and for religion as a focus of group identity, see now Parker (1998a). Cf. the case of the people of Apis and Marea on the borders of Libya and Egypt, 2. 18, whose resentment at being Egyptian focuses on ritual taboos.

[16] The prominence of ritual in Herodotus' accounts of foreign religions is emphasized by Linforth (1926: 8), J. Z. Smith (1978: 244–9), Darbo-Peschanski (1987: 39 ff.), Burkert (1990), Gould (1994: 98 ff.), Feeney (1998: 78). Weeks (1982: 64) asserts that Herodotus 'may have been willing to include mentions of cultic differences because it fitted his scepticism on such matters'. The difference in religious customs is played upon at Anaxandrides fr. 40 KA, E. *Hel.* 800, 1065–6, 1240 ff.; E. *Rhes.* 703 suggests interestingly that peoples are distinguished by the order in which they rank the gods.

[17] See esp. Linforth (1926: 13). See also Sourdille's remarks on the flimsy basis of many of Herodotus' identifications (1910: 386); Sourdille's procedure is to correct Herodotus' identifications in favour of his own (e.g. pp. 145 ff. on Apis and Epaphus) or to supply an identification where Herodotus has omitted to (p. 172 on Heracles).

(2. 46. 4).[18] Although in some rare cases Herodotus feels able to sketch the historical circumstances in which a god's 'name' and rites were transferred from one people to another, such identifications appear more often to be taken for granted.[19] Only in one case—the identification of Aphrodite Xeinie as Helen,[20] on the grounds that Helen had spent time with the Egyptian Proteus, and that the epithet Xeinie for Aphrodite was unique (2. 112. 2)—does Herodotus present an equation overtly as his own innovation.[21] Given the lengthy contacts between Greece and Egypt,[22] it is likely that the vast majority of such identifications had been long established by both Greeks and Egyptians for their mutual convenience, that Herodotus' speculations on Helen are ingenious variations on a well-worn theme.

This picture of a tolerant universalism must be qualified, however. On a number of occasions in the *Histories,* it appears to be the gods themselves rather than their shrines that distinguish the Greeks from foreigners; the principle of identification, so deep-rooted elsewhere, is momentarily forgotten.[23] In many of these cases, the apparent lapse can be explained by its context. Apis is described as 'the god of the Egyptians' even

[18] Cf. also 4. 108. 2, referred to below.

[19] Linforth (1926: 18), Hall (1989: 183). As Rudhardt observes (1992*b*: 224–5) (cf. the emphasis of Lachenaud (1978: 194)), it is impossible to explain identification solely in terms of the diffusion of knowledge of the gods. Herodotus only employs the explanation of diffusion in a few cases (1. 131. 3, 2. 50). He never offers any such historical explanation e.g. of how the Scythians came to worship the same gods as the Greeks (even though, given the existence of a surviving Greek population in Scythia with temples to Greek gods, 4. 108. 2, such a hypothesis might have been attractive). See also for the process of identification Mora (1985: 101).

[20] See here Fehling (1989: 64–5) on Herodotus' 'fictitious proof', but for the (earlier) association of Helen and Astarte, see Rebuffat (1966), Mora (1985: 89), Lloyd iii. 46 ff., Pritchett (1993: 63–71).

[21] As Linforth points out (1926: 15), Herodotus does not draw the same conclusion in the case of the unique epithet Zeus Stratios, 5. 119; at 2. 112. 2 it is perhaps the combination of 'evidence' that has forced his speculation. Linforth continues to describe 2. 112. 2 as the only identification made by Herodotus (pp. 15–6)—ultimately unknowable (if likely).

[22] For earlier contacts between Greece and Egypt, see Austin (1970), Lloyd i. 1 ff., and now Braun (1982*b*: 32 ff.). For earlier Greek ideas of Egyptian religion: Mora (1985: 186–8). See also now *SEG* 37. 994.

[23] Linforth (1926: 3).

as, through Cambyses' fatal injury, he shows his orbit to be
unlimited (3. 64. 3). When Croesus terms Apollo 'the god of the
Greeks' (1. 87. 3, 90. 2) or asks Delphi 'if it is customary for the
Greek gods to be ungrateful' (1. 90. 4), his scorn is born of the
mistaken sense of having been deceived.[24] Apollo, whom he had
formerly honoured above all gods (1. 90. 2), is subsequently, of
course, vindicated: the whole episode illustrates again precisely
the universality of the Greek god's power. Other instances of
such expressions, however, are more problematic. Aristagoras
begs Cleomenes 'by the Greek gods' to free the Ionians from
their slavery (5. 49. 3). Hegesistratus makes a similar appeal for
Greek freedom by their 'common gods' (9. 90. 2). The Corinthian Soclees calls on the Spartans not to restore tyrannies 'by
the Greek gods' (5. 92. η5), and Hippias then calls on 'the same
gods' in reply (5. 93. 1). In two other cases, moreover, similar
phrases come from Herodotus' own mouth.[25] In the town of
Gelonus in Scythia, the Budini have 'shrines, built in the Greek
manner, of Greek gods' (Ἑλληνικῶν θεῶν ἱρὰ Ἑλληνικῶς κατασ-
κευασμένα, 4. 108. 2), a fact he then explains by the Budini being
in origin Greek.[26] In another instance, foreign cults give way to
foreign gods. The Caunians decide to terminate the 'foreign
cults' established in their territory (ἱρῶν ξεινικῶν), to 'worship
only their ancestral gods' (τοῖσι πατρίοισι μοῦνον χρᾶσθαι θεοῖσι)
and to expel—physically, by striking the air with their spears—
'foreign gods' (ξεινικοὺς θεούς, 1. 172. 2).[27]

A number of foreign gods, moreover, prove untranslatable.

---

[24] As Linforth observes (1926: 23), there may also have been 'a little
naughty, Hellenic pride in emphasizing the Hellenic nature of the Delphic
Apollo who had tricked Croesus so prettily'.

[25] Contrast Burkert (1990: 24–5).

[26] Cf. 2. 91. 4–6: the presence of Greek rites in Egypt is put down,
according to the Egyptians, to the instructions of Perseus.

[27] See, however, Parker (1996: 158–9 and n. 20), arguing on the basis of
Apollophanes' use of the term xenikos for Asclepius (fr. 6 KA), that xenikoi
theoi 'are not identical with "foreign gods"' (i.e. non-Greek gods): 'The
essential distinction is not between Greek and non-Greek gods, but between
those traditionally honoured in Athenian public cult and all others.' The
rationale behind the Caunians' action is not alien to the Greeks: cf. 5. 67
(Cleisthenes' expulsion of Adrastus), 2. 30. 4 ('Deserters' leave ancestral
gods), 8. 41. 3 (Athena deserts Athens), 8. 111. 3 (Andrian 'gods' refuse to
leave). For (Athenian) wariness in introducing new gods, see Rudhardt
(1992b), Parker (1996: ch. 9).

Cybebe and Pleistorus are both termed 'local gods' (ἐπιχωρίης
θεοῦ, 5. 102. 1; cf. 9. 119. 1); Herodotus is uncertain also as to
whether Salmoxis is a man or a local daimon of the Getae
(δαίμων . . . ἐπιχώριος, 4. 96. 2).[28] The description of Cybebe as
a local god (despite her established identification with
Demeter, the Great Mother and Aphrodite[29]) may be explicable by its context: the Greeks' accidental destruction of her
temple in the course of the Ionian Revolt. With Pleistorus and
Salmoxis, it appears that their reduced status is related to the
barbaric nature of their rites, in both cases involving forms of
human sacrifice.[30] The Egyptians, it should be noted, the
people above all who applied themselves to the proper worship
of the gods, could not conceivably, in Herodotus' view, have
practised human sacrifice (2. 45. 2).[31]

Though Herodotus' judgement on Cambyses may reveal
then a belief that men should not actively mock or violate the
sacred customs of others, that they should give the benefit of the
doubt to the gods worshipped by foreign peoples, disapproval is

[28] Cf. Linforth (1926: 2): 'it never seems to occur to the Greek traveler to
doubt their [foreign gods'] existence.'

[29] See Edwards (1993), Robertson (1996: 304), *OCD*[3] s.v. 'Cybele'. Aphrodite: Charon of Lampsacus *FGH* 262 F 5.

[30] Linforth (1926: 23–4). A parallel case might be the burying alive of
upper-class Persian children by Amestris 'to gratify the so-called god under
the ground' (τῷ ὑπὸ γῆν λεγομένῳ εἶναι θεῷ ἀντιχαρίζεσθαι, 7. 114. 2): if 'so-
called' reflects anything more than the equivalent of modern inverted
commas, then that reserve may be the function of Amestris' cruelty. An
interesting counter-example is Iphigenia, identified with a Taurian goddess
with rites no less barbarous than Pleistorus (human sacrifice of shipwrecked
foreigners), 4. 103. 1–2. Possibly, however, as Linforth suggested, the fact
that the identification is made in this instance only by the Taurians is
significant. At E. *IT* 35 ff., 386 ff., the goddess to whom the Taurians sacrifice
Greeks is Artemis whilst Iphigenia is her reluctant priestess. Iphigenia cannot
believe that the rites are welcome to the goddess, or that the gods are capable
of evil, but imagines that the Taurians are merely passing the responsibility
for their murders onto Artemis. For an excellent discussion of the Iphigenia
myth in relation to Attic cult, see Sourvinou-Inwood (1997: 171–5). For a
fantastic reconstruction of the cult of Pleistorus, see Fol and Mazarow (1977:
25). For the issue of Herodotean invention in the context of Iphigenia, see
predictably Fehling (1989: 50 n. 5), Pritchett (1993: 195).

[31] It was not inconceivable to Herodotus' uncle Panyassis: Matthews (1974:
126–7), Braun (1982*b*: 53). For the exploitation of the theme of Heracles
abroad by comic poets, see Long (1986: 56–7).

still apparently an available option: indeed the designation of a god as local seems itself a mark of disapproval. Herodotus' comments on Cambyses have been described by John Gould as 'an argument for respecting the traditions of all cultures', but this should not be mistaken for an all-out cultural relativism.[32] Babylonian temple prostitution, for example, is described by Herodotus as the 'most shameful of customs' (ὁ δὲ δὴ αἴσχιστος τῶν νόμων, 1. 199. 1).[33]

A clear line is also drawn at worshipping foreign gods. There is no suggestion that Cambyses should have become a devotee of Apis—as in actual fact he may have done. Greek festivals, of course, were limited to Greeks (5. 22, 8. 65. 4). The Greeks in Egypt likewise required the Hellenion; the Aeginetans, the Samians, and the Milesians built their own shrines there to Zeus, Hera, and Apollo respectively (2. 178).[34] The belief in the identity of one's own and others' gods is all very well in theory— but not in practice.[35] When foreigners do attempt to propitiate Greek gods, it is frequently the case that no good comes of it. The Scythian king Scyles, in the habit of spending whole months within the city of the Borysthenites (4. 78. 4), is on the verge of his initiation into the rites of the Bacchic Dionysus when 'the god' destroys his palace with lightning (4. 79. 2); his people then discover his initiation, revolt, and kill him. Xerxes' propitiation of Athena Ilias and the heroes of Troy appears to have met with divine displeasure in the form of a panic attack (7. 43. 2). When, after the occupation and destruction of Athens,

[32] Gould (1994: 93).

[33] See also e.g. his views on sex or imagined sex in temples, 2. 64, 1. 181. 5–182 (for which see Ch. 3). Rudhardt (1992b: 222–4; 1991: 50), citing 1. 199, suggests that Herodotus never disapproves of foreign customs *only* on the grounds of their being foreign. See also the remarks of Burkert (1990: 24) (and of Asheri and Lloyd in the following discussion, pp. 33–4), distinguishing e.g. between an ethnographic and a moral relativism.

[34] Rudhardt (1992b: 236–8) similarly explains the Athenians' wariness at the introduction of foreign cults by the argument that they recognized the legitimacy of cults of foreign gods, but only in their traditional place. Contrast Lateiner (1989: 51): '*Nomos* is king of all . . . except that he who knows this truth is already semi-detached from the shackles of his society. The privileged few include Herodotus and anyone willing to be liberated by his work from the tyranny of parochial values'! (The exclamation mark is mine.)

[35] Adrastus, however, requests purification according to the 'native' i.e. Lydian customs, 1. 35. 1.

Xerxes orders Athenian exiles to sacrifice on the Acropolis, the gesture is met by the sudden sprouting of the sacred olive tree, a symbol of Athenian resurgence (8. 54–5).

Of course, in this last instance, Xerxes' reception may have something to do with his earlier destruction of the temples of the Acropolis (8. 53. 2). There is a sense, however, in which Persians in particular cannot win: against the strong pattern of their destruction of Greek shrines (cf. 6. 25. 2, 32, 96, 101. 3), isolated instances of piety seem lost and inexplicable (6. 97. 2, 6. 118, 7. 197). While Greeks burn the temple of Cybebe by accident,[36] Persian sacrilege is presented as an inevitable function of their restless expansionism. Paradoxically then, the imagined intolerance of foreign peoples appears itself to become a cause of Greek contempt.

The same phenomenon can be seen in a weaker form with other peoples. A recurrent feature of Herodotus' account of the Scythians is their violent disapproval of others' customs (4. 76. 1, 77. 2, 80. 5). In addition to the case of Scyles, for example—where curiously it appears that the god responsible for the destruction of his palace appears to be of the same mind as the majority of the Scythians[37]—there is the story of Anacharsis who, having made a vow in Cyzicus that he would institute a festival to the Mother of the Gods if he returned home safely, returned, was reported to the king and promptly shot dead with an arrow (4. 76. 7). One class of people whom Herodotus has difficulties in understanding, or indeed in conceiving of as such, are monotheists. The adherents of Salmoxis recognized no other god (4. 94. 4):[38]

These Thracians, when there is thunder and lightning, shoot arrows up into sky and threaten the god (ἀπειλέουσι τῷ θεῷ), for they consider no other god to exist but their own[39] (οὐδένα ἄλλον θεὸν νομίζοντες εἶναι εἰ μὴ τὸν σφέτερον).

---

[36] Parker (1983: 168 n. 133).   [37] Cf. Lachenaud (1978: 200).

[38] Salmoxis has no Greek name but two Scythian names, prompting Hartog (1978: 38–9) to speak of his doubled 'alterité'. For the meaning of the alternative name 'Gebeleizis' and its associations with the sky, see Mora (1985: 171 and n. 19). For reconstructions of 'Geto-Dacian religion', see Treptow (1992), Hartog (1978), and Eliade (1972) (22 n. 1 for further bibliography); for Zalmoxis as bear, see Carpenter (1946: 112 ff.).

[39] See here Fahr (1969: 42 ff.).

Unless we suppose that they are shooting arrows against their own god[40]—in which case it is hard to see how their monotheism serves as a rationale for their behaviour—it appears that the Getae's reponse to storms is an unconscious acknowledgement that their rejection of foreign gods cannot, in fact, be justified.[41] A similar contradiction may be evident in Herodotus' understanding of another people. The Massagetai, he says, 'revere' only the sun (σέβονται), to whom they sacrifice horses—'the thinking behind this being that they give the swiftest of living things to the swiftest of the gods' (1. 216. 4). Unless the Massagetai, as Herodotus understood it, acknowledged the existence of gods but chose only to worship the sun, it seems that he has slipped unconsciously into ascribing a polytheistic rationale to a monotheistic people.

There were other grounds also for Greek condescension. There is no evidence that the Persians considered their kings to be gods, or that the *proskynesis* performed to the King— probably the blowing of a kiss while leaning forward—constituted a form of worship.[42] The Greeks, however, persisted in maintaining otherwise, as the story of two Spartans who volunteer to die in Persia in expiation of the wrath of Talthybius demonstrates (7. 136. 1):

And when they came to Susa into the King's presence and the guards ordered them to fall down and do obeisance, and went so far as to use force to compel them, they refused and said they would never do such a thing, even were their heads thrust down to the ground; for it was not their custom to perform *proskynesis* to a man, and they had not come to Persia for that purpose.

The Greeks, by contrast, know to maintain the proper boundaries between men and gods.

In another way also their knowledge sets them apart from other peoples. The Greeks derived the names of almost all of

[40] Daicoviciu (1944–5: 93).

[41] Hartog (1978: 39). The Getae believed that they were themselves immortal, that they 'made themselves immortal' (see Linforth (1918) for the term ἀθανατίζοντες), and that after death they went to Salmoxis, 4. 94. 1. It is their valour, 4. 93, that makes the Getae worthy of immortality—according to Coman (1981: 264 ff.).

[42] See e.g. Bickermann (1963), Hall (1989: 91; 1996: 121); see further Harrison (2000: 87–91).

their gods from Egypt (2. 50. 1). (How the Egyptian and Greek names came to be different is the subject of Appendix 2.) At the same time, however, Herodotus provides a lengthy list of exceptions: Poseidon, the Dioscuri, Hera, Hestia, Themis, the Charites, and the Nereids. With the exception of Posei-don—of whom the Greeks learnt from the Libyans—these other gods Herodotus believes to have been named by the Pelasgians, the pre-Greek inhabitants of Greece (2. 50. 2–3). Though Herodotus then may scorn the Greeks—in comparison with the Egyptians, at least—as late starters in the knowledge of the gods (2. 53. 1), by his own day the policy of giving refuge to gods who came their way has ensured that the Greeks have caught up with, and indeed overtaken, the Egyptians. Though Egypt may still demand respect as a museum of certain aspects of Greek heritage, in the case of other peoples it is hard not to see a patronizing glint behind the formula 'alone of the gods' (1. 216. 4, 2. 29. 7, 3. 8. 3, 5. 7).[43] Certain Libyans sacrifice only to the sun and moon (4. 188). The Ausaeans are not even aware of the universality of their gods. Ausaean girls fight with one another, 'saying that they perform these ancestral rites for their native god—whom we call Athena' (τῇ αὐθιγενέϊ θεῷ λέγουσαι τὰ πάτρια ἀποτελέειν, τὴν Ἀθηναίην καλέομεν, 4. 180. 2).[44] Misguid-edly they imagine that their divinity is unique to them, but Herodotus knows better.

One final question needs to be addressed—undoubtedly a central one. Herodotus' procedure in discussing foreign peo-ples—of focusing on differences in ritual practice rather than differences in belief—has been taken as evidence of the cen-trality of ritual to Greek religion in general.[45] John Gould indeed has gone further still and spoken of how Herodotus 'almost' identifies 'religion with ritual process'.[46] Even in what

[43] Linforth (1926: 3): 'an instinctive feeling that the wider and more generous polytheism of the Greeks is one of the features of their superior civilization.' See also Hemberg (1950: 76). Cf. Aesch. *Suppl.* 921–3: the Egyptian herald reveres the daimones of the Nile but not (by implication—and to Pelasgus' disapproval) the gods of the Greeks. Aeschylus' choice of the term 'daimon' to describe the Egyptian gods might imply their relegation to a second division of divinities.

[44] For twentieth-century parallels to this ritual around Marrakesh, see Camps (1985: 52–3).

[45] See above, n. 16.   [46] Gould (1994: 106).

is perhaps the most 'theological' section of his work, his investigation into the nature of Heracles, Herodotus' conclusion is phrased noticeably in terms of approval for correct ritual action, not correct belief: those men are correct who sacrifice to one Heracles as a god and propitiate another as a hero (2. 44. 5). This picture of the centrality of ritual must be significantly qualified, however. Even if Herodotus chooses when describing foreign peoples' customs only to do so in terms of the bare bones of what they do rather than what they say, certain assumptions underpin these accounts: that different peoples mean the same by sacrifice, oaths, or divination, for example, even if they perform them differently.[47] We are reminded of these underlying similarities on those (rare) occasions when Herodotus points out deviant assumptions, for example that the Persians unlike the Greeks do not consider (ἐνόμισαν) their gods to be anthropomorphic (1. 131. 1) or that the Getae consider (νομίζοντες) no god to exist but their own. Another underlying assumption of Herodotus' descriptions of foreign religion is that such religious practices are a subset of *nomoi* or customs.[48] There is, of course, no Greek word for, no tidy conception of, anything approximating to our 'religion'. When we say then, on the basis of Herodotus' descriptions of foreign peoples, that Herodotus (by implicit comparison with a modern 'Christian' definition of religion) identifies religion with ritual process, it is questionable whether we are comparing like with like.

The identification of Greek and foreign gods clearly matters. It matters enough indeed, as we have seen, for such equations to have been made in the face of what seem insuperable obstacles.[49] Of course, such identifications found no reflection in cult action. But to suppose on this basis that the 'principle of identification', in Linforth's phrase, was somehow secondary to

[47] Cf. Rudhardt (1981: 24).

[48] Evans (1965: 143), Mora (1985: 27), Rudhardt (1992b: 221 ff.); Rudhardt concludes with the question: 'n'y a-t-il donc pas de religion . . ., ou bien tout y est-il religieux?'

[49] Cf. Linforth (1926: 13): 'the power of attraction was greater than the power of repulsion'; however (p. 20), 'Intense nationalism forbids the recognition of universal gods. It is only in times of peace and relaxed emotions that the philosophic mind can perceive identities between the gods of different peoples.'

the 'principle of differentiation' merely takes for granted precisely the point that is at issue, the centrality of ritual. Clearly this discussion has ramifications also for the identification of gods within the Greek world: the identification—implicit in the name of the god—of two local cults of, say, Athena clearly means *something,* regardless of whether their devotees were distinct.[50]

Rather than asking then whether the principle of diffentiation or of identification is predominant, it is necessary to see both in combination, and to try to explain the dissonance between them. Quite simply, a completely liberal attitude to foreign religions is unsustainable. Differences in ritual, necessitating a continuing separation in cult practice, provide the necessary flexibility for the universalism of Greek religion (both within and beyond the Greek world) to be maintained.[51] Similar techniques, we should remember, are required even in religions which place a greater emphasis on their uniformity: 'the St. George we have is not the same saint as comes from Cappadocia. Ours is from right here.'[52]

[50] See esp. a marvellous passage of Sourvinou-Inwood (1997: 165–70).

[51] Cf. Rudhardt (1992*b*: 230–1).

[52] A modern Greek parallel cited by Versnel (1981: 17). Cf. the words of Thomas More (quoted by K. Thomas 1971: 29): '"Of all Our Ladies I love best Our Lady of Walsingham".'

Fate and Human Responsibility

'The concept of man as an independent moral agent', it has been written, is 'fundamental to Herodotus' view of historical causation.'[1] Other principles, however, other themes of the *Histories* appear to conflict with this. Man, as we have seen, is characterized repeatedly as blind and impotent. He is buffeted by chance reversals beyond control or foresight. He is also subject to fate. Herodotus' sense of fatalism cuts across all the forms of divine intervention discussed so far; it colours his entire understanding of causation.

The most prominent expression of man's responsibility is also the clearest statement of the predetermination of human life: the Pythia's reply to Croesus.[2] Croesus, after his defeat by Cyrus, had sent messengers to Delphi to ask the god if he was ashamed of having encouraged him to imagine that he would defeat Cyrus (1. 90. 4), and to ask if it was the custom of Greek gods to be ungrateful. The god, through the Pythia, replied that Croesus had no cause for complaint (1. 91. 4): the god had told him that a great empire would be destroyed; he ought to have asked whose empire was intended, his own or Cyrus'. By his initial interpretation, and then by his failure to check its

---

[1] Lloyd iii. 3; cf. A. B. Lloyd (1988*b*: 29), 'the concept of fate does not . . . in any way impair man's responsibility as a moral agent'; Lateiner (1984: 272), and (with a slight difference of emphasis) (1989: 207), all human actions are both free and determined; free will is stressed esp. also by Huber (1963: part II), and Perisinakis (1987: 17 ff.). Shimron, e.g. (1989: 28), and Maddalena (1950: esp. 65 ff.) both see free will and fate as irreconcilable (except, in Maddalena's view, through Herodotus' conviction in the mystery of human life). For a sensible, balanced discussion of fate, see Marinatos (1982). Lachenaud tabulates different forms of necessity (1978: 95–6).

[2] Whether or not Herodotus' account of Croesus is no more than a Delphic apologia, as Parke (1967*b*: 70), Défradas (1954: 208 ff.), La Bua (1976: 187), Elayi (1979*b*: 143 ff.) claim, is irrelevant here; but see now Flower's counter-arguments (1991: 70–3).

meaning by a second enquiry, he showed himself 'responsible' for his own fate (αἴτιον). When Croesus heard the Pythia's reply, he 'realized that the error was his own rather than the god's' (1. 91. 6). The Pythia's attribution of responsibility to Croesus is not a casual one. Her reply answers Croesus' earlier claim that 'the god of the Greeks' was responsible for his disaster in having encouraged him in his campaign (1. 87. 3). It also recalls his words to Adrastus after the death of Atys, reassuring him that he was not 'responsible for this evil' (τοῦδε τοῦ κακοῦ αἴτιος), but that one of the gods was responsible, who long before had 'shown him what was to be' (προεσήμαινε τὰ μέλλοντα ἔσεσθαι, 1. 45. 2).[3] The story of Croesus appears then almost to constitute an affirmation of human responsibility.

Other elements in the Pythia's message are hard to reconcile, however[4]—not least her first words (1. 91. 1): 'It is impossible even for a god to flee his allotted fate' (Τὴν πεπρωμένην μοῖραν ἀδύνατά ἐστι ἀποφυγεῖν καὶ θεῷ). Croesus paid the price for the fault of his ancestor in the fifth generation (ἁμαρτάδα ἐξέπλησε), in other words of Gyges. The oracle which confirmed Gyges in power in Lydia, recorded long before in Book 1 by Herodotus (1. 13. 2), had spoken of how tisis would descend on his fifth descendant—a prophecy that was predictably forgotten 'until it was fulfilled' (πρὶν δὴ ἐπετελέσθη).[5] If Croesus' end were already minutely pre-plotted, what difference would correct interpretation have made?

Another contradiction is arguably more blatant still. Loxias had been eager to delay the disaster of Sardis until the next generation. In the event he had been unable to bring the Fates

[3] Pippidi (1960: 83) sees fate as absolving the characters of responsibility here—and more justifiably perhaps at 6. 135 (for which see below, this chapter). The unity of the Croesus story, its 'literary architecture', is well brought out by Stahl (1975), Lombardo (1990: 193). See further, Ch. 2.

[4] Audiat (1940: 5) by contrast sees this passage as evidence of Herodotus' clarity of thought: 'on verra avec quelle tranchante netteté l'historien sait, quand il le faut, aligner des arguments.' Shimron expects an absurd degree of consistency here (1989: 49). Evans sees a contradiction also between the idea of nemesis, 1. 34. 1, and that of moira, 1. 91. 1: (1991: 31).

[5] As Fornara remarks (1990: 31), it was unnecessary for Herodotus to make this remark, 'to go out on a limb'; Fornara sees this remark as polemical rather than as a reflex narrative habit. Cf. 1. 19. 2: no account was paid (λόγος οὐδεὶς ἐγένετο) of the destruction of the temple of Athena, until Alyattes was struck down with disease.

(*Μοίρας*) round to this scheme (1. 91. 2). He did, however, succeed in delaying the capture of Sardis by three years: 'let Croesus know then that he was captured three years later than was allotted' (τοῦτο ἐπιστάσθω Κροῖσος ὡς ὕστερον τοῖσι ἔτεσι τούτοισι ἁλοὺς τῆς πεπρωμένης, 1. 91. 3). He also then came to Croesus' rescue when he was on the point of death by fire. The Pythia gives Croesus to imagine that Apollo had moved mountains to win him three years' reprieve. How is it that Apollo manages to mitigate and delay Croesus' fate even to this extent?

A legalistic justification—only partly satisfying—can be found for this second set of contradictions. Though the remark that Croesus' capture came three years later than was 'allotted' seems jarring, nothing in the final outcome of Croesus' career contradicts the terms of the oracle given to Gyges. Capture and the loss of his kingdom still constitute a substantial *tisis*. Delay by three years is also, in one sense, neither here nor there: the important dividing line is that between the fifth and sixth generations. This conclusion is supported by a number of other passages in the *Histories*. The voice that addressed Aristodicus of Cyme, after he had disturbed the nests under the eaves of the temple of Branchidae, told him that the order to expel the suppliant Pactyes had been made 'so that, committing an act of sacrilege', Aristodicus 'should be destroyed *more quickly*' (ἵνα γε ἀσεβήσαντες θᾶσσον ἀπόλησθε, 1. 159. 4), and never come again to enquire about the surrender of suppliants. (The Cymeans, not wishing to be destroyed by expelling Pactyes, pass him on instead to the safe-keeping of the Mytileneans—revealing, it seems, the god's ouburst as counter-productive.[6]) Similarly, a dream advised Sabacus to cut all the priests in Egypt in half, but he realized that the gods were showing him the dream 'as a pretext' (ὡς πρόφασιν, 2. 139. 2) so that he should commit an act of sacrilege and be punished for it. He did not do as the dream advised, however; but, remembering an oracle that prophesied that he would be king of Egypt for fifty years, voluntarily (ἑκὼν) left

---

[6] According to Maddalena (1950: 80) Aristodicus also manages to sidestep divine deceit; but 'it is not the god who comes off second best, but the Cymaeans', Brown (1978: 72). That Sabacus is the only man to avert 'divine causality' is a rare insight of Giraudeau (1984: 88).

Egypt as soon as his time expired. The basic skeleton of events
is preordained: he was bound to be king for fifty years (δέοι).
But against that backdrop, there is again some room for human
error: if he had followed the advice of his dream, his departure
from Egypt might have been involuntary—and less pleasant.

In another case, it appears at first that a man can defy fate.
Mycerinus learnt from the oracle of Buto that he would die in
the seventh year (2. 133. 1). Like Croesus, he reproached the
god: his father and uncle before him—men who had closed
temples, paid no heed to the gods, and destroyed numerous of
their subjects—had lived long lives, whereas 'he, having been
pious, was about to die quickly like this' (αὐτὸς δ' εὐσεβέων
μέλλοι ταχέως οὕτω τελευτήσειν, 2. 133. 2). The oracle replied
that it was precisely because of his piety that his life would be
short (2. 133. 3):

For he had not done what it was necessary for him to do (οὐ γὰρ
ποιῆσαί μιν τὸ χρεὸν ἦν ποιέειν). For it was fated (δεῖν) that Egypt should
be harshly treated for one hundred and fifty years: this was a lesson
that the two men who had been king before him had learnt, but not
him.

Not even a god can escape his 'allotted fate' (Τὴν πεπρωμένην
μοῖραν), the Pythia tells Croesus (1. 91. 1). Artabanus, his
dream assures him, will be punished for attempting to 'turn
aside what must be' (ἀποτρέπων τὸ χρεὸν γενέσθαι, 7. 17. 2)—he
is damned either way, of course. The same lesson is learnt by
Amasis (3. 43. 1),[7] given by the dying Cambyses (3. 65. 3),[8] and
again (with a slight difference of emphasis[9]) by an anonymous
Persian at the Theban banquet: whatever is bound to come
from the god, it is impossible for a man to turn aside (ὅ τι δεῖ
γενέσθαι ἐκ τοῦ θεοῦ, ἀμήχανον ἀποτρέψαι ἀνθρώπῳ, 9. 16. 4). And
yet Mycerinus appears to have done exactly that.

---

[7] ἔμαθε ὅτι ἐκκομίσαι τε ἀδύνατον εἴη ἀνθρώπῳ ἄνθρωπον ἐκ τοῦ μέλλοντος
γίνεσθαι πρήγματος.

[8] ἐν τῇ γὰρ ἀνθρωπηίῃ φύσι οὐκ ἐνῆν ἄρα τὸ μέλλον γίνεσθαι ἀποτρέπειν.

[9] Here 'fate' is seen as coming from the gods, whereas at 1. 91 fate (τὴν
μοῖραν) is inescapable even for the gods. Compare H. Il. 16. 431 ff., where
Hera dissuades Zeus from intervention. Cf. e.g. Soph. El. 696–7, Aesch. Sept.
719 (no man can flee kaka from gods), E. Rhes. 634–5 (impossible to do more
than pepromenon; not themis to do so). This contradiction is eliminated in
Virgil by the assimilation of fate with Jupiter: Heinze (1993: 236).

τὸ χρεὸν arguably here means less 'what shall happen' than 'what ought to happen', what men ought to do, not according to any moral rules but according to a preordained pattern of how events would turn out.[10] Fate, it appears, is a plot with a number of alternative endings, one that allows for (a limited number of) different contingencies, for human error and for human choice, as well as divine intervention.[11] Had Mycerinus learnt his lesson and behaved as he ought (in this instance by behaving impiously) he might have avoided his punishment altogether and lived a long life like his fathers; Egypt would have suffered its due dose of misfortune. By failing to do so, Mycerinus earned an early death, presented again as an immutable fact. Even so he manages to delay his death and prove the oracle wrong—if only by sophistry: he drank and partied night and day, so that, making his nights into days, he should live twelve years rather than six (2. 133. 4–5).[12]

   To observe the fundamental flexibility of Herodotus' conception of 'what must be' does not, however, help us with the basic contradiction at the heart of the Pythia's message. Is it possible that Croesus' responsibility was not for his fall in general but for the manner of it—that, if he had managed to read the oracles correctly, his come-uppance would have taken some other form? The Pythia is more specific, however. Croesus may have been saved from death by Apollo's favour, his date with destiny postponed, but in other ways the manner of his fall was predetermined in detail: Apollo delayed *the fall of Sardis* and *the capture of Croesus* by three years (1. 91. 3), and he did so before Croesus triggered his downfall by misinterpreting the oracles. The implication is that, had he ascertained that it was his own empire that was destined to be destroyed, it would have made little difference to the outcome.[13]

   Ultimately this is not a contradiction that can be pushed

---

[10] Cf. 5. 89. 3.

[11] The situation is similar to that described by Heinze (1993: 238) of the *Aeneid*: 'only the main outlines of what happens are regarded as laid down by *fatum*, and the rest is left in the balance for the time being, so that it is possible for Jupiter to be swayed by human prayers or divine requests.'

[12] Pherus' punishment is also for a limited period, 2. 111. 2.

[13] Flower (1991: 73) fails apparently fully to grasp the difficulties of this passage: 'this explanation . . . absolves Croesus of any blame, except for his failure to understand the full implications of the oracles he received.'

through to any point of resolution. We must accept that the inconsistency that is so striking to modern eyes simply never appeared as such to Herodotus,[14] that—in so far as we can talk at all of a single 'belief in fate' on Herodotus' part—this was not a worked-through thesis but an unrationalized collection of attitudes and responses. At 1. 91, as we have seen, *moira* is inescapable even for the gods whereas the anonymous Persian sees 'what must be' as deriving 'from the god'. This distinction is clearly not one that can be ascribed to national difference, nor is it the product of lengthy theological reflection. In the words of Geoffrey de Ste Croix, 'Just what a *peprōmenē moira* was, and by what machinery it worked, or for that matter how the Moirai operated and on what principles, and how they made their decisions prevail, I do not suppose Herodotus or any other pious Greek cared to think out to the very bottom.'[15]

A further contradiction is that, in two other instances, divine intervention appears after all to absolve an individual from responsibility.[16] The first story is that of the Parian priestess Timo, who advised the Athenian Miltiades as to how he might capture the island of Paros (6. 134 1). Acting on her advice, Miltiades entered the precinct of Demeter Thesmophoros (as he was forbidden to do), but then panicked, and in jumping back over the wall incurred the wound from which he died (6. 134. 2, 136. 2–3).[17] When Miltiades then fled the island, the Parians plotted their vengeance against Timo and sent to Delphi (6. 135):

[14] Cf. Legrand (1932: 133), Lateiner (1989: 143), seeing Herodotus' lack of solution as no failure on his part; contrast Shimron (1989): for whom there is no doubt that Herodotus 'thought about this difficulty' (p. 28), but 'his only way out of the dilemma was not to try to solve it' (p. 56).

[15] De Ste Croix (1977: 142).

[16] Adkins (1960: 123).

[17] He did not manage to perform whatever further act of sacrilege he was planning, 6. 134. 2. Cf. Ael. fr. 44 with the comments of Parker (1983: 179): 'In both cases the goddess prevents the impiety but punished the intent; the existence of the stories proves the intensity of the taboo.' For the idea of *to abaton*, see Parker (1983: 167 and n. 132). The word φανῆναι implies, according to Stein, ad loc., and Macan (iv. 1. 390) that a φάσμα 'in the shape of Timo had misled Miltiades'; this would absolve her more clearly of responsibility. For variant traditions of Miltiades' expedition to Paros, and of Miltiades' wound, see Kinzl (1976).

They sent to enquire whether they should put to death the priestess of the goddesses, for having made known to the enemy the means of capturing her country, and for having revealed to Miltiades sacred things not to be revealed to the male sex (τὰ ἐς ἔρσενα γόνον ἄρρητα ἱρὰ ἐκφήνασαν Μιλτιάδῃ). But the Pythia did not allow them, saying that Timo was not responsible for this, but that it was fated that Miltiades should not end well, and that she had appeared to him as a guide to misfortunes (ἡ δὲ Πυθίη οὐκ ἔα, φᾶσα οὐ Τιμοῦν εἶναι τὴν αἰτίην τούτων, ἀλλὰ δεῖν γὰρ Μιλτιάδεα τελευτᾶν μὴ εὖ, φανῆναί οἱ τῶν κακῶν κατηγεμόνα).

The parallel between Timo and Croesus is perhaps not perfect. Timo may have given the bad advice, but it was Miltiades who *acted* on that advice. Timo's position is perhaps analogous to the Pythia rather than to Croesus himself: Miltiades ought to have checked her advice, or (like Sabacus or Aristodicus) simply should not have listened to any advice to commit sacrilege.[18]

In a second case, however, the story of Euenius, 'the negligent nightwatchman' (9. 93–4),[19] the contradiction with the story of Croesus is less equivocal. The Apollonians blind Euenius in punishment for his falling asleep while watching their sacred flocks, so allowing wolves to eat about sixty of them. A blight then strikes their land and cattle. The oracles of Delphi and Dodona tell them that the reason for this is that they have punished Euenius for something for which not he but the gods were responsible, for it was they, the gods, who had set the wolves upon the sheep; divine retribution will continue, the Apollonians are told, until they have paid Euenius compensation; the gods will in addition give Euenius and his descendants a gift themselves, one which would make many men call him blessed—as it transpired, the gift of prophecy. Euenius himself chooses what form the compensation from the Apollonians should take, but without knowing of the oracles they have been given and in answer to a hypothetical question of what compensation he *would* choose. The well-worn term 'dual

---

[18] As it turned out, it was his sacrilege that led to his death: he incurs the injury from which he later dies—an injury to the thigh—shortly after his entry into the precinct, and as a result of his panic at committing this act of sacrilege. Cf. Cambyses' similar end, 3. 29, 64, with Gammie (1986: 191). Another tyrant incurs a thigh wound, Histiaeus, 6. 5. 2, but without such fateful consequences.

[19] In the phrase of A. Griffiths (1999).

determination' is clearly inadequate to describe the complex interrelation of human and divine causation in an episode such as this. In so far as the gods' responsibility absolves Euenius of fault it is also in plain contradiction of the story of Croesus (1. 91. 1).[20]

In all the passages reviewed so far, the course of fate is revealed explicitly and in retrospect through oracles—or, in the case of the various proverbial remarks on the impossibility of averting fate, through the generalizing prophetic remarks of Solonian wise men. More often, however, the pattern of fate is revealed through brief, suggestive glimpses, left implicit through the course of Herodotus' narrative. One such implicit pattern is the pattern of human error. The moral of the story of Glaucus, as we saw in Chapter 4, may be precisely that moralizing is useless, that any amount of persuasion, any number of cautionary tales will not prevent a man from contemplating or committing an act of sacrilege. Given the certainty of divine retribution, why, we have also to ask, would anyone in his right mind choose to draw it upon himself? The answer is that, in varying degrees, they are not in their right minds. Alexander 'knew certainly that he would not be punished' (ἐπιστάμενον πάντως ὅτι οὐ δώσει δίκας, 1. 3. 1). Cambyses must, in Herodotus' view, have been mad to mock the sacred rites and customs of the Egyptians (3. 38. 1). And at some point the same conclusion seems to have been drawn concerning Cleomenes.

Moreover, though it is in no way stated or suggested in the course of the story of Croesus that the misinterpretation or neglect of oracles or prophecies is fated, misinterpretation in the *Histories* as a whole is so common as itself to constitute a pattern;[21] correct interpretation (such as that of Themistocles) or the disarming of a conditional prophecy (Sabacus or Aris-

---

[20] The function of the story, of course, is to explain Euenius' gift of prophecy; it is perhaps important then that he should seem an innocent victim. Euenius' responsibility may just possibly have been mitigated by his crime having been one of *omission* rather than *commission*.

[21] Darbo-Peschanski (1987: 75); see further above, Ch. 5. Compare also the Greeks' disbelief at the idea that Helen was not in Troy, 2. 120. 5, or Thersander's remark, 9. 16. 4–5, that his knowledge is useless. This is clearly a common pattern in Greek literature generally, embodied in the story of Cassandra.

todicus) is correspondingly rare. Clearly this neglect or misinterpretation of prophecies serves other functions: tales of
neglect and punishment (while punishment may be presented
as fated) provide cautionary tales of the need to take proper
care of prophecies; actual neglect at the same time allows for
the *post-eventum* supply of appropriate prophecies. Such
misinterpretations also, however, serve to illustrate the inevitability of the action. Just as in film car-chases, when a
signpost shows the hazard (a low bridge, a dead end street)
that the hero is rushing blindly towards, so the oracle or
prophecy shows both the route on which the character is set
and, by implication, the turning which he might (if what?)
have taken to avoid it. In the case of Croesus, we have a whole
series of such missed turnings. The story of the dreams that
come to Xerxes and Artabanus is also relevant here: is this
episode intended to emphasize the failure of the Persians
(unlike Sabacus, like Croesus) to see through the gods' plan
to tempt them into invading Europe—again, according to
Themistocles at least, something impious in itself
(8. 109. 3)—or is it rather intended to emphasize the inevitability of their action? Even if theoretically Xerxes and
Artabanus might have resisted the temptations of their
dreams, on another level the dramatic irony of Herodotus'
narrative—seen most clearly in Xerxes' question to Artabanus
of how he would have acted had no dream appeared to him
(7. 47)—strongly suggests a sense of inevitability.

Herodotus' fatalism is revealed also in his frequent observation that x or y was 'bound to come to a bad end'. Like the
expression 'divine chance' (discussed in Chapter 3) with which
it frequently occurs, such remarks occur characteristically in
the context of an event, insignificant in itself, deemed to be
significant in the light of its consequences.[22] Cypselus, for

---

[22] Cf. also 1. 8. 2 (Candaules), 2. 133. 3 (Mycerinus), 2. 161. 3 (Apries),
4. 79. 1 (Scyles), 5. 33. 2 (Naxians), 6. 64 (Demaratus), 6. 135. 3 (Miltiades),
9. 109. 2 (Artaynte). The words are in Herodotus' own mouth, except 2. 133. 3
and 6. 135. 3, spoken by the oracles of Buto and of Delphi respectively. For
various interpretations, see Lang (1984a: ch. 4); Fornara (1990: 37), remarks
'an integral part of . . . Herodotus' metaphysical system'. Contrast Lateiner
(1989: 197); Darbo-Peschanski (1987: 62–3); Bowden (1992: p. xxv), proverbs
explain nothing, Derow (1994: 76), Herodotus *knew* that 'the explanation of
human affairs has to be done at the human level'.

example, survived an early death by the 'divine chance' of a timely smile: his first assassin was seized by pity, and so the baby Cypselus was passed from man to man along the line, while no one of the assassins had the courage to do the deed himself (5. 92. γ3–4). For it was 'necessary for evils to shoot up for Corinth from the offspring of Eetion' (ἔδει δὲ ἐκ τοῦ Ἠετίωνος γόνου κακὰ ἀναβλαστεῖν, 5. 92. δ1). Similarly, a chance remark of Ariston's (6. 63. 2), that it was impossible that he was the father of his wife's child, resulted ultimately in the deposition of Demaratus: 'it was necessary apparently that these things should come to light and put an end to the kingship of Demaratus' (ἔδει δέ, ὡς οἶκε, ἀνάπυστα γενόμενα ταῦτα καταπαῦσαι Δημάρητον τῆς βασιληίης, 6. 64). The deduction that a character or a city is bound to meet a bad end depends, of course, on hindsight. Once that end has been discovered, every twist in the career of the man or city in question then becomes illustrative of their impending fate; mere chance takes on a greater weight. The tendency to look back for the moment of ignition of any course of events is not always so clearly flagged. The dark tone of the remark with which Herodotus marks the first (fateful?) contact between Athens and Persia in the course of the Ionian Revolt—that the Athenians' sending of twenty ships was the 'beginning of evils' for both Greeks and barbarians (5. 97. 3)—arguably suggests a similar fatalism.

The miraculous fulfilment of an oracle or other form of divination often shows the pattern of fate falling into place. During the siege of Babylon, Zopyrus overheard a Babylonian's contemptuous remark that 'when mules give birth to foals, then you'll capture us' (3. 151. 2). When he later saw—nineteen months later—one of his mules actually giving birth to a foal, Zopyrus put two and two together, realized that the Babylonian's remark and the fact of the mule giving birth to a foal had been σὺν . . . θεῷ (3. 153. 2), and understood that Babylon, despite the length of the siege, was 'fated to be captured' (ὡς δέ οἱ ἐδόκεε μόρσιμον εἶναι ἤδη τῇ Βαβυλῶνι ἁλίσκεσθαι, 3. 154. 1). In this case, the delay in the fulfilment of the Babylonian's chance remark seems to add weight to the original prophecy. In other cases, fulfilment of an oracle or dream—or indeed of divine retribution—appears to derive significance from following immediately. Herodotus' passing remark that an event followed 'not long after' often again reflects the way in which the unfolding of his narrative is also the unfolding of a plan of fate—as on one occasion Herodotus makes explicit. After introducing Candaules, his excessive love for his wife, and his trusted lieutenant Gyges, Herodotus continues (1. 8. 2): 'not much time passing—for it was necessary for Candaules to suffer misfortune ($\chi\rho\hat{\eta}\nu$ $\gamma\grave{\alpha}\rho$ $K\alpha\nu$-$\delta\alpha\acute{\upsilon}\lambda\eta$ $\gamma\epsilon\nu\acute{\epsilon}\sigma\theta\alpha\iota$ $\kappa\alpha\kappa\hat{\omega}\varsigma$)—he said to Gyges the following words.'

It is not only through such reflex narrative habits that the *Histories* are suffused with fatalism. A similar tendency to look for a pattern beneath events is revealed most clearly in two stories of omens. Two misfortunes that occur to the Chians (6. 27)—the death of two large groups of schoolchildren in a plague and through the collapse of a schoolhouse—demonstrate for Herodotus how when 'great evils are about to occur to a city or a people' there tend to be signs in advance. The earthquake at Delos allows Herodotus the opportunity for a prophetic glimpse of the future (6. 98): the earthquake was a sign from the god to men 'of the evils that would be' ($\tau\hat{\omega}\nu$ $\mu\epsilon\lambda\lambda\acute{o}\nu\tau\omega\nu$ $\acute{\epsilon}\sigma\epsilon\sigma\theta\alpha\iota$ $\kappa\alpha\kappa\hat{\omega}\nu$). The observation that more misfortunes occurred to the Greeks in the next three generations, 'both from the Persians and from the chief Greeks waging war concerning the leadership', than in the twenty preceding generations leads to the judgement that 'there was nothing unreasonable in Delos being shaken when it had never been shaken before'. Just as this flash-forward provides a quasi-prophetic glimpse of future misfortunes of the time of Herodotus' writing,[23] the implied flashback at the end of the *Histories* to Protesilaus and the Trojan war, and to the beginning of the *Histories,* serves to remind the reader that the clash of Asia and Europe has happened before and that it will happen again.

As we saw in Chapter 2, the tendency to 'look to the end'—whether it be of the history of a city or of a man's life—and to emphasize the reversals in human fortune is a deep-rooted one. Such Solonian reversals may be presented as unpredictable (1. 32. 1), but in retrospect—or in moments of striking lucidity,

[23] For such flash-forwards, see esp. Fornara (1971*a*: esp. ch. 5); cf. also Carrière (1988: 246 ff.).

calm before the storm, such as the Theban banquet—chance
reversals are envisaged as forming part of a less random plan, as
'what is bound to come from the god' (9. 16. 4). Apries, the
most fortunate of any Egyptian king save Psammetichus,
thought that his power was so safely established that no god
could end his rule (2. 169. 3), but the Egyptians revolted, and
the man assigned to quash the rebellion, Amasis, instead
became its leader: Apries 'was bound to come to a bad end'
(οἱ ἔδεε κακῶς γενέσθαι, 2. 161. 3). Though it is only in a handful
of instances that Herodotus makes this explicit by the use of a
'proverbial expression', every instance of reversal of fortune,
every observation that a man was not 'fortunate in all respects',
or that a city was 'at its peak', may also—like the slow
unfolding of the fate revealed by oracles—constitute to him a
demonstration of the unfolding of at least a loosely conceived
pattern.

It scarcely needs to be said that Herodotus employs the
language of human choice and autonomy. In the words of
Lloyd, Herodotus 'shows a keen interest in human motivation
and attributes to his characters a wide range of human impulses
to action, e.g. greed, pity, social obligation, love of freedom,
lust for power or territorial aggrandisement, cowardice and
national pride . . .'.[24] Indeed human action and motivation often
appear garishly overdrawn: people do not simply do things in
the *Histories,* but they conceive a desire and then concoct a
cunning plan.[25] Herodotus tends also to pile on different
motives without establishing any clear priority.[26] So, for example, Croesus opted to invade Cappadocia because of his
desire for land, and also because of his wish to avenge Cyrus on
behalf of Astyages; at the same time he relied greatly on the
oracle he had been given by Delphi (1. 73. 1). Similarly
Aristagoras decided to revolt from Persia because of his fears
that he could not afford the cost of his expedition against
Naxos, that he would therefore not be able to fulfil his promises

[24] Lloyd iii. 3.
[25] See e.g. 1. 96. 2, 3. 120. 1, 5. 62. 2; for examples of secret communication, 1. 123. 4, 5. 35. 2, 7. 239. 2–3, with Lewis (1996: 145–6). For 'brave
gestures', see Flory (1978*b*), S. Said (1980: 92 ff.), Brown (1981), Dewald
(1985: 53 ff.).
[26] Pelling (1991: 139).

to Artaphernes, and that he would therefore be ousted from his rule of Miletus (5. 35. 1); at the same time, a message arrived from Histiaeus (tattooed on the head of Histiaeus' most trusted slave) counselling revolt: 'all these things coming together occurred at the same time to Aristagoras' (5. 36). With a few small changes—by removing, for example, the references to Croesus' reliance on oracles (with the substitution perhaps of an economic motive), or with the expunging of folktale elements such as Histiaeus' tattooed slave—it might be imagined that these ascriptions of motivation differ little from the equivalent passages in modern history-writing. This impression would be misleading, however. The landscape of causation in the *Histories* is very clearly a foreign country.

It is clear, first, that in many instances human agency and motivation are not incompatible with parallel divine causes. Herodotus, it is often said, provides a 'perfectly good set of human motives' in addition to divine causes;[27] to separate them out, however, is essentially an artificial exercise.[28] Men, as we saw in Chapter 4, may be the agents of divine retribution: Sabacus might have received his punishment for an act of sacrilege from gods or men (2. 139. 2). The miracle of the rumour arriving from Plataea to Mycale was effective in so far as it lifted the morale of the Greek fighters (9. 100. 2, 101. 3). As evidence of the proposition that Ariston's chance remark 'was bound to come to light and put an end to Demaratus' kingship', Herodotus adduces the hatred of Cleomenes for Demaratus—Cleomenes, of course, the engineer of Demaratus' deposition through his bribery of Delphi. Fate, in one instance, is fulfilled through an almost caricaturedly deliberate human effort: Zopyrus' reaction to the discovery that the fall of Babylon was fated was not to sit back and wait for the city to fall, but to concoct a cunning plan, based on his own self-mutilation, whereby to capture it. Though misinterpretation and human error may recur with a regularity that suggests the futility of any attempt to interpret correctly, this does not

---

[27] Pelling (1991: 139–40); cf. de Ste Croix (1977: 144); conversely Immerwahr argues (1966: 312) that the majority of human actions are paralleled by divine causation.

[28] As Cobet writes (1986: 9), 'we have to accept the *coexistence* in Herodotus of extra-human causes on different, but partly interconnected levels'.

prevent characters from preaching the need for proper deliberation: Themistocles indeed espouses the belief that divinity is
more likely to advance human plans if they are reasonable
(8. 60. γ).

It is possible also that 'fate'—what is bound to occur—can be
worked out through patterns of forced human action.[29] The
very piling on of causes so characteristic of Herodotus may
reflect a fatalistic conception of causation. The convergence of
a number of factors that persuades Aristagoras to revolt is, in
one sense, psychologically plausible: Aristagoras had dug
himself into a hole from which a rash and damaging revolt
seemed the only escape. But the coincidence of causes, in
particular the timely arrival of Histiaeus' messenger, may to
Herodotus and to his audience have seemed more than purely
accidental: as we have seen, fateful coincidences, chances with
disproportionate consequences, are often imagined to be
divine.

The choice faced by Aristagoras—to revolt or not to revolt—
is arguably one of a number of choices in the *Histories* that is,
for all intents and purposes, illusory. The events surrounding
the birth and exposure of Cyrus (1. 107–22) are marked by the
repeated unwillingness of each individual involved to execute
the decision to kill him: Cyrus is passed from one person to
another, just as later the baby Cypselus is passed from hand to
hand by his appointed assassins (5. 92. γ3). As Harpagus, the
man chosen by Astyages to do the deed, describes his dilemma
(1. 109. 4), 'it is necessary (δεῖ) for my safety that this boy
should die, but it is necessary (δεῖ) that one of Astyages' and not
my men should be his killer.' Harpagus then co-opts the
swineherd Mitradates to kill Cyrus. Mitradates' dilemma is
solved in turn by his wife's news, introduced almost casually,
that the baby she had been carrying had been still-born that
very day. Now he can satisfy Harpagus by returning the body
of a child, whilst giving his own child a royal burial. Effectively
there is no choice to be made.[30] The divine or fated nature of

---

[29] See Kroymann (1970: esp. 175), esp. on Gyges, for the argument that
moira is the unbreakable link between cause and effect. A similar line is
pursued by Hecabe at E. *Hec.* 864 ff..

[30] Cf. Maddalena (1950: 65): 'Tutti gli eventi sono concatenati in modo
strano, e pure fatalmente: ogni azione . . . lo avvicina e prepara.'

this chain of events is suggested by Herodotus a number of times: Mitradates' wife had given birth that day 'according to a daimon' (κατὰ δαίμονα, 1. 111. 1); Astyages tells Cyrus that he has survived by his own *moira* (1. 121); and Cyrus' natural parents subsequently put it about that Spako (or 'Bitch'), the wife of Mitradates, was indeed a dog rather than a woman, so that his survival 'should seem more divine' (ἵνα θειοτέρως δοκέῃ, 1. 122. 2)—the implication being that his survival had been, at least to an extent, the result of divine involvement. Another illusory choice is that offered to Gyges by Candaules' wife. Candaules' wife, because of the Lydian *nomos* by which even male nakedness is regarded with disapproval (1. 10. 3), is ashamed to have been seen naked by a man other than her husband (1. 10. 2). The choice she offers to Gyges is either to kill Candaules and marry her, or to be killed himself (1. 11. 2). As C. H. Sisson writes in his poem *The Queen of Lydia*,[31] 'The choice was easy: no one dies | Rather than sleep beside a girl.' 'He chose to survive', Herodotus writes simply (αἱρέεται αὐτὸς περιεῖναι, 1. 11. 4). 'You compel me', Gyges replies, 'to kill my master against my will' (οὐκ ἐθέλοντα). Herodotus again makes plain that the sequence of events by which Candaules fell was fated: his love was so excessive that he persuaded Gyges to view his wife; this was an illustration of how he was 'bound to suffer misfortune' (χρῆν γὰρ Κανδαύλῃ γενέσθαι κακῶς, 1. 8. 2).

There is some evidence, moreover, that certain forms of human motivation are divinely inspired. So, for example, the desire for imperial expansion ascribed to Croesus (1. 73. 1) is, in the different context of the Persian invasion, portrayed by Xerxes as being a *nomos* inspired by 'the god' (7. 8. a):[32]

Men of Persia, I shall not be the first to introduce this custom among you but adopt it, having received it. For as I discover from older men, we have never remained inactive since we wrested power from the Medes and Cyrus overthrew Astyages. But the god so leads us on that to us that busy ourselves a great deal things happen for the better (ἀλλὰ θεός τε οὕτω ἄγει καὶ αὐτοῖσι ἡμῖν πολλὰ ἐπέπουσι συμφέρεται ἐπὶ τὸ ἄμεινον).

---

[31] C. H. Sisson, *Collected Poems* (Manchester, 1984), 106–7. The same point is made e.g. by Immerwahr (1954: 36), Stahl (1975: 2).

[32] For this passage, see Ch. 2; cf. Dem. 4. 42 (god inspired restless activity in Philip).

The Persians' *nomos* of restless expansion is seen almost as an act of propitiation, rewarded by increasing good fortune. At the same time, the apparent conviction that this fortune will continue, like Cyrus' similar conviction (1. 205. 2), suggests to the reader (what of course s/he knows already) that Xerxes and the Persians will in fact suffer a reverse.

Other forms of motivation are likewise seen as external forces acting upon men.[33] Fear, as we have seen in Chapter 3, is sent down by the god just as thunder is. Love is never said explicitly to be of divine origin, but frequently, at least, has fateful consequences.[34] Most famously, Alexander's desire for a Greek wife (1. 3. 1) attracted retribution, in Herodotus' own view, in the form of the complete destruction of Troy (2. 120. 5).[35] The initial spark for the affair of Gyges and Candaules' wife, and for Candaules' fated fall (1. 8. 2), was Candaules' excessive passion for his wife: 'this Candaules', Herodotus begins his account, 'conceived a desire ($\dot{\eta}\rho\dot{\alpha}\sigma\theta\eta$) for his own wife, and being so in love considered his wife to be by far the most beautiful of all women' (1. 8. 1)—a conviction he felt obliged to share with his lieutenant Gyges. A similar pattern can be seen in the orgy of sex and slaughter into which Xerxes' court explodes at the end of the *Histories* (9. 108–113).[36] This affair is triggered by Xerxes' passion for his brother Masistes' wife (9. 108. 1). Artaynte's bad end and the end of her house 'was bound' to occur ($\ddot{\epsilon}\delta\epsilon\epsilon$, 9. 109. 2), as becomes evident from her request for the very cloak given to Xerxes by his wife Amestris.

In a number of ways also divinity sanctions or reinforces the *status quo* of Herodotus' world. The story of the Cnidian

---

[33] For such motivation as externalized, see Dover (1974: 208).

[34] According to Hall (1989: 208), in Herodotus 'the transgressive desire denoted by the term *eros* is attributed only to tyrants and kings'; see also Benardete (1969: 137–8 and n. 9). Love leading to disaster: E. *Hipp.*, esp. 41–2, 438–42, 538–44; cf. also e.g. Aesch. *Eum.* 365, E. *Rhes.* 859, *Med.* 627 ff., *IA* 808 ff. For love as divine: H. *Il.* 3. 380 ff., 14. 197 ff., *Od.* 4. 261 ff., Xen. *Symp.* 8. 37. For the analogy of love and madness or disease: Prodicus DK 84 B 7, E. *IA* 557, *Hipp.* 1268–81, Ar. *Thesm* 1116–8. For love used by analogy of money or power: 1. 96. 2, 3. 53. 4, 3. 123. 1, Thuc. 6. 24. 3, Plut. *Per.* 20. 4; cf. also the 'terrible desire' that seized Mardonius to sack Athens for a second time, 9. 3. 1, or Xerxes to see Pergamum, 7. 43. 1.

[35] Cf. 2. 129–32 (Mycerinus), 6. 62. 1 (Ariston), 5. 18–21 (Persian ambassadors), 3. 31–2 (Cambyses), 5. 92. η, 3. 50–53 (Periander).

[36] For Masistes, see Wolff (1964), Sancisi-Weerdenburg (1983).

ditch—the aborted attempt of the Cnidians to separate their city from the mainland of Asia (1. 174. 3–4)[37]—implies strongly the moral that man should let his environment be. The Cnidians' project is met with an unnatural number of injuries. Herodotus' telling of the story concludes with the oracular judgement that 'Zeus would have made [Cnidus] an island, had he wished to'. Xerxes' punishment of the Hellespont similarly, or rather the speech which accompanied it, is said by Herodotus to be 'impious' (ἀτάσθαλα, 7. 35. 2).[38] Conversely, the tendency of Persian kings to try patronizingly to appropriate nature, by for example gold-plating a plane tree as a reward for its beauty (7. 31), is presented as, at the very least, ridiculous.[39] On one occasion, Herodotus makes similar ideas explicit. The balance of power that he perceives between different species—the way, as he sees it, in which more savage animals reproduce in smaller numbers than the timid[40]—he ascribes to the 'divine foresight', to providence (3. 108. 2). Although Herodotus can scarcely be said to have a well-defined notion of a retributive world order,[41] there is clearly an affinity between this statement and his belief in the mutability of human fortune. There is also an affinity with his belief in divine retribution: as revealed by the story of Pheretime, eaten inside-out by worms as punishment for an excessive act of vengeance, in the interaction between men also the gods (or the divine) guarantee equilibrium.[42]

[37] See Ch. 3; see also Ch. 2 for 2. 14. 2, 7. 102. 1. The Egyptian king Pherus is struck blind after throwing his spear, Canute-like, into the sea, 2. 111. 2: for blindness as a characteristically Egyptian divine punishment, see de Meulenaere (1953: 255 ff.).

[38] Cf. 1. 189; for rivers as divine limits, see Asheri (1990: 135–6), Lateiner (1989: ch. 6; = 1985a).

[39] For Greek love of plane-trees and the suggestion that Xerxes was 'peforming a religious act', see Stubbings (1946). Aelian, VH 2. 14, mocks Xerxes more explicitly. The opening scene of Handel's Xerxes sees him seated at the foot of the plane tree, singing: 'Ombra mai fu | di vegetabile | cara ed amabile | soave più.' Cf. Darius' inscription, 4. 91. 2, to the river Tearus 'from the best and most beautiful man' to 'the best and most beautiful water'.

[40] But 'if lions bred in this way there would be no lions', Redfield (1985: 104): the theory 'answered his hunger for symmetry'.

[41] For the exaggerated ascription to Herodotus of ideas of cosmic equilibrium, see Ch. 4.

[42] See Falus (1977: 376), connecting this passage with 8. 13; Lateiner (1989: 195), connecting to ison with tisis; and for the gods as guarantors of nature

Herodotus may also consider that human *nomoi* are similarly sanctioned by the divine.[43] Human infringements of *nomoi* are often characterized as impious. So, for example, Cambyses' order to burn the body of Amasis was, Herodotus says, 'impious' (3. 16. 2–4) as it breached both the Egyptian and the Persian *nomos*. It has been suggested on the basis of this passage that Herodotus may have believed only universal *nomoi* to be divine: what distinguishes Cambyses' crimes was that they breached the customs of more than one people.[44] Certainly the fact that Cambyses' act breached both his own and the Egyptians' customs compounds his offence, but a similar respect for all customs can be seen elsewhere. Herodotus' conclusion to his description of Persian sacrifice seems to suggest a pious fear of the consequences of his questioning Persian customs, akin to his religious discretion at 2. 3. 2 (1. 140. 3).[45]

It is tempting, finally, to try to draw together the different strands of Herodotus' fatalism into a single synthesis: to seek to explain the contradiction at the heart of the story of Croesus in terms of the fated nature of misinterpretation, or to suggest that, if both the default settings of human behaviour (the fulfilment of *nomoi* or of patterns of vengeance, the respect of

Immerwahr (1966: 311). De Sanctis (1936: 5) suggests that divine *pronoia* never impinges on human affairs; cf. also the caution of G. E. R. Lloyd (1979: 32 n. 108), 'what must remain in some doubt is the extent to which Herodotus saw nature as a *universal* principle, and *all* natural phenomena as law-like.'

[43] For gods as sanctioning laws, see Dover (1974: 255 ff.), Davies (1988: 384). Evans asserts (1991: 24) that Herodotus 'has broken almost entirely with the ancient view that nomoi were ordained by Heaven'; see also Waters (1971: 99), remarking that 'there is no instance of νόμος as the manifestation of divine will'. Cf. Heraclitus DK 22 B 114 (all human *nomoi* are nourished by one divine one). For the meanings of *nomos* in the *Histories,* see esp. Humphreys (1987); also, for Book 1, Konstan (1983).

[44] Evans (1965: 147), adducing the Spartans' killing of Persian heralds, punished by Talthybius, an act described by Xerxes as in contravention of the 'customs of all men' (τὰ πάντων ἀνθρώπων νόμιμα), 7. 136. 2.

[45] καὶ ἀμφὶ μὲν τῷ νόμῳ τούτῳ ἐχέτω ὡς καὶ ἀρχὴν ἐνομίσθη, ἄνειμι δὲ ἐπὶ τὸν πρότερον λόγον. Herodotus' hunger for symmetry in his descriptions of foreign customs, as in his descriptions of geography, may also possibly reflect a belief that this order was to some extent planned. See esp. Redfield (1985: 103 ff.). For geographical symmetry, see Ch. 7.

nature etc.), and the exceptions to this rule (actions motivated by, for example, fear, love, or a desire for empire) are each equally the result of the divine, we can talk of a complete divine coverage of human affairs, to insinuate that all human actions are, more or less loosely, divinely motivated or sanctioned. Such temptations should be resisted. The vague sense of fate pervading Herodotus' narrative, suggested by proverbial remarks such as that a man 'was bound to come to a bad end' must be distinguished from the more 'theological' tenor of the Pythia's statements of 1. 91. Herodotus' proverbial remarks are no 'integral part' of a 'metaphysical system', in the words of Fornara,[46] nor do they reflect a conscious aversion to expressing a view 'about the properties and function of "fate"';[47] rather they constitute a reflex response to a repeated historical pattern. Even the apparently more 'theological' term *moira* can be used in a loose, 'proverbial' sense—as when Cyrus survives 'by his *moira*' (1. 121), or when Polycrates and Arcesilaus fulfil their respective *moirai* through their deaths (3. 142. 1, 4. 164. 4). Against the background of this confusion of causation,[48] the question (with which this chapter began) of whether free will or fate, human or divine causation, was predominant is simply unanswerable.

One final question that should be raised is that of Herodotus' moralism. Herodotus' emphasis on the possibility of divine retribution, his concentration on the bad ends of powerful men, have frequently been described as 'moralizing'—a charge which Kenneth Waters's 1971 monograph *Herodotos on Tyrants and Despots* is dedicated to refuting. However, the abiding fatalism of the *Histories* has consequences here also. Herodotus' stories of divine retribution certainly imply the moral that certain actions have certain consequences, a *descriptive* moral; they are not so clearly, however, moral in the sense of being *prescriptive*. The difference can be neatly summed up by looking at the words of the dream which appeared to Hipparchus on the eve of his death (5. 56):

---

[46] Fornara (1990: 37).

[47] Immerwahr (1954: 33).

[48] Gould (1989: 71), in the course of his excellent discussion of fate, cites Ieuan Lewis on the 'luxuriant multiplicity' of the perception of causes among the Azande.

'Endure, lion, suffering the unendurable with an enduring heart. No man who acts unjustly shall avoid vengeance' (οὐδεὶς ἀνθρώπων ἀδικῶν τίσιν οὐκ ἀποτίσει).

Now, when day dawned, Hipparchus openly entrusted these things to the dream-interpreters. But then he renounced the dream and went on to conduct the procession—in which he died.

Is the phrase that 'no man who acts unjustly shall avoid vengeance' a threat, a commandment, or is it simply a statement of fact? This distinction might seem pedantic: after all, even if such statements were indeed only descriptive, a belief in the inevitability of retribution for certain actions might still *in practice* have operated as a deterrent. However, that men cannot act to avert their fate (as Hipparchus cannot) is, as we have seen, not an incidental truth but a conscious and repeated message of the *Histories*.

Modern historians are very prone to rush to judgement on Herodotus' behalf—to suppose that his remark on the Athenian contribution to the Ionian revolt as the 'beginning of evils' (5. 97. 3) constitutes an indictment, that he disapproved of war or tyranny, or that he was preaching for or against the new expansionist empire of Pericles and the Athenians.[49] Such one-line judgements seem but a crude paraphrase of Herodotus' nuanced irony. They also miss the resigned detachment at the heart of his conception of the past.

[49] See most recently Arieti (1995: p. x), Moles (1996: 278).

Epilogue

'There can be little doubt', wrote Ivan Linforth in 1924, 'that Herodotus must plead guilty of a charge of skepticism in religion.'[1] More often, as we have seen, it has been from a charge of credulity that Herodotus has been defended. It has been the purpose of this study to show that both these positions—both Herodotus the pioneer, fully abreast of his age, and Herodotus the 'last great exponent of the archaic world-view' (to rob that accolade from Sophocles[2])—are equally caricatures.

Certain passages of the *Histories* have been described in the course of this book as 'evangelizing'—the story of Artayctes and Protesilaus, for example, with its implied moral that the gods may still intervene in human affairs. Other stories have more explicit morals: Pheretime's death, for instance, is an example of how excessive vengeances are punished by the gods. Such passages have been seen recently as evidence of a conscious conservatism on Herodotus' part, a polemical desire to reawaken an archaic religious sense in his audience.[3] In general, however, the most powerful impression that should be taken away from the study of Herodotus' beliefs is of their complexity and of the assurance with which he holds them. In the case of his belief in divination, for example, Herodotus can accept all or some of the following propositions—that seers are often motivated by greed, that even Delphi could be bribed, that some oracles, some prophets, are just not very good, that collections of prophecies are often tampered with, that ambassadors misrepresent oracles, that oracles are recycled, misapplied, and invented after the event, that dreams may be

---

[1] Linforth (1924: 286).
[2] Dodds (1951: 49).
[3] See esp. Fornara (1990).

deceptive and often only reflect the concerns of the day, that
oracles are characteristically ambiguous—and still protest his
belief in the truth of prophecies (8. 77) and his unwillingness to
listen to those who deny that truth.

The assurance, the rooted nature, of Herodotus' beliefs, has
important implications for the understanding of religious
change. These can only be hinted at here. To continue with
the example of divination, modern studies often appear to
envisage Greek belief as something fragile, even provisional.
'Private intrigues' like the Alcmeonid bribery of Delphi 'may
have helped', it has been suggested, 'to crack the facade of
infallibility.'[4] Both the experience of the Persian wars (in
particular, the alleged Medism of Delphi) and the disaster of
the Athenian expedition to Sicily have been credited as turning
points in the status, respectively, of oracles or of seers.[5] More
generally, a common view holds that democracy was 'not a
fertile soil for oracles and seers', that the everyday discussion of
political affairs in the assembly somehow dispelled the need to
consult any higher authority.[6] Reversals, however, such as the
revelation of Alcmeonid bribery or the Sicilian disaster can
easily be explained with the tools at Herodotus' disposal: the
corruption of a priestess does not necessarily stigmatize the
institution as a whole; seers are notoriously corrupt and self-
serving; as for the Medism of Delphi, as Herodotus' account
shows, the advice of the oracle to the Athenians to 'flee to the
ends of the earth' was comfortably accommodated with their
subsequent victory. As Douglas Johnson's recent treatment of
Nuer prophets reveals, within a culture in which the possibility
of divination is taken for granted apocalyptic reversals may
make no obvious dent on belief in divination. So, for example,
after what appears to have been a failed attempt at reconcili-
ation with the 'Turuk' (or British), the prophet Guek and

---

[4] Whittaker (1965: 29).

[5] Persian wars: H. A. Shapiro (1990: 345). Sicilian expedition: Bremmer
(1993: 157; 1994: 90), N. D. Smith (1989: 153); contrast Garland (1984: 82),
Mikalson (1991: 92).

[6] As e.g. Burkert (1985a: 116), Parker (1985: 322–3), Bremmer (1993: 157).
The jokes about prophecy in Aristophanes' *Knights*, 109 ff., 960 ff., 997 ff. (cf.
e.g. *Pax* 1063 ff., *Lys.* 768 ff., *Av.* 959 ff.), suggest that prophecies may have
played a large part of the ordinary Athenian's experience of the assembly
(Dover 1972: 76).

thirty other men were shot in a battle by the British. Even this humiliating failure, however, had no impact on DENG (Guek's divinity), nor did it devalue Guek's past career or make the Nuer more wary of prophecy.[7]

DENG did not fail as a divinity; rather it was Guek who failed as DENG's prophet, and the Lou are still trying to answer the question of why he failed. Some say that it was merely because he chose to listen to members of his age-set rather than his divinity. Others say that DENG abandoned Guek out of displeasure with his having sex with women who came to be cured of barrenness. Yet others claim that Pok had advised Guek to meet the troops by going around the eastern side of the Mound (the side of good things), but Guek went out by the western side (the side of bad things) instead. There are still others who insist—improbably—that Guek's attempted sacrifice before the battle was intended as a peace offering, an appeasement to his divinity that was misunderstood.

As for the alleged erosion of divination by democracy, the interpretation of oracles in no way precludes such rational deliberation but rather depends upon it. As is illustrated most graphically by the story of Themistocles and the wooden wall, the democratic assembly of Athens—the *sanctum sanctorum* of Greek secular rationality—was also a fitting venue for the textual analysis of the advice of Apollo. Themistocles, Herodotus continues to say, also made 'another judgement' that was beneficial to the Athenians, on the best use of the silver from Laureion—an archetypally everyday political question, we might say, but envisaged no differently by Herodotus from Themistocles' more famous insight. There is no necessary reason then why democratic decision-making and divination should have been incompatible.

It would be foolish, of course, to assume on the basis of Herodotus a completely static picture of Greek divination, or of Greek religion in general. The differences between a democratic city such as Athens and a city such as Sparta in which the control of oracles was the prerogative of the kings must surely have been reflected in differing attitudes to divination, and in differing practices: it is only reasonable to suppose then that the democratization of decision-making in Athens also had

[7] D. H. Johnson (1994: 199).

some impact. The public failure of the Athenian seers at the
time of the Sicilian expedition clearly, from Thucydides'
account, led to a good deal of introspection. The evidence
often adduced in support of a decline in the popularity of
divination after Sicily, the relative lack of references to prophets in the comedies of Aristophanes after that date, may—
though the evidence for a clear comparison is hardly available—reflect *a* change, that politicans and people were more
wary of the presentation of such prophecies in political contexts. Such change as occurred, however, was almost certainly
much more piecemeal than a general 'decline in divination'.

We must be wary also of mistaking variety for change.
Thucydides, at least, was one Greek whose views of prophecy
were very different from those of Herodotus,[8] but as his
profession of faith in prophecy at 8. 77 reveals, Herodotus
was well aware of the existence of such sceptical opinions. The
difference between the two historians need not then reflect any
shift of opinion in the course of the twenty years, say, between
the times at which they wrote, but rather the difference of
outlook of intellectual contemporaries.[9] In a number of other
ways also, Herodotus can be seen to accommodate, to anticip-
ate sceptical viewpoints. His apparent wariness concerning
myths or rituals of gods sleeping with mortal women parallels
the concerns dramatized in Euripides and Aristophanes.[10] In
his statement that all men know equally about the gods (2. 3. 2),
Herodotus, as Walter Burkert has observed, 'essentially agrees
with' (or at least, we may qualify, is some way towards) the
scepticism of Protagoras:[11] the uncertainty of any knowledge of
the divine is almost a commonplace in Greek literature. And
Herodotus' understanding of divine retribution—with the
delay in retribution for crimes, with his parallel conception
of the divine as unjust and capricious—provides answers in
advance for both the question of unjust suffering and of

[8] An extreme scepticism is posited by e.g. Powell (1979), Badian (1989:
98), Hornblower (1991); contrast Oost (1975), Marinatos (1981*a*: esp. ch. 4;
1981*b*), Jordan (1986), Dover (1988).
[9] For the vexed question of the date(s) of Herodotus' publication, see e.g.
Fornara (1971*b*; 1981), Cobet (1977), Sansone (1985), W. A. Johnson (1995),
but esp. now the excellent comments of Hornblower ii. 25–8.
[10] See Ch. 3.   [11] Burkert (1985*a*: 313).

unpunished crimes. The famous statement in a fragment of Euripides that the impious prosper, perjurers go unpunished, and the conclusion drawn that there are therefore no gods in heaven,[12] can (except perhaps for that final step) to a large extent be paralleled in earlier writers. This is not to deny any innovation to the religious sceptics of the late fifth century, only to assert again that their scepticism was rooted in traditional attitudes—that Herodotus and Protagoras, Herodotus and Thucydides were quite able to breathe the same air.

To return to the evidence of Herodotus' religious conservatism, another possible interpretation exists. Such cautionary tales form part of what we might describe as a self-generating religious culture, the on-going process of the reinforcement of shared values. Daughters, we may fancifully imagine, were told the story of Pheretime—the woman who ventured too far into a man's world—on their mothers' knees.[13] We are dealing, however, with more than just a set of isolated morals—that perjurers do not escape punishment, that oracles should not wilfully be neglected and so on—but rather a complete religious outlook: awareness of the gods, acquiescence to fortune, acknowledgement of human impotence and blindness. The message that the gods are still present in human affairs was not, in other words, unique to Herodotus but one which echoed through Greek life.

[12] E. fr. 286.
[13] For religious education, see Bremmer (1995: 30–5).

APPENDIX 1

Cooper on the 'intrusive oblique infinitive'

Cooper has argued that 'the intrusion of oblique infinitives into certain O. O. constructions where they do not regularly occur indicates an attempt to indicate reserve vis-à-vis the reported speaker, to put distance between himself and the report, to avoid responsibility for the matter or opinion therein represented'.[1] As this is a view that has achieved a surprising currency,[2] and which no one to my knowledge has troubled to refute, it might be worthwhile briefly to highlight some of the problems and contradictions in Cooper's thesis.

The impression given by Cooper, for example in the passage cited above, is that wherever there is an 'intrusive oblique infinitive', Herodotus intends to distance himself from his report. Cooper is setting out to disprove the position 'that Classical Greek possesses no means to suggest reserve or comment on the part of the reporter'. On the evidence of Cooper's attempts to pin down this phenomenon, it might at least be wise to conclude that Classical Greek possesses no *clear* means. Many of Cooper's interpretations are open to serious question. He presumes, for example, that Herodotus' reaction to certain material is critical merely on the basis of the nature of the material in question: 'In the first division . . . fall relations of dreams, myths and unlikely reports. This first category is *thus* made up of reports for which the reporter feels no hostility but only a certain bemused and incredulous detachment' (my italics).[3] In those cases where Cooper imagines that the O. O. infinitive has been 'postponed on religious grounds', his reconstruction of Herodotus' thought processes is frighteningly speculative.

Certainly unwilling to deny the subjective reality, or even the possible genuine religious significance of such an experience, Herodotus appropriately begins the account with finite verb forms. Still, being too prudent not to realize that what he is dealing with may after all have been illusions, he indicates this

[1] Cooper (1974: 24).
[2] See Gould (1994: 96), Darbo-Peschanski (1985: 108), and Lateiner (1989: 23).
[3] Cooper (1974: 29).

reserve by finally switching over to the infinitive. The motivation here is the *determination of the author to maintain a pious but enlightened attitude towards all religious matters.*[4]

It is not only the 'fantastic or incredible turn of a report', moreover, that may be responsible for the phenomenon, as Cooper himself admits. It may be 'merely a sense of offended delicacy—whether this be real or merely affected'; it might be employed merely on 'euphemistic grounds'.[5] One example given is the Samian explanation of how it was that the mixing-bowl sent by the Spartans to Croesus came into their possession (1. 70. 3):

> But the Samians themselves say that when those Lacedaimonians who were bringing the bowl came too late and discovered that Sardis and Croesus had been taken, they sold the bowl in Samos, and that the private citizens who bought it dedicated it in the Heraion (αὐτοὶ δὲ Σάμιοι λέγουσι ὡς ἐπείτε ὑστέρησαν οἱ ἄγοντες τῶν Λακεδαιμονίων τὸν κρητῆρα, ἐπυνθάνοντο δὲ Σάρδις τε καὶ Κροῖσον ἡλωκέναι, ἀπέδοντο τὸν κρητῆρα ἐν Σάμῳ, ἰδιώτας δὲ ἄνδρας πριαμένους ἀναθεῖναί μιν ἐς τὸ Ἥραιον)

Cooper accepts that Herodotus 'found the story credible', and so he concludes that the infinitive 'ἀναθεῖναι signals a sense of shame, real or affected, for the all too typical Spartan venality'.[6] Given the impossibility of his primary explanation of the intrusive infinitive, in terms of reserve or distance, Cooper seems to have jumped to the most compatible alternative.

More important perhaps for our purposes is that Cooper does (despite his general assertions on the reserve or distance implied by the intrusive infinitive) envisage alternative interpretations as possible: as well as a sense of offended delicacy, for example, there is the possibility of the 'formulaic intrusion of the O. O. infinitive accompanied by γάρ'—or by expressions similar in meaning to γάρ.[7] It must be conceded then as a possibility that in cases such as 1. 70. 3 (cited above) the intrusive oblique infinitive might be similarly free of any implications of distance, that it might serve the same explanatory

---

[4] Cooper (1974: 51–2), the italics are Cooper's own; see also his two examples of 'intrusion postponed on religious grounds' (p. 61), and his fanciful discussion of 1. 59. 1–2 (p. 72): 'the religious phenomenon itself is reported with strict objectivity. The human interpretations and political applications of the religious phenomenon then come in for more cavalier treatment—being related in terms of infinitives.'

[5] Id. (1974: 28 n. 8).

[6] Id. (1974: 55); for other examples, see pp. 55–6.

[7] Id. (1974: 56–9, 61–5); see also his idea of Herodotus' use of extended 'free narratival infinitive' as an 'extra-grammatical idea of citation' (pp. 65 ff.), the reserve implicit in which cannot, at least, be so pronounced.

function in the absence of γάρ or similar expressions as when accompanied by them.

Another obstacle to Cooper's argument is that, in the case of one of his examples of infinitival subordinate clauses in O. O., Herodotus explicitly approves of the version reported in O. O. (τῷ μάλιστα λεγομένῳ αὐτὸς πρόσκειμαι, 4. 11. 1).[8] Cooper's justification of this seems over-sophisticated. It must be remembered, he says, that this is an 'alternate version' (the 'dubiety' implied by which 'often brings the use of the intrusive infinitive with it'): 'in this case the intrusive infinitive δόξαι is used of that part of the account which might arouse objections in the hearers—to wit the passage and initial implementation of the mutual suicide motion in the Cimmerian nobles' council. The impression is rather that Herodotus feels he is strengthening his case for his favored version by understating it . . . [The] intrusive infinitive is only a kind of litotes which does not necessitate a reevaluation of the proper significance of the idiom.'

On other occasions Herodotus expresses his disapproval of a version which contains an 'intrusive infinitive' within O. O. (e.g. 7. 220. 1–2). Cooper cites Herodotus' disapproval as if it constituted evidence that the intrusive infinitive indicates reserve or distance.[9] One can as easily, however, use the passage to prove the opposite: if the technique of intrusive oblique infinitives were a sufficiently clear indication of distance, there would be no need for Herodotus to make this reserve explicit.

[8] Id. (1974: 42); Cooper's justification, p. 42 n. 20. Cf. also 6. 84. 1, merely quoted by Cooper, p. 43.

[9] Id. (1974: 64).

APPENDIX 2
The names of the gods[1]

Herodotus, as we have seen in Chapter 8, identifies foreign gods with those of the Greeks. In many cases he merely describes a foreign god by a Greek name; but in a significant number of cases, most frequently in his account of Egypt, he also gives both the Greek and foreign name alongside one another. At the same time, however—despite then his evident awareness that the names of foreign gods differed—he advances the thesis that the Greek names of the gods came from Egypt (2. 50):

Almost all the names of the gods came from Egypt to Greece (σχεδὸν δὲ καὶ πάντων τὰ οὐνόματα τῶν θεῶν ἐξ Αἰγύπτου ἐλήλυθε ἐς τὴν Ἑλλάδα). For that they came from the barbarians I found by investigation to be true, and I think that they arrived especially from Egypt. For except for Poseidon and the Dioscuri, as I explained before, and Hera and Hestia and Themis, and the Graces and the Nereids, the names of the other gods the Egyptians have always had in their land (τῶν ἄλλων θεῶν Αἰγυπτίοισι αἰεί κοτε τὰ οὐνόματά ἐστι ἐν τῇ χώρῃ). I say what the Egyptians themselves say. Those gods whose names (τὰ οὐνόματα) the Egyptians say they do not know, these seem to me to have been named (ὀνομασθῆναι) by the Pelasgians, except Poseidon, for this god they discovered from the Libyans (τοῦτον δὲ τὸν θεὸν παρὰ Λιβύων ἐπύθοντο). No other people except the Libyans have possessed Poseidon's name (οὔνομα ἔκτηνται) from the beginning, and they have always honoured this god.

How are we to square these two apparently contradictory positions?

One solution that has often been adopted is that Herodotus here does not mean by 'names of the gods' the names of the gods, but the practice, the habit, of giving names to those gods, the recognition of them as distinct.[2] By this argument, the statements that 'this god [the Greeks] discovered from the Libyans' and that they derived the name of Poseidon from the Libyans are equivalent.[3] When Herodotus says,

[1] An earlier version of this appendix, with a greater emphasis on linguistic questions than on the meaning of 'the names of the gods', forms a part of Harrison (1998a).

[2] See esp. Linforth (1926: 18–19), foreshadowed (1924: 275), restated (1940); Rudhardt (1992b: 227–8); also Wiedemann on 2. 50. 1 (p. 230), Legrand ii. 96 n. 3, Hemberg (1950: 76), J. G. Griffiths (1970: 30) (cf. pp. 518–9), Vandiver (1991: 84 n. 4).

[3] Cf. Herodotus' remark that the Egyptians deny knowledge of the names

however, that the Persians call the circle of the sky 'Zeus'—just as when
he uses a Greek name for a god whose native name has already been
given (e.g. 4. 67. 2, 127. 4)—he in fact means that they called it the
Persian *for* 'Zeus'.

This solution has the advantage of solving the immediate contradiction, but it gives rise to a number of even greater problems. The
main proponent of this solution, Ivan Linforth, claimed that there
was no confusion between this 'technical meaning' and the 'ordinary
sense of the word', whereby for instance the Greeks 'name' Horus
Apollo.[4] But this definition of name as 'practice of naming' in fact
makes a nonsense of a number of neighbouring passages.[5] In his
subsequent account of the Pelasgians' discovery of the names of the
gods, Herodotus says that they had 'not yet heard' the names (οὐ γὰρ
ἀκηκόεσάν κω, 2. 52. 1). Before they heard the names of the gods, the
Pelasgians simply called the gods '*theoi*', the reason for this being that
they had arranged (θέντες) affairs in the cosmos—an etymology
apparently put forward in all seriousness.[6] If we were to assume
that the Pelasgians merely called them the Pelasgian for *theoi*,
Herodotus' etymology of the term (unless he were to assume that
the Pelasgian term for *theoi* somehow had a parallel etymology?)
would be difficult to explain.[7] Linforth's solution is often paraphrased
by saying that οὔνομα means more than just name: the name and

of Poseidon and the Dioscuri and that those gods were not received by the
Egyptians among the other gods, 2. 43. 2. For the argument that recognition is
distinguished from naming by Herodotus, see Lattimore (1940: 364); *contra*
e.g. Linforth (1926: 19).

[4] Linforth (1926: 19).

[5] See esp. Lattimore (1940) for 2. 52 (pp. 359–60). See also Meyer (1892–9:
i. 194), Diels (1910: 16), Lloyd ii. 203–5; Gould (1994: 104) appears (without
explicitly addressing the question) to interpret οὔνομα as name. Even Linforth
admits that Herodotus' statement (on his construction) 'at first sight . . . seems
hopelessly loose thinking' (1926: 18).

[6] As recognized by Burkert (1990: 28–9), Lloyd ii. 245. On Herodotus'
etymology of *theoi*, see Diels (1910: 19), judging the etymology false, though
see now Petersmann (1990; 1992: esp. 139–41). This passage appears to show
that he considers the Pelasgians 'to have spoken a language nearly akin to the
Greek' (Rawlinson ii. 96); but see 1. 58–9, where Herodotus argues that the
Pelasgians spoke a barbarian language: see further Harrison (1998a). A
number of scholars read too much into Herodotus' words: Usener (1896:
279), How and Wells, ad loc., Immerwahr (1966: 312), Burkert (1985b: 130).
For other theories, see Myres (1907: 198), usefully summarized by Lloyd
ii. 243–5, Gomme (1913: 230), Fehling (1989: 89–90).

[7] For the possibility that Herodotus conceived of foreign languages merely
as collections of alternative names without any structure, proposed by Burkert
(1970: 453), see Harrison (1998a).

personality.[8] But, as Lattimore argued, it might mean something *more* than 'name', but it is hard to see how it can mean anything less: 'if Herodotus means to tell us that the Pelasgians derived from Egypt everything about the gods *except* their names, he is deliberately emphasizing the most misleading of possible terms.'[9]

Another neighbouring passage rendered mystifying by the definition of 'names' as the 'practice of naming' is Herodotus' discussion of the nature of Heracles (2. 43. 1–4). Herodotus is concerned to show that, far from it being the case that the Egyptians took the name of Heracles from the Greeks, the Greeks took 'the name Heracles' and gave it to the son of Amphitryon. Even if Herodotus had merely said 'the name' rather than 'the name Heracles', it is surely very unlikely that he could mean that the Greeks picked up from the Egyptians the 'practice of giving a name' to a mortal already recognized as an individual.[10] As proof of his argument of the Egyptian origin of the name, moreover, Herodotus adduces the Egyptian descent of the Greek Heracles' parents: the point would surely be blunted if 'name' were not intended literally. The obvious conclusion then is that Herodotus believes Heracles to be an Egyptian name.[11] The same conclusion is suggested by his subsequent travels: his discovery of a temple of Heracles in Tyre (2. 44. 1), or a temple of Heracles with the eponym 'the Thasian' (2. 44. 3), or of a temple of Heracles in Thasos set up by the island's Phoenician founders (2. 44. 4). A similar context is offered by Herodotus for the introduction of the name of Dionysus from Egypt to Greece (2. 49): it was Melampus who brought the

[8] See e.g. Stein and How and Wells, ad loc., Parke (1967a: 57), Ferguson (1981: 8), Mora (1987: 47). Lloyd also unexpectedly adopts this definition, ii. 232 ('names and concepts'), 245 ('names and personalities'), presumably on the grounds that (p. 204, following Lattimore 1939: 359) 'οὔνομα may mean "name + personality" but it must mean at least "name"'.' Cf. the various definitions of Sourdille: (1910: 3), 'sons différents'; (1910: 4), 'les différents personalités divines'; (1910: 18), paraphrasing 'il a nommé' as 'rapporte des particularités'; (1925: 294–5), the names of festivals e.g. 2. 48, 62. 1, 171. 1, the mere mentioning of sacred stories (cf. 1910: 17–8).

[9] Lattimore (1939: 359–61).

[10] Further support for the literal interpretation of 'the name' can be taken from Herodotus' account of the introduction to Egypt of the names of Dionysus and Pan, 2. 146. If more was known by the Greeks of the lives of Dionysus and Pan, Herodotus says, then it might be said (as in the case of Heracles) that these were in fact men who had taken the names of previously existing gods (ἔφη ἄν τις καὶ τούτους ἄλλους γενομένους ἄνδρας ἔχειν τὰ ἐκείνων οὐνόματα τῶν προγεγονότων θεῶν, 2. 146. 1). This would be very difficult to understand except with the ordinary sense of the word 'name'.

[11] As concluded e.g. by Rawlinson ii. 79, Lloyd ii. 201 ff., Finley (1978: 23), Weeks (1982: 66).

name and sacrifices of Dionysus to Boeotia, with the help of the
middleman Cadmus of Tyre. It may not be unrelated also that
Herodotus believed the Greek alphabet to be in origin Phoenician
(5. 58. 1–2).[12]

There are a number of other gods also for whom no Egyptian
names are given: Athena, Ares, Heracles, Hermes, Hephaestus, Leto,
Typhon, the Moon, and the Sun. In the case of sun and moon,
Herodotus' omission may be understandable—he might reasonably
be expected to have taken it as given that the Egyptians used Egyptian
words—but in other cases it is less clear. Hephaestus is referred to so
frequently in Book 2 that we might perhaps reasonably expect an
Egyptian name for him.[13] In the case of Leto and Typhon, moreover,
Herodotus has the perfect opportunity to introduce their Egyptian
names. In his telling of the story of how Leto had hidden Apollo from
Typhon, he uses these Greek names side by side with the Egyptian
names Isis and Osiris (2. 156. 4–5). He concludes with a list of
translations of god-names, equating 'Apollo' with 'Horus', 'Demeter'
with 'Isis', and 'Artemis' with 'Bubastis'. Leto and Typhon are given
no Egyptian name. It is, of course, possible that Herodotus knew or
guessed that Egyptian names existed for these gods, but simply did
not know what they were, but it is at least as possible that his omission
reflects a belief that these actually were the Egyptian names.[14] The
superficial resemblance between the names of Leto and the town
associated with her and the site of her oracle, Buto, may possibly have
deceived him.[15]

Even if we accept, however, that in the case of certain gods
Herodotus believed that the Greek names were used by the Egyptians, in other cases the contradiction remains unresolved. How is it
that he can believe both that the name 'Dionysus', for example,
derived from Egypt, and that 'Dionysus' is the Greek name for
Osiris (2. 144. 2)? Richmond Lattimore suggested that the solution
lay in the fact that gods can have more than one name. Herodotus
switches quite casually between the names 'Aphrodite' and 'Ourania'
(1. 131. 3), sometimes calling her 'Ourania' alone (3. 8), sometimes
'Aphrodite' (1. 199. 1–3, 4. 67. 2), and sometimes by both names

[12] Cf. Hecataeus *FGH* 1 F 21 (the Phoenician name for Danaë, Dana).

[13] Herodotus' apparent ignorance of Hephaestus' Egyptian name is doubly
surprising in the light of the fact that it was mentioned by Hecataeus: frag. 327
bis, Mette (1985: 33).

[14] He is able to admit the existence of a foreign name without giving it:
4. 180. 2.

[15] Gardiner (1944: 30). Compare Herodotus' apparent confusion of Bastit
(the Egyptian 'name' of Artemis) with the town Bubastis: see Sourdille (1910:
122).

(4. 59). In general, however, his manner of making equations—his remarks that the Egyptians 'call' Zeus 'Amon' (καλέουσι, 2. 42. 5; cf. 1. 131. 3, 199. 3; 2. 46. 4), that in 'the Greek language' Bubastis is 'Artemis' (κατὰ Ἑλλάδα γλῶσσάν, 2. 137. 5; cf. 2. 59. 2, 144. 2, 153, 156. 5; 4. 59. 2), or that the Greeks 'name' Horus 'Apollo' (ὀνομάζουσι, 2. 144. 2; cf. 4. 59. 2, 3. 8. 3)[16]—suggests a translation of equivalent names, not that the Egyptians or Scythians have, as it were, another name tucked away. In one instance, that of the Ausaean maidens who fight for their native god 'whom we call Athena' (τὴν Ἀθηναίην καλέομεν, 4. 180. 2), the possibility of both names being used alongside one another is specifically excluded. His translations of gods' names are performed in precisely the same way as his translations of more humdrum pieces of vocabulary, for example his observation that *piromis* is 'in the Greek language *kalos kagathos*' (2. 143. 1).[17] Are we to assume in these cases that the Egyptians in fact used the term *kalos kagathos* alongside *piromis*—or that they were all bilingual?

Two other similarly bold solutions must be aired and dismissed. Could it be that those gods for whom Herodotus offers Egyptian names—Apollo, Artemis, Demeter, Dionysus, Epaphus, Pan and Zeus—are simply the exceptions to a general rule that the Greek and Egyptian names are identical? Herodotus offers his own list of exceptions, however (2. 50. 2), a list so specific, including minor deities such as the Nereids alongside Hera, that it would be very curious if he had overlooked divinities such as Apollo, Artemis, and Dionysus, let alone Zeus. Another possibility is that Herodotus' contradiction can be explained by the existence of two sets of Egyptian names. If the names of the Egyptian gods, for example Horus, 'the lofty one', were in fact taboo names,[18] might Herodotus have thought that the Greeks' names were the real, unmentionable, Egyptian names? We should resist, however, any presumption that Herodotus knew much more than he wanted to disclose. Herodotus repeatedly mentions the name of Osiris despite a considerable display of reluctance to do precisely that: surely then he would at least have mentioned the existence of other names, had he known them.[19]

We should not struggle too officiously to maintain Herodotus'

---

[16] Cf. 2. 42. 2: Osiris 'whom they say to be Dionysus' (τὸν δὴ Διόνυσον εἶναι λέγουσι). This could, taken very literally, be seen as evidence that the Egyptians called Dionysus by both names; a more likely reconstruction is that Herodotus' Egyptians were reporting what they considered an established identification, that they were merely aware of the existence of the Greek name.

[17] For Herodotus' foreign vocabulary, see further Harrison (1998a).

[18] See e.g. Morenz (1973: 21 ff.).

[19] 2. 86. 2, 132. 2, 170. 1. For Herodotus' reticence, see Ch. 7.

consistency. There are, however, some ways of softening, or helping to understand, the contradiction: these lie in his understanding of the nature of language. Very simply, Herodotus knows that language changes. This is evident, for example, from a number of frequently repeated expressions in the course of the *Histories*, for example when he introduces a city or people as 'now called *x*' or 'formerly called *y*',[20] or when he gives details of how the names of different peoples have changed, almost always as a result of a (Greek) mythical eponymous ancestor.[21] Given Herodotus' acknowledgement of language change, perhaps then he thought (or might have thought, had someone confronted him with his contradiction) that the Egyptians had once used the Greek names, but that, having imparted these to the Greeks, and the names having fallen out of use in Egypt, they had begun to use different names.[22] There is a vast gulf in time, according to Herodotus, between the introduction to Greece of the names of the gods and his own day: knowledge of Dionysus came to Greece sixteen hundred years before his lifetime, knowledge of Pan around eight hundred years (2. 145. 4).

More interestingly, there are a number of passages in the *Histories* which are suggestive of the idea, famously proposed in Plato's *Cratylus,* of the natural appropriateness of names, a 'certain rightness of names (ὀρθότητά τινα τῶν ὀνομάτων), the same both for Greeks and barbarians'.[23] Similar ideas may, for example, lie behind his discussion of the origins of the names of the continents (4. 45. 2–5):

I cannot work out why it is, since the earth is all one, that there should be three names set upon it (ἐπ᾽ ὅτευ μιῇ ἐούσῃ γῇ οὐνόματα τριφάσια κεῖται), all having the eponyms of women; nor why for boundaries the Egyptian river Nile is given as one and the Colchian river Phasis as another—though there

[20] See 1. 57. 1 (Thessaliotis), 2. 99. 4 (Memphis), 2. 111. 3 ('Red soil'), 2. 113. 2 (Canobic mouth), 2. 156. 4 (floating island), 4. 8. 3 (Scythian territory), 4. 160. 1 (Barca), 7. 94 (Achaea), 7. 108. 3 (Briantike), 8. 43 (Doris), 8. 44. 2 (Hellas), 8. 46. 1 (Aegina). For examples in Herodotus' contemporaries, esp. Hecataeus and Pherecydes, see Fowler (1996: 73 n. 86).

[21] 1. 94. 7, 171. 5, 173. 3; 2. 42. 5; 7. 61. 2–3, 62. 1, 73, 74. 1, 75. 2, 91, 92, 94, 95. 1; 8. 44. 2. For this 'mythological colonisation' of foreign peoples, see Braun (1982a: 29–31) Hall (1989: 36), Fowler (1996: 73 and n. 82).

[22] As suggested by Lloyd, ii. 204–5.

[23] P. *Crat.* 383a–b. For the *Cratylus* and its philosophical background, see Classen (1976), Levin (1995), but esp. Baxter (1992). The idea of the appropriateness of names is ascribed in the dialogue itself to Prodicus (384b) and to Euthyphro (396d–e, 428c), but Baxter (1992: ch. 5) stresses the wide range of targets against whom Plato is arguing: Plato 'is battling against what he sees as a culture-wide mistaken belief in the power of names' (p. 107).

are those who speak for the Maeetian river Tanaïs and the Cimmerian ferries. Nor can I find out the names of those who established these boundaries or from where they got these eponyms. For instance, Libya is said by many Greeks to have that name from Libya, a woman native to that land, and Asia has its name by attribution to Prometheus' wife. Yet the Lydians claim a share in the name Asia too, in that they say Asia was so called from Asies, the son of Cotys, the son of Manes, from whom the tribe of Asiads in Sardis is called; and so, according to them, the name is not from Prometheus' wife at all. But about Europe, no one knows whether it is surrounded by water, nor is it known whence came its name or who it was that gave it its name, unless we say that the country gots its name from Tyrian Europe, being before then without a name like the other lands. But this woman appears to be from Asia and did not arrive in this land which is now called by the Greeks Europe, but only as far as from Phoenicia to Crete and from Crete to Lycia. That is enough said. We will use the established names for these things.

Clearly Herodotus has some problems with the conventional names, even though he decides ultimately to opt for them. At the same time, however, there is a lingering idea here that the distinctions of language *should* reflect real rather than merely arbitrary distinctions; he wants the names to make sense and is disappointed that they do not. The same idea that names can be appropriate to the object named can be seen perhaps more baldly behind an odd, apparently throw-away, remark that the names of the Persians fitted their bodies and magnificence (τὰ οὐνόματά σφι ἐόντα ὅμοια τοῖσι σώμασι καὶ τῇ μεγα-λοπρεπείῃ, 1. 139).[24]

There are a number of parallels between the question of the names of the continents and that of the names of the gods. As well as just trying to find names that are loosely appropriate to the objects named, Herodotus is also keen in this passage to ascertain the one original source of any name. The etymologies of the Greeks and the Lydians are alternatives, but there are no alternative names: Asia is called 'Asia' by both Lydians and Greeks. In the same way, just as Herodotus goes back and looks for the first inventor or the first instance of any number of phenomena,[25] so he also looks for the origins of the names of the gods, and seems to assume that that there is an authentic name which was held from the beginning.[26] Some peoples always possessed the names of certain gods. Herodotus distinguishes, for example, between those gods to whom the Persians

---

[24] Immerwahr asserts (1966: 186 n. 111) that Herodotus' statement 'should refer to the length and peculiar sound of the names, not to their meaning'.

[25] For 'firsts' in Herodotus, see Ch. 7.

[26] Though contrast the common idea of gods as 'many-named': e.g. Aesch. *PV* 212, Soph. *OC* 42–3 (cf. Aesch. *Eum.* 418), Soph. *Ant.* 1115, fr. 941 Radt, E. *Hipp.* 1–2, *Bacch.* 275–6.

sacrificed 'from the beginning',[27] and Aphrodite to whom they learnt
to sacrifice (1. 131. 3). The names of the majority of the gods, he says,
had always been in Egypt (2. 50. 2), and the Libyans are the only
people to have possessed the name of Poseidon 'from the beginning'
(2. 50. 3). In the case of those gods who have no obvious origin,
Herodotus attempts to find one almost by a process of elimination:
those gods of whose names the Egyptians deny knowledge Herodotus
reckons (with the exception of Poseidon) 'to have been named',
presumably named for the first time, by the Pelasgians. Another
parallel between the names of the continents and the names of the
gods (in particular with his discussion of the Pelasgians' discovery of
the names of the gods) is that just as the Pelasgian gods were once
anonymous, so were the continents until the lifetimes of the women
after whom they are named.[28] Finally, Herodotus' resolution that he
should give the benefit of the doubt to the current names of the
continents is reminiscent of a common attitude to the names of the
gods: 'Zeus', say the Chorus in Aeschylus' *Agamemnon* (160–5),
'whoever Zeus may be, if this name is pleasing to him, by this
name I address him. I can compare with him, measuring all things
against him, none but Zeus.'[29] The implication of such passages is not
that names are merely conventional, but rather that, should the right
name be hit upon, a name indeed has a certain power.

  These parallels between Herodotus' discussion of the names of the
gods and of the continents suggest that he may, in his discussion of
the gods' names, have been thinking instinctively in terms of a single
set of authentic names. However, how might he have accounted for
the existence of other names in parallel to the authentic names? A very
similar objection was advanced against the idea of the natural
appropriateness of names, first by Hermogenes in the *Cratylus* and
later by Sextus Empiricus,[30] that different cities and different peoples
use different names for the same thing. Other arguments were

[27] As Rudhardt remarks, however (1992*b*: 225–6), it is relatively easy to
know the sun, moon, stars, etc. from the beginning.
[28] Peoples, by contrast, seem usually to have had a name before their
current name: see above, n. 21. Ion also was anonymous before his identity
was discovered: E. *Ion* 1372–3.
[29] For other instances of this uncertainty concerning the names of the gods,
see Pulleyn (1994: 17–25), concluding that names had no magical power. His
suggestion that philosophical influence may lie behind some such instances of
uncertainty (e.g. E. fr. 912. 2 Nauck, *Tro.* 884, *Bacch.* 275) is undermined by
Aesch. *Ag.* 160–5 (as Pulleyn acknowledges). Moreover, expressions of fear
concerning 'theological' speculation such as P. *Crat.* 400d–401a, 407d–e, *Phil.*
12c, cannot be dismissed as merely or exclusively philosophical in tone.
[30] P. *Crat.* 385d–e, Sext. Emp. *adv. math.* 1. 45; cf. *Pyrrh. Hyp.* 2. 214.

advanced by Democritus: the existence of homonyms and of synonyms and the fact that names may change.[31] The *Cratylus* itself provides a number of responses to these criticisms. One response is to hold that different names for the same thing can capture its essence equally well. As Socrates argues, 'if different lawgivers do not embody it [the name] in the same syllables, we must not forget this ideal name on that account; for different smiths do not embody the form in the same iron, though making the same instrument for the same purpose, but so long as they reproduce the same ideal, though it be in different iron, still the instrument is as it should be, whether it be made here or in foreign lands.'[32] As T. M. J. Baxter puts it, 'a Greek name and a barbarian name of completely different letters and syllables can be qualitatively equivalent by reproducing the same idea'.[33] Another possibility, however, is that some names might be artificial and conventional, and by extension that there are two levels of language: Hermogenes' name, for example, since he is not really 'born from Hermes' must either not be his name or be merely a conventional name.[34]

What evidence does Herodotus present on these questions? The first passage that may be relevant is the famous story of Psammetichus' language test in Book 2 (2. 2–3). Psammetichus wished to settle the question of who were the oldest people of mankind. And so he gave two new-born children to a shepherd, with instructions that

[31] Democritus DK 68 B 26. Diodorus Cronus took a more practical approach to disproving the 'natural appropriateness of names' by giving the names *men* and *de* to his sons, the name *allamēn* to a servant, and Theognis to his daughter: Giannantoni ii. F6–7.

[32] P. *Crat.* 389d–390a. Cf. Arist. *de interpr.* 1. 16a: names may not be the same among all peoples, but the 'impressions of the soul' are the same for all men, as are the *pragmata* that the impressions represent. For the gradual Greek distinction of name and thing, see further Burkert (1985*b*), Salvadore (1987). Cf. also the charming argument of Epicurus, *Letter to Herodotus* 75–6, tr. Chilton (1962: 161), maintaining the idea of the naturalness of language in such a way as to account for linguistic differences: 'And so names were not originally brought into being by arbitrary determination, but men's own natures in their different races, feeling their particular emotions and receiving their particular impressions, emitted in their particular fashion the air forced out by each of these emotions and impressions with the added differences caused by the places of the abode of the nations at the time. Then later by common agreement in their different races particular names were settled on so as to make their meanings less ambiguous to one another and more briefly expressed.' Diogenes of Oenoanda criticized the idea of the naturalness of names as absurd, 'in fact . . . more absurd than any absurdity as well as being quite impossible': see Chilton, p. 163.

[33] Baxter (1992: 44).   [34] Cf. Baxter (1992: 10).

no word should be spoken to them, but that they should be left alone in a room and fed by goats introduced from time to time into their room. After two years the shepherd was met one day by the two children crying out '*bekos*' as they held out their hands. When this occurred repeatedly, the shepherd reported this to the king, who in turn ascertained that '*bekos*' was the Phrygian name for bread. So the Egyptians concluded that the Phrygians were the oldest people in the world and also (without any proof to this effect) that they, the Egyptians, were the second oldest people.[35] What are the implications of this story? First, it presupposes that the first language will have been spoken by the first people: Herodotus does not entertain the possibility that there might have been an older people still who had no language.[36] More importantly, one language emerges, given the absence of other 'nurturing influences', as the default setting, the natural, authentic language of men. That such an idea had a wider currency is suggested also by its refutation in the *Dissoi Logoi*:[37] if a small (Greek) child were transported to Persia, we are told, he would speak Persian—and vice versa. The story is also reminiscent of an idea expressed in the *Cratylus,* referred to below, that certain names (whose etymologies are impossible to discover) are derived from barbarian languages older than Greek.

Another passage that sheds further light on Herodotus' idea of the relationship between different languages is that in which he translates the names of the Persian Kings (6. 98. 3):

These names mean in the Greek language: Darius worker (ἐρξίης), Xerxes warrior (ἀρήιος), and Artaxerxes great warrior (μέγας ἀρήιος). Thus rightly (ὀρθῶς) the Greeks would call them in their own language.[38]

[35] For the story of Psammetichus, see Kassel (1991: 66–7), but esp. now Vannicelli (1997). Similar experiments are ascribed also to Frederick II of Germany, James IV of Scotland, and the Moghul emperor Akbar: see esp. Sulek (1989). The experiment of James IV of Scotland (on the isle of Inchkeith in the Firth of Forth) ends, in the account of Robert Lindesay of Pitscottie's *The Histories and Chronicles of Scotland* (ed. Aeneas J. G. Mackay, Edinburgh, 1899) i. 237, in the Herodotean judgement: 'Sum sayis they spak goode hebrew bot as to my self I knew not bot be the authoris reherse.' For later parallels to the idea of 'natural language', e.g. that different languages retained elements of the original, perfect language created by Adam, see Baxter (1992: 65–72), E. Said (1978: 135–8).

[36] A possibility raised at least in theory by Euripides, *Suppl.* 201–4 (god first gave intelligence to men and then language, the messenger of *logoi*), or by references to non-verbal communication, e.g. E. *IA* 465–6, *Or.* 1245 (cf. Soph. *Ant.* 700), 4. 111 ff.

[37] *Dissoi Logoi* DK 90 B 6 (12).

[38] See Schmitt's suggestion (1977: 243–4) that Herodotus reveals know-

Herodotus presumes that the names of the Kings mean something, that they therefore have a Greek equivalent. A. B. Cook made the intriguing suggestion, however,[39] that Herodotus' translations of the Kings' names have been distorted in transmission, and should read instead: Darius ἀρήιος, Xerxes ἐρξίης, and Artaxerxes κάρτα ἐρξίης. This may be thought to be asking a lot of textual transmission: first that ἀρήιος and ἐρξίης are confused, and then that the situation is rationalized by Artaxerxes becoming κάρτα ἀρήιος; then, though this is less important, that κάρτα is replaced by the more common μέγας. There are other areas of doubt: the confusion may, of course, not be in the manuscript tradition, but be Herodotus' own or that of his source (though whether the ideas of language underlying this passage are those of Herodotus or of his source is, arguably, not very important). Against the first objections is the powerful argument of the uncanny phonetic resemblance between the names and their Greek 'translations'. Moreover, why, as Cook asked, 'should Herodotus have used the excessively rare word ἐρξίης, unless he wished to bring out what he took to be the obvious etymology of Xerxes?'

If Cook's theory is correct, Herodotus appears to envisage not only that these Persian names have a meaning which can be rendered in Greek, but that their meaning can only be discovered through their Greek etymologies. It is for this reason, because the Persian names mean something in Greek (rather than simply because of the appropriateness of their meanings), that Herodotus can say that the Greeks call the Kings 'rightly in their own language'.[40] Were these Persian names, however, exceptional in that their meaning could be

ledge of the real Iranian etymology of Darius' name at 3. 82. 5. For the real meaning of the Persian kings' names, see Hofmann-Kutschke (1907: esp. 174–6), Schmeja (1975), with an alternative explanation of the Herodotean etymology.

[39] A. B. Cook (1907), accepted now by Rosén. Contrast Benardete (1969: 162), arguing that Herodotus 'thus denies that their looks can tell one anything at all. Translation from Persian to Greek cannot be done by likeness of letters to letters, but it depends on the sameness of meanings.'

[40] The meanings of the Kings' names may, of course, alternatively or in addition be appropriate to the characters of the respective kings (cf. 1. 139). Cf. 4. 59. 2 where the Scythians are said to have named Zeus 'Papaios' most correctly or most appropriately (ὀρθότατα). One possible explanation is that Herodotus knew that Papaios meant 'father' in Scythian and Api 'mother': see above, Ch. 8; however, we might ask why it is that Herodotus does not mention the meaning of 'Papaios' if he knew of it. The appropriateness of Papaios' name could consist simply in a similarity of ritual between Zeus and Papaios (in other words, he is saying that the identification of the two gods is a good one).

understood through Greek, or can we make any judgement about a
general relationship between Greek and Persian, for example that
Persian is a distorted, corrupt version of Greek?

The possibility that only a few Persian names might have been
imagined to have had Greek derivations is arguably supported by the
barbarian derivations of the *Cratylus*: only a handful of Greek words
are imagined to be in origin barbarian words on the grounds that they
do not allow of a Greek etymology. The words are notably Greek-
sounding: πῦρ, ὕδωρ, κύων (*Crat.* 410a), σοφία (412b), κακόν (416a), or
ἀλγηδών (419c). However, that Herodotus envisaged a broader relationship between Greek and Persian is suggested by the fact that the
assimilation of Persian names to Greek words was a very much more
widespread practice amongst the Greeks.[41] Some of these are what one
might term weak cases of assimilation, the mere moulding of Persian
names into recognizable and convenient forms, for example the name
Androbazus, influenced by the Greek *andro-*, Artabes, influenced by
ἀρτάβη, the Persian measure, or Artibios, influenced by the Greek
word βίος. Others, however, one might describe as examples of
'ideologically charged' assimilation: Habrokomes, influenced by the
Greek *habro-*, soft,[42] Harmamithres influenced by the Greek ἅρμα for
chariot,[43] Harpagus, the name of the Median general who ravaged the
coast of Asia Minor for Cyrus, influenced by the Greek ἁρπαγή,
plunder, and Cyrus himself, influenced by τό κῦρος, supreme authority.[44] Great play is made in Herodotus' account of the name of Cyrus,
of whether, for example, the baby Cyrus was indeed Cyrus:[45] 'the baby
named Cyrus', Herodotus says on two occasions, before correcting
himself, and saying that he had another name and not Cyrus (1. 113. 3;
cf. 1. 114. 4). His name is subsequently discovered at the same time as
his kingship is revealed through his free manner of speech: his name
has encoded within it his royal authority. Most ideologically charged
of all, however, is the name of the Persians themselves, meaning in
Greek 'destroyers', something picked up on in Aeschylus' *Persians* as
well as in two of the most famous oracles of the time of the Persian
wars (7. 220. 4, 8. 77. 1, Aesch. *Pers.* 65).[46]

[41] In general, see Immerwahr (1966) s.v. etymologies, Schmitt (1967;
1976), Armayor (1978d), Mayrhofer (1979) index sect. 3. 3 (iii. 23–4).

[42] For *habro-* compound names, see Schmitt (1975), Hall (1993: esp. 122–3).

[43] The transition from *Arbamithra may, Schmitt (1976: 31), have been
'facilitated in that the original *arba- has been brought up to the indigenous
names containing the name of the lunar god *Arma* in Asia Minor'.

[44] The pun is made explicit by Numenios of Tarsus, *Anth. Pal.* 2, 28.

[45] Cf. Immerwahr (1966: 163 n. 38).

[46] Cf. Immerwahr (1966: 44 n. 85), Moreau (1992–3: 39), esp. Couch (1931:
270–3).

Such word-plays appear too frequently to be merely the self-conscious product of literary artists, but are rather the reflection of a more deep-rooted idea of language.[47] Greek names too were significant in their meanings. 'Who would have thought', Sophocles' Ajax cries (430–3; cf. 914), 'that my name would come to harmonise with my sorrows' [the cry *aiai*]?[48] It was not only mythical characters whose names were so significant, moreover. The story of Hegesistratus, whose name was taken as an omen of the success of the Mycale expedition (9. 91), shows that even in relatively everyday contexts a name might be thought to indicate its bearer's destiny.[49] Greek names, in general, are unusually meaningful, and stories in the *Histories* of how an individual came by his name (5. 92. ε1, 6. 63. 3) suggest that the Greeks were conscious of this, even perhaps that children were named with a view to the fulfilment of their ominous names.[50]

When the Greeks saw meaning in Persian names then, they were doing no more than they did in relation to their own names—except for the presumption perhaps that the meaning of Persian names was not similarly evident to Persians.[51] Clearly not all Persian names were susceptible to Greek etymologizing. However, a sufficient number of Persian names are believed to reveal their meaning in Greek (and *only* in Greek) to suggest some belief that, presumably in the distant past, there was a link between the Greek and Persian languages.

[47] See the comments of Fowler (1996: 72 n. 77) on the distinction between popular and 'scientific' etymology. For the differences between ancient and modern etymology, see Baxter (1992: 57–65).

[48] Other more or less likely word-plays or 'speaking names' in the *Histories,* including both Greek names and Hellenized foreign names: Atys and Adrastus (Immerwahr 1966: 158 n. 25, Hellmann 1934: 62); Tellus (Immerwahr 1966: 156–7 n. 21); Deiphon (Immerwahr 1966: 301); Prexaspes (Powell 1937: 104, Immerwahr 1966: 163 n. 38); Proteus (Powell 1937: 104); Leonidas (Immerwahr 1966: 260–1 n. 69); the seers Teisamenus, Hegesistratus, and Hippomachus (Immerwahr 1966: 294–5 and n. 164); Callimachus (Immerwahr 1966: 250 n. 37; cf. Myres 1953: 208); Peisistratus (Immerwahr 1966: 196); Astyages (Immerwahr 1966: 162 n. 37); Deioces (Flory 1987: 124); Telesarchus (Flory 1987: 145); Phye (Flory 1987: 128). For etymologies in Hellanicus and other authors, esp. fragmentary historians, see Fowler (1996: 73 nn. 78–9), noting an 'obvious concentration of this activity in the later part of the fifth century'. For other genres, see further Harrison (1998*a*).

[49] Cf. Plut. *Nic.* 1. 2.

[50] For wish-fulfilment in naming in antiquity, see Erskine (1995: 371); see also Immerwahr (1966: 295 n. 164), Hornblower (1992*a*: 189 and n. 72), for the suggestion that seers or generals were chosen for their names.

[51] Cf. Herodotus' observation that the Persians had not noticed that all their names ended in the same letter, 1. 139.

This is not to say that Herodotus could not tell the difference between Greek and foreign names in his own day. Indeed he comments that the name of the northern river 'Eridanus' is transparently Greek, and so cannot be a barbarian name but must have been invented by some poet (3. 115. 2). However, as the *Cratylus* demonstrates repeatedly, names were believed to undergo significant distortion over time: it is only by a certain rearrangement, just as with Herodotus' etymology of the Persian Kings' names, that the meaning of a Greek name can be teased out. As we have seen, perfectly Greek-sounding words in the *Cratylus* are ascribed an unknown barbarian etymology. In order to maintain then, for example, that Herodotus really did believe that the Greek gods' names came from Egypt, it is not necessary to believe him totally lacking in any sense of the difference between Greek and Egyptian. As we have seen, he knew that the Egyptians had different names both for the gods and for other things. The names of the gods that came from Egypt might, in Herodotus' view, have arrived in a rather different form from that in which he knew them in his own day.[52]

[52] Some clue to the degree of corruption of these names can perhaps be gleaned from Hecataeus' statement, *FGH* 1 F 21, that the Phoenicians pronounced Danaë as Dana.

Bibliography

Abbreviations of journals are as in *L'Année Philologique*.

ABRAMENKO, A. (1995), 'Polykrates' Aussenpolitik und Ende. Eine Revision', *Klio* 77, 35–54.

ADKINS, A. (1960), *Merit and Responsibility* (Oxford).

AFRICA, T. (1982), 'Worms and the Death of Kings: a Cautionary Note on Disease and History', *ClAnt* 13, 1–17.

ALEXANDRESCU, P. (1980), 'La Nature de Zalmoxis selon Hérodote', *DHA* 6, 113–22.

ALONSO-NUÑEZ, J. M. (1988), 'Herodotus' Ideas about World Empires', *AncSoc* 19, 125–33.

ALVAR, J. (1995), 'Matériaux pour l'étude de la formule *sive deus, sive dea*', *Numen* 32, 236–73.

ALY, W. (1921), *Volksmärchen Sage und Novellen bei Herodot und seinen Zeitgenossen* (Göttingen).

AMANDRY, P. (1950), *La Mantique apollinienne à Delphes. Essai sur le fonctionnement de l'Oracle* (Paris).

ARIETI, J. A. (1995), *Discourses on the First Book of Herodotus* (Lanham, Md).

ARMAYOR, O. K. (1978a), 'Did Herodotus ever go to the Black Sea?', *HSPh* 82, 45–62.

——(1978b), 'Herodotus' Catalogues of the Persian Empire in the Light of the Monuments and the Greek Literary Tradition', *TAPhA* 108, 1–9.

——(1978c), 'Did Herodotus Ever Go to Egypt?', *JARCE* 15, 59–73.

——(1978d), 'Herodotus' Persian Vocabulary', *AncW* 1, 147–56.

——(1980), 'Sesostris and Herodotus' Autopsy of Thrace, Colchis, Inland Asia Minor, and the Levant', *HSPh* 84, 51–74.

——(1985), *Herodotus' Autopsy of the Fayoum: Lake Moeris and the Labyrinth of Egypt* (Amsterdam).

ASHERI, D. (1990), 'Herodotus on Thrace and Thracian Society', in W. Burkert *et al.*, *Hérodote et les peuples non-grecs*, Fondation Hardt Entretiens 35 (Geneva), 131–69.

——(1993), 'Erodoto e Bacide. Considerazioni sulla fede di Erodoto negli oracoli (Hdt. VIII 77)', in M. Sordi (ed.), *La profezia nel mondo antico*, *CISA* 19, 63–76.

ASHERI, D. (1998), 'Platea vendetta delle Termopili: alle origini di un motivo teologico erodoteo', in M. Sordi (ed.), *Responsibilità perdono e vendetta nel mondo antico, CISA* 24, 65–86.

AUBRIOT, D. (1991), 'Serment et conceptions religieuses', *Kernos* 4, 91–103.

AUDIAT, J. (1940), 'Apologie pour Hérodote (1. 32)', *REA* 42, 3–8.

AUSTIN, M. M. (1970), *Greece and Egypt in the Archaic Age, PCPhS* Suppl. 2.

——(1990), 'Greek tyrants and the Persians, 546–479 BC', *CQ* 40, 289–306.

AVERY, H. C. (1972*a*), 'Herodotus 6. 112. 2', *TAPhA* 103, 15–22.

——(1972*b*), 'Herodotus' Picture of Cyrus', *AJPh* 93, 529–46.

AYO, N. (1984), 'Prolog and Epilog: Mythical History in Herodotus', *Ramus* 13, 31–47.

BADIAN, E. (1989), 'Plataea between Athens and Sparta', in H. Beister and J. Buckler (eds.), *Boiotika* (Munich), 95–111.

BALCER, J. M. (1987), *Herodotus and Bisitun* (Stuttgart).

BARNES, J. (1982), *The Presocratic Philosophers* (London).

BARTH, H. (1968), 'Zur Bewertung und Auswahl des Stoffes durch Herodot (Die Begriffe θῶμα, θωμάζω, θωμάσιος und θωμαστός)', *Klio* 50, 93–110.

BAXTER, T. M. J. (1992), *The* Cratylus. *Plato's Critique of Naming, Philosophia Antiqua* vol. 58 (Leiden).

BEARD, M., and M. CRAWFORD (1985), *Rome in the Late Republic* (London).

BEARD, M., J. NORTH, and S. PRICE (1998), *Religions of Rome, vol. i. A History* (Cambridge).

BELOCH, J. (1890), 'Wann lebten Alkaeos und Sappho?', *RhM* 45, 465–73.

——(1924), *Griechische Geschichte* (Berlin).

BENARDETE, S. (1969), *Herodotean Inquiries* (The Hague).

BÉRARD, J. (1941), *La Colonisation grecque de l'Italie et de la Sicile dans l'antiquité* (Paris).

BERNAL, M. (1987), *Black Athena* (London).

BIANCHI, U. (1980), 'Iside dea misterica. Quando?', in G. Piccaluga (ed.), *Perennitas. Studi in onore di A. Brelich* (Rome), 9–36.

BICKERMANN, E. J. (1963), 'A propos d'un passage de Charès de Mytilène', *PP* 18, 241–55.

——and H. TADMOR (1978), 'Darius I, Pseudo-Smerdis and the Magi', *Athenaeum* 56, 239–61.

BISCHOFF, W. (1932), *Der Warner bei Herodot* (diss. Marburg), repr. in Marg, 302–19.

BJÖRK, G. (1946), '῍Οναρ ἰδεῖν. De la perception de rêve chez les anciens', *Eranos* 44, 306–14.

BLEEKER, C. J. (1965), 'Initiation in Ancient Egypt', in C. J. Bleeker (ed.), *Initiation, Numen* Suppl. 10, 49–58.

BOEDEKER, D. (1987), 'The two faces of Demaratus', *Arethusa* 20, 185–201.

—— (1988), 'Protesilaos and the End of Herodotus' *Histories'*, *ClAnt* 7, 30–48.

—— (1993), 'Hero Cult and Politics in Herodotus. The Bones of Orestes', in C. Dougherty and L. Kurke (eds.), *Cultural Poetics in Archaic Greece. Cult, Performance, Politics* (Cambridge), 164–77.

BOER, W. DEN (1957), 'The Delphic Oracle concerning Cypselus (Hdt. v, 92β, 2)', *Mnemosyne* 10, 339.

—— (1967), 'Herodot und die Systeme der Chronologie', *Mnemosyne* 20, 30–60.

BOHRINGER, F. (1979), 'Culte d'athlètes en Grèce classique: propos politiques, discours mythiques', *REA* 81, 5–18.

BORGEAUD, P. (1988), *The Cult of Pan in Ancient Greece,* tr. K. Atlass and J. Redfield (Chicago).

BOSSY, J. (1985), *Christianity in the West 1400–1700* (Oxford).

BOWDEN, H. (1991), 'Herodotos and Greek Sanctuaries' (unpubl. Oxford D. Phil. thesis).

—— (1992), Introduction to Everyman edition of Rawlinson's translation (London).

BOWIE, A. M. (1993), 'Homer, Herodotus and the "Beginnings" of Thucydides' *History'*, in H. D. Jocelyn and H. Hurt (eds.), *Tria Lustra. Essays and Notes Presented to John Pinsent* (Liverpool), 141–7.

BOWRA, C. M. (1963), 'Arion and the Dolphin', *MH* 20, 121–34.

—— (1964), *Pindar* (Oxford).

BRAUN, T. F. R. G. (1982a), 'The Greeks in the Near East', *CAH* III² pt. 3, 1–31.

—— (1982b), 'The Greeks in Egypt', *CAH* III² pt. 3, 32–56.

BRAUND, D. (1998), 'Herodotus on the Problematics of Reciprocity', in C. Gill, N. Postlethwaite, and R. Seaford (eds.), *Reciprocity in Ancient Greece* (Oxford), 159–80.

BRELICH, A. (1958), *Gli Eroi Greci* (Rome).

BREMMER, J. (1982), 'Literacy and the Origins of Greek Atheism', in J. den Boeft and A. H. M. Kessel (eds.), *Actus. Studies in honour of H. L. W. Nelson* (Utrecht), 43–55.

—— (1987), 'What is a Greek Myth?', in J. Bremmer (ed.), *Interpretations of Greek Mythology* (London), 1–9.

BREMMER, J. (1993), 'Prophets, Seers and Politics in Greece, Israel and Early Modern Europe', *Numen* 40, 150–83.

——(1994), *Greek Religion,* Greece and Rome New Surveys in the Classics 24 (Oxford).

——(1995), 'The Family and Other Centres of Religious Learning in Antiquity', in J. W. Drijvers and A. A. MacDonald (eds.), *Centres of Learning* (Leiden), 29–38.

BRIANT, P. (1996), *Histoire de l'empire perse* (Paris).

BRILLANTE, C. (1990), 'Myth and History', in L. Edmunds (ed.), *Approaches to Greek Myth* (Baltimore), 91–138.

BROWN, T. S. (1965), 'Herodotus Speculates about Egypt', *AJPh* 86, 60–76.

——(1978), 'Aristodicus of Cyme and the Branchidae', *AJPh* 99, 64–78.

——(1981), 'Aeneas Tacticus, Herodotus and the Ionian revolt', *Historia* 30, 385–93.

——(1982), 'Herodotus' Portrait of Cambyses', *Historia* 31, 387–403.

——(1989), 'Solon and Croesus (Hdt. 1. 29)', *AHB* 3, 1–4.

BRUIT ZAIDMAN, L., and P. SCHMITT PANTEL (1992), *Religion in the Ancient Greek City,* tr. P. Cartledge (Cambridge).

BRUNIUS-NILSSON, E. (1955), *ΔAIMONIE.* An Inquiry into a Mode of Apostrophe in Old Greek Literature (Uppsala).

BUNNENS, G. (1969), 'Les Presages orientaux et la prise de Sardes. A propos d'Hérodote, I, 84', in *Mélanges . . . M. Rénard,* Collection Latomus 102 (Brussels).

BURKERT, W. (1965), 'Demaratos, Astrabakos und Herakles. Königsmythos und Politik zur Zeit der Perserkriege (Herodot VI, 67–69)', *MH* 22, 166–77.

——(1970), 'La Genèse des choses et des mots. Le papyrus de Derveni entre Anaxagore et Cratyle', *Les Études Philosophiques,* 443–55.

——(1972), *Lore and Science in Ancient Pythagoreanism* (Cambridge, Mass.).

——(1981), 'ΘΕΩΝ ΟΠΙΝ ΟΥΚ ΑΛΕΓΟΝΤΕΣ. Götterfurcht und Leumannsches Missverständnis', *MH* 38, 195–204.

——(1985*a*) *Greek Religion: Archaic and Classical,* tr. J. Raffan (Oxford).

——(1985*b*), 'Herodot über die Namen der Götter: Polytheismus als historisches Problem', *MH* 42, 121–32.

——(1985*c*), 'Das Ende des Kroisos: Vorstufen einer Herodoteischen Geschichtserzählung', in C. Schläubin (ed.), *Catalepton. Festchrift B. Wyss* (Basel), 4–15.

——(1990), 'Herodot als Historiker fremder Religionen', in W.

Burkert *et al.*, *Hérodote et les peuples non-grecs*, Fondation Hardt Entretiens 35 (Geneva), 1–39.

——(1995), 'Lydia between East and West or How to Date the Trojan war: A Study in Herodotus', in J. B. Carter and S. P. Morris (eds.), *The Ages of Homer. A Tribute to Emily Townsend Vermeule* (Austin), 139–48.

BURN, A. R. (1962), *Persia and the Greeks* (London).

BURY, J. B. (1895–6), 'The Campaign of Artemisium and Thermopylae', *ABSA* 2, 83–104.

——(1902), 'The Epicene Oracle concerning Argos and Miletus', *Klio* 2, 14–25.

BUXTON, R. (1994), *Imaginary Greece. The Contexts of Mythology* (Cambridge).

CAMPS, G. (1985), 'Pour une lecture naïve d'Hérodote. Les récits libyens (IV. 168–199)', *SStor* 7, 38–59.

CARBONELL, C.-O. (1985), 'L'Espace et le temps dans l'oeuvre d'Hérodote', *SStor* 7, 138–49.

CAREY, C. (1982), 'Notes on Aristophanes' *Peace*', *CQ* 32, 465–7.

CARPENTER, R. (1946), *Folktale, Fiction and Saga in the Homeric Epics* (Berkeley).

CARRIÈRE, J.-C. (1988), 'Oracles et prodiges de Salamine: Hérodote et Athènes', *DHA* 14, 219–75.

CARTLEDGE, P. (1990), 'Herodotus and the "the other": A Meditation on Empire', *EMC* 34, 27–40.

——(1992), Introduction to L. Bruit Zaidman and P. Schmitt Pantel (1992).

CATLING, H. W., and H. CAVANAGH (1976), 'Two Inscribed Bronzes from the Menelaion, Sparta', *Kadmos* 15, 145–57.

CAWKWELL, G. L. (1992), 'Early Colonisation', *CQ* 42, 289–303.

CHANTRAINE, P. (1952), 'Le Divin et les dieux chez Homère', in H. J. Rose *et al.*, *La Notion du Divin depuis Homère jusqu'à Platon*, Fondation Hardt Entretiens 1 (Geneva), 47–94.

CHIASSON, C. (1982), 'Tragic Diction in Herodotus: Some Possibilities', *Phoenix* 36, 156–61.

——(1983), 'An Ominous Word in Herodotus', *Hermes* 111, 115–18.

——(1986), 'The Herodotean Solon', *GRBS* 27, 249–62.

CHILTON, C. W. (1962), 'The Epicurean Theory of the Origin of Language: A Study of Diogenes of Oenoanda. Fragments X and XI (W)', *AJPh* 83, 159–67.

CHRIST, M. (1994), 'Herodotean Kings and Historical Inquiry', *ClAnt* 13, 167–202.

CLANCHY, M. T. (1993), *From Memory to Written Record. England 1066–1307* (Oxford, 2nd. edn.).

CLASSEN, C. J. (1976), 'Study of Language among Socrates' Contemporaries', in *Sophistik, Wege der Forschung* Bd. 187 (Darmstadt), 215–47.

CLINTON, K. (1986), 'The Author of the Homeric Hymn to Demeter', *OAth* 16, 43–9.

COBET, J (1977), 'Wann wurde Herodots Darstellung der Perserkriege publiziert?', *Hermes* 105, 2–27.

——(1986), 'Herodotus and Thucydides on War', in I. S. Moxon, J. D. Smart, A. J. Woodman (eds.), *Past Perspectives* (Cambridge), 1–18.

COLLINGWOOD, R. G. (1946), *The Idea of History* (Oxford).

COMAN, I. G. (1981), 'L'Immortalité chez les Thraco-Géto-Daces', *RHR* 198, 243–78.

CONNOR, W. R. (1985), 'The Razing of the House in Greek Society', *TAPhA* 115, 79–102.

——(1987), 'Tribes, Festivals and Processions: Civic Ceremonies and Political Manipulation in Archaic Greece', *JHS* 107, 40–50.

——(1988), '"Sacred" and "Secular". Ἱερά καὶ ὅσια and the Classical Athenian Concept of the State', *AncSoc* 19, 161–88.

——(1993), 'The *Histor* in History', in R. M. Rosen and J. Farrell (eds.), *Nomodeiktes. Greek Studies in Honour of Martin Ostwald* (Ann Arbor), 3–15.

COOK, A. B. (1907), 'Nomen Omen', *CR* 21, 169.

COOK, J. M. (1983), *The Persian Empire* (London).

COOPER, G. L. (1974), 'Intrusive Oblique Infinitives in Herodotus', *TAPhA* 104, 23–76.

CORCELLA, A. (1984), *Erodoto e l'analogia* (Palermo).

COUCH, H. N. (1931), 'Three Puns on the Root of *perthō* in the *Persae* of Aeschylus', *AJPh* 52, 270–3.

COULET, C. (1992), 'Réflexions sur la famille de *ΔΙΚΗ* dans l'*Enquête* d'Hérodote', *REG* 105, 371–84.

CRAHAY, R. (1956), *La Littérature oraculaire chez Hérodote* (Paris).

CUMONT, F. (1902), 'Le Dieu Orotalt d'Hérodote', *RA* 40, i. 297–300.

DAICOVICIU, C. (1944–5), 'Herodot si pretinsul monotheism al Getilor', *Apulum* 2, 90–3.

DARBO-PESCHANSKI, C. (1985), 'Les logoi des autres dans les *Histoires* d'Hérodote', *QS* 22, 105–28.

——(1987), *Le Discours du particulier. Essai sur l'enquête hérodotéene* (Paris).

DAUX, G. (1957), 'Mys au Ptôion (Hérodote, VIII, 133)', *Hommages W. Déonna* (Bruxelles), 157–62.

DAVIES, J. K. (1988), 'Religion and the State', *CAH* IV², 368–88.

DAWSON, W. (1986), 'Herodotus as a Medical Writer', *BICS* 33, 87–96.

DÉFRADAS, J. (1954), *Les Thèmes de la propagande delphique* (Paris).

DELCOURT, M. (1944), *Oedipe ou la légende du conquérant* (Liège).

DEMONT, P. (1988), 'Hérodote et les pestilences (Note sur HDT. VI. 27; VII. 171 et VIII. 115–117)', *RPh* 62, 7–13.

DEPUYDT, L. (1995), 'Murder in Memphis: The Story of Cambyses' Mortal Wounding of the Apis Bull (ca. 523 B. C. E.)', *JNES* 54, 119–26.

DEROW, P. S. (1994), 'Historical Explanation: Polybius and his Predecessors', in S. Hornblower (ed.), *Greek Historiography* (Oxford), 73–90.

——(1995), 'Herodotus Readings', *ClassicsIreland* 2, 29–51.

——and W. G. FORREST (1982), 'An inscription from Chios', *ABSA* 77, 79–92.

DETIENNE, M. (1963), *La Notion de* Daïmôn *dans le Pythagorisme Ancien* (Liège, Paris).

——(1986), *The Creation of Mythology,* tr. M. Cook (Chicago).

DEVELIN, R. (1985), 'Herodotus and the Alkmaeonids', in J. W. Eadie and J. Ober (eds.), *The Craft of the Ancient Historian. Essays in honour of Chester G. Starr* (Lanham, Md.), 125–39.

DEWALD, C. (1985), 'Practical Knowledge and the Historian's Role in Herodotus and Thucydides', in M. H. Jameson (ed.), *The Greek Historians. Papers Presented to A. E. Raubitschek* (Palo Alto, Calif.), 47–63.

——(1987), 'Narrative Surface and Authorial Voice in Herodotus' *Histories*', *Arethusa* 20, 147–50.

——(1993), 'Reading the World: Interpretation of Objects in Herodotus' *Histories*', in R. M. Rosen and J. Farrell (eds.) *Nomodeiktes. Greek Studies in honour of Martin Ostwald* (Ann Arbor), 55–70.

——(1997), 'Wanton Kings, Pickled Heroes and Gnomic Founding Fathers: Strategies of Meaning at the End of Herodotus' *Histories*', in D. H. Roberts, F. M. Dunn, and D. Fowler (eds.), *Classical Closure* (Princeton), 62–82.

——(1998), Introduction to Herodotus *The Histories,* tr. R. Waterfield (Oxford), pp. ix–xli.

DIELS, H. (1910), 'Die Anfänge der Philologie bei den Griechen', *Neue Jahrbuch fur Philologie* 25, 1–25.

DIESNER, H. (1961), 'Skythische Religion und Geschichte bei Herodot', *RhM* 104, 202–12.

DIETRICH, B. C. (1965), *Death, Fate and the Gods* (London).

DILLERY, J. (1992), 'Darius and the Tomb of Nitocris (Hdt. 1. 187)', *CPh* 87, 30–8.

DILLERY, J. (1996), 'Reconfiguring the Past: Thyrea, Thermopylae and Narrative Patterns in Herodotus', *AJPh* 117, 217–54.

DOBSON, M. (1979), 'Hdt. 1. 47. 1 and the *Hymn to Hermes*: A Solution to the Test Oracle', *AJPh* 100, 349–59.

DODDS, E. R. (1951), *The Greeks and the Irrational* (Berkeley).

——(1960), Euripides *Bacchae* (2nd edn., Oxford).

DOVER, K. J. (1972), *Aristophanic Comedy* (Berkeley).

——(1974), *Greek Popular Morality in the Time of Plato and Aristotle* (Oxford).

——(1988), 'Thucydides and Oracles', in *The Greeks and their Legacy. Collected Papers*, vol. 2 (Oxford), 65–73.

——(1998), 'Herodotean Plausibilities', in M. Austin, J. Harries, and C. Smith (eds.), *Modus Operandi. Essays in honour of Geoffrey Rickman* (London), 219–25.

DOWDEN, K. (1992), *The Uses of Greek Mythology* (London).

DREWS, R. (1973), *Greek Accounts of Eastern History* (Cambridge, Mass.).

DUCAT, J. (1995), 'Un rituel samien', *BCH* 119, 339–68.

DUCHESNE-GUILLEMIN, J. (1967/8), 'Religion et politique, de Cyrus à Xerxes', *Persica* 3, 1–9.

DUCREY, P. (1968), *Le Traitement des prisonniers de guerre dans la Grèce antique* (Paris).

DUNBABIN, T. J. (1948), 'Minos and Daidalos in Sicily', *PBSR* NS 3, 16, 1–18.

DYSON, G. W. (1929), '*ΛΕΟΝΤΑ ΤΕΚΕΙΝ*', *CQ* 23, 186–95.

EASTERLING, P. (1973), 'Presentation of Character in Aeschylus', *G&R* 20, 3–19.

——(1988), 'Tragedy and Ritual: "Cry 'Woe, Woe' but may the Good Prevail" ', *Metis* 3, 87–109.

EDMUNDS, L. (1990), 'Introduction: The Practice of Greek Mythology', in his *Approaches to Greek Myth* (Baltimore), 1–20.

EDWARDS, M. J. (1990), 'Herodotus and Mithras: *Histories* I. 131', *AJPh* 111, 1–4.

——(1991), 'Xenophanes Christianus', *GRBS* 32, 219–28.

——(1993), 'Cybele among the Philosophers: Pherecydes to Plato', *Eranos* 91, 65–74.

ELAYI, J. (1978), 'Le Rôle de l'Oracle de Delphes dans le conflit gréco-perse d'après "Les Histoires" d'Hérodote' (1ère partie), *IA* 13, 93–118.

——(1979a), 'Deux oracles de Delphes: les réponses de la Pythie à Clisthène de Sicyone, et aux Athéniens avant Salamine', *REG* 92, 224–30.

—— (1979b), 'Le Rôle de l'Oracle de Delphes dans le conflit gréco-perse d'après "Les Histoires" d'Hérodote' (suite), *IA* 14, 67–151.

ELIADE, M. (1972), *Zalmoxis. The Vanishing God*, tr. W. R. Trask (Chicago).

ELSE, G. (1949), 'God and Gods in Early Greek Thought', *TAPhA* 80, 24–36.

ERSKINE, A. (1995), 'Rome in the Greek World: The Significance of a Name', in A. Powell (ed.), *The Greek World* (London), 368–82.

EVANS, J. A. S. (1965), '*Despotes Nomos*', *Athenaeum* 43, 142–53.

—— (1978), 'What Happened to Croesus?', *CJ* 74, 34–40.

—— (1988a), 'The "Wooden Wall" again', *AHB* 2, 25–30.

—— (1988b), 'The Story of Pythius', *LCM* 13/9, 139.

—— (1991), *Herodotus. Explorer of the Past* (Princeton).

—— (1992), Review of Fehling (1989), *EMC* 36, 57–60.

EVANS-PRITCHARD, E. E. (1956), *Nuer Religion* (Oxford).

—— (1965), *Theories of Primitive Religion* (Oxford).

—— (1976), *Witchcraft, Oracles and Magic among the Azande*, abridged from 1937 edn. by E. Gillies (Oxford).

FAHR, W. (1969), *ΘΕΟΥΣ NOMIZEIN. Zum Problem der Anfänge des Atheismus bei den Griechen*, Spudasmata 26 (Hildesheim).

FALUS, R. (1977), 'Hérodote III 108–109', *AAntHung* 25, 371–6.

FARNELL, L. R. (1921), *Greek Hero Cults and Ideas of Immortality* (Oxford).

FEBVRE, L. (1982), *The Problem of Unbelief in the Sixteenth Century. The Religion of Rabelais*, tr. Beatrice Gottlieb (Cambridge, Mass.).

FEENEY, D. (1998), *Literature and Religion at Rome* (Cambridge).

FEHLING, D. (1989), *Herodotus and his 'Sources'. Citation, Invention and Narrative Art*, tr. J. G. Howie (Leeds).

FERGUSON, J. (1981), 'Herodotus as a Source for Greek Religion' (Part I), *MusAfr* 7, 1–22.

FINLEY, M. I. (1975), 'Myth, Memory and History', in his *The Use and Abuse of History* (London), 11–33.

—— (1978), *The World of Odysseus* (London, 4th edn.).

FISHER, N. R. E. (1992), *Hybris. A Study in the Values of Honour and Shame in Ancient Greece* (Warminster).

FLACELIÈRE, R. (1946), 'Plutarque et les oracles Béotiens', *BCH* 70, 199–207.

—— (1965), *Greek Oracles* (London).

FLORY, S. (1969), 'The Personality of Herodotus', *Arion* 8, 99–109.

—— (1978a), 'Laughter, Tears and Wisdom in Herodotus', *AJPh* 99, 145–53.

—— (1978b), 'Arion's Leap: Brave Gestures in Herodotus', *AJPh* 99, 411–21.

FLORY, S. (1980), 'Who Read Herodotus' *Histories?*', *AJPh* 101, 12–28.
——(1987), *The Archaic Smile of Herodotus* (Detroit).
FLOWER, H. I. (1991), 'Herodotus and Delphic Traditions about Croesus', in M. A. Flower and M. Toher (eds.), *Georgica. Greek Studies in Honour of George Cawkwell* (London), 57–77.
FOL, A., and I. MAZAROW (1977), *Thrace and the Thracians* (London).
FONTENROSE, J. (1968), 'The Hero as Athlete', *ClAnt* 1, 73–104.
——(1978), *The Delphic Oracle. Its Responses and Operations with a Catalogue of Responses* (Berkeley).
——(1988), *Didyma. Apollo's Oracle, Cult and Companions* (Berkeley).
FORNARA, C. W. (1971*a*), *Herodotus. An Interpretative Essay* (Oxford).
——(1971*b*), 'Evidence for the Date of Herodotus' Publication', *JHS* 91, 25–34.
——(1981), 'Herodotus' Knowledge of the Archidamian War', *Hermes* 109, 149–56.
——(1983), *The Nature of History in Ancient Greece and Rome* (Berkeley).
——(1990), 'Human History and the Constraint of Fate in Herodotus', in J. W. Allison (ed.), *Conflict, Antithesis, and the Ancient Historian* (Columbus, Ohio), 25–45.
FORREST, W. G. (1968), *A History of Sparta* (London).
——(1969), 'The Tradition of Hippias' Expulsion from Athens', *GRBS* 10, 277–86.
——(1979), 'Motivation in Herodotos: The Case of the Ionian Revolt', *International History Review* 1, 311–22.
——(1982), 'Delphi 750–500 BC', *CAH* III² pt. 3, 305–20.
——(1984), 'Herodotus and Athens', *Phoenix* 38, 1–11.
FOWLER, R. L. (1996), 'Herodotus and his Contemporaries', *JHS* 116, 62–87.
FRANÇOIS, G. (1957) *Le Polytheisme et l'emploi au singulier des mots ΘΕΟΣ, ΔΑΙΜΩΝ* (Paris).
FRISCH, P. (1968), *Die Traüme bei Herodot* (Diss. Köln).
FRITZ, K. VON (1967), *Die griechische Geschichtsschreibung* (2 vols., Berlin).
GABBA, E. (1981), 'True History and False History', *JRS* 71, 50–62.
GAMMIE, J. G. (1986), 'Herodotus on Kings and Tyrants: Objective Historiography or Conventional Portraiture?', *JNES* 45, 171–95.
GARBRAH, K. (1986), 'On the ΘΕΟΦΑΝΙΑ in Chios and the Epiphany of Gods in War', *ZPE* 65, 207–10.
GARDINER, A. H. (1944), 'Horus the Behdetite', *JEA* 30, 23–60.

GARLAND, R. S. J. (1984), 'Religious Authority in Archaic and Classical Athens', *ABSA* 79, 75–123.

GARNSEY, P. (1984), 'Religious Toleration in Classical Antiquity', in W. J. Sheils (ed.), *Studies in Church History* 21, 1–27.

GÄRTNER, H. A. (1983), 'Les Rêves de Xerxès et d'Artabane chez Hérodote', *Ktema* 8, 11–18.

GEERTZ, C. (1973), 'Religion as a Cultural System', in his *The Interpretation of Cultures* (New York), 87–125.

GEORGES, P. B. (1986), 'Saving Herodotus' Phenomena', *ClAnt* 5, 14–59.

——(1994), *Barbarian Asia and the Greek Experience* (Baltimore).

GERMAIN, G. (1956), 'Le Songe de Xèrxes et le rite babylonien du substitut royal' (Étude sur Hérodote, VII 12–18)', *REG* 69, 303–13.

GERNET, L. (1981), 'Marriages of Tyrants', in his *The Anthropology of Ancient Greece* (Baltimore), 289–302.

GHIMADEYEV, R. A. (1986), *ΗΡΩΣ ΗΡΟΔΟΤΟΣ*', *VDI* 179, 77–84.

GIANOTTI, G. (1988), 'Ordine e simmetria nella rappresentazione del mondo: Erodoto e il paradosso del Nilo', *QS* 27, 51–92.

GIRAUDEAU, M. (1984), *Les Notions juridiques et sociales chez Hérodote* (Paris).

GLADIGOW, B. (1985–6), 'Präsenz der Bilder. Präsenz der Götter', *VRel* 4–5, 114–33.

——(1990), 'Epiphanie, Statuette, Kultbild', *VRel* 7, 98–121.

GOMME, A. W. (1913), 'The Legend of Cadmus and the Logographi', *JHS* 33, 53–72, 223–45.

——(1954), *The Greek Attitude to Poetry and History* (Berkeley).

GORDON, R. L. (1979), 'The Real and the Imaginary: Production and Religion in the Graeco-Roman World', *Art History* 2, 5–34.

GOTTSCHALK, H. B. (1980), *Heraclides of Pontus* (Oxford).

GOULD, J. (1985), 'On Making Sense of Greek Religion', in P. Easterling and J. V. Muir (eds.), *Greek Religion and Society* (Cambridge), 1–33.

——(1989), *Herodotus* (London).

——(1991), *Give and Take in Herodotus. The Fifteenth J. L. Myres Memorial Lecture* (Oxford).

——(1994), 'Herodotus and Religion', in S. Hornblower (ed.), *Greek Historiography* (Oxford), 91–106.

GRANT, J. R. (1983), 'Some Thoughts on Herodotus', *Phoenix* 37, 283–98.

GRIFFITHS, A. (1989), 'Was Cleomenes Mad?', in A. Powell (ed.), *Classical Sparta. Techniques behind her Success* (London), 51–78.

GRIFFITHS, A. (1999), 'Euenius, the Negligent Nightwatchman', in R. Buxton (ed.), *From Myth to Reason? Studies in the Development of Greek Thought* (Oxford), 169–82.

GRIFFITHS, J. G. (1970), *Plutarch's De Iside et Osiride* (Wales).

—— (1991), *The Divine Verdict. A Study of Divine Judgement in the Ancient Religions* (Leiden).

GRONINGEN, B. A. VAN (1953), *In the grip of the past. An Essay on an Aspect of Greek Thought* (Leiden).

—— (1956), 'Un oracle de Delphes (Hérodote IV 159³)', *Mnemosyne* 9, 295.

GROTE, G. (1888), *A History of Greece,* vol. iii (4th edn., London).

GROTEN, F. J. (1963), 'Herodotus' Use of Variant Versions', *Phoenix* 17, 79–87.

GUTHRIE, W. H. C. (1962), *A History of Greek Philosophy,* vol. i (Cambridge).

HALL, E. (1989) *Inventing the Barbarian. Greek Self-Definition through Tragedy* (Oxford).

—— (1993), 'Asia Unmanned: Images of Victory in Classical Athens', in J. Rich and G. Shipley (eds.), *War and Society in the Greek World* (London), 107–33.

—— (1994), 'Drowning by Nomes: The Greeks, Swimming and Timotheus' *Persians*', in H. A. Khan (ed.), *The Birth of the European Identity: The Europe–Asia Contrast in Greek Thought, Nottingham Classical Literature Studies* 2 (Nottingham), 44–80.

—— (1996), Aeschylus *Persians* (Warminster).

HALLIDAY, W. R. (1910–11), 'A Note on the ΘΗΛΕΑ ΝΟΥΣΟΣ of the Scythians', *ABSA* 17, 95–102.

HALLPIKE, C. R. (1979), *The Foundations of Primitive Thought* (Oxford).

HAMMOND, N. G. L. (1955), 'Studies in Greek Chronology of the Sixth and Fifth Centuries B.C.', *Historia* 4, 377–411.

HANDS, A. R. (1965), 'On Strategy and Oracles 480/79', *JHS* 85, 56–61.

HARRISON, T. (1997), 'Herodotus and the Certainty of Divine Retribution', in A. B. Lloyd (ed.), *What is a God? Studies in the Nature of Greek Divinity* (London), 101–22.

—— (1998a), 'Herodotus' Conception of Foreign Languages', *Histos* 2.

—— (1998b), 'Aeschylus, Atossa and Athens', in E. Dąbrowa (ed.), *Ancient Iran and the Mediterranean World* (Kraków), 69–86.

—— (1999a), *Templum mundi totius*: Ammianus and a Religious Ideal of Rome', in E. D. Hunt and J. W. Drijvers (ed.), *The Late Roman World and its Historian: Interpreting Ammianus Marcellinus* (London), 178–90.

——(1999*b*), 'Sicily in the Athenian Imagination: Thucydides and the Persian Wars', in C. J. Smith and J. Serrati (eds.), *Ancient Sicily* (Edinburgh), 84–96, 199–201.

——(2000), *The Emptiness of Asia. Aeschylus'* Persians *and the History of the Fifth Century* (London).

HARTOG, F. (1978), 'Salmoxis, le Pythagore des Gètes, ou l'autre de Pythagore?', *ASNP* 8, 15–39.

——(1988), *The Mirror of Herodotus. The Representation of the Other in the Writing of History,* tr. J. Lloyd (Berkeley and Los Angeles).

HARVEY, F. D. (1966), 'The Political Sympathies of Herodotus', *Historia* 15, 254–5.

——(1991), 'Herodotos, I, 78 and 84: Which Telmessos?', *Kernos* 4, 245–58.

HAUVETTE, A. (1894), *Hérodote, historien des Guerres Médiques* (Paris).

HAVELOCK, E. A. (1969), 'Dikaiosune: An Essay in Greek Intellectual History', *Phoenix* 23, 49–70.

——(1978), *The Greek Concept of Justice* (Cambridge, Mass.)

HEIDEL, W. A. (1935), *Hecateus and the Egyptian Priests in Herodotus Book II,* American Academy of Arts and Sciences Memoirs 18/2, 53–134.

HEINZE, R. (1993), *Virgil's Epic Technique,* tr. H. and D. Harvey and F. Robertson (Bristol).

HELLMANN, F. (1934), *Herodots Kroisos-Logos* (Berlin).

HEMBERG, B. (1950), *Die Kabiren* (Uppsala).

HERMAN, G. (1987), *Ritualized Friendship and the Greek City* (Cambridge).

HERZFELD, M. (1982), 'Divining the Past', *Semiotica* 38, 169–75.

HOFMANN-KUTSCHKE, A. (1907), 'Iranisches bei den Griechen', *Philologus* 66, 173–91

HOOKER, J. T. (1989), 'Arion and the Dolphin', *G&R* 36, 141–6.

HORNBLOWER, S. (1983), *The Greek World 479–323 BC* (London).

——(1987), *Thucydides* (London).

——(1992*a*), 'The Religious Dimension to the Peloponnesian War, or What Thucydides Does Not Tell Us', *HSPh* 94, 169–97.

——(1992*b*), 'Thucydides' Use of Herodotus', in J. M. Sanders (ed.), *Philolakon. Laconian Studies in honour of Hector Catling* (London), 141–54, repr. in Hornblower, ii. 122–36.

HORST, P. W. VAN DER (1994), 'Silent Prayer in Antiquity', *Mnemosyne* 41, 1–25.

HUBER, L. (1963), *Religiöse und politische Beweggründe des Handelns in der Geschichtsschreibung des Herodot* (diss. Tübingen).

HUMPHREYS, S. C. (1987), 'Law, Custom and Culture in Herodotus', *Arethusa* 20, 211–20.

HUNTER, V. (1982), *Past and Process in Herodotus and Thucydides* (Princeton).

HUXLEY, G. (1979), 'Bones for Orestes', *GRBS* 20, 145–8.

IMMERWAHR, H. I. (1954), 'Historical Action in Herodotus', *TAPhA* 85, 16–45.

——(1956), 'Aspects of Historical Causation in Herodotus', *TAPhA* 87, 41–80.

——(1957), 'The Samian Stories of Herodotus', *CJ* 52, 312–22.

——(1960), '*Ergon*: History as a Monument in Herodotus and Thucydides', *AJPh* 81, 261–90.

——(1966), *Form and Thought in Herodotus* (Cleveland, Ohio).

JACOBY, F. (1909), 'Über die Entwicklung der griechischen Historiographie', *Klio* 9, 80–123, repr. in H. Bloch (ed.), *Abhandlungen zur griechischen Geschichtsschreibung von F. Jacoby* (Leiden, 1956), 16–64.

——(1913), 'Herodotos', *RE* Suppl. 2, 205–519.

——(1949), *Atthis* (Oxford).

JOHNSON, D. H. (1994), *Nuer Prophets* (Oxford).

JOHNSON, W. A. (1995), 'Oral Performance and the Composition of Herodotus' *Histories*', *GRBS* 36, 229–54.

JONES, W. H. (1913), 'A Note on the Vague use of θεός', *CR* 27, 252–5.

JORDAN, B. (1986), 'Religion in Thucydides', *TAPhA* 116, 119–47.

KASSEL, R. (1991), *Kleine Schriften* (Berlin).

KAZAROW, I. (1940), 'Zu Herodot V, 4', *PhW*, 410–11.

KEARNS, E. (1989), *The Heroes of Attica, BICS* Suppl. 57 (London).

——(1990a), 'Between God and Man: Status and Function of Heroes and their Sanctuaries', in A. Schachter *et al.*, *Le Sanctuaire Grec*, Fondation Hardt Entretiens 37 (Geneva), 65–99.

——(1990b), 'Saving the City', in O. Murray and S. R. F. Price (eds.), *The Greek City from Homer to Alexander* (Oxford), 323–44.

KEBRIC, R. B. (1983), *The Paintings in the Cnidian Lesche and their Historical Context* (Leiden).

KESSELS, A. H. M. (1978), *Studies on the Dream in Greek Literature* (Utrecht).

KINZL, K. H. (1976), 'Miltiades' Parosexpedition in der Geschichtsschreibung', *Hermes* 104, 280–307.

KIRCHBERG, J. (1965), *Die Funktion der Orakel im Werke Herodots* (Göttingen).

KIRK, G. S. (1970), *Myth. Its Meaning and Functions in Ancient and Other Cultures* (Cambridge and Berkeley).

——(1973), 'On Defining Myth', *Phronesis* Suppl. vol. 1, 61–9.

KLEES, H. (1964), *Die Eigenart des griechischen Glaubens an Orakel und Seher* (Stuttgart).

KLEINGÜNTHER, A. (1933), Πρῶτος Εὑρετής, *Philologus* Suppl. 26 (Leipzig), 43–65.

KNOX, B. M. W. (1952), 'The Lion in the House (*Agamemnon* 717–36 [Murray])', *CPh* 47, 17–25.

KÖHNKEN, A. (1988), 'Der dritte Traum des Xerxes bei Herodot', *Hermes* 116, 24–40.

KONSTAN, D. (1983), 'The Stories in Herodotus' *Histories*: Book I', *Helios* 10, 1–22.

——(1987), 'Persians, Greeks and Empire', *Arethusa* 20, 59–74.

KRISCHER, T. (1965), 'Herodots Proimion', *Hermes* 93, 159–67.

——(1974), 'Herodots Schlusskapitel, seine Topik und seine Quellen', *Eranos* 72, 93–100.

KROYMANN, J. (1970), 'Götterneid und Menschenwahn', *Saeculum* 21, 166–79.

KUHRT, A. (1995), *The Ancient Near East c. 3000–330 B. C.* (2 vols., London).

——and S. SHERWIN-WHITE (1987), 'Xerxes' Destruction of Babylonian Temples', in H. Sancisi-Weerdenburg and A. Kuhrt (eds.), *Achaemenid History II. The Greek Sources* (Leiden), 69–78.

KUKOFKA, D.-A. (1991), 'Das *MAPTYPION MEΓIΣTON* der Sybariten (Herodot, 5, 43–46)', *Hermes* 119, 374–80.

LABARBE, J. (1957), *La Loi navale de Thémistocle* (Paris)

——(1986), 'Le Manteau de Syloson', *CCC* 7, 7–27.

LA BUA, V. (1976), 'Sulla fine di Creso', *Studi di Storia Antica offerti degli allievi a Eugenio Manni* (Rome), 177–92.

LACHENAUD, G. (1978), *Mythologies, religion et philosophie de l'histoire dans Hérodote* (Lille and Paris).

LANG, M. L. (1968), 'Herodotus and the Ionian Revolt', *Historia* 17, 24–36.

——(1984a), *Herodotean Narrative and Discourse* (Cambridge, Mass.).

——(1984b), 'Herodotus: Oral History with a Difference', *PAPhS*, 93–103.

LATEINER, D. (1977), 'No Laughing Matter. A Literary Tactic in Herodotus', *TAPhA* 107, 173–82.

——(1980), 'A Note on *ΔIKAΣ ΔIΔONAI* in Herodotus', *CQ* 30, 30–2.

——(1982), 'A Note on the Perils of Prosperity in Herodotus', *RhM* 125, 97–101.

——(1984), 'Herodotean Historiographical Patterning: The Constitutional Debate', *QS* 20, 157–84.

LATEINER, D. (1985*a*), 'Limit, Propriety and Transgression in the *Histories* of Herodotus', in M. H. Jameson (ed.), *The Greek Historians. Papers presented to A. E. Raubitschek* (Palo Alto, Calif.), 87–100.

—— (1985*b*), 'Polarità: il principio della differenza complementare', *QS* 22, 79–103.

—— (1986), 'The Empirical Element in the Methods of the Early Greek Medical Writers and Herodotus: A Shared Epistemological Response', *Antichthon* 20, 1–20.

—— (1989), *The Historical Method of Herodotus* (Toronto).

—— (1990), 'Deceptions and Delusions in Herodotus', *ClAnt* 9, 230–46.

LATTIMORE, R. (1939*a*), 'The Wise Adviser in Herodotus', *CPh* 34, 24–35.

—— (1939*b*), 'The Second Storm at Artemisium', *CR* 53, 57–8.

—— (1940), 'Herodotus and the Names of the Egyptian Gods', *CPh* 35, 357–65.

—— (1958), 'The Composition of the *History* of Herodotus', *CPh* 53, 9–21.

LAVELLE, B. M. (1993), *The Sorrow and the Pity. Prolegomena to a History of Athens under the Peisistratids c. 560–510 B.C.* (Stuttgart).

LEGRAND, Ph.-E. (1932), *Hérodote* (Paris).

—— (1937), 'Hérodote, croyait-il aux oracles?', *Mélanges P. Desroussaux* (Paris), 275–84.

LEVIN, S. B. (1995), 'What's in a Name? A Reconsideration of the *Cratylus'* Historical Sources and Topics', *Ancient Philosophy* 15, 91–115.

LEWIS, S. (1996), *News and Society in the Greek Polis* (London).

LEYDEN, W. M. VON (1949–50), 'Spatium historicum. The Historical Past as Viewed by Hecataeus, Herodotus and Thucydides', *Durham University Journal* 11, 89–104.

L'HOMME-WÉRY, L.-M. (1994), 'Solon, Libérateur d'Éleusis dans les "Histoires" d'Hérodote', *REG* 107, 362–80.

LIEBESCHÜTZ, J. H. W. G. (1979), *Continuity and Change in Roman Religion* (Oxford).

LIENHARDT, G. (1956), 'Religion', in H. L. Shapiro (ed.), *Man, Culture and Society* (New York), 382–401.

—— (1961), *Divinity and Experience. The Religion of the Dinka* (Oxford).

LIESHOUT, R. G. A. VAN (1970), 'A Dream on a *KAIPOΣ* of History. An Analysis of Herodotus *Hist.* VII 12–19; 47', *Mnemosyne* 23, 225–49.

—— (1980), *Greeks on Dreams* (Utrecht).

LIGOTA, C. R. (1982), '"This story is not true." Fact and Fiction in Antiquity', *JWI* 45, 1–13.

LINFORTH, I. M. (1918), '*OI AΘANATIZONTEΣ* (Herodotus iv. 93–6)', *CPh* 13, 22–33.

——(1924), 'Herodotus' Avowal of Silence', *University of California Publications in Classical Philology* 7/9, 269–92.

——(1926), 'Greek Gods and Foreign Gods in Herodotus', *University of California Publications in Classical Philology* 9/1, 1–25.

——(1928), 'Named and Unnamed Gods in Herodotus', *University of California Publications in Classical Philology* 9/7, 201–43.

——(1940), 'Greek and Egyptian Gods (Herodotus II. 50 and 52)', *CPh* 35, 300–1.

LLOYD, A. B. (1988*a*), 'Herodotus on Cambyses. Some Thoughts on Recent Work', in A. Kuhrt and H. Sancisi-Weerdenburg (eds.), *Achaemenid History III. Method and Theory* (Leiden), 55–66.

——(1988*b*), 'Herodotus' Account of Pharaonic History', *Historia* 37, 22–53.

——(1990), 'Herodotus on Egyptians and Libyans', in W. Burkert *et al., Hérodote et les peuples non-grecs,* Fondation Hardt Entretiens 35 (Geneva), 215–53.

——(1995), 'Herodotus on Egyptian Buildings. A Test Case', in A. Powell (ed.), *The Greek World* (London), 273–301.

LLOYD, G. E. R. (1979), *Magic, Reason and Experience* (Cambridge).

——(1990), *Demystifying Mentalities* (Cambridge).

LLOYD, M. (1984), 'Croesus' Priority: Herodotus 1. 5. 3', *LCM* 9/1, 11.

——(1987), 'Cleobis and Biton (Herodotus, 1. 31)', *Hermes* 115, 22–8.

LLOYD-JONES, H. (1956), 'Zeus in Aeschylus', *JHS* 76, 55–67.

——(1971), *The Justice of Zeus* (Berkeley).

——(1976), 'The Delphic Oracle', *G&R* 23, 60–73.

LOMBARDO, M. (1990), 'Erodoto storico dei Lidi', in W. Burkert *et al., Hérodote et les peuples non-grecs,* Fondation Hardt Entretiens 35 (Geneva), 171–214.

LONG, T. (1986), *Barbarians in Greek Comedy* (Corbendale and Edwardsville, Ill.).

LONIS, R. (1979), *Guerre et religion en Grèce à l'époque classique. Recherches sur les rites, les dieux, l'idéologie de la victoire* (Paris).

LORAUX, N. (1985), 'La Cité, l'historien, les femmes', *Pallas* 32, 7–29.

MACAN, R. W. (1927), 'Herodotus and Thucydides', *CAH* V[1], 398–419.

MCCARTNEY, E. S. (1940), 'Engineering Superstitions Comparable to that Recorded by Hdt. I. 174', *CPh* 35, 416–20.

——(1941), 'Modern Analogues to Ancient Tales of Monstrous Races', *CPh* 36, 390–4.

MACINTYRE, A. (1970), 'Is Understanding Religion Compatible with believing?', in B. R. Wilson (ed.), *Rationality* (Oxford), 62–77.

MACTOUX, M.-M. (1993), 'Phobos à Sparte', *RHR* 210, 259–304.

MADDALENA, A. (1942), *Interpretazioni Erodotee* (Padova).

——(1950), 'L'umano e il divino in Erodoto', in V. E. Alfieri and M. Untersteiner (eds.), *Studi di Filosofia Greca . . . in onore di R. Mondolfo* (Bari), 57–84.

MALKIN, I. (1987), *Religion and Colonization in Ancient Greece* (Leiden).

MALLOWAN, M. (1972), 'Cyrus the Great (558–529 B. C.)', *Iran* 10, 1–17, revised version in I. Gershevitch (ed.), *Cambridge History of Iran*, ii (Cambridge, 1985), 392–400.

MARINATOS, N. (1981*a*), *Thucydides and Religion* (Königstein).

——(1981*b*), 'Thucydides and Oracles', *JHS* 91, 138–40.

——(1982), 'Wahl und Schicksal bei Herodot', *Saeculum* 33, 258–64.

MARINCOLA, J. (1997), *Authority and Tradition in Ancient Historiography* (Cambridge).

MASSON, O. (1950), 'A propos d'un rituel hittite pour la lustration d'une armée', *RHR* 137, 5–25.

MATHIEU, G. (1931), 'Dikaios d'Athènes', *REA* 33, 97–108.

MATTHEWS, V. J. (1974), *Panyassis of Halikarnassos* (Leiden).

MAURIZIO, L. (1995), 'Anthropology and Spirit Possession: A Reconsideration of the Pythia's Role at Delphi', *JHS* 115, 69–86.

MAXWELL-STUART, P. G. (1976), 'Pain, Mutilation, and Death in Herodotus VII', *PP* 31, 356–62.

MAYRHOFER, M. (1979), *Iranisches Personennamenbuch I. Die Altiranischen Namen* (Wien).

MEIGGS, R. (1957), 'Herodotus', *History Today* 7/11 (Nov.).

MERKELBACH, R. (1984), *Mithras* (Königstein).

METTE, H. J. (1985), 'Die "Kleinen" griechischen Historiker heute', *Lustrum* 27, 33–8.

MEULENAERE, H. DE (1949), 'Nota a Erodoto, II, 174', *Athenaeum* 27, 299–301.

——(1953), 'La Légende de Phérus', *CE* 55, 248–60.

MEULI, K. (1935), 'Scythica', *Hermes* 70, 121–76.

MEYER, E. (1892–9), *Forschungen zur Alten Geschichte* (Halle).

MIKALSON, J. D. (1983), *Athenian Popular Religion* (Chapel Hill).

——(1989), 'Unanswered Prayers in Greek Religion', *JHS* 109, 81–98.

——(1991), *Honor Thy Gods. Popular Religion in Greek Tragedy* (Chapel Hill).

MILLER, M. (1965), 'Herodotus as Chronographer', *Klio* 46, 109–28.

MILLER, M. C. (1997), *Athens and Persia in the Fifth Century* (Cambridge).

MITCHEL, F. (1956), 'Herodotus' Use of Genealogical Chronology', *Phoenix* 10, 48–69.

MOLES, J. (1993), 'Truth and Untruth in Herodotus and Thucydides', in C. Gill and T. P. Wiseman (eds.), *Lies and Fiction in the Ancient World* (Exeter), 88–121.

——(1996), 'Herodotus Warns the Athenians', *Papers of the Leeds International Latin Seminar* 9, 259–84.

MOMIGLIANO, A. (1966), *Studies in Historiography* (London).

——(1978), 'Greek Historiography', *H&T* 17/1, 1–8.

——(1984), 'Persian Empire and Greek Freedom', in *Settimo Contributo* (Rome), 61–75, originally published in A. Ryan (ed.), *The Idea of Freedom. Essays in Honour of Isaiah Berlin* (Oxford, 1979), 139–51.

——(1985), 'Herodotus Today', *SStor* 7, 3–5.

MORA, F. (1981), 'I "Silenzi Erodotei"', *Studi Storico-Religiosi* 5/2, 209–22.

——(1985), *Religione e Religioni nelle Storie di Erodoto* (Milan).

——(1987), 'Religious Silence in Herodotus and the Athenian Theatre', in M. G. Ciani (ed.), *The Regions of Silence: Studies in the Difficulty of Communicating* (Amsterdam), 41–65.

MOREAU, A. (1992–3), 'Le Songe d'Atosse', in P. Ghiron-Bistagne, A. Moreau, and J.-C. Turpin (eds.), *Les Perses d'Eschyle* (Montpellier), 29–51.

MORENZ, S. (1973), *Egyptian Religion,* tr. A. E. Keep (London).

MORGAN, C. (1990), *Athletes and Oracles: The Transformation of Olympia and Delphi in the Eighth Century BC* (Cambridge).

MORRIS, B. (1987), *Anthropological Studies of Religion. An Introductory Text* (Cambridge).

MORRIS, I. (1993), 'Poetics of Power: The Interpretation of Ritual Action in Archaic Greece', in C. Dougherty and L. Kurke (eds.), *Cultural Poetics in Archaic Greece. Cult, Performance, Politics* (Cambridge), 15–45.

MOSSMAN, J. M. (1995), *Wild Justice. A Study of Euripides' Hecuba* (Oxford).

MUIR, J. V. (1985), 'Religion and the New Education', in P. Easterling and J. V. Muir (eds.), *Greek Religion and Society* (Cambridge), 191–218.

MÜLLER, D. (1981), 'Herodot—Vater des Empirismus? Mensch und Erkenntnis im Denken Herodots', *Gnomosyne. Festschrift W. Marg* (Munich), 299–318.

MUNSON, R. V. (1986), 'The Celebratory Purpose of Herodotus: The Story of Arion in Histories 1. 23–24', *Ramus* 15, 93–104.

MUNSON, R. V. (1991), 'The Madness of Cambyses (Herodotus 3. 16–38)', *Arethusa* 24, 43–65.

MURRAY, O. (1980), *Early Greece* (London).

——(1987), 'Herodotus and Oral history', in H. Sancisi-Weerdenburg and A. Kuhrt (eds.) *Achaemenid History II. The Greek Sources* (Leiden), 93–115.

MUSSIES, G. (1988), 'Identification and Self-Identification of Gods in Classical and Hellenistic Times', in J. van den Broek *et al.*, *Knowledge of God in the Graeco-Roman World* (Leiden), 1–18.

MUSTI, D. (1990) 'La teoria delle età e i passaggi di *status* in Solone', *MEFRA* 102, 11–35.

MYRES, J. L. (1907), 'A History of the Pelasgian Theory', *JHS* 27, 170–225.

——(1908), 'Herodotus and Anthropology', in R. R. Marett (ed.), *Anthropology and the Classics. Six Lectures delivered before the University of Oxford* (Oxford), 121–68.

——(1953), *Herodotus. The Father of History* (Oxford).

NEVILLE, J. W. (1977), 'Herodotus on the Trojan war', *G&R* 4, 3–12.

NEWBERRY, P. E. (1928), 'The Pig and the Cult-Animal of Set', *JEA* 14, 211–25.

NICKAU, K. (1990), 'Mythos und Logos bei Herodot', in W. Ax (ed.), *Memoria Rerum Veterum. Festschr. C. J. Classen* (Stuttgart), 83–100.

NISBET, R. G. M., and M. HUBBARD (1970) *A Commentary on Horace: Odes Book 1* (Oxford).

NOCK, A. D (1942), 'Religious Attitudes of the Ancient Greeks', *Proceedings of the American Philosophical Association* 85, 472–82.

——(1944), 'The Cult of Heroes', *HThR* 37, 141–73.

OGDEN, D. (1997), *The Crooked Kings of Ancient Greece* (London).

OOST, S. I. (1975), 'Thucydides and the Irrational: Sundry Passages', *CPh* 50, 186–96.

OOTEGHEM, J. VAN (1940), 'L'Anneau de Polycrate', *LEC* 9, 311–14.

OSBORNE, R. (1994), 'Archaeology, the Salaminioi and the Politics of Sacred Space in Archaic Attica', in S. Alcock and R. Osborne (eds.), *Placing the Gods* (Oxford), 143–60.

PACKMAN, Z. M. (1991), 'The Incredible and the Incredulous: The Vocabulary of Disbelief in Herodotus, Thucydides and Xenophon', *Hermes* 119, 399–414.

PALLI BONET, J. (1956), 'Los Heraldos, Taltibio y Eurípides', *Helmantica* 7, 345–55.

PANITZ, H. (1935), *Mythos und Orakel bei Herodot* (Greifswald).

PARKE, H. W. (1962), 'A Note on αὐτοματίζω in Connexion with Prophecy', *JHS* 82, 145–6.

——(1967a), *The Oracles of Zeus* (Oxford).

——(1967b), *Greek Oracles* (London).

——(1984), 'Croesus and Delphi', *GRBS* 25, 209–32.

——(1985), *The Oracles of Apollo in Asia Minor* (London).

——and D. E. W. WORMELL (1956), *The Delphic Oracle*, 2 vols. (Oxford).

PARKER, R. C. T. (1983), *Miasma. Pollution and Purification in Early Greek Religion* (Oxford).

——(1985), 'Greek States and Greek Oracles', in P. Cartledge and D. Harvey (eds.), *CRUX. Essays presented to G.E.M. de Ste. Croix* (Exeter), 298–326.

——(1987), 'Myths of Early Athens', in J. Bremmer (ed.), *Interpretations of Greek Mythology* (London), 187–214.

——(1989), 'Spartan Religion', in A. Powell (ed.), *Classical Sparta. Techniques behind her Success* (London), 142–72.

——(1992), 'The Origins of Pronoia: A Mystery', in *Apodosis. Essays presented to Dr. W. W. Cruickshank* (London), 84–94.

——(1996), *Athenian Religion. A History* (Oxford).

——(1997), 'Gods Cruel and Kind: Tragic and Civic Ideology', in C. Pelling (ed.), *Greek Tragedy and the Historian* (Oxford), 213–35.

——(1998a), *Cleomenes on the Acropolis. An Inaugural Lecture delivered before the University of Oxford on 12 May 1997* (Oxford).

——(1998b), 'Pleasing Thighs: Reciprocity in Greek Religion', in C. Gill, N. Postlethwaite, and R. Seaford (eds.), *Reciprocity in Ancient Greece* (Oxford), 105–25.

PEARSON, L. (1939), *Early Ionian Historians* (Oxford).

——(1941), 'Credulity and Scepticism in Herodotus', *TAPhA* 72, 335–55.

——(1954), 'Real and Conventional Personalities in Greek History', *JHI* 15, 136–45.

PELLING, C. (1991), 'Thucydides' Archidamus and Herodotus' Artabanus', in M. A. Flower and M. Toher (eds.), *Georgica. Greek Studies in Honour of George Cawkwell* (London), 120–42.

——(1997), 'Aeschylus' *Persae* and History', in C. Pelling (ed.), *Greek Tragedy and the Historian* (Oxford), 1–19.

PELLIZER, E. (1993), 'Periandro di Corinto e il forno freddo', in R. Pretagostini (ed.), *Tradizione e Innovazione nella cultura greca da Omero all' età ellenistica. Scritti in onore di B. Gentili*, vol. 2 (Rome), 801–11.

PEMBROKE, S. (1967), 'Women in Charge: The Function of Alternatives in Early Greek Tradition and the Ancient Idea of Matriarchy', *JWI* 30, 1–35.

PERISINAKIS, I. N. (1987), Η έννοια του πλούτου στην Ἱστορίη του Ηροδότου (Ioannina).

PETERSMANN, H. (1990), 'Les Dieux anciens et leur professions', *Ktema* 15, 75–80.

—— (1992), 'Beobachtungen zu den Apellativen für "Gott"', in K.-F. Kraft, E.-M. Lill, and U. Schwab (eds.), *triuwe. Studien zur Sprachgeschichte und Literaturwissenschaft. Gedächtnisbuch für Elfriede Stutz* (Heidelberg), 127–141.

PFISTER, P. (1953), 'Zalmoxis', in G. E. Mylonas and D. Raymond (eds.), *Studies presented to D. M. Robinson*, vol. 2 (St Louis, Mo.), 1112–23.

PHILLIPS, C. R. (1986), 'The Sociology of Religious Knowledge in the Roman Empire to A. D. 284', *ANRW* II. 16. 3, 2677–773.

PICARD, C. (1952), 'Apollon et son Clergé pouvaient-ils être polyglottes', *RA* 39, 84–9.

PIPPIDI, D. M. (1960), 'Sur la philosophie de l'histoire d'Hérodote', *Eirene* 1, 75–92.

PLEKET, H. W. (1981), 'Religious History as the History of Mentality: The "Believer" as Servant of the Deity in the Greek World', in H. S. Versnel (ed.), *Faith, Hope and Worship. Aspects of Religious Mentality in the Ancient World* (Leiden), 152–92.

PLESCIA, J. (1970), *The Oath and Perjury in Ancient Greece* (Tallahassee, Fla.).

—— (1972), 'Herodotus and the Case for Eris (strife)', *PP* 27, 301–11.

POHLENZ, M. (1937), *Herodot, der erste Geschichtsschreiber des Abendlandes* (Leipzig).

PÖTSCHER, W. (1958), 'Götter und Gottheit bei Herodot', *WS* 71, 5–29.

POWELL, A. (1979), 'Thucydides and Divination', *BICS* 26, 45–50.

POWELL, J. E. (1937), 'Puns in Herodotus', *CR* 51, 103–5.

—— (1939), *The History of Herodotus* (Oxford).

PRAKKEN, D. W. (1940), 'Herodotus and the Spartan King Lists', *TAPhA* 71, 460–72.

PRANDI, L. (1993), 'Considerazioni su Bacide e le raccolte oracolari greche', *CISA* 19, 51–62.

PRICE, S. R. F. (1984), *Rituals and Power* (Cambridge).

—— (1985), 'Delphi and Divination', in P. E. Easterling and J. V. Muir (eds.), *Greek Religion and Society* (Cambridge), 128–54.

PRITCHETT, W. K. (1982), *Studies in Ancient Greek Topography* (Berkeley).

—— (1993), *The Liar School of Herodotus* (Amsterdam).

PULLEYN, S. J. (1994), 'The Power of Names in Classical Greek Religion', *CQ* 44, 17–25.

—— (1997), *Prayer in Greek Religion* (Oxford).

RAAFLAUB, K. A. (1987), 'Herodotus, Political Thought, and the Meaning of History', *Arethusa* 20, 221–48.

RADERMACHER, L. (1898), 'Euripides und die Mantik', *RhM* 53, 497–510.

RAUBITSCHEK, A. E. (1939), '*"Εργα μεγάλα τε καὶ θωμαστά*', *REA* 41, 217–22.

——(1960), 'The Covenant of Plataea', *TAPhA* 91, 178–83.

——(1989), 'What the Greeks Thought of their Early History', *AncW* 20, 39–45.

REBUFFAT, R. (1966), 'Hélène en Égypte et le romain égaré (Hérodote, II, 115 et Polybe, III, 22–24)', *REA* 68, 245–63.

REDFIELD, J. (1985), 'Herodotus the Tourist', *CPh* 80, 97–118.

RHODES, P. J. (1981), *A Commentary on the Aristotelian* Athenaion Politeia (Oxford).

——(1994), 'In Defence of the Greek Historians', *G&R* 41, 156–71.

ROBERT, L. (1950), 'Le Carien Mys et l'oracle de Ptöon (Hérodote, VIII, 135)', *Hellenica* 8, 23–38.

ROBERTSON, N. (1987), 'The True Meaning of the "Wooden Wall"', *CPh* 82, 1–20.

——(1992), *Festivals and Legends: The Formation of Greek Cities in the Light of Public Ritual* (Toronto).

——(1996), 'The Ancient Mother of the Gods. A Missing Chapter in the History of Greek Religion', in E. N. Lane (ed.), *Cybele, Attis and Related Cults. Essays in Memory of M. J. Vermaseren* (Leiden), 293–304.

ROMILLY, J. DE (1971), 'La Vengeance comme explication historique dans Hérodote', *REG* 4, 314–37.

——(1977), *The Rise and Fall of States According to Greek Authors* (Ann Arbor).

ROMM, J. (1989), 'Herodotus and Mythic Geography: The Case of the Hyperboreans', *TAPhA* 119, 97–113.

——(1992), *The Edges of the Earth in Ancient Thought. Geography, Exploration and Fiction* (Princeton).

RUDHARDT, J. (1981), 'Sur la possibilité de comprendre une religion antique', in his *Du mythe, de la religion grecque et de la compréhension d'autrui* (Geneva), 13–32.

——(1991), 'Comprendre la religion grecque', *Kernos* 4, 47–59.

——(1992a), *Notions Fondamentales de la Pensée Religieuse et Actes Constitutifs du Culte dans la Grèce Classique* (2nd edn., Paris).

——(1992b), 'Les Attitudes des Grecs a l'égard des religions étrangères', *RHR* 209, 219–38.

RUSTEN, J. S. (1983), '*ΓΕΙΤΩΝ ΉΡΩΣ*. Pindar's Prayer to Heracles (*N.* 7. 86–101), and Greek Popular Religion', *HSPh* 87, 289–97.

SAID, E. (1978), *Orientalism* (London).

SAID, S. (1980), 'Guerre, intelligence et courage dans les Histoires d'Hérodote', *AncSoc* 11, 83–117.

——(1981), 'Darius et Xerxes dans les *Perses* d'Eschyle', *Ktema* 6, 17–38.

SAINTE CROIX., G. E. M. DE (1977), 'Herodotus', *G&R* 24, 130–48.

SALMON, A. (1956), 'L'Expérience de Psammétique (Hérodote II, 2)', *LEC* 24, 321–9.

SALMON, J. (1997), 'Lopping off the Heads? Tyrants, Politics and the *Polis*', in L. G. Mitchell and P. J. Rhodes (eds.), *The Development of the Polis in Archaic Greece* (London), 60–73.

SALVADORE, M. (1987), *Il Nome, la persona. Saggio sull' etimologia antica* (Genoa).

SANCISI-WEERDENBURG, H. (1983), 'Exit Atossa: Images of Women in Greek Historiography on Persia', in A. Cameron and A. Kuhrt (eds.), *Images of Women in Antiquity* (London), 20–33.

SANCTIS, G. DE (1936), 'Il "logos" di Creso e il Proemio della Storia Erodotea', *RFIC* ser. 2, 15, 1–14.

SANSONE, D. (1985), 'The Date of Herodotus' Publication', *ICS* 10, 1–9.

——(1991), 'Cleobis and Biton in Delphi', *Nikephoros* 4, 121–32.

SCHADEWALDT, W. (1962), 'Das Religiös-Humane als Grundlage der geschichtlichen Objektivität bei Herodot', in Marg, 185–201.

SCHMEJA, H. (1975), 'Dareios, Xerxes, Artaxerxes. Drei persische Königsnamen in griechischer Deutung (Zu Herodot 6, 98, 3)', *Sprache* 21, 184–8.

SCHMID, W., and O. STÄHLIN (1934), *Geschichte der griechischen Literatur* (Munich).

SCHMITT, R. (1967), 'Medisches und persisches Sprachgut bei Herodot', *ZDMG* 117, 119–45.

——(1975), 'Bakchylides *abrobatas* und die Iranier-Namen mit Anlaut *ABRA/O-*', *Glotta* 53, 207–16.

——(1976), 'The Medo-Persian Names of Herodotus in the Light of New Evidence from Persepolis', *AAntHung* 24, 25–35.

——(1977), 'Die Verfassungsdebatte bei Herodot 3, 80–82 und die Etymologie des Dareios-Namens', *Historia* 26, 243–4.

SCHREINER, J. H. (1981), 'The Exile and Return of Peisistratus', *SO* 56, 13–17.

SCHWABL, H. (1969), 'Herodot als Historiker und Erzähler', *Gymnasium* 76, 253–72.

SEALEY, R. (1957), 'Thucydides, Herodotus, and the Causes of War', *CQ* 7, 1–12.

——(1975), 'The Causes of the Peloponnesian War', *CPh* 70, 89–109.

——(1976), 'The Pit and the Well: The Persian Heralds of 491 B. C.', *CJ* 72, 13–20.

SEBEOK, T. A., and E. BRADY (1979), 'The Two Sons of Croesus: A Myth about Communication in Herodotus', *QUCC* NS 1, 7–22.

SEGAL, C. (1971), 'Croesus on the Pyre', *WS* NS 5, 39–51.

SHAPIRO, H. A. (1990), 'Oracle-Mongers in Peisistratid Athens', *Kernos* 3, 335–45.

SHAPIRO, S. O. (1994), 'Learning through Suffering: Human Wisdom in Herodotus', *CJ* 89, 349–55.

——(1996), 'Herodotus and Solon', *ClAnt* 15, 348–64.

SHIMRON, B. (1973), 'πρῶτος τῶν ἡμεῖς ἴδμεν', *Eranos* 71, 45–51.

——(1989), *Politics and Belief in Herodotus* (Stuttgart).

SINGOR, H. W. (1987), 'Tegea en het gebeente van Orestes (Hdt I 66–68)', *Lampas* 20, 182–203.

SINOS, R. (1993), 'Divine Selection: Epiphany and Politics in Archaic Greece', in C. Dougherty and L. Kurke (eds.), *Cultural Poetics in Archaic Greece. Cult, Performance, Politics* (Cambridge), 73–91.

SKORUPSKI, J. (1973), 'Science and Traditional Religious Thought', *Philosophy of the Social Sciences* 3. 2, 97–116, 3. 3, 209–30.

——(1976), *Symbol and Theory* (Cambridge).

SMITH, J. Z. (1978), *Map is not Territory. Studies in the History of Religion* (Leiden).

SMITH, N. D. (1989), 'Diviners and Divination in Aristophanic Comedy', *ClAnt* 8, 140–58.

SNODGRASS, A. (1980), *Archaic Greece* (London).

SOLERI, G. (1960), 'Politeismo e monoteismo nel vocabolario teologico della letteratura greca da Omero a Platone', *Rivista di Studi Classici* 8, 24–56.

SOLMSEN, L. (1943), 'Speeches in Herodotus' Account of the Ionic Revolt', *AJPh* 64, 194–207.

——(1944), 'Speeches in Herodotus' Account of the Battle of Plataea', *CPh* 39, 241–53.

SOMVILLE, P. (1989), 'Jeux de mots et sens du sacré dans la religion grecque', *Kernos* 2, 199–211.

SOURDILLE, C. (1910), *Hérodote et la religion d'Égypte* (Paris).

——(1925), 'Sur une nouvelle explication de la discrétion d'Hérodote en matière de religion', *REG* 38, 289–305.

SOURVINOU-INWOOD, C. (1997), 'Tragedy and Religion: Constructs and Readings', in C. Pelling (ed.), *Greek Tragedy and the Historian* (Oxford), 161–86.

SOUTHERN, R. W. (1990), *St. Anselm. A Portrait in a Landscape* (Cambridge).

SPERBER, D. (1975), *Rethinking Symbolism* (Cambridge).

SPEYER, W. (1980), 'Die Hilfe und Epiphanie einer Gottheit, eines Heroen und eines Heiligen in der Schlacht', in E. Dassmann and K. S. Frank (eds.), *Pietas. Festschrift B. Kötting* (Münster), 55–77.

STAAL, F. (1989), *Rules without Meanings* (Frankfurt).

STADTER, P. (1992), 'Herodotus and the Athenian *Arche*', *ASNP* 22. 3–4, 781–809.

——(1998), 'Herodotus and the North Carolina Oral Narrative Tradition', *Histos* 1.

STAHL, H.-P. (1975), 'Learning through Suffering?', *YClS* 24, 1–36.

STARR, C. G. (1966), 'Historical and Philosophical Time', *H&T* Beiheft 6, 24–35.

——(1968a), *The Awakening of the Greek Historical Spirit* (New York).

——(1968b), 'Ideas of truth in early Greece', *PP* 23, 348–59.

——(1989), 'The Birth of History', *PP* 44, 446–62.

STERN, J. (1989), 'Demythologization in Herodotus: 5. 92.η', *Eranos* 87, 13–20.

STRASBURGER, H. (1955), 'Herodot und das Perikleische Athen', *Historia* 5, 1–23.

——(1956), 'Herodots Zeitrechnung', *Historia* 5, 129–61.

STUBBINGS, F. H. (1946), 'Xerxes and the Plane Tree', *G&R* 15, 63–7.

SUAREZ DE LA TORRE, E. (1992), 'Les Pouvoirs des devins et les récits mythiques: l'exemple de Mélampous', *LEC* 60, 3–21.

SULEK, A. (1989), 'The Experiment of Psammetichus: Fact, Fiction, and Model to Follow', *JHI* 50, 645–51.

TAMBIAH, S. J. (1968), 'The Magical Power of Words', *Man* 3, 175–208.

THOMAS, K. (1971), *Religion and the Decline of Magic* (London).

THOMAS, R. (1989), *Oral Tradition and Written Record in Classical Athens* (Cambridge).

——(1992), *Literacy and Orality in Ancient Greece* (Cambridge).

——(1997), 'Ethnography, Proof and Argument in Herodotus' *Histories*', *PCPhS* 43, 128–48.

TRAUTWEIN, P. (1890), 'Die Memoiren des Dikaios', *Hermes* 25, 527–66.

TREPTOW, K. (1992), *From Zalmoxis to Jan Palach. Studies in East European History* (New York).

TREVES, P. (1941), 'Herodotus, Gelon and Pericles', *CPh* 36, 321–45.

TRÜDINGER, K. T. (1918), *Studien zur Geschichte der griechisch-römischen Ethnographie* (Basel).

USENER, H. (1896), *Götternamen. Versuch einer Lehre von der religiösen Begriffsbildung* (Bonn).

VANDIVER, E. (1991), *Heroes in Herodotus. The Interaction of Myth and History, Studien zur klassischen Philologie* Bd. 56 (Frankfurt).

VANNICELLI, P. (1993), *Erodoto e la Storia dell' alto e medio Arcaismo (Sparta—Tessaglia—Cirene)* (Rome).

——(1997), 'L'esperimento linguistico di Psammetico (Herodot. II. 2): c'erà una volta il frigio', in *Frigi et Frigio. Monografie scientifiche—Serie Scienze umane et sociale* (Rome, CNR), 201–17.

VEEN, J. E. VAN DER (1993), 'The Lord of the Ring. Narrative Technique in Herodotus' Story of Polycrates' Ring', *Mnemosyne* 46, 433–57.

——(1995), 'A Minute's Mirth', *Mnemosyne* 48, 129–45.

——(1996), *The Significant and the Insignificant. Five Studies in Herodotus' View of History* (Amsterdam).

VERDIN, H. (1982), 'Hérodote et la politique expansionniste des Achéménides. Notes sur Hdt. VII. 8', in J. Quaegebeur (ed.), *Studia Paulo Naster Oblata II. Orientalia Antiqua* (Louvain), 327–36.

VERNANT, J. P. (1980), *Myth and Society in Ancient Greece*, tr. J. Lloyd (Brighton).

VERSNEL, H. S. (1977), 'Polycrates and his Ring. Two Neglected Aspects', *Studi Storico-Religiosi* 1, 17–46.

——(1981), 'Religious Mentality in Ancient Prayer', in H. S. Versnel (ed.), *Faith, Hope and Worship. Aspects of Religious Mentality in the Ancient World* (Leiden), 1–64.

——(1987), 'What Did Ancient Man See When He Saw a God?', in D. van der Plas (ed.), *Effigies Dei. Essays on the History of Religions* (Leiden), 42–55.

——(1990a), *Inconsistencies in Greek and Roman Religion*, vol. 1 (Leiden).

——(1990b), 'What's sauce for the goose is sauce for the gander: myth and ritual, old and new', in L. Edmunds (ed.), *Approaches to Greek Myth* (Baltimore), 23–90.

VEYNE, P. (1981), 'Between Myth and History, or the Weaknesses of Greek Reason', *Diogenes* 113, 1–30.

——(1988), *Did the Greeks Believe in their Myths? An Essay on the Constitutive Imagination*, tr. P. Wissing (Chicago).

VIDAL-NAQUET, P. (1960), 'Temps des dieux et temps des hommes', *RHR* 157, 55–80, tr. as 'Divine time and human time', in his *The Black Hunter* (Baltimore, 1986), 39–60.

VISSER, M. (1982), 'Worship your Enemy: Aspects of the Cult of Heroes in Ancient Greece', *HThR* 75, 403–28.

WALLINGA, H. T. (1991), 'Polycrates and Egypt: The Testimony of the *Samaina*', in H. Sancisi-Weerdenburg and A. Kuhrt (eds.), *Achaemenid History VI. Asia Minor and Egypt: Old Cultures in a New Empire* (Leiden), 179–97.

WALSER, G. (1983), 'Der Tod des Kambyses', in H. Heinen (ed.), *Althistorische Studien . . . H. Bengston* (Wiesbaden), 8–18.

WARDMAN, A. E. (1960), 'Myth in Greek Historiography', *Historia* 9, 403–13.

——(1961), 'Herodotus on the Cause of the Greco-Persian Wars (Herodotus, I, 5)', *AJPh* 82, 133–50.

WATERS, K. H. (1966), 'The Purpose of Dramatisation in Herodotus', *Historia* 15, 155–71.

——(1970), 'Herodotus and the Ionian Revolt', *Historia* 19, 504–8.

——(1971), *Herodotus on Tyrants and Despots. A Study in Objectivity* (Wiesbaden).

——(1972), 'Herodotus and politics', *G&R* 19, 136–50.

——(1974), 'The Structure of Herodotus' Narrative', *Antichthon* 15, 1–10.

——(1985), *Herodotos the Historian: His Problems, Methods and Originality* (London and Sydney).

WEEKS, N. K. (1982), 'Herodotus and Egypt. Discerning the Native Tradition in Book II', in G. H. R. Horsley (ed.), *Hellenika. Essays in Greek History and Politics* (North Ryde, NSW), 63–8.

WÉRY, L. M. (1966), 'Le Meurtre des hérauts de Darius en 491 et l'inviolabilité du héraut', *AC* 35, 468–86.

WEST, S. (1985), 'Herodotus' Epigraphical Interests', *CQ* 35, 278–305.

——(1987), 'And it Came to Pass that Pharaoh Dreamed: Notes on Herodotus 2. 139, 141', *CQ* 37, 262–71.

——(1988), 'The Scythian Ultimatum (Herodotus iv 131, 132)', *JHS* 108, 207–11.

——(1991), 'Herodotus' Portrait of Hecataeus', *JHS* 111, 144–60.

——(1992), 'Sesostris' Stelae (Herodotus 2. 102–106)', *Historia* 41, 117–20.

WHITE, M. E. (1969), 'Herodotus' Starting Point', *Phoenix* 23, 39–48.

WHITTAKER, C. R. (1965), 'The Delphic Oracle. Belief and Behaviour in Ancient Greece—and Africa', *HThR* 58, 21–47.

WIKARJAK, J. (1963), 'Elementy Polemiczne w Dziele Herodota', *Eos* 53, 41–55.

WILAMOWITZ-MOELLENDORFF, U. VON (1931–2), *Der Glaube der Hellenen* (Berlin).

WILL, E. (1953), 'Sur la nature de la mantique pratiquée à l'Héraion de Pérachora', *RHR* 143, 145–69.

WILSON, J. A. (1970), *Herodotus in Egypt* (Leiden).

WOLFF, E. (1964), 'Das Weib des Masistes', *Hermes* 92, 51–8.

WOOD, H. (1972), *The Histories of Herodotus: An Analysis of the Formal Structure* (The Hague).

WOODMAN, A. J. (1988), *Rhetoric in Classical Historiography: Four Studies* (London).

YUNIS, H. (1988), *A New Creed. Fundamental Religious Beliefs in the Athenian Polis and Euripidean Drama, Hypomnemata* 91 (Göttingen).

ZGUSTA, L. (1953), 'Zwei skythische Götternamen ΠΑΠΑΙΟΣ und ΑΠΓ', *Archiv Orientální* 21, 270–1.

—— (1955), *Die Personennamen griechischer Städte der nördlichen Schwarzmeerküste* (Prague).

ZOGRAPHOU, G. (1995), 'L' Argumentation d'Hérodote concernant les emprunts faits par les Grecs à la religion égyptienne', *Kernos* 8, 187–203.

General Index

References in footnotes to the names of modern scholars, ancient authors, or individuals who do not feature in the *Histories*, are cited here only when they are the subject of sustained discussion.

Index of Passages of Herodotus cited

I. 1: 199 n. 64
I. 1–2. 1: 205
I. 1–5: 200 n. 68
I. 1–5. 2: 31
I. 2. 1: 201
I. 3. 1: 61, 104, 230, 238
I. 4. 4: 81 n. 48, 121
I. 5. 3–6. 2: 198
I. 5. 3–4: 31–2, 62
I. 5. 3: 75 n. 33, 202 n. 76, 203 n. 82
I. 5. 4: 33
I. 6. 2: 202, 203 n. 82
I. 6. 3: 202
I. 8. 1: 54, 238
I. 8. 2: 231 n. 33, 233, 237, 238
I. 10. 2: 237
I. 10. 3: 237
I. 11. 2: 237
I. 11. 4: 237
I. 13: 156 n. 122
I. 13. 2: 152 n. 112, 157, 224
I. 14. 1: 199
I. 14. 2: 201
I. 15: 199
I. 16. 2: 199
I. 17–22: 199
I. 19: 115 n. 41
I. 19. 1: 100, 230
I. 19. 2: 224 n. 5
I. 19. 3: 148 n. 98, 155
I. 20: 142 n. 69
I. 21. 4: 155
I. 22. 4: 205
I. 23–4: 76
I. 23: 75 n. 33, 201, 203 n. 82
I. 23. 1: 76
I. 24. 8: 76
I. 26. 1: 201 n. 71
I. 27. 1: 202
I. 27. 3: 171 n. 53
I. 29. 1: 38, 55
I. 30. 1: 33, 38, 47

I. 30. 2: 33
I. 30. 3: 34
I. 30. 4–5: 34
I. 31. 1: 34
I. 31. 2: 34, 53
I. 31. 3: 34–5, 41, 50, 129, 169 n. 44, 172, 174
I. 31. 4–5: 80
I. 31. 4: 34, 174
I. 31. 5: 34–5
I. 32: 36 n. 13
I. 32. 1: 35, 45, 48, 50, 171, 172, 175, 177, 191, 233
I. 32. 3: 50 n. 51
I. 32. 4: 35, 51, 58
I. 32. 5: 35, 48
I. 32. 6: 36, 41, 52 n. 53, 58
I. 32. 7: 36
I. 32. 9: 36, 37, 46, 50, 117, 172, 175 n. 67
I. 33: 36, 129
I. 34. 1: 36, 40, 123, 175 n. 67, 224 n. 4
I. 34. 2: 41
I. 35. 1: 217 n. 35
I. 39: 135 n. 48
I. 43. 2: 41, 58, 124, 170 n. 47, 175 n. 67, 224
I. 45. 3: 41
I. 46. 2ff.: 134 n. 46
I. 47. 2: 27 n. 110, 70
I. 47. 3: 41 n. 30
I. 48. 1: 79
I. 48. 2: 70
I. 49: 27 n. 110, 145 n. 84
I. 50–4: 61
I. 50. 1: 62, 80, 171
I. 51: 184 n. 8
I. 53. 1: 70 n. 18
I. 53. 2: 144
I. 54. 1: 62
I. 56. 1: 62
I. 57. 1: 27 n. 112, 256 n. 20